GOVERNING FORTUNE

Governing Fortune

• • • • • • • • • • • • • • • • • •

CASINO GAMBLING IN AMERICA

Edward A. Morse and Ernest P. Goss

The University of Michigan Press　Ann Arbor

Copyright © by the University of Michigan 2007
All rights reserved
Published in the United States of America by
The University of Michigan Press
Manufactured in the United States of America
∞ Printed on acid-free paper

2010   2009   2008   2007   4   3   2   1

A CIP catalog record for this book is available from the British Library.

Library of Congress Cataloging-in-Publication Data

Morse, Edward A., 1962–
      Governing fortune : casino gambling in America / Edward A. Morse
and Ernest P. Goss.
          p. cm.
      ISBN-13: 978-0-472-09965-8 (cloth : alk. paper)
      ISBN-10: 0-472-09965-5 (cloth : alk. paper)
      ISBN-13: 978-0-472-06965-1 (pbk. : alk. paper)
      ISBN-10: 0-472-06965-9 (pbk. : alk. paper)
      1. Casinos—Economic aspects—United States.   2. Casinos—
Social aspects—United States.   3. Gambling—Economic aspects—
United States.   4. Gambling—Social aspects—United States.
I. Goss, Ernest, 1950–   II. Title.

HV6711.M67   2007
338.4'77950973—dc22   2006028160

PREFACE

This book explores the legal and economic environment of casino gambling in the United States. The authors draw upon their respective backgrounds to offer important (and often interrelated) insights to those wrestling with the policy dilemmas presented by legalized gambling. Rather than providing a polemic against gambling or an apology for it, this book is designed to provide an analysis of the industry to allow policymakers and interested citizens to make informed and thoughtful choices. By evaluating what is known—as well as the limits of that knowledge—this book casts additional light on the costs and benefits of legalized casino gambling and the policy decisions affecting its regulation.

After a brief examination of the historical roots of casino gambling in chapter 1, chapter 2 explores the growth of casino gambling generally, including both commercial and tribal casinos. Casino ownership has become a corporate enterprise, and this chapter also explores the major players in this industry and marketplace perceptions of its future prospects.

Casino gambling is often touted for its ability to create jobs, to generate tax revenues, and to encourage economic growth. As in other contexts, visible effects from investment and legal changes are often accompanied by invisible ones, which can be difficult to measure and evaluate. These benefits and costs are the subject of chapters 3 through 5. Chapters 3 and 4 examine the benefits claimed from casinos, focusing particularly on taxes and economic development. The conclusions are surprising. For example, casinos appear to create jobs but not growth in personal income. While casinos provide new sources for tax collections, their impact on tax relief is dubious.

Chapter 5 explores problem gambling and surveys significant research into social costs associated with gambling. It is critical of the industry's approach toward social costs, which exploits the limits on social science research methods and the complex causes of human social problems. Although there is still much to be learned, available research suggests that these costs are significant counterweights to the putative benefits of the industry—a risk that policymakers have been willing to ignore for the purpose of political gain from expanded casino gambling.

Chapters 6 through 11 explore the regulatory environment in which casinos operate, including the respective roles of state, federal, and tribal governments in designing and enforcing gambling laws. Gambling regulation has generally been left to the states, though federal influence is also evident, particularly in matters involving Native American tribes and those touching upon constitutional issues. This regulatory structure is not without its problems: interstate competition affects both the economics of gambling as well as its impact on citizens. States have generally used their preeminent regulatory position to foster a partnership with the industry that enhances industry profits and government revenues, paying little attention to efforts to curtail the effects of problem gambling. Early efforts toward adopting limits or constraints in some states have largely been abandoned in favor of industry-friendly rules.

Challenges to state sovereignty come from technology and the market forces of international competition. Chapter 10 explores the challenges presented by the Internet, including an analysis of recent World Trade Organization proceedings affecting the impact of international trade agreements on the continued viability of federal and state laws governing gambling. Tribal gaming also presents a potential challenge to state sovereignty that the federal government has encouraged and protected, and these issues are explored in chapter 11.

Chapter 12 concludes with an examination of liability issues affecting the future of the gaming industry, including lawsuits from victims of problem gambling behaviors and their potential impact on government approaches to regulation. Earlier approaches to regulation, which helped to foster the growth of this industry, may now need to be changed to address the real problem of social costs. This chapter outlines an innovative proposal involving individual licensing as a means to balance the liberty interests of individuals against the social costs generated from problem gambling behavior.

CONTENTS

FIGURES

TABLES

I. A Brief History of Gambling in America

Gambling has a long and ambivalent track record. At various points in history, gambling has been despised and criminalized, tolerated, and embraced—often at the same time. An appreciation of the historical development of social attitudes and government policies toward gambling is a helpful beginning point in understanding the current state of affairs with regard to casino gambling. Despite government efforts to stamp it out, gambling remains a persistent part of the human experience. History shows us that what cannot be defeated is often assimilated. This is the case with gambling in America.

EARLY ENGLISH HISTORY

English common law, which was influential in the formation of laws pertaining to gambling in the United States, reflects the deep historical roots of gambling as a leisure activity. The common law, which reflects customary practices, did not proscribe gambling per se.[1] Early statutes affecting gambling practices were aimed at perceived collateral effects of gambling, some of which seem curious by current standards. For example, an English statute in 1388 directed men subject to military service to abandon their pursuit of games, including tennis, football, and dice, based on the concern that such activities detracted from their military preparedness.[2] Similar concerns that men were gambling instead of practicing their archery skills provided the basis in 1541 for additional statutes prohibiting games, including cards and dice.[3] Significantly, these statutes did not outlaw gaming altogether, as games played at home during Christmastime were expressly allowed. Public gaming, on the other hand, was often thought to result in a breach of the peace resulting in an assorted list of crimes.[4]

Despite attempts to constrain gambling behavior through legal proscriptions, commoners and nobility alike retained their affection for gambling.[5] The ascension of the Stuarts to the throne in 1603 signaled an era of expansive gambling practices in both private and public forums. Gambling had become "a national pastime" that respectable persons found difficult to avoid in ordinary social intercourse.[6] However, the proliferation of gambling among the aristocrats raised concerns about adverse effects on the social structure through the loss of family estates through high-stakes wagering.[7] These concerns prompted statutory reforms in 1664 and later in 1710 that were aimed at regulating gambling rather than absolutely prohibiting it.[8] For example, notes and other security agreements given in payment of gambling debts were declared void; losers of sums over ten pounds could sue to recover their losses within three months, and if they failed to do so a third party could sue for treble damages.[9] However, these statutes retained a royal privilege for gambling within the royal palaces during the residence of the Queen.[10]

The disparate treatment of the royals and their subjects exposed the absence of an articulated moral foundation for prohibition apart from instrumental goals in preserving public order. The propriety of that public order was also drawn into question. Some argued that gambling put the rights of Englishmen at risk by jeopardizing the estates of the aristocracy, who were thought to be a bulwark against the excesses of the Crown.[11] Others looked at the propensity for gambling to circulate property as having positive effects on the social order, as it allowed for the redistribution of wealth.[12] Risk-taking behavior in military officers was also thought to have a salutary effect on their ability to lead.[13]

As the industrial and mercantile economy continued to grow, economic considerations grew to have a significant role in setting the parameters for gambling behavior. Government policy that would emerge across the sea in the American colonies would be influenced primarily by these considerations, though the religious worldviews of the early founders also had some effects in shaping social and ultimately government views about gambling.

GAMBLING IN COLONIAL AMERICA

Economics played a pivotal role in early prohibitions against gaming in the New World. Just as their English counterparts needed militia with strong archery skills, the American colonists needed productive citizens to withstand the rigors and hardship of early colonization efforts. Assuming that gambling undermined the colonists' work ethic, some of the colonies sought to limit gambling through legal measures. During its first year of existence, the Massachusetts Bay Colony outlawed dice, cards, and other games thought to induce the colonists toward idle or unprofitable use of time.[14] In fact, early statutes in both Massachusetts and Connecticut even went so far as to proscribe idleness as a punishable offense.[15]

Though such provisions now seem quite odd in a society where leisure is an important value—perhaps even rising to the level of a human right—the struggles of the times arguably may have demanded it. Difficult winters, diseases, and other travails presented a battle for survival.[16] Those who failed to engage in productive activities drained the resources of the larger group, which had little margin to maintain a safety net for those who could work but chose not to work. Of course, this public position abated as economic prosperity was achieved. For example, a Massachusetts statute in 1737 officially recognized an appropriate role for moderate pursuit of social games (though not gambling) in a manner consistent with a pursuit of other gainful activity: "All lawful games and exercise should not be otherwise used than as innocent and moderate recreations, and not as trades or callings, to gain a living or make unlawful advantage thereby."[17]

It should be noted that not all of the American colonies had similar approaches toward idleness. In New York, which was initially settled by the Dutch, gambling was commonplace.[18] The arrival of English rule in 1660 apparently had only modest effects on gambling, as it was not until 1741 that the first antigambling statute was enacted. Like many other statutes of this kind, it was enacted in response to the negative consequences of frequent public gambling.[19] Similar laws arose in other states, which focused not only on disorderly conduct associated with gambling houses but also on the negative effects on family welfare from gambling losses and the perceived corruption of youth.[20]

The southern colonies were also more tolerant toward gambling, and some commentators attribute this to the influence of the landed aristocracy, who emphasized and valued the pursuit of pleasure, as compared to the New England farmers' emphasis upon the importance of hard work in economic prosperity.[21] Gambling among plantation owners was thought to be common, and it suited their pursuit of a carefree lifestyle detached from the rigors of daily farmwork.[22] Even in Virginia, which took a more restrictive approach toward gambling than other southern colonies, public gambling was outlawed but gambling in private homes was permitted. As one commentator suggested, this legislation "did not really strike a blow at the way of life of the tidewater aristocrats; if anything, prohibitions of public gambling struck at the pleasures of the poor, who, unlike the rich, did not have the space in their own houses for large-scale gaming."[23]

Lotteries were also common. Their utility as fund-raising devices in support of public works and charitable pursuits allowed lotteries to flourish during early colonial periods.[24] Lotteries helped to finance projects at universities, including Harvard, Yale, and Princeton, as well as public works projects such as roads, schools, and river transportation. Even churches were built through lottery financing.[25]

THE EARLY REPUBLIC

As the nation emerged from the Revolutionary War, legislators in the Northeast continued to be hostile to gambling as a commercial or professional activity.[26] Public gambling and professional gamblers were the primary targets of antigambling laws.[27] Private game playing that did not involve wagering was allowed, but these activities occurred in a social environment that championed honest labor as the means to success and looked with skepticism on attempts to provide a shortcut to riches.[28]

Despite the benign treatment of gambling in English common law, the developing law in the United States turned more strongly against it. For example, in *Irwin v. Williar,* the Supreme Court observed: "In England, it is held that the contracts, although wagers, were not void at common law, and that the statute has not made them illegal, but only non-enforceable, [citation omitted] while generally, in this country, all wagering contracts are held to be illegal and void as against public policy."[29] In a Massachusetts case, Justice Holmes characterized wagering contracts as void as against public policy because they are "vicious."[30]

The common law concept of public nuisance also grew to encompass the maintenance of a gambling house as an activity that interfered with public morals, a classification shared with houses of prostitution and other activities classified as "indecent" and "profane."[31] However, gambling houses were also associated with disturbances and quarrels, particularly if cheating was involved, which also affected the public peace.[32] In this sense, the gambling house shared some characteristics with another public nuisance, the "common scold"—"a troublesome and angry person who, by brawling and wrangling among his or her neighbors, breaks the public peace, increases discord, and [by so doing] becomes a public nuisance to the neighborhood."[33]

As populations migrated westward, the frontier presented many new opportunities for gambling practices to develop outside the constraining effects of the established social order of the early colonies. Nevertheless, public gambling, and in particular gambling of a professional nature, was specifically targeted as being a threat to the public good once a legal establishment began to emerge. For example, an 1823 act in Kentucky was specifically targeted toward professional gambling activities:

> The object of the legislature[ ] was not to suppress gaming generally; but to pr[o]scribe a particular species of gambling, by punishing, rigorously, a notorious class of professional gamblers. Former laws were deemed sufficient for discountenancing the ordinary games of chance. But a more public and severe sanction was ascertained to be necessary for the extirpation of a vice, which had taken deep root, and was seen and felt to be peculiarly pernicious and demoralizing.[34]

The Missouri Supreme Court provided a similarly harsh description of the business of running a gambling operation, along with a more tolerant view of the individual gambler:

> To set up, or keep, or carry on a faro-bank . . . is an offense a great deal more injurious to the public morals, than the act of betting upon the gambling device so set up or conducted. The former is followed as a profession, and its professors go about, seducing the unwary, and holding out temptations to dissipation and vice, and leading thousands to ruin. The latter offense is committed often in the thoughtlessness of the moment—to amuse an idle hour, and without a clear perception of the corrupting associations and vicious habits to which the practice so often tends.[35]

However, in other states, an individual gambler's conduct was considered equally reprehensible. An early Tennessee statute provided that one convicted of gambling lost his right to hold public office for a period of five years.[36] As a Tennessee court explained, dark assumptions about gambling underlay this decision:

> Governments legislate to suppress general evils, without reference to possible or probable exceptions. Gaming, as a general evil, leads to vicious inclinations, destruction of morals, abandonment of industry and honest employment, a loss of self-control and respect. Frauds, forgeries, thefts, make up the black catalogue of crime, the closing scene of which generally ends in highway robbery and murder. The American and European journals are full of cases of the most distressing nature; of bankers, merchants, clerks to banking institutions, men in almost every description of trust, public and private, becoming bankrupts and thieves, to the ruin of themselves and others. Look for the source of their misfortune; you find it in lotteries, loo, faro, thimble, dice and the like.[37]

In the frontier regions west of the Mississippi, gambling flourished before formal governmental control was established. The nature of that control ranged from prohibition to regulation, depending on the state. In plains states such as Kansas and Nebraska, which were dominated by local farming communities, absolute bans were enacted soon after territorial statutes were granted.[38] However, rather than attempt to curtail idleness or sloth, these laws focused on the disruption of social order and other excesses associated with public gambling.[39] There was no particular aversion to private forms of gambling, and light penalties tended to be applied toward those who were unfortunate enough to be caught.[40] Horse racing, which would have a tendency to reflect progress in animal husbandry that was useful to the plains farmers and ranchers, even enjoyed a preferential status when it came to enforcement of gambling debts.[41]

In the far West, where farming communities were not the dominant political structure, early governments embraced licensing and regulation as a means of limiting the disruptive effects of cheating and other violent consequences associated with gambling.[42] Montana, for example, imposed substantial fees on gambling operators for each establishment and each faro, poker, or roulette table.[43] Cheating (and violence) still existed under this scheme,[44] which apparently involved little more than an attempt by the government to raise money from gambling activity. Eventually, even these states gradually enacted antigambling legislation, though the public sentiment against gambling was comparatively weak. Penalties were modest, reflecting a more laissez-faire approach toward regulation than in states with orientations toward farming communities.[45]

TRANSITIONS TO MODERN LEGALIZED GAMBLING: THE NEVADA EXPERIENCE

Nevada merits special attention in this historical discussion due to its pre-eminence as a gambling destination and its long-standing acceptance of commercialized gambling. However, early Nevada settlers possessed conflicting value systems: Mormon pioneers held strong antigambling views, while prospectors seeking the mother lode were quite tolerant of the risk taking associated with gambling and apparently practiced it with alacrity.[46] Congress established the Nevada Territory in 1861, and its first territorial governor pushed through a statute banning all gambling and imposing stiff penalties, which included both fines and prison terms.[47] To the consternation of the territorial governor (and probably others, including the Mormon pioneers), gamblers flouted these laws. Soon after Nevada achieved statehood in 1864, the state legislature substantially reduced the penalties for gambling, and in 1869 it took the further step of legalizing gambling.[48]

The legalization position was accompanied by a system of licensing and regulation, which was ostensibly motivated by the desire to curtail, if not eliminate, gambling altogether. The license fees, which ranged from $250 to $500 every three months, were thought to be sufficiently high to make it impractical for most gambling establishments to carry on their businesses. As a committee report stated, "[V]ery few, if any[,] will be able or willing to pay the heavy license required, and the practicable result will be: to close once and forever hundreds of low dens and 'dead falls' which now disgrace our principal towns."[49] The legislators' predictions were wildly erroneous, however, and gambling (primarily of a small stakes variety) remained a common activity in Nevada towns.

In addition to imposing license fees, which generated revenue to support government services, regulations controlled other aspects of gambling as well. For example, Nevada prohibited minors from gambling and provided their parents with the right to pursue a civil action for damages against the owner of a gambling establishment who permitted a minor to gamble.[50] Nevada legislation also limited gambling activities to the back room or to upper floors, where available.[51] Thus, despite legalization of gambling, Nevada's public policy toward gambling reflected sufficient social concern to keep it out of the reach of children and out of public display.

One additional regulation added in 1877 is particularly noteworthy in its concern for the social consequences of gambling: it prohibited debtors and men with wives and dependent minor children from gambling.[52] Those who gambled with such persons were guilty of a misdemeanor.[53] The extent to which the state enforced this provision is unclear, but it furnishes an interesting approach toward addressing the consequences of excessive gambling losses—a topic that will be taken up later.

Oddly enough, the permissive attitude toward other forms of gambling in early Nevada history did not extend to lotteries, which were expressly prohibited by the Nevada Constitution.[54] The Nevada Supreme Court rebuffed early legislative efforts to authorize a lottery to raise funds for state government. In *Ex Parte Blanchard,* the court reasoned that English statutes declaring lotteries to be a public nuisance were part of the common law in Nevada and that Nevada's constitutional provisions proscribing lotteries withheld legislative power to authorize a lottery.[55] Thus, a statute enabling a lottery for the seemingly beneficent purpose of "providing means to erect an insane asylum" was held to be unconstitutional.

A similar enabling provision was also rebuffed in a later case on similar grounds, with some additional moralizing by the court:

> We are of opinion that the facts stated in the articles of incorporation, in the statute, and in the information, show that the scheme is one whereby the legislature of this state, in consideration of the sum of $250,000, to be placed in the state treasury, to the credit of the "insane and charitable fund," attempted to authorize the managers of the "Nevada Benevolent Association" to enrich their own pockets, at the expense of the people of this and other states, by holding out promises of the great and sudden gains that might be acquired by the ticket-holders; that golden prizes would be "the lure to incite the credulous and unsuspecting into this scheme."[56]

Thus, public law seemed to express the sentiment that private casino-style games offered a sporting chance, while lotteries represented a corrupt exercise of government power that took advantage of its weaker citizens. (Though some might criticize this position as anomalous, it is not completely devoid of a foundation given the low payouts associated with the typical state-run lottery.)

Nevada's era of regulated legalized gambling ended abruptly in 1909 when the legislature once again banned gambling and imposed severe penalties.[57] Over the next two decades, which included the implementation of Prohibition with the ratification of the Eighteenth Amendment in 1919, individuals frequently violated both antigambling and antialcohol laws without significant consequences, albeit in private clubs and other locations outside of public view.[58]

However, in 1931, the Nevada legislature once again passed a legalization bill that ushered in the modern era of regulated casino gambling in the state.[59] Instead of prospectors, these modern casinos drew in patrons from California and eventually from other states, as they enjoyed an effective monopoly on legalized casino gambling in the United States until New Jersey approved casino gambling in 1976 and opened its first casinos two years later.[60] During the ensuing period, regulatory efforts would be refined and strengthened to address concerns about corruption and other criminal activity. Moreover, gambling would become entrenched as a legitimate business and entertainment option in that state and, ultimately, in many others that sought to emulate the Nevada model.

THE MODERN ERA

Though states other than Nevada had generally retained the approach of imposing criminal sanctions on gambling activities, notable exceptions began to emerge. Horse racing was a popular exception, which was sometimes considered "sport" in order to circumvent otherwise applicable gambling restrictions.[61] Unlike casino-style games, horse racing also supported an industry that had other economic impacts extending beyond the track, including breeders, farms, and feed stores. These arguments may have helped to distinguish horse racing from other forms of gambling that remained legally prohibited.

Economic needs of state and local governments also affected the acceptance of pari-mutuel betting on horse races. Some attribute the Great Depression as a catalyst for legalization, as states sought new revenue sources to address fiscal shortfalls.[62] Charitable gambling, such as bingo, also grew to be widely accepted as a fund-raising method.[63] Here, stakes were generally limited, and profits went to what could be considered "good causes" rather than into private coffers. Nevertheless, constitutional amendments were sometimes required to permit even charitable gambling, thus reflecting very strong antigambling sentiments that had to be overcome.[64]

Fiscal interests have undoubtedly played a significant—if not the most significant—role in this metamorphosis from gambling as taboo to gambling as a tool of the state.[65] State lotteries taught the important lesson that significant revenues could be gained from willing participants, some of whom were already being served by illegal numbers rackets. State lotteries have enjoyed explosive growth in the latter part of the twentieth century and into the twenty-first, taking in more than $48.8 billion in 2004 in forty-one states and the District of Columbia, up from $45.18 billion in 2003.[66] Per capita spending on lotteries in these states averages $183, ranging from a low of $9.27 in sparsely populated North Dakota to $1,370.95 in Rhode Island, where video lottery terminals (close cousins of slot machines) are allowed.[67] Of this $48.8 billion in 2004 revenues, an estimated $13.9 billion was returned to the states, with the remainder paying for expenses for the promotion of the lottery and the prizes awarded to players.[68]

Casinos also offer significant potential for public revenues, though the model for earning those revenues is typically different. States have chosen to license private firms to run casinos and to impose taxes on gaming activities.[69] In 2004, commercial casinos posted gross gaming revenues (defined as the amount wagered minus payouts to winning players) of nearly $29 billion,[70] with an additional $16.2 billion estimated for tribal casinos.[71] As of 2005, commercial casino gambling is currently available in only eleven states, while twenty-eight states allow tribal casinos.[72]

Many other states have more limited gambling activities, such as keno, bingo, card rooms, pull-tabs, and horse or dog racing. Few states have resisted legalization of gambling in some form, with Utah and Hawaii being the most notable exceptions. When all is totaled, estimated spending on gambling in the United States ranges from $72 billion to as much as $100 billion, depending on how the base is measured.[73] By comparison, Americans spend each year approximately $9.5 billion at the movies, $10.3 billion at theme parks, $23.8 billion on DVD and video rentals, and $51 billion on cable television.[74] Though $100 billion is less than 1 percent of the gross domestic product in the United States (which in 2004 was about $12 trillion), it is nevertheless a large figure. Moreover, it does not include illegal gambling, which still exists as an illicit alternative.

The history of gambling in America discussed here is considerably abbreviated, but it does permit us to make some general observations. First, a desire to gamble seems deeply rooted in human experience. Despite some moral objections to gambling, belief in luck has had a powerful influence in American culture.[75] A demand for gambling is likely to continue to exist for the foreseeable future, as patrons continue to be attracted by the hope that they will be lucky.

Government has at various times attempted to prohibit gambling through criminal sanctions, which have focused primarily on professional or commercial operations. However, laws of this nature have not always enjoyed widespread public acceptance. Regulating gambling, rather than letting it freely propagate according to market demands, is emerging as the dominant governmental approach. What might have started on a small scale with bingo or charitable operations has eventually expanded to more lucrative gambling options.

Government has thus chosen to exploit the public's belief in luck rather than repress it. In the case of lotteries, government itself is the operator and promoter. When commercial gambling operations are involved, gambling no longer involves a sterile redistribution of resources among participants. Instead, it becomes a means for gambling providers to reap substantial profits. Government has effectively harnessed this profit motivation to turn casinos into tools for tax collection, and in the process traditional characterizations of gambling as a vice have been overturned in favor of more positive characterizations.

Despite the fact that social costs have had a significant role in the legal suppression of gambling throughout its history, policymakers have given only limited attention to the nature and extent of social costs in designing regulations for the industry. From a political perspective, a "see no evil" approach is understandable: costs associated with the gambling industry are diffused and difficult to measure, whereas benefits (such as jobs and tax revenues) are tangible and quantifiable.[76] Interstate competition magnifies pressures toward legalization, as gambling proponents cite significant gaming tax revenue losses to the state from patrons willing to cross state lines to gamble.

Resistance to these pressures is not always futile, as evidenced by the fact that many states are without casinos and have relatively limited options for legal gambling. However, continued resistance is also difficult. Political pressures from interstate competition, growing antitax sentiments, and libertarian values of personal freedom all potentially contribute to an expanding role for legalized gambling, despite uncertainties about social costs. Unfortunately for the industry, as well as for the states that have enjoyed its largesse, in some locations the market is maturing, and much of the easy money has already been made. For most Americans, a casino is now within an easy traveling distance—and the prospects of gambling on the Internet may bring it even closer to home.

In 1999, the National Gambling Impact Study Commission urged policymakers to slow the expansion of gambling so that researchers and government could learn more about the social impacts of gambling, stating in part:

> The members of the Commission agree that there is a need for a "pause" in the growth of gambling. The purpose of the pause is not to wait for definitive answers to the subjects of dispute, because those may never come. Instead the purpose of this recommended pause is to encourage governments to do what, to date, few, if any, have done: to survey the results of their decisions and to determine if they have chosen wisely; to ask if their decisions are in accord with the public good, if harmful effects could be remedied, if benefits are being unnecessarily passed up.[77]

That recommendation was essentially ignored, as gambling continued to expand. However, the social science community has continued to learn about the industry, and it has produced some disturbing results about some of the negative social impacts of the industry. The regulatory environment has also continued to change, as the industry and government begin to deal with these looming social issues.

The chapters that follow explore some of these social and economic impacts of the casino gambling industry, as well as the regulatory environment in which they occur. Policymakers face difficult choices in the years ahead, and the discussion that follows is designed to provide a basis for reflection and understanding of this industry and the dilemmas that it presents.

2. Casino Expansion in the United States

From 1931 until 1976, Nevada held an effective monopoly on legalized casino gambling in the United States. However, that monopoly soon began to fracture as other states changed their approaches toward the gambling industry. New Jersey became the first state outside of Nevada to add casinos by legalizing casino gambling in Atlantic City in 1976 and opening its first casino two years later. It was more than a decade before other states began what has become a landslide in the expansion of U.S. commercial casinos.[1] Indian tribes soon joined in, adding casino facilities in thirty-three states between 1987 and 2005. Gambling supporters in the eleven commercial casino states and the thirty-three tribal casino states viewed casinos as an efficient device for generating tourism and economic development, as well as tax revenues for state and local governments.

Perhaps more emphatically, Indian tribes embraced gambling as a means to achieve economic development and to provide jobs for unemployed tribal members. In many cases, the close proximity of gambling opportunities across state lines influenced decisions for legalization as governments sought to compete for the gambling dollars of citizens from neighboring states. This legislative design of cross-border competition is evidenced by the fact that the vast majority of commercial casinos outside of Nevada are within two miles of state borders. Thus, many government officials viewed casinos as a reaction to the lure of casinos directly across the state line.

Since its expansion outside of Nevada and New Jersey, casino gambling has proven to be a growth industry with its pattern of growth highly resilient to negative conditions in the general economy. Even the tragic events of September 11, 2001, brought only a temporary setback for the industry, as patrons soon returned to gaming. Although reductions in air travel affected

Nevada casinos negatively, other venues reachable by automobile posted gains, allowing the casino industry to post overall growth even during that economically troubled year.[2]

Over the past decade, Americans' gambling losses at casinos grew at a rate twice that of the growth in the overall economy. In 2004, revenues for commercial casinos reached nearly $29 billion, up more than 7 percent from $27 billion in 2003.[3] Racetrack casinos—"racinos"—reflected an even stronger growth in revenues, taking in $2.9 billion in 2004, up more than 30 percent from $2.2 billion in 2003. As of 2004, the American Gaming Association reported a total of 445 commercial casinos operating in eleven states and twenty-four racinos operating in seven states.[4]

Tribal casinos have also experienced phenomenal growth. In 2004, there were 228 tribes operating 405 gaming facilities in thirty states.[5] These tribal facilities collected approximately $19 billion in gaming revenues in 2004. This reflects a 14.3 percent compound annual growth rate since 1997—dramatically higher than commercial casinos' growth of 6.8 percent annually.[6] However, not all of the tribal facilities are full-service casinos, as some include card rooms, bingo, or more limited forms of gambling. Class III casinos, which offer gaming opportunities that are comparable to those of commercial casinos (i.e., those owned by private firms), are available in twenty-three states.[7]

The following discussion explores casino growth in greater detail, focusing first on commercial casinos, next on their counterparts run by the Indian tribes, and then on racetrack casinos or racinos. The final section of this chapter examines how the explosive growth in casino gambling has affected firms that own the commercial casinos and manage the tribal casinos.

COMMERCIAL CASINOS

Figure 2.1 shows states that currently have legalized commercial casino gaming along with the date that the first casino was constructed in the state. Years of legalization were Nevada in 1931; New Jersey in 1976; Iowa, Louisiana, and South Dakota in 1989; Colorado, Illinois, and Mississippi in 1990; Indiana and Missouri in 1993; and Michigan in 1996. Pennsylvania and Florida will soon join these states, as both states legalized slot machines in 2004. Pennsylvania will allow up to sixty-one thousand slot machines at locations across the state.[8]

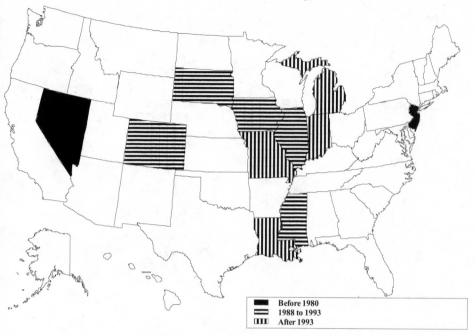

Fig. 2.1. First year of commercial casino operations

Figure 2.2 details the location of commercial casinos by county for 2003. Fifty-seven counties in the United States currently offer commercial casino gaming. Outside of Nevada, most commercial casino activity is located near either a river or a body of water, which often also forms a geographic border between states. In part, this is due to the fact that many states use public nostalgia for riverboat gambling to support the expansion of casino gambling. However, this also reflects the reality of cross-border competition for gambling patrons. For example, most of Iowa's thirteen casinos are located on the state's border with Nebraska (four casinos) and on the state's border with Illinois (seven casinos). Only two of Iowa's thirteen casinos are located more than three miles from the state border.[9]

Table 2.1 shows gross casino revenues by state between 1999 and 2004, along with the annual growth rate from 1999 to 2004. Iowa and Indiana experienced the most rapid growth during this period, with annual growth rates of 16.6 percent and 16.5 percent, respectively. New Jersey experienced the slowest annual growth rate during this period at 3.7 percent.

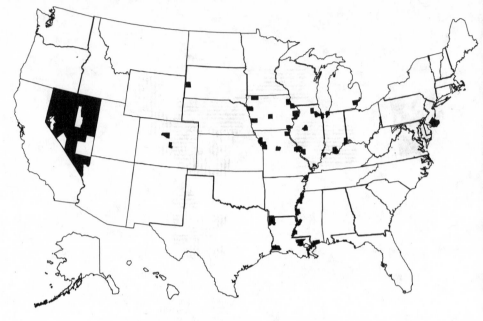

Fig. 2.2. Commercial casino counties, 2003

TABLE 2.1.   Commercial casino AGR by state and growth rate, 1999–2004

	AGR (in millions of dollars)						Compound Annual Growth (%)
	1999	2000	2001	2002	2003	2004	1999–2004
Colorado	479.0	631.8	631.8	719.7	698.2	725.9	8.7
Illinois	1,100.0	1,700.0	1,800.0	1,800.0	1,709.0	1,718.0	9.3
Indiana	1,100.0	1,700.0	1,800.0	2,100.0	2,229.0	2,369.0	16.6
Iowa	496.0	887.0	922.9	972.3	1,024.0	1,064.0	16.5
Louisiana	1,300.0	1,800.0	1,800.0	2,000.0	2,017.0	2,163.0	10.7
Michigan	N.A.	743.6	1,000.0	1,100.0	1,130.0	1,189.0	12.5
Mississippi	2,200.0	2,649.0	2,701.0	2,700.0	2,700.0	2,781.0	4.8
Missouri	853.0	997.7	1,100.0	1,300.0	1,330.0	1,473.0	11.5
Nevada	8,100.0	9,600.0	9,500.0	9,400.0	9,625.0	10,562.0	5.5
New Jersey	4,000.0	4,300.0	4,300.0	4,360.0	4,490.0	4,807.0	3.7
South Dakota	44.0	51.8	58.6	66.3	70.4	78.0	12.1
U.S.	19,672.0	25,060.9	25,614.3	26,518.3	27,022.6	28,929.9	8.0
As % of U.S. GDP	2.12	2.55	2.54	2.53	2.46	2.47	

Source: American Gaming Association and U.S. Bureau of Economic Analysis.

This difference may be explained, in part, by the fact that Iowa and Indiana are newer casino markets, whereas Atlantic City, New Jersey, is a more mature market, having casinos that have operated since 1978. Michigan, the latest state to add casinos to its economic mix, experienced growth of 12.5 percent per year between 2000 (the first full year of operation) and 2004. Nationwide, commercial casino revenues, termed "adjusted gross receipts" (AGR),[10] grew from $8.3 billion in 1990 to $28.9 billion in 2004. This reflects a compounded yearly growth rate of almost 8 percent—more than three times the rate of inflation and more than twice the rate of U.S. economic growth as measured by the nation's gross domestic product.

Revenues per casino visitor also vary significantly among the commercial casino states. Table 2.2 lists attendance and average revenue per visitor by state for 2004. Spending per casino visitor ranged from $27 in Missouri to $209 in Nevada.[11] The average visitor across the United States spent $91 per casino visit in 2004. However, the 319 million visits or attendance came from 54.1 million individuals. Thus, on average, each individual who visited a casino in 2004 lost $535 for the full year.

Table 2.3 ranks casino locations across the United States based on 2004 AGR. While locations in Nevada and New Jersey, states with the older

TABLE 2.2.   Commercial casino attendance and AGR per visitor, 2004

	Attendance	Compound Annual Growth 2001–4 (%)	AGR per Casino Visitor ($)
Colorado	N.A.	N.A.	N.A.
Illinois	15,300,000	−6.6	112
Indiana	26,730,000	10.5	89
Iowa	19,540,000	0.2	54
Louisiana	40,890,000	−3.8	53
Michigan	N.A.	N.A.	N.A.
Mississippi	55,260,000	−0.9	50
Missouri	54,200,000	4.5	27
Nevada	50,500,000	0.6	209
New Jersey	33,230,000	0.8	145
South Dakota	N.A.	N.A.	N.A.
U.S.	319,000,000	−0.4	91

Source: American Gaming Association.
N.A. = not available

casinos, are ranked highly, new casino locations in Indiana, Michigan, and Mississippi have moved up rapidly in the rankings. Proximity to large population bases appears to be a significant factor in the AGR potential of commercial casino facilities. This also suggests the importance of local patronage to the successful casino.

TRIBAL CASINOS

The development of tribal casino gambling traces its roots to the Supreme Court's 1987 decision in *California v. Cabazon Band of Mission Indians,*[12] where the Court held that the state of California lacked authority to apply its regulatory statutes to gambling activities conducted on Indian reservations.[13] Tribal sovereignty in these matters was subordinate only to the federal government, and state power to regulate was thus dependent on congressional authorization. Congress quickly responded to this decision in 1988 by en-

TABLE 2.3.   Ranking of casinos by location, 2001, 2003, 2004

	Rank			
2004	2003	2001	Location	2004 AGR ($)
1	1	1	Las Vegas—Strip	5.555 billion
2	2	2	Atlantic City, NJ	4.806 billion
3	3	3	Chicagoland (IL, IN)	2.346 billion
4	4	N.A.	Connecticut (Indian)	1.646 billion
5	6	5	Tunica, MS	1.199 billion
6	5	4	Detroit, MI	1.189 billion
7	8	6	Biloxi, MS	911.45 million
8	7	7	Reno/Sparks, NV	903.45 million
9	9	8	Southeast Indiana	885.90 million
10	11	10	St. Louis (MO, IL)	848.41 million
11	10	9	Shreveport, LA	835.51 million
12	12	12	Boulder Strip (NV)	791.69 million
13	14	13	Kansas City, MO	701.39 million
14	13	11	Las Vegas—Downtown	663.28 million
15	15	15	New Orleans	608.80 million
16	16	14	Laughlin, NV	595.32 million
17	17	16	Black Hawk, CO	524.04 million
18	18	19	Lake Charles, LA	462.07 million
19	19	18	Council Bluffs, IA	418.18 million
20	24	N.A.	Charlestown, WV (racino)	360.23 million

Source: Innovation Group, October 2001, 2003, 2004.
N.A. = not available

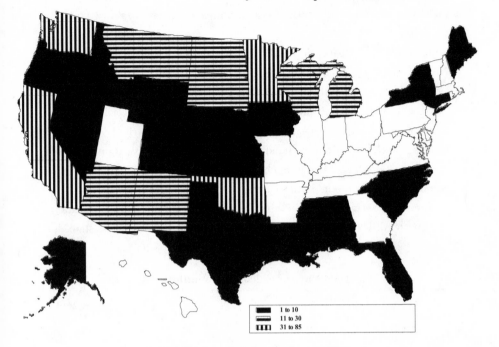

Fig. 2.3. Number of tribal casinos by state, 2004

acting the Indian Gaming Regulatory Act (IGRA),[14] which attempted to balance the interests of the states and of the tribes located within their geographical borders.

The IGRA was intended to accomplish several policy goals, which included (1) promoting tribal economic development and self-sufficiency; (2) providing a regulatory base to protect Indian gaming from organized crime, to ensure that the tribe is the beneficiary of the gaming operation, and to ensure the fairness and honesty of the gaming operation; and (3) establishing the National Indian Gaming Commission to assist in these purposes.[15] The IGRA essentially recognized tribal rights to operate gaming facilities on their reservations commensurate with the types of gaming that could otherwise be operated under state law.

Figure 2.3 shows the number of tribal casinos in each state as of 2004.[16] There were 405 tribal gaming facilities in the United States in 2004 compared to 385 in 2003. In 2004, Oklahoma had the largest number of tribal casinos at 85, followed by California at 56 and Minnesota and Washington each with 31. Class III tribal casino facilities are located in 192 counties across the United States.

Table 2.4 lists tribal casino AGR (i.e., wagers less winnings) by state from 2002 to 2004. California had the highest AGR at $5.3 billion, followed by Connecticut at $2.2 billion and Arizona at $1.5 billion. The data indicate that tribal casino AGR is quickly approaching that of commercial casinos. In some of these states, tribes have been granted exclusive rights to operate casinos, which have often included opportunities to exploit gaming markets with large population bases. Such operations can provide significant economic benefits for their tribal owners.

The top five states listed in table 2.4 all have exclusive gaming relationships with tribal governments, with no commercial casinos in the state. In-

TABLE 2.4.   Tribal AGR by state, 2002–4 (in millions of dollars)

State	2002	2003	2004	Growth 2002–4 (%)
Alaska	8.1	8.4	8.5	4.9
Arizona	1,094.2	1,218.3	1,533.7	40.2
California	3,678.1	4,699.9	5,324.3	44.8
Colorado	54.1	55.2	57.4	6.1
Connecticut	2,054.4	2,157.0	2,231.9	8.6
Florida	572.1	642.0	862.0	50.7
Idaho	94.2	103.9	140.0	48.6
Kansas	165.0	169.8	171.3	3.8
Louisiana	444.1	448.1	372.7	−16.1
Michigan	965.0	969.9	971.0	0.6
Minnesota	1,309.4	1,326.8	1,343.3	2.6
Montana	15.0	15.5	16.3	8.7
Nevada	45.0	44.0	51.6	14.7
New Mexico	576.9	613.6	707.4	22.6
New York	275.0	577.3	730.5	165.6
North Dakota	89.0	95.0	96.9	8.9
Oklahoma	461.1	641.8	939.3	103.7
Oregon	418.9	433.9	460.1	9.8
South Dakota	44.5	50.0	53.0	19.1
Washington	707.8	888.0	987.5	39.5
Wisconsin	980.7	991.5	1,004.1	2.4
Other states	850.0	872.1	974.3	14.6
All states	14,902.6	17,022.0	19,037.1	27.7

Source: Indian Gaming Industry Report, 2005–6.

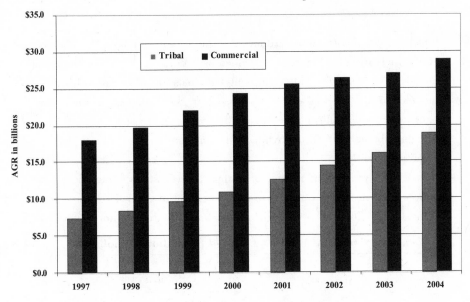

Fig. 2.4. Tribal versus commercial AGR, 1997–2004

terestingly, between 2002 and 2004, tribal AGR growth in states without commercial casinos was much higher than in states with commercial casinos. Collectively, tribal AGR in states with no commercial casinos grew by 44.5 percent, while tribal AGR in states with commercial casinos actually declined by 3.0 percent between 2002 and 2004. This indicates the importance of exclusive agreements between the tribes and the states in terms of producing higher growth rates in gambling revenue.

Tribal casino AGR has been growing at a rate that even surpasses the healthy growth rate of their commercial counterparts. Figure 2.4 attests to the rapid growth in casino gambling in terms of AGR. The aggregate AGR from tribal casinos increased from $8.2 billion in 1997 to more than $19.0 billion in 2004, an annual growth rate of nearly 14.2 percent. In contrast, the growth rate for commercial casinos slowed somewhat during this period to an average of 6.8 percent per year. Significantly, if these growth trends continue, the gap in AGR between commercial and tribal casinos will soon no longer exist. This growth trend is certainly not surprising given the favorable tax treatment afforded tribal casinos—a topic that is explored in greater detail in chapters 4 and 11.

RACINOS

Racetrack casinos (racinos) are an increasingly important segment of the U.S. casino market. A racino is defined as a horse-racing track that also includes slot machines, video gambling terminals, or other casino features. Included in the category are also dog-racing tracks that offer the same gambling opportunities. Proponents assert that racinos allow states to derive the economic benefits of gaming while containing gaming expansion to current racetrack facilities.

In 2004, twenty-four racinos operating in seven states generated $2.78 billion in AGR, which was up from $2.20 billion in 2003. However, more than $190 million of the increase was produced by the addition of four ra-

TABLE 2.5.   Racino AGR by state, 2002–4 (in millions of dollars)

State	2002	2003	2004	Growth 2002–4 (%)
Delaware	565.9	502.0	553.32	−2.2
Iowa	316.1	330.3	337.48	6.8
Louisiana	114.6	168.9	280.97	145.2
New Mexico	141.3	149.8	149.68	5.9
New York	N.A.	N.A.	192.45	N.A.
Rhode Island	281.0	333.5	383.8	36.6
West Virginia	596.0	717.1	882.4	48.1
Total	2,014.9	2,201.6	2,780.1	38.0

Source: American Gaming Association, yearly surveys.
N.A. = not available

TABLE 2.6.   Top racino markets, 2004 (in millions of dollars)

Rank	Top Markets	2004
1	Charlestown, WV	360.24
2	Providence, RI	304.77
3	Dover/Harrington, DE	297.70
4	Delaware Park/Wilmington, DE	261.60
5	Chester, WV	255.73
6	Wheeling, WV	192.12
7	Des Moines, IA	161.47
9	Council Bluffs, IA	133.94
9	Lake Charles/Vinton, LA	128.39
10	Shreveport, LA	84.24

Source: American Gaming Association, 2004 survey.

cinos in New York in 2004. Also 2004 marked the first full year of operation for two of Louisiana's three racinos.

Table 2.6 lists the top racino markets for 2004. As presented, Charlestown, West Virginia, was the largest racino market at $360.24 million in 2004 AGR. In fact, Charlestown's racino AGR was significant enough to place this market in twentieth place in terms of overall casino markets for 2004, up from twenty-fourth place in 2003.

Table 2.7 provides comparative data for commercial casinos, tribal casinos, and racinos for 2004. While there were more commercial casinos in 2003 than tribal casinos, the number of casinos added in the past few years clearly favors tribal casinos, with all 192 tribal casinos added in the past fifteen years. During this same period of time, only 175 commercial casinos were created. Table 2.7 also shows that a significant difference exists in the share of AGR going to government coffers, with 16.4 percent of commercial AGR paid to state and local governments but only 6.1 percent of tribal AGR being paid to state and local governments in lieu of taxes. (These tax differentials are the product of limits on the state taxing powers accorded to Indian tribes, a topic addressed in greater detail in chapter 11.)

Table 2.7 also shows the significantly higher tax rate paid by racinos, whose average tax rate is more than double that of commercial casinos. However, Iowa racinos sued the state of Iowa, claiming that the state's practice of taxing racetrack gambling at a higher rate than riverboat gambling violated

TABLE 2.7.   Comparison of commercial casinos, tribal casinos, and racinos

	Commercial	Tribal	Racinos
Number of casinos, 2004	445	405	24
Total 2004 AGR (in billions of dollars)	28.9	19.0	2.8
AGR per casino (in millions of dollars)	65.0	47.0	115.8
AGR growth, 2002–4 (%)	9.1	27.7	38.0
Taxes or revenue sharing, 2004 (in billions of dollars)	4.7	0.9	1.1
Effective tax or revenue sharing rate, 2003 (%)	16.4	4.7	38.6

Sources: Authors' calculation based on American Gaming Association surveys and *Indian Gaming Industry Report.*

Note: For Iowa and Louisiana, the AGA includes racino AGR with casino AGR. The total tribal casinos of 405 includes Class II (no slots or table games) and Class III (slots and/or table games).

the Fourteenth Amendment's Equal Protection Clause. The Iowa Supreme
Court ultimately agreed with the industry on state constitutional grounds,
despite a temporary victory for the state in the U.S. Supreme Court.[17]

INDUSTRY LEADERS

While casino gambling has expanded rapidly in the United States, the companies owning and/or managing the casinos have likewise grown at a brisk
rate. Table 2.8 lists the largest casino firms in the United States according to
market capitalization. Also listed in table 2.8 are the return on equity and
current price-earnings ratios of each firm. For companies earning a positive
income, the price-earnings ratio is calculated by dividing the current price

TABLE 2.8.   Casino leaders in market capitalization, 2005

Name of Company	Stock Exchange Symbol	Market Capitalization (in millions of dollars)[a]	Return on Equity (%)[b]	Price-Earnings Ratio[c]
Las Vegas Sands Corp.	LVS	12,700	42.8	26.8
MGM Mirage	MGM	10,200	13.4	29.0
International Game Tech	IGT	9,600	20.2	25.4
Harrah's Entertainment	HET	7,700	3.8	16.9*
Caesars Entertainment Inc.	CZR	6,400	2.9	68.5
Wynn Resorts LTD	WYNN	4,800	−17.1	39.6*
Boyd Gaming Corp.	BYD	4,800	20.5	30.1
Station Casinos	STN	4,300	31.4	32.1
Penn National Gaming	PENN	2,700	21.8	32.2
Scientific Games	SGMS	1,900	21.7	32.7
Ameristar Casinos	ASCA	1,410	21.4	22.0
Argosy Casino	AGY	1,360	22.4	17.5
Aztar Casino	AZR	1,130	6.2	18.4
Isle of Capri	ISLE	774.2	4.1	77.3
Century Casinos	CNTY	102	12.9	24.8
Diamonds	DIA	N.A.	N.A.	16.2
Spyders	SPY	N.A.	N.A.	16.0

Source: Reuters and Yahoo.com.

[a]Market capitalization is equal to the number of shares of stock outstanding multiplied by
the stock price.

[b]Return on equity is equal to the profits divided by total net worth of the firm.

[c]The price-earnings ratio is calculated by dividing the price of the stock by the earnings
over the past year.

*Indicates forward price-earnings ratio.

N.A. = not available

by last year's operating income. For companies with a negative income, the price-earnings ratio is calculated by dividing the current price by next year's income as estimated by analysts tracking the stock.[18]

Las Vegas Sands, with a market capitalization of $12.7 billion, is the largest publicly traded casino company listed on the New York Stock Exchange or the NASDAQ Exchange. Las Vegas Sands also had the highest return on equity at 42.8 percent, but not the highest price-earnings ratio. Despite having a return on equity of only 2.9 percent, Caesars had the highest price-earnings ratio of 68.5. Typically a high price-earnings ratio stems from high projected earnings growth rate or lower risk as assessed by investors. The median price-earnings ratio for the casino firms listed in table 2.8 is 30.0. This compares to 16.2 for the thirty Dow Jones industrial firms traded as Diamonds and 16.0 for the five hundred firms that make up the Standard and Poor's Index and traded as Spyders.[19] This data suggest that investors are estimating higher growth, or lower risks, for casinos than for other large firms in the United States.

Table 2.9 shows casino revenues by year for the casino companies listed in table 2.8.[20] As presented, Pennsylvania National Gaming experienced the highest rate of annual growth at 108.9 percent, and Station Casinos experienced the lowest rate of annual growth at 2.8 percent. Harrah's, with over $4 billion in casino revenues, was the top casino company. However, among the ten firms, only Station Casinos had a lower growth rate in revenues than Harrah's. Growth rates for firms listed in table 2.9 are considerably higher than casino AGR. In fact, the revenue growth of Pennsylvania National Gaming was roughly ten times that of casino AGR across the United States, while revenue growth of Las Vegas Sands was more than four times that of U.S. casino AGR. AGR is just one component of casino revenues, with other revenues coming from the sale of food and beverages and other items.

Table 2.10 lists casino revenues as a percentage of total revenues by year by company. Pennsylvania National Gaming casino revenue as a percentage of total revenue was the highest among the companies at 87.0 percent, while International Game Tech was the lowest at 46.8 percent. Table 2.10 shows clearly that casino revenues represent a significant and, in some cases, preponderant share of total company sales or revenues. However, five of the ten firms experienced a decline in casino revenues as a share of total revenues. In

TABLE 2.9. Casino revenues, 1997–2004 (in thousands of dollars)

	Las Vegas Sands	Harrah's	Caesars	International Game Tech	Boyd Gaming Corp.	Penn National Gaming	MGM Mirage	Station Casinos	Ameristar Casinos	Century Casinos
1997	N.A.	1,338,003	1,832	282,820	323,707	5,712	457,206	600,847	173,077	19,096,857
1998	N.A.	1,660,313	1,587	347,099	722,124	37,396	410,605	509,149	216,345	19,036,621
1999	N.A.	2,424,237	2,269	353,064	733,677	55,125	873,781	764,089	247,416	22,726,004
2000	N.A.	2,852,048	3,480	401,014	868,983	159,589	1,913,733	807,880	286,438	27,703,000
2001	227,240	3,235,761	3,271	374,942	912,427	366,166	2,163,808	659,276	551,648	30,096,000
2002	256,484	3,688,416	3,337	882,432	1,045,082	494,271	2,189,720	638,113	678,642	30,607,000
2003	272,804	3,853,150	3,212	1,059,539	1,073,736	976,411	2,075,569	648,664	760,376	31,869,000
2004	708,564	4,077,694	2,872	1,163,416	1,454,884	992,088	2,223,965	730,584	856,901	N.A.
Annual growth rates (%)	46.1	17.3	6.6	22.4	24.0	108.9	25.4	2.8	25.6	8.9

Source: Authors' calculations from Reuters and Yahoo! data.

N.A. = not available

addition to casino revenues, total revenues include food and drink sales, hotel rentals, and entertainment ticket sales.

Table 2.11 lists operating income as a percentage of revenues for all companies reporting results. This measure of profitability ranged from 14.6 percent to 49.1 percent. For 2004, Las Vegas Sands experienced the highest rate at 49.1 percent, and International Game Tech had the second highest rate at 32.8 percent. Interestingly, these two firms earned a high proportion of their revenues from noncasino sources. The firms that depended more heavily on casino revenues tended to experience lower earnings rates.

In order to accomplish the revenue growth listed in table 2.9, casinos spend heavily on advertising and promotion. According to Christiansen Capital Advisors, the casino industry currently spends 2.5 percent of casino

TABLE 2.10.   Casino revenues as a percentage of total revenues

	Las Vegas Sands	Harrah's	Caesars	International Game Tech	Boyd Gaming Corp.	Penn National Gaming	MGM Mirage	Station Casinos	Ameristar Casinos	Century Casinos
1997	N.A.	75.7	71.2	38.0	64.7	5.1	51.3	73.0	78.1	94.0
1998	N.A.	75.9	68.9	42.1	67.6	24.3	48.9	73.6	75.5	94.6
1999	N.A.	73.2	71.4	38.0	67.8	32.2	58.1	75.6	76.2	93.8
2000	N.A.	74.8	71.1	39.9	69.4	54.3	54.4	76.3	77.4	93.1
2001	36.1	75.7	71.4	31.3	74.6	70.5	49.0	72.3	83.2	89.8
2002	39.0	76.0	71.7	47.8	77.0	75.2	49.1	73.7	84.2	90.7
2003	37.0	75.5	72.1	49.8	77.0	84.0	48.0	70.1	83.5	88.4
2004	56.3	75.4	68.3	46.8	75.3	87.0	47.6	69.3	84.0	N.A.

Source: Authors' calculations from Reuters and Yahoo! data.
N.A. = not available

TABLE 2.11.   Net operating income as a percentage of revenue

	Las Vegas Sands	Harrah's	Caesars	International Game Tech	Boyd Gaming Corp.	Penn National Gaming	MGM Mirage	Station Casinos	Ameristar Casinos	Century Casinos
1997	N.A.	12.1	7.8	25.7	11.6	8.7	21.4	10.2	12.6	0.0
1998	N.A.	13.2	13.1	26.6	11.6	12.6	15.7	9.4	1.1	3.2
1999	N.A.	14.5	12.6	12.5	12.6	10.4	14.0	2.9	7.9	9.6
2000	N.A.	7.4	14.2	26.6	14.3	15.6	15.3	22.9	−6.1	13.5
2001	20.7	13.6	8.9	33.0	9.5	15.0	14.2	15.4	17.3	17.5
2002	24.3	16.1	12.3	28.8	12.1	15.5	17.2	16.8	14.3	18.4
2003	25.3	14.2	10.3	31.3	10.7	15.8	16.5	15.2	15.4	20.2
2004	49.1	14.6	14.8	32.8	15.3	18.7	20.4	24.4	15.6	N.A.

Source: Authors' calculations from Reuters and Yahoo! data.
N.A. = not available

revenues on advertising and promotion.[21] In an effort to lure increasing numbers of patrons, casinos continue to spend heavily on new promotions. The promotion competition between casinos tends to get pretty intense, especially in the major markets. For example, eight casinos compete for gambling patrons in the Chicago area. One of the large casino companies, Harrah's, recently initiated its $1,000,000 Treasure Hunt. Customers at Harrah's properties nationwide throughout the year earned an entry into the contest by the frequency of their gambling visits. The customers earned an opportunity to travel to Las Vegas on November 10, 2005, to search for a treasure chest containing $1 million in a remote desert location. This is an example of Harrah's efforts to increase repeat business.

At the Grand Victoria Casino in Elgin, Illinois, all dice players have to do is roll each of the six point numbers (4, 5, 6, 8, 9, and 10) during a single "hand" of their roll at a live craps game. Should the shooter roll all the numbers at least once before rolling a 7 the player wins a bonus payment of four thousand dollars in cash.

In 2002, Majestic Star in Detroit ran a promotion on table games entitled "Money for Nothing, Chips for Free." On Thursdays from January to October 2002, the staff members at Majestic Star randomly selected a table every ten minutes. Every player at that table who was using his or her Club Majestic card received free gaming chips, in amounts ranging from five to one hundred dollars.

Caesars in Tunica, Mississippi, offers what they term Grand One Players Club. By earning thirty thousand or more slot points or six hundred hours of rated play on table games with a twenty-five-dollar average bet or the equivalent, players can join the Grand One Players Club. Play must be accumulated in a twelve-month period. Patrons earn a 25 percent cash back bonus seven days a week. They also earn free spa services, including one free spa or salon service per month, VIP restaurant seating, VIP valet retrieval, VIP self-parking, VIP show seating, VIP hotel check-in, VIP reservation services, preferred tee times at Cottonwoods golf course, free room upgrade, invitation to private Grand One member events, and extra sweepstakes entry tickets. Final membership is determined by a combination of various play criteria and management approval.

Table 2.12 shows casino promotion spending by company from 1997 to 2004. Interestingly, Las Vegas Sands, the most profitable casino, grew their casino promotion budget at a rate much slower than all of its competitors, except for Station Casinos. Thus, the two low-growth casino firms, in terms of promotion spending, were the two casinos with the highest operating income as a percentage of revenues. It may be that low-earning casinos responded to their low earnings by increasing their promotion spending. Table 2.13 lists casino promotion spending as a percentage of revenues.

In order to investigate the relationship among promotion spending, operating income, and casino income, we calculate correlation coefficients between each relationship. A correlation coefficient measures the degree to which two variables are linearly related or associated. As the strength of the

TABLE 2.12.   Casino promotion spending

	Las Vegas Sands	Harrah's	Boyd Gaming Corp.	Penn National Gaming	MGM Mirage	Station Casinos	Ameristar Casinos	Century Casinos
1997		$147,432	$44,308		$63,733	$53,426	$15,530	
1998		$184,477	$93,772		$66,219	$49,176	$22,071	$753,063
1999		$286,539	$94,547		$112,560	$67,892	$24,618	$672,153
2000		$340,438	$98,268		$286,343	$67,659	$28,224	$653,120
2001	$42,594	$565,758	$120,656		$407,071	$72,816	$36,598	$755,000
2002	$34,208	$717,628	$128,547	$27,713	$428,318	$73,281	$108,406	$3,943,000
2003	$44,856	$782,050	$141,459	$74,324	$415,643	$67,365	$128,272	$4,424,000
2004	$61,514	$862,806	$198,033	$65,615	$434,384	$67,857	$165,461	$4,657,000
Growth (%)	13.0	28.7	23.9	54.0	31.6	3.5	40.2	35.5

Source: Authors' calculations based on data from Reuters.

TABLE 2.13.   Casino promotion spending as a percentage of casino revenues

	Las Vegas Sands	Harrah's	Boyd Gaming Corp.	Penn National Gaming	MGM Mirage	Station Casinos	Ameristar Casinos	Century Casinos
1997		11.0	13.7		13.9	8.9	9.0	
1998		11.1	13.0		16.1	9.7	10.2	4.0
1999		11.8	12.9		12.9	8.9	10.0	3.0
2000		11.9	11.3		15.0	8.4	9.9	2.4
2001		17.5	13.2		18.8	11.0	6.6	2.5
2002	17.3	19.5	12.3	5.6	19.6	11.5	16.0	12.9
2003	14.0	20.3	13.2	7.6	20.0	10.4	16.9	13.9
2004	10.8	21.2	13.6	6.6	19.5	9.3	19.3	

Source: Authors' calculations based on data from Reuters.

relationship between two variables increases, so does the correlation coefficient. A correlation coefficient can range between -1, perfectly and negatively related to $+1$, perfectly and positively related. A correlation coefficient of 0 means that there is no linear relationship between the variables. For example, the correlation coefficient between the temperature measured in Fahrenheit and centigrade is $+1$.

Table 2.14 lists correlation coefficients between each of the variables. According to the results, operating income and promotion spending are positively related with a small correlation coefficient of 0.163. On the other hand, operating income and casino revenues are negatively related with a larger correlation coefficient of -0.496, and operating income and casino revenues are also negatively associated with a correlation coefficient of -0.454. Perhaps low-earning casinos, in order to remedy the problem, are spending more aggressively on promotion. Moreover, casinos that make a large share of their revenues from noncasino activities appear to be earning higher operating incomes.

Almost 300 tribal casinos and 175 commercial casinos have been constructed during the past fifteen years, with more on the way. For many Americans, access to casino gambling is more convenient than ever. Though the growth of commercial casinos appears to have slowed somewhat, tribal casinos are continuing to expand. Tax and legal structures appear to be contributing to this disparate growth, as tribes have achieved competitive advantages over their commercial counterparts in building and opening new operations.

Although some states have benefited from tribal operations through the granting of exclusive rights (a topic explored further in chapter 11), those with both commercial and tribal facilities must draw the vast majority of state revenues from commercial operations. Thus, a shift toward tribal gam-

TABLE 2.14.   Correlation coefficients, 1997–2004

	Promotion Spending	Operating Income	Casino Revenue
Promotion spending	1.000		
Operating income	0.163	1.000	
Casino revenues	−0.496	−0.454	1.000

Source: Authors' calculations.

ing potentially threatens an important source of tax revenues. Moreover, the potential for stagnation of casino collections as markets mature should awaken government officials to the danger of heavy reliance on growing revenue streams from casino operations. The nature and extent of those revenues, and their rising importance in each of the casino states, are considered in chapter 3.

Company financial statements indicate that casino company earnings and revenues have been growing robustly since 1997. Furthermore, investors are rewarding casino companies by bidding up the stock prices of the companies to the point where their price-earnings ratios are significantly above market averages. This indicates that investors expect casino profits to continue to grow at a pace exceeding that of the average publicly listed corporation.

3. Tax Revenues from Casinos

As presented in chapter 2, legalized casino gambling has emerged as a significant growth industry in the United States. State and local governments are willing participants in this expansion as they have increasingly looked to casino gambling as a new source of tax revenues, with citizens generally supporting the expansion of gambling. For many citizens, funding government activities with "voluntary" casino tax collections presents an attractive alternative to raising traditional or noncasino taxes. Additionally, with the promise of job and income growth, states have embraced gambling and casino wagering as tonics to remedy economic lethargy. However, it is unclear whether the addition of casino gambling actually reduces the tax burdens of citizens and is a net benefit to the community. Certainly the economic benefits or costs of casino expansion may depend on whether the added casinos are tribal or commercial.

TRIBAL CASINO PAYMENTS

Given significant differences between the taxes paid by commercial casinos and the payments in lieu of taxes paid by tribal casinos, the benefits to the community are likely to depend crucially on whether the casino is commercial or tribal. Indian tribes occupy an unusual legal status in our federal system. Tribes possess a limited sovereignty consistent with their status as "domestic dependent nations."[1] This sovereignty has limited state and local governments' ability to obtain funds via taxation from the operation of tribal casinos. The legal consequences of tribal status are discussed at length in chapter 11.

According to estimates by Meister in his 2005–6 *Indian Gaming Industry Report*, tribal casinos, despite any legal responsibility to pay state and local

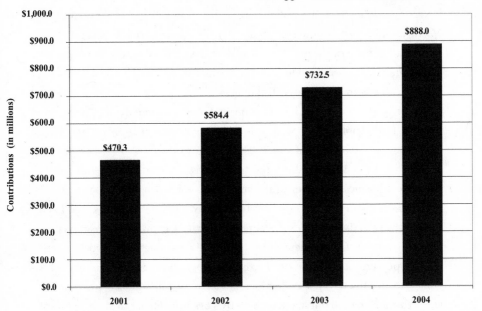

Fig. 3.1. Tribal casino contributions to state and local government, 2001–4 (in millions of dollars)

casino taxes, contributed $888.0 million to state and local governments on 2004 AGR of $19.0 billion.[2] This represents an average "tax" rate of 4.7 percent. Figure 3.1 shows that tribal contributions to state and local government tax coffers have risen from $470.3 million in 2001 to $888.0 million in 2004.

Despite the IGRA limits on state taxing powers, states have been allowed to negotiate gaming compacts that extract a payment for granting exclusive gaming rights to tribal interests. For example, this model is followed in Connecticut, which has no commercial casinos but two tribal casinos. By granting exclusive rights to the tribes, Connecticut reaped $411.4 million in payments in lieu of taxes from these two casinos in 2004, or approximately 46 percent of total tribal contributions to state and local governments in 2004. Thus, the two Connecticut casinos racked up an average of $205.7 million in tax receipts while the remaining 403 tribal casinos brought in an average of slightly less than $1.2 million in tax revenue.

Table 3.1 shows tribal casino contributions to state and local governments by state for 2003 and 2004. As listed, California and Connecticut accounted for almost 70 percent of total tribal contributions to state and local governments in 2004. Two of the states listed in table 3.1, Louisiana and Michigan, also had commercial casinos within their borders. Several other states had tribal casinos but did not report any tribal casino contributions. These include Colorado, Florida, Iowa, Kansas, Montana, Nevada, North Dakota, Oklahoma, and South Dakota.

As presented in table 3.1, Wisconsin tribes expanded their payments from casino gambling to state and local governments at the strongest pace in the nation between 2003 and 2004. Wisconsin Potawatomi tribal officials contend that the $40.5 million the tribe paid to the state in 2003 made it the largest business taxpayer in the state that year.[3]

Table 3.2 lists effective tax rates by state by year for tribal casinos. Even though the effective tax rates remain low, they have grown each year. As presented for 2004, Connecticut collected the highest rate from tribal casinos at 20.3 percent and Minnesota netted the lowest rate at 1.2 percent. This wide gap in effective tax collections is easily explained. As stated earlier, tribal casinos opened pursuant to the IGRA are not subject to state and local taxes on gaming revenues. State taxing powers are limited to recovering amounts necessary to cover regulatory costs, with amounts above this as

TABLE 3.1.   Tribal contributions to state and local governments, 2003, 2004

	2003 ($)	2004 ($)	Growth 2003–4 (%)
Connecticut	396,400,000	411,400,000	3.8
California	131,600,000	153,200,000	16.4
Arizona	26,100,000	70,100,000	168.6
Wisconsin	16,700,000	68,000,000	307.2
New York	39,000,000	57,100,000	46.4
New Mexico	36,900,000	39,500,000	7.0
Michigan	31,500,000	31,400,000	−0.3
Minnesota	16,100,000	16,100,000	0.0
Washington	8,900,000	9,900,000	11.2
Oregon	8,900,000	9,500,000	6.7
Louisiana	10,200,000	8,500,000	−16.7
Idaho	5,200,000	7,000,000	34.6
Alaska	300,000	300,000	0.0
*Other states	4,700,000	6,000,000	27.7
Total all states	732,500,000	888,000,000	21.2

Source: Indian Gaming Industry Report 2005–6.

purely voluntary contributions. Thus, tribal casinos not only fail to generate gaming taxes, but they may also erode the tax base through competition with commercial activities.

As listed in table 3.2, California's tribal casinos, with an average tax rate of 3.6 percent in 2004, represent an important contrast to Connecticut's. In March 2000, California governor Gray Davis signed unbreakable twenty-year compacts with sixty-one tribes, giving them a monopoly casino industry. However, in June 2005 Governor Davis's replacement, Governor Arnold Schwarzenegger, announced deals with five of California's casino-owning Indian tribes to provide the state with $150–200 million annually.[4] Schwarzenegger, like many other U.S. governors, is bumping up against increasing demands for state dollars while at the same time facing the barrier of tribal sovereignty. Politicians in states with commercial casinos are experiencing a much more positive environment, at least in terms of casino tax receipts.

COMMERCIAL CASINO TAX COLLECTIONS

As stated earlier, tax rates on commercial casinos are typically more than five times those of tribal casinos, depending on the state. Table 3.3 shows the

TABLE 3.2.   Tribal casino payments in lieu of taxes as a percentage of AGR, 2001–4

	2001	2002	2003	2004
Connecticut	20.7	19.7	19.6	20.3
New York	N.A.	N.A.	7.1	10.4
New Mexico	0.4	6.0	6.0	6.5
Wisconsin	2.7	2.4	1.5	6.3
Idaho	1.2	1.1	4.4	5.9
Arizona	N.A.	N.A.	2.1	5.8
California	0.8	2.0	3.1	3.6
Michigan	3.4	3.5	3.6	3.6
Alaska	3.9	3.7	3.6	3.6
Oregon	2.3	2.1	2.1	2.2
Louisiana	2.3	2.1	2.1	1.7
Washington	0.5	1.1	1.2	1.3
Minnesota	1.2	1.2	1.2	1.2
Other states	0.3	0.1	0.1	0.2
Total	3.7	3.9	4.3	5.2

Source: Author calculations based on Meister data.

N.A. = not available

legislated casino tax rates on commercial casinos in each state where they exist. Marginal tax rates range from 6.25 percent in Nevada to as much as 70 percent in Illinois. In addition to tax rates on AGR, many states also assess admission fees for each gambler, but these admission fees are paid by the casino from the proceeds of the casino and are not dependent on the gambling losses, or AGR, of the casino patron. However, the experience of each state has varied as widely as the characteristics of the populations of the states.

Based on the rates listed in table 3.3, the American Gaming Association (AGA) estimates that commercial casinos paid $4.7 billion in wagering taxes alone in 2004—a figure that does not include income, property, and sales taxes that casinos also contribute to public coffers. This represents an average tax rate on AGR of 16.4 percent. The 445 commercial casinos operating in eleven states have become an increasingly powerful tax-generating engine for specific locales of the United States, with tax collections from casinos

TABLE 3.3.   **Legislated casino tax rates by state, 2005**

Colorado	Graduated tax rate with a maximum tax of 20% on gross gaming revenue
Illinois	Graduated tax rate from 15% to 70% of gross gaming revenue, $3–5 per patron admissions tax
Indiana	Graduated tax rate from 15% to 35% of gross gaming revenue, $3 per patron admissions tax
Iowa	Graduated tax rate with a maximum tax of 22% on gross gaming revenue
Louisiana	Riverboat casinos: 21.5%; land-based casino: $60 million annual tax or 21.5% of gross gaming revenue, whichever is greater; racetrack casinos: 18.5% tax on gross gaming revenue,[3] 18% of net revenue paid to horsemen
Michigan	24% tax on gross gaming revenue (11.9% to city of Detroit, 12.1% to state of Michigan); effective tax rate of 23.02% (including taxes and fees)
Mississippi	Graduated tax rate with a maximum state tax of 8% on gaming revenue; up to 4% additional tax on gaming revenues may be imposed by local governments
Missouri	20% tax on gross gaming revenue, $2 per patron admission fee per excursion split between home dock community and the state
Nevada	Graduated tax rate with a maximum tax of 6.75% on gross gaming revenue; additional fees and levies may be imposed by counties, municipalities, and the state, adding approximately 1% to the tax burden
New Jersey	8% tax on gross gaming revenue plus a community investment alternative obligation of 1.25% of gross gaming revenue (or an investment alternative 2.5% on gross gaming revenue), 4.25% tax on casino ancillaries effective July 1, 2003*
South Dakota	8% tax on gross gaming revenue, gaming device tax of $2,000 per machine per year

Source: American Gaming Association, 2005 survey.

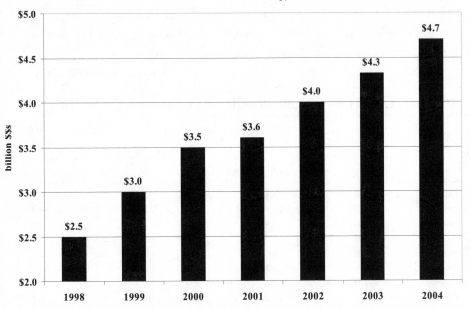

Fig. 3.2. Commercial casino wagering taxes paid, 1998–2004 (in billions of dollars)

growing much faster than overall tax collections. Figure 3.2 shows how casino tax collections have grown between 1998 and 2004.

As presented in figure 3.2, tax collections from casinos increased from $2.5 billion in 1998 to $4.7 billion in 2004, a growth of 88.0 percent or a compound yearly growth rate of 11.1 percent. According to the U.S. Census Bureau, from 1998 to 2004 the annual compound growth rate for federal tax collections was only 0.1 percent and was 3.8 percent for state taxes.

Table 3.4 shows tax collections from casino gambling by state. As listed for 2004, Nevada collected the largest sum at $887.0 million, while South Dakota collected the smallest sum at $11.9 million. Michigan, opening its commercial casinos in 1999, experienced the highest yearly growth rate at 70.0 percent, while Mississippi experienced the lowest annual growth rate at 4.4 percent.

Table 3.5 presents average tax rates by state from 1998 to 2004. The average tax rate is calculated as tax collections from casinos divided by the total net gambling revenues, or AGR, of casinos. As listed in table 3.5, Illinois levied the highest average tax rate at 46.7 percent, while Nevada assessed the lowest tax rate on casino revenues at 8.4 percent for 2004. Table

3.5 also indicates the stability of tax revenues as a percentage of AGR, with the average tax rate increasing by slightly more than three percentage points in the five-year period. As presented, the average tax rates on AGR for all casino states rose from 13.2 percent in 1998 to 16.4 percent in 2004. Ad-

TABLE 3.4.   Commercial tax collections (in millions of dollars), 1998–2004

	1998	1999	2000	2001	2002	2003	2004	Compound Yearly Growth 1998–2004 (%)
Colorado	63.0	728.0	82.1	92.0	98.2	95.6	99.6	8.7
Illinois	337.0	419.0	512.0	555.2	666.1	719.9	801.7	16.4
Indiana	370.0	425.0	453.5	492.6	544.7	702.7	760.5	13.7
Iowa	96.0	214.0	206.3	216.9	249.3	209.7	252.7	16.9
Louisiana	315.0	324.0	381.0	374.8	414.2	448.9	436.9	7.3
Michigan	N.A.	30.0	170.8	219.3	249.1	250.2	279.4	70.0
Mississippi	262.0	302.0	320.0	322.6	331.7	325.0	333.0	4.4
Missouri	251.0	275.0	304.0	322.7	357.6	369.0	403.1	8.1
Nevada	586.0	635.0	707.6	688.0	718.7	776.5	887.0	5.8
New Jersey	319.0	330.0	342.0	342.4	403.7	414.5	470.7	5.4
South Dakota	3.4	3.7	4.8	4.5	5.1	5.5	11.9	10.3
All casino states	2,602.4	3,685.7	3,484.1	3,631.0	4,038.4	4,317.5	4,736.5	10.7

Source: American Gaming Association, 1998–2004 surveys.

N.A. = not available

TABLE 3.5.   Average tax rate on AGR for commercial casinos by state, 1998–2004 (%)

	1998	1999	2000	2001	2002	2003	2004
Colorado	13.2	11.4	13.0	14.6	13.6	13.7	13.7
Illinois	30.6	29.9	30.1	30.8	37.0	42.1	46.7
Indiana	33.6	28.3	26.7	27.4	25.9	31.5	32.1
Iowa	19.4	25.0	23.3	23.5	25.6	20.5	23.7
Louisiana	24.2	23.1	21.2	20.8	20.7	22.3	20.2
Michigan	N.A.	18.1	23.0	21.9	22.6	22.1	23.5
Mississippi	11.9	12.1	11.9	11.9	12.3	12.0	12.0
Missouri	29.4	29.3	30.5	29.3	27.5	27.7	27.4
Nevada	7.2	7.1	7.4	7.2	7.6	8.1	8.4
New Jersey	8.0	7.9	8.0	8.0	9.3	9.2	9.8
South Dakota	7.7	7.7	9.3	7.7	7.7	7.7	15.3
U.S.	13.2	13.4	13.9	14.2	15.2	16.0	16.4

Source: Author calculations based on American Gaming Association data. Tax rate is equal to total gaming taxes paid divided by AGR.

N.A. = not available

ditionally, it must be noted that these percentages do not include admission fees, which are not considered part of AGR. The data in table 3.5 suggest that the national recession encouraged legislators to revisit this financial source to help solve the state and local fiscal crisis, with the average tax rate growing by a full percentage point between 2001 and 2002.

Table 3.6 shows the relative dependence of each commercial casino state on casino tax collections, with Nevada and Mississippi depending more heavily on casino tax generation to finance government activities than other casino states. In terms of the share of taxes collected from casinos, states ranged from 1.1 percent for South Dakota to 18.7 percent for Nevada. Data indicate that each state's casino tax collections grew more quickly than other tax receipts, thus showing an increasing reliance among the casino states on casino taxes. Iowa experienced the largest increase in casino taxes as a percentage of total tax collection, growing by 2.9 percentage points in six years.

Data in the preceding tables understate the increasing dependence of states on casino tax collections. For example, on June 23, 2005, Pennsylvania governor Edward G. Rendell issued the following statement after the Pennsylvania Supreme Court issued a ruling in *Pennsylvanians Against Gambling Expansion Fund, Inc. et al., v. Commonwealth of Pennsylvania, et al.,* upholding Act 71, which expanded gaming in Pennsylvania.

TABLE 3.6.   Casino taxes as a percentage of total tax collections, 1998–2004

	1998	1999	2000	2001	2002	2003	2004
Colorado	1.0	1.1	1.1	1.3	1.4	1.4	1.4
Illinois	1.7	2.0	2.1	2.4	3.0	3.2	3.1
Indiana	3.6	4.0	4.3	4.7	5.2	6.0	6.4
Iowa	2.0	4.3	4.0	4.2	5.0	4.1	4.9
Louisiana	5.3	5.4	5.7	5.1	5.9	6.2	5.4
Michigan	N.A.	0.1	0.7	1.0	1.1	1.0	1.2
Mississippi	5.9	7.4	7.2	6.6	6.6	6.4	6.5
Missouri	3.0	3.2	3.5	3.6	4.1	4.2	4.4
Nevada	18.3	20.6	21.2	19.7	21.9	18.4	18.7
New Jersey	1.9	1.9	1.8	1.8	2.1	2.0	2.2
South Dakota	0.5	0.5	0.6	0.5	0.5	0.5	1.1
All casino states	2.6	2.9	3.1	3.2	3.6	3.7	3.9

Source: Authors' calculations based on American Gaming Association and U.S. Census Bureau data.

N.A. = not available

The Administration is incredibly pleased that the Supreme Court upheld the majority of Act 71, which legalizes slot machine gaming in the commonwealth. It is a complete vindication of the Act, the process and the hard work and thoughtful drafting that many people put into creating this bill.[5]

And in 2004, the Michigan House of Representatives passed a bill doubling the tax rate on Detroit's three casinos, pushing it to 36 percent. The Michigan casinos warned that, if taxed at the higher rate, they would not build the new hotels they had promised for downtown Detroit and would have to reduce marginal operations, such as table games, with resulting job losses. Furthermore, casino officials made the case that such action could actually result in lower tax collections for the state, as it did in Illinois when the state raised taxes on its riverboat casinos and the state experienced a 6.6 percent drop in gaming revenues. In the end both sides compromised, and Michigan governor Jennifer Granholm signed a bill that increased tax rates on casinos from 18 percent to 24 percent.

But does increasing the casino tax rate produce higher casino tax collections? Just as expressed by Michigan casino leaders, Illinois presents an interesting case on the sensitivity of gambling tax collections to changes in gambling tax rates. In 2003, the Illinois legislature and the governor implemented a top-tax rate of 70 percent on AGR. Illinois's new wagering tax ranged from 15 percent of AGR up to $25 million, but it increased to 37.5 percent on AGR between $25 million and $50 million and escalated to 70 percent for AGR over $250 million. Prior to 1998, Illinois's wagering tax had held steady at a flat 20 percent when the state began to tap the industry for added revenues and implemented massive tax hikes, first a 50 percent rate in 2002 followed by the more recent increase to 70 percent in 2003.

Figure 3.3 profiles Illinois effective tax rates and Illinois AGR as a percentage of U.S. AGR from 1998 to 2004. As presented, from 1998 to 2001, when Illinois effective tax rates on casino AGR ranged from 25.9 percent in 1998 to 30.8 percent in 2001, Illinois expanded its relative position in the United States, growing from 5.6 percent of U.S. AGR in 1998 to 7.0 percent in 2001. However, beginning in 2002, the first year of the large tax hike, Illinois's growth in AGR moved below U.S. AGR, with its share dropping to 5.9 percent by 2004. These data, at least superficially, indicate the sensitivity of gambling revenues to tax rates on AGR.

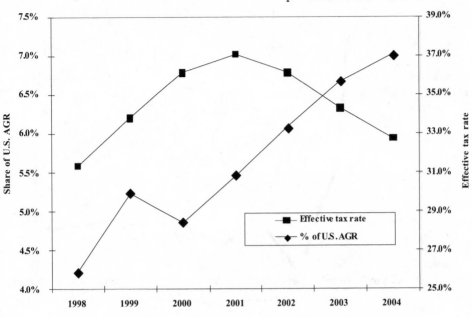

Fig. 3.3. Illinois casino tax rates and AGR as percentage of U.S. AGR, 1998–2004

Figure 3.4 shows average tax rates versus percentage of U.S. AGR for the eleven commercial casino states for 2004. There appears to be a negative relationship. That is, higher casino tax rates produce lower casino market shares.

HOW ARE CASINO TAXES SPENT?

Each commercial casino state has enacted legislation that specifies how casino tax collections will be spent. The spending targets vary widely and are often used to support popular causes, in addition to sharing revenues with state and local governments. For example, Colorado directs that regulatory costs must first be repaid from gaming revenues, after which 28 percent is distributed for the purpose of funding historical preservation grants. Such grants would be important for the purpose of developing tourism.[6] The remainder is divided between state and local governments. In contrast, Illinois allows local governments to share 5 percent of AGR and half the admission tax, but the remainder of its substantial tax collections goes to the state.[7]

Indiana's code contains a complex set of directions for revenue disposition, which vary by the type of casino involved. A substantial portion of these revenues—up to 37.5 percent—is required to be deposited in a special

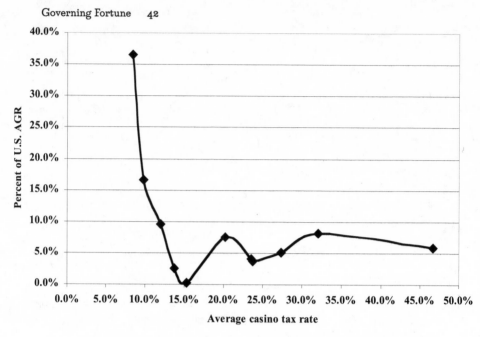

Fig. 3.4. Average casino tax rates versus percentage of U.S. AGR for 2004

property tax replacement fund.[8] Both state and local governments potentially benefit from gaming revenues according to complex formulas apparently designed to mollify different political constituencies.

Both Iowa[9] and Louisiana[10] share requirements that a portion of their
casino revenues be deposited into a fund designated to address problem
gambling. In Iowa, a special fund is also available to fund community improvements.[11] Targeted spending benefits in Louisiana include education and
law enforcement. Michigan shares similar policy goals, as its laws specify
that the distribution of casino tax revenue shall go to K–12 public education
in Michigan and to capital improvements, youth programs, and tax relief in
the city of Detroit.[12] Michigan's casino legislation also creates certain funds
for the operation of the Michigan Gaming Control Board to license, regulate, and control casino gaming and funds for compulsive gambling prevention programs and other casino-related state programs.[13]

As these varying provisions illustrate, funding important public activities
like historical preservation or education can involve providing additional tax
revenues instead of tax relief. However, when the funds are primarily available to the state general fund, or when they are designated for the purpose

of tax relief, the political promise inherent in casino gambling deserves closer scrutiny.

DO CASINOS GENERATE TAX RELIEF?

Each year the AGA surveys approximately one thousand adults from across the nation to gauge attitudes toward casino gambling in America. In the surveys between 1996 and 2005, the AGA asked respondents whether they thought legalized casino gambling was a good way to add to tax collections without raising noncasino patrons' taxes. Figure 3.5 shows the percentage of survey participants who agreed that this was an effective methodology of tax generation. As displayed, 67.0 percent of those surveyed in 2005 agreed with this taxing methodology.

While over the past decade between 60 and 70 percent of Americans judged casinos as a good method of raising tax collections, it is debatable whether casinos provide any tax relief for taxpayers in the state. To combat local opposition, politicians appear to have taken the position that it is good policy to attract casino spending from other states. The location of new casinos reflects the targeted goal of attracting cross-border patronage. Outside of Nevada, a high share of commercial casinos is within close proximity of the state border. Political leaders consider these cross-border patrons as a rich deposit of tax revenues from nonconstituents. Moreover, to the extent that gambling produces social costs, these costs are likely to return home along with the gambler, thus becoming a drain on another jurisdiction's social services. Iowa, for example, receives roughly 50 percent of its casino tax collections from four of its thirteen casinos that are located less than one mile from its border with Nebraska.[14]

Unfortunately, the quest for tourism-funded gambling has been hard to achieve, and it is not always possible to raise revenues from residents of other states. As casinos proliferate, interest in tourism for the purpose of gambling understandably wanes. As a result, casino revenues (and associated taxes) come increasingly from local patrons. Local patronage still generates gambling taxes from willing participants, which might be viewed as politically preferable to forced exactions from the general population. Governor Rendell of Pennsylvania announced that the tax revenue from the sixty-one thousand slot machines allowed by recent legislation would be used to provide property tax relief. Clearly, political leaders in Pennsylvania, much like

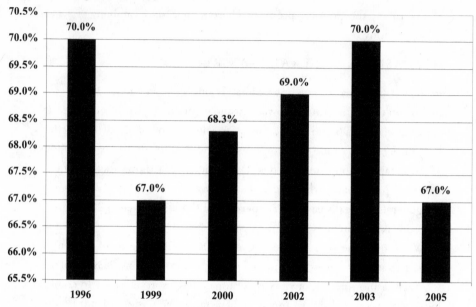

Fig. 3.5. Percentage of Americans who think legalized casinos are a good way of generating tax collections (*Source:* AGA Surveys, 1996–2005)

their counterparts in other states, view gambling as a ready and willing source of tax dollars. However, expanded gambling also presents a concern that local citizens (including those who do not participate in gambling at all) may also be bearing some hidden social costs. To this extent casinos would provide little tax relief.

Table 3.7 shows taxes as a percentage of personal income from 1998 to 2004. In 1998, noncasino taxes as a percentage of personal income were 6.6 percent in noncasino states and 6.1 percent in casino states. However, by 2004, the rate had dropped to 6.1 percent for noncasino states and 5.8 percent for casino states. Thus during the period of rapid growth in casino revenues and tax collections, the effective tax rate in noncasino states dropped more than in casino states. While this is certainly not definitive, it does suggest that casinos have not played an important role in reducing the tax burden for taxpayers in casino states.

Table 3.8 provides a measure of the extent to which casinos provide relief from local taxes. The table shows taxes per one thousand dollars of personal income for casino states and for noncasino states for 1991 and 2001. The year

1991 was chosen because, except for Nevada and New Jersey, no casinos had opened in any states at that time. The year 2001 was selected because it was the latest year for which both state and local tax data were available.

For property taxes, noncasino states clearly had a more positive experience than casino states. In terms of state property taxes, noncasino state taxes, per one thousand dollars in personal income, declined by 51.2 percent while casino state taxes actually rose by 75.0 percent. For local property taxes, much the same is calculated, with noncasino state taxes declining by 32.0 percent and casino state taxes declining by a much smaller 13.4 percent. Much the same trend is detected in other taxes. For example, sales taxes per one thousand dollars of personal income in noncasino taxes declined by 29.7 percent and 17.6 percent for state and local sales taxes, respectively. But for noncasino states, sales taxes per one thousand dollars of personal income declined by a much lower 2.4 percent and 3.5 percent for state and local taxes, respectively. This same pattern is observed in income taxes and overall taxes, as noncasino state taxes, per one thousand dollars of personal income, dropped by much higher rates than casino state taxes.

Table 3.9 contains data for the same two time periods, 1991 and 2001. Only categories for which the definition of spending did not change between the two years are listed. Data indicate that noncasino states reduced their

TABLE 3.7.   Noncasino taxes as a percentage of personal income, 1998–2004

	1998	1999	2000	2001	2002	2003	2004
Colorado	5.1	5.2	5.0	4.7	4.4	4.2	4.2
Illinois	5.4	5.5	5.9	5.5	5.3	5.3	5.6
Indiana	6.7	6.7	6.1	5.9	5.7	6.2	6.0
Iowa	6.7	6.5	6.4	6.2	5.8	5.8	5.3
Louisiana	5.8	5.8	6.1	6.4	5.8	5.8	6.2
Michigan	N.A.	7.4	7.8	7.5	7.3	7.6	7.3
Mississippi	7.6	6.7	6.9	7.2	7.4	7.0	6.8
Missouri	5.8	5.8	5.5	5.6	5.2	5.1	5.0
Nevada	5.0	4.3	4.3	4.3	3.9	4.9	4.9
New Jersey	5.7	5.7	5.7	5.6	5.5	5.8	5.7
South Dakota	4.2	4.1	4.4	4.6	4.8	4.7	4.5
Total casino states	6.1	6.0	6.1	5.9	5.7	5.8	5.8
All noncasino states	6.6	6.6	6.7	6.5	6.1	6.1	6.1

Source: Author calculations from U.S. Census Bureau data.

N.A. = not available

education spending per $1,000 of personal income at a much higher rate than noncasino states. Noncasino states reduced their education spending by 16.7 percent for state expenditures and 0.6 percent for local expenditures. Casino states actually increased their relative education spending at the state level by

TABLE 3.8.   Taxes per $1,000 of personal income, casino versus noncasino states, 1991, 2001

	State Taxes		Local Taxes	
	Noncasino States	Casino States	Noncasino States	Casino States
Property, 1991	$1.78	$0.66	$34.90	$38.90
Property, 2001	$0.87	$1.15	$23.74	$33.67
Percent change	−51.2	75.0	−32.0	−13.4
General sales, 1991	$23.13	$20.95	$4.97	$4.26
General sales, 2001	$16.26	$20.46	$4.09	$4.11
Percent change	−29.7	−2.4	−17.6	−3.5
Income—individual & corp., 1991	$26.93	$24.57	$3.10	$0.92
Income—individual & corp., 2001	$19.37	$22.63	$2.15	$0.78
Percent change	−28.1	−7.9	−30.7	−15.1
All taxes, 1991	$70.76	$62.67	$47.40	$47.01
All taxes, 2001	$48.72	$59.60	$33.51	$41.86
Percent change	−31.1	−4.9	−29.3	−11.0

Source: Authors' calculations based on U.S. Census Bureau data.

TABLE 3.9.   Government spending per $1,000 of personal income, casino versus noncasino states, 1991, 2001

	State Spending		Local Spending	
	Noncasino States	Casino States	Noncasino States	Casino States
Education, 1991	$5.81	$6.78	$2.05	$2.37
Education, 2001	$4.84	$7.02	$1.48	$2.36
Percent change	−16.7	3.5	−28.1	−0.6
Parks and recreation, 1991	$0.55	$0.60	$2.70	$2.78
Parks and recreation, 2001	$0.09	$0.22	$0.49	$0.85
Percent change	−83.4	−63.6	−82.0	−69.4
Housing and community development, 1991	$0.34	$0.32	$3.64	$1.74
Housing and community development, 2001	$0.05	$0.06	$0.37	$0.30
Percent change	−85.9	−80.8	−89.9	−82.9

Source: Authors' calculations based on U.S. Census Bureau data.

3.5 percent but reduced their relative education spending at the local level by 0.6 percent. Given that in many states, a high share of casino revenues goes to education, this is not surprising.

Much the same pattern is calculated for parks and recreation and housing and community development spending with expenditures per $1,000 of personal income declining at a faster pace for noncasino states than for casino states.

Another method of examining the impact of casinos on taxes is to analyze the change in the relative size of state and local government before and after the introduction of a casino. The location quotient (LQ) is one of the most frequently used tools in economic geography to examine how a particular change, in this case a new casino, changes the distribution of employment. This technique compares the county economy to the state economy, in the process attempting to identify specializations in the local economy. To calculate the LQ you simply divide the county's share of employment in an industry by the state's share of employment in the same industry. Equation (1) below indicates how the LQ is calculated.

LQ = % of county employment in industry K / % of state

employment in industry K.   (1)

According to equation (1), an LQ of 1.0 indicates that a county has its expected share of employment in industry K. On the other hand, suppose a county has 10 percent of its workforce in state and local government and the state has only 5 percent of its workforce in state and local government. In this case the LQ is 2.0, indicating that the county has twice its expected share of employment in state and local government. Casino opponents argue that casinos produce an increase in the size of the local police force, thus precipitating an increase in the county's LQ for government workers. However, irrespective of casinos, a county's LQ may be greater than 1.0. For example, a county with a state prison would likely have an LQ for government greater than 1.0.

But by comparing a county's LQ for state and local government employment before and after the addition of a casino, one can determine the extent to which the size of government expanded to accommodate the increased social services demands produced by the casino or contracted due to economies of scale for the delivery of social services. Alternatively, a decline in the LQ indicates that the county's nongovernment sectors grew more robustly than these same industries at the state level, pointing to potential benefits to the county's taxpayers from casino operations.

Table 3.10 compares casino counties by state for the year before casinos were added and for 2003. As presented, five of ten states[15] experienced little change in the relative size of government between the introduction of casinos and 2003. Iowa, Illinois, Indiana, Michigan, and Missouri had LQs in 2003 virtually the same as LQs prior to the introduction of casinos. On the other hand, four states experienced a reduction in the relative size of the government sector after the introduction of casinos. Colorado, Mississippi, New Jersey, and South Dakota all experienced a relative decline in the size of the government sector upon the introduction of casinos. Only Louisiana saw the relative size of its government sector expand significantly with the introduction of casinos.

Data in table 3.10 provide evidence that casino counties in Colorado, Mississippi, New Jersey, and South Dakota grew the relative size of their nongovernment workforce at a much faster pace than noncasino counties in the state, with significant declines in the LQ for government. On the other hand, casino counties in Louisiana, with a significant increase in the LQ for government, expanded the relative size of their government workforce at a much faster pace than noncasino counties in the state.

However, average LQs for casino counties in the state likely mask changes for a particular county. As listed in table 3.11, the impacts at the individual

TABLE 3.10.   Average government location quotients for casino counties before casino operations and in 2003

Casino Counties in	First Year of Casino Operations	LQ before Casinos	LQ in 2003
Colorado	1991	1.36	0.86
Iowa	1991	0.72	0.72
Illinois	1991	1.04	1.04
Indiana	1995	0.97	0.96
Louisiana	1993	0.87	0.95
Michigan	1998	0.98	0.99
Missouri	1994	0.77	0.77
Mississippi	1992	0.82	0.69
New Jersey	1978	1.30	0.94
South Dakota	1989	1.14	0.90

Source: Author calculations from U.S. Bureau of Economic Analysis.

TABLE 3.11. Impact of casino on goverment location quotient

State	County	FIPS	Year Casino Opened	LQ before Casino	LQ in 2003	Change
IL	Rock Island	17161	1992	0.79	0.88	0.09
LA	Orleans	22071	1994	0.93	1.02	0.09
IA	Lee	19111	1991	0.82	0.90	0.09
MO	Jackson	29095	1994	0.88	0.94	0.06
MO	Clay	29047	1994	0.91	0.97	0.06
IN	Lake	18089	1996	1.02	1.07	0.05
MO	St Charles	29183	1994	0.74	0.79	0.05
MO	Buchanan	29021	1994	1.06	1.12	0.05
LA	Caddo	22017	1994	0.90	0.94	0.05
MS	Greenville	28151	1994	0.98	1.01	0.03
IA	Woodbury	19193	1993	0.77	0.80	0.03
IA	Dubuque	19061	1991	0.48	0.51	0.03
IL	Tazewell	17179	1991	0.88	0.90	0.02
LA	Calcasieu	22019	1993	0.88	0.90	0.02
IL	Kane	17089	1991	0.97	0.98	0.01
MS	Adams	28001	1993	0.81	0.82	0.01
IA	Clinton	19045	1991	0.76	0.77	0.01
LA	East Baton Rouge	22033	1994	1.29	1.30	0.01
MO	Platte	29165	1994	0.60	0.61	0.01
IN	Vanderburgh	18163	1995	0.64	0.65	0.01
IA	Polk	19153	1995	0.74	0.73	−0.01
IA	Osceola	19143	2000	0.74	0.73	−0.01
IA	Scott	19163	1991	0.66	0.63	−0.03
MO	St Louis	29189	1994	0.65	0.61	−0.04
IL	Will	17197	1992	1.33	1.27	−0.05
LA	Jefferson	22051	1994	0.62	0.56	−0.06
MO	Lewis	29111	2001	1.29	1.22	−0.07
IA	Pottawattamie	19155	1996	0.95	0.88	−0.08
MS	Hancock	28045	1992	0.76	0.67	−0.09
MS	Harrison	28047	1992	0.74	0.64	−0.09
MS	Warren	28149	1993	0.69	0.60	−0.10
IN	LaPorte	18091	1997	1.30	1.19	−0.10
MO	Cooper	29053	1996	1.44	1.32	−0.12
IL	St Clair	17163	1993	1.10	0.96	−0.14
IN	Harrison	18061	1998	1.09	0.94	−0.15
LA	Bossier	22015	1994	0.91	0.76	−0.15
IA	Clayton	19043	1994	1.02	0.86	−0.15
IN	Dearborn	18029	1996	1.18	1.01	−0.17
MO	Pemiscot	29155	1995	2.18	1.99	−0.18
SD	Lawrence	46081	1989	1.14	0.90	−0.24
CO	Teller	8119	1991	1.30	1.02	−0.28
IL	Massac	17127	1993	1.53	1.25	−0.28
MS	Coahoma	28027	1994	1.36	1.06	−0.30
NJ	Atlantic	34001	1978	1.30	0.94	−0.35
IN	Switzerland	18155	2000	1.46	1.01	−0.45
MS	Tunica	28143	1992	0.92	0.32	−0.60
IN	Ohio	18115	1996	1.67	0.93	−0.74
CO	Gilpin	8047	1991	1.79	0.59	−1.20

Source: Author calculations based on U.S. Bureau of Economic Analysis data.

county level before and after the opening of a casino are more enlightening. According to the results, twenty-one counties experienced an increase in the relative size of government, with Rock Island County in Illinois seeing the largest rise in the size of government. On the other hand, twenty-seven counties saw a decline in the relative size of government before and after the introduction of casinos, with Gilpin County in Colorado experiencing the largest decline in the relative size of government.

How do casino counties that appeared to benefit from casinos in terms of the relative size of government differ from those that did not? Table 3.12 lists answers to that question by comparing counties in which the LQ for government increased (column 1) to counties in which the LQ for government decreased (column 2). As presented, counties that benefited tended to have a smaller population, lower density, and lower per capita income. Furthermore, counties in which the LQ for government declined experienced higher income, population, and employment growth over the course of the decade than counties in which the LQ for government increased.

Results in table 3.12 are not unexpected. They indicate that counties like Gilpin in Colorado, which was small in population, income, and employment before the casino opening, tended to benefit more than counties that were large in terms of population, income, and employment before the casino opening, such as Orleans in Louisiana, a county large in all three of these factors.

TABLE 3.12.   **Profile of gainers and losers in casino counties**

	Increased Relative Size of Government	Decreased Relative Size of Government
Population before casino	154,200	31,735
Population density before casino (persons per square mile)	281	64
Population growth, 1990–2003 (%)	3.5	7.4
Per capita income before casino ($)	17,657	15,461
Per capita income growth, 1990–2003 (%)	60.9	67.9
Employment before casino	84,056	13,224
Employment/population, 2003 (%)	58.8	53.6
Employment growth, 1990–2003 (%)	10.9	22.7

Source: U.S. Bureau of Labor Statistics, U.S. Census Bureau, U.S. Bureau of Economic Analysis.

State and local governments have become increasingly dependent on gambling taxes to support spending. From the data, it is clear that states derive significant tax advantages from commercial casinos in comparison to tribal casinos, with the tax rate almost four times as high for commercial casinos. Only Connecticut's 20.0 percent rate rivals that of commercial casino states.

While tax collections from casinos have grown dramatically over the years, data suggesting significant benefits to the taxpayer in the casino state are less compelling. Taxpayers in casino states did not experience benefits in terms of taxes as measured against personal income. Moreover, data indicate that casinos have no perceptible impact on property taxes. However, with only sixty-one commercial casino counties, impacts are difficult to detect.

Data indicate that the benefits to the taxpayer are likely dependent on the characteristics of the county before the opening of the casinos. Data suggest that counties with smaller and less dense populations and lower per capita income tend to benefit from casinos more than otherwise situated counties.

4. Casinos as Economic Development Tools

Local and state governments look at casinos as sources of taxes, gamblers see casinos as entertainment venues, and pathological gamblers gauge casinos as adversaries. Other entertainment providers view casinos as competitors but with inherent and insurmountable advantages. A wide swath of policymakers asserts that casinos create economic opportunities in the form of more jobs and higher pay for area residents. These casino advocates argue that casinos promote tourism, create jobs, spur economic development, and generate additional tax revenue for education and other needs. However, other policymakers and researchers contend that casinos simply rearrange employment in the area, offering no significant change in employment opportunities or in income gains. In the previous chapter, we examined the casino as a tool to reduce or alter relative tax burdens. In this chapter, we investigate casino contributions to economic development as defined by job growth, income growth, and changes in unemployment rates.

In a 2004 study published by the Federal Reserve of St. Louis, researchers examined the impact of casinos on economic development.[1] The lead researcher, Thomas Garrett, concluded that casinos create true economic development only when there is an increased "value" to society. He found that the addition of casinos into an area may produce business bankruptcy and higher levels of unemployment for the areas, thus reducing value. He found that the net change in local area jobs may be less than the additional casino jobs. At the same time, however, he noted that casino gaming may increase total employment when casinos indirectly generate noncasino jobs in the local area as a result of increased demand for noncasino goods and services. Furthermore, he concluded that casinos may have a positive impact on area income when previously unemployed workers become employed or when individuals move into the area to take new casino jobs. A portion of the added income will then be spent on locally provided goods and services such as housing and entertainment.

In a 2005 research study, Garrett and Nichols, examining three destination casino areas, concluded that casinos do indeed export bankruptcy to the state in which the casino patron resides.[2] Using survey data, the authors calculated the number of visits from each state to casino resort destinations in Nevada, New Jersey, and Mississippi and found strong evidence that states having more residents who visit out-of-state casino resorts have higher bankruptcy filings. And in a 2005 study, Goss and Morse found that, after an initial increase in personal bankruptcy rates, counties that legalized casino gambling experienced lower personal bankruptcy rates during the first several years of casino operations.[3] However, the researchers concluded that those rates then increase, rising above those of noncasino counties after nine years of operations. By the thirteenth year of casino operations, the estimated bankruptcies per one thousand in population are 6.7 for counties that added casinos compared to 5.2 for noncasino counties. For the period of time covered by their analysis, this amounts to a compound annual growth rate in personal bankruptcies that is 2.3 percent higher for the county that added a casino than for an equivalent noncasino county.

Focusing on tribal casinos in a 1998 study, the Economics Research Group concluded that casinos make important job contributions to an area.[4] In examining 214 tribes, they found that the unemployment rate had fallen by 13 percent for tribes with casinos while there was no change for tribes without casinos. And in investigating four tribal casino locations, they measured significant declines in the unemployment rate before and after the casino opened. They calculated that for the Ho-Chunk tribe in Wisconsin, the rate declined from 19 percent to 6 percent; for the Oneida tribe, also in Wisconsin, the unemployment rate decreased from 19 percent to 4 percent; for the Chippewa tribe in Michigan, the rate dropped from 49 percent to 32 percent; and for the Sioux tribes in North Dakota and South Dakota, the unemployment rate plummeted from 62 percent to 29 percent.

In a 1998 study of one hundred communities, forty of which had casinos, the National Opinion Research Center (NORC) at the University of Chicago reported that communities with a casino within a fifty-mile radius experienced a 1 percent decline in their unemployment rate, a 17 percent decrease in unemployment insurance benefit payments, and a 13 percent drop in per capita welfare costs. In comparing reservations with casinos against reservations without casinos, Taylor and Kalt found that between 1990 and 2000 real per capita income grew by 36 percent, 21 percent, and 11 percent for tribes with casinos, tribes without casinos, and the United States, respectively.[5] During the same period the researchers calculated that unemployment rates declined by 4.8 percent, 1.8 percent, and 0.5 percent for tribes with casinos, tribes without casinos, and the United States, respectively. Clearly, their evidence implies significant positive economic development impact for tribal populations with casinos.

Goss concluded that yearly operation of an Omaha, Nebraska, casino would add $17.5 million in yearly wages and salaries, $58.4 million in yearly sales and support, and 1,008 jobs for the metropolitan area, with roughly $27.0 million in tax collections added each year.[6] However, for the rest of Nebraska outside of Omaha, he estimated that yearly operation of an Omaha, Nebraska, casino would reduce yearly wages and salaries by $6.3 million, yearly sales by $24.7 million, and jobs by 613.[7] He found that an Omaha, Nebraska, casino would likely increase the yearly crime rate by 1.5 percent to 7.9 percent but would have negligible impacts on the area's poverty rate. The primary reason for the low impact on crime and other social parameters is due to the fact that the Omaha Metropolitan Statistical Area (MSA) had three exisiting casinos on the Iowa side of the MSA.

The remainder of this chapter investigates casinos as business entities and as instruments of economic development. The next section investigates how this rapid growth in overall gambling revenues has affected the size of the casino.

THE TYPICAL U.S. CASINO

As presented in earlier chapters, the casino industry is a high-growth industry, with AGR expanding at a compound annual growth rate of 8.0 percent over the past five years. Typically, companies experiencing high growth, such as casinos, tend to pay less attention to cost cutting. However, when revenue growth slows, corporations, including casinos, begin to focus on costs and the bottom line. To date, casinos have yet to experience significant pullbacks in growth and have consequently paid less attention to costs and more consideration to revenues.

Just as casino AGR has expanded, the average size of U.S. casinos has increased steadily since 1998. Table 4.1 profiles casino size from 1998 to 2003 based on data from the U.S. Census Bureau's *County Business Patterns*. In 1998, the average stand-alone casino in the United States employed 201 workers. By 2003, the average stand-alone casino employed 265 workers. During this same period of time, casino hotels grew from an average workforce of 988 employees in 1988 to 1,208 employees in 2003. Furthermore, in 1998, 11.4 percent of stand-alone casinos employed more than 500 workers, while 30.6 percent employed fewer than 5 workers. By 2003, 15.9 percent of stand-alone casinos had employment levels greater than 500, but only 17.7 percent had workforces less than 5 workers. In 1998, 47.8 percent of casino hotels employed more than 500 workers and 10.2 percent employed fewer than 5 workers. By 2003, 59.2 percent of casino hotels employed more than 500 workers while only 6.3 percent employed fewer than 5 workers.

During this time span, U.S. casino employment rose by 11.0 percent per year, while the annual payroll increased by 16.4 percent per year. Consequently, average pay for stand-alone casino workers climbed from $21,792 in 1998 to $25,134 in 2003.[8] Table 4.2 shows casino employment and pay trends between 1998 and 2003. For casino hotels, average pay grew from $23,771 in 1998 to $26,121 in 2003. For both stand-alone and casino hotels, average pay was significantly higher than for the average firm in the amusement and recreation industry and in the accommodation industry. The inescapable fact from the data in tables 4.1 and 4.2 is that stand-alone casinos and casino hotels are

TABLE 4.1.   Average employment size for casinos, 1998–2003

	Average Number of Employees per Casino		Percentage with 1–4 Employees		Percentage with More than 500 Employees	
	Stand-alone Casinos	Casino Hotels	Stand-alone Casinos	Casino Hotels	Stand-alone Casinos	Casino Hotels
1998	201	988	30.6	10.2	11.4	47.8
1999	235	1,071	27.5	10.8	13.9	50.2
2000	280	1,082	23.6	10.4	15.5	48.6
2001	278	976	26.5	9.9	15.5	45.7
2002	292	907	23.3	15.9	15.5	44.4
2003	265	1,208	17.7	6.3	15.9	59.2

Source: Authors' calculations from U.S. Census Bureau, *County Business Patterns.*

growing in employment size and average pay, making them even more prized by the economic development community and politicians.

Table 4.3 lists the number of casinos, number of casino workers, and percentage of the workforce employed by commercial casinos in each state for the year 2004 as reported by the AGA. Supporters of casino expansion often point to the positive economic contributions of casinos, particularly in the area of employment. According to the AGA, 445 commercial casinos in eleven states employed 349,210 workers in 2004, for an average of 785 workers per casino. These workers earned an aggregate of $11.837 billion, or an average of just over $33,600 per worker.[9] AGA data differ from U.S. Census data due to different definitions of casinos and methodology used to count employment.

The average number of workers per casino ranged from 51 in South Dakota to 3,793 in New Jersey. The impact of casino employment is clearly more significant in Nevada than in any other state, as over 17 percent of its workforce is employed in casinos. Mississippi places a distant second, with approximately 3 percent of its workforce employed in casinos, with other states trailing far behind. However, it should be noted that table 4.3 overstates the number of casino workers since it includes hotel and lodging employees. There is a significant difference between the numbers reported by the AGA and by the U.S. Census Bureau. The AGA lists 445 commercial casinos while the U.S. Census Bureau reports 562 casinos. This difference may stem from the number of smaller casinos in some states, particularly South Dakota, that are not counted as casinos by the AGA. These smaller casinos are often simply a portion of a restaurant or convenience store that has been designated as a casino and separated from the rest of the establishment.

TABLE 4.2. Employees and payroll for U.S. casinos, 1998–2003

	Number of employees		Annual pay per employee ($)			
	Stand-alone Casinos	Casino Hotels	Stand-alone Casinos	Casino Hotels	Amusement & Recreation	Accommodation
1998	119,820	291,489	21,792	23,771	15,449	17,586
1999	128,446	298,890	23,956	25,546	16,360	18,530
2001	150,218	311,576	23,913	26,135	16,858	19,453
2002	156,151	296,839	25,664	26,402	17,241	19,634
2003	163,956	301,909	25,134	26,121	17,591	20,113

Source: Authors' calculations from U.S. Census Bureau, *County Business Patterns.*

Data in the preceding tables show, to no one's surprise, that casinos create gambling jobs. However, the salient economic development question is, What impact do casinos have on the size of the noncasino workforce and on the value of income in the area where the casino is located?

Of course casinos have added casino jobs. However, opponents of casinos argue that they cannibalize other jobs in the leisure and hospitality industry. In order to investigate this issue, we once again calculate location quotients.[10] An LQ less than 1.0 indicates that the state has less than the nation in the leisure and hospitality industry exclusive of casino jobs. An LQ greater than 1.0 indicates that the state has a larger share of total employment in leisure and hospitality than the nation, again exclusive of casino jobs. Table 4.4 lists LQs for each casino state for the year before casinos were opened in the state and for 2005. Leisure and hospitality data were not available for Nevada and New Jersey for the year preceding casinos opening in those states. Additionally, reliable data were not available for racino states.

Data presented in table 4.4 indicate that in three states, Colorado, Iowa, and South Dakota, casinos appeared to draw jobs from noncasino firms. However, for the remaining six states, and for casino states in total, casinos appeared to not pull jobs from other firms in the leisure and hospitality industry and instead increased the state's share of employment in noncasino

TABLE 4.3.   Commercial casino employment by state, 2004

State	Number of Casinos	Number of Casino Workers	Casino Employment as % of Total Workforce
Colorado	46	7,703	0.3
Illinois	9	8,628	0.2
Indiana	10	17,377	0.6
Iowa	13	8,799	0.6
Louisiana	18	20,048	1.1
Michigan	3	7,572	0.2
Mississippi	29	28,932	2.7
Missouri	11	11,200	0.4
Nevada	258	191,620	17.7
New Jersey	12	45,501	1.2
South Dakota	36	1,830	0.5
Total	445	349,210	1.3

Source: American Gaming Association and U.S. Bureau of Labor Statistics.

TABLE 4.4.   Leisure and hospitality location quotients for casino states before casino opening and for 2005

	Year Casinos Opened	LQ before Casinos	LQ for 2005
Colorado	1991	1.21	1.14
Illinois	1991	0.87	0.93
Indiana	1995	0.89	0.94
Iowa	1991	0.91	0.90
Louisiana	1993	0.83	0.89
Michigan	1998	0.95	0.97
Mississippi	1992	0.33	0.80
Missouri	1994	0.99	1.00
South Dakota	1989	1.12	1.07
All casino states		0.93	0.96

Source: Authors' calculations based on U.S. Bureau of Labor Statistics data.

leisure and hospitality firms. Of course, this result could stem from increases in casino jobs reducing jobs outside of leisure and hospitality.

DO CASINOS CREATE NONCASINO JOBS AND HIGHER INCOME?

Critics of casinos argue that increases in employment tied to gambling are offset by losses in other nongambling entertainment firms. In addition, others argue that casinos tend to make a location less desirable for other nongambling establishments, thereby failing to increase overall employment or to actually reduce noncasino employment. Table 4.5 shows employment growth from 1995 to 2002 for noncasino counties compared to counties that added casinos in 1993 and 1994. Casino counties are further divided into tribal and commercial casinos.

As presented, counties that added a tribal casino in 1993 or 1994 experienced much stronger employment growth than either noncasino counties or commercial casino counties. The superior employment growing experience of tribal casinos may stem from the fact that tribal casinos are more likely to locate in rural or nonurban counties and will attract casino patrons and dollars from outside the county. This finding is consistent with findings in chapter 3. But, importantly, data in table 4.5 indicate that noncasino counties grew their employment at almost twice the rate of commercial casino counties.

Table 4.6 compares per capita income growth for noncasino counties, tribal casino counties, and commercial casino counties. Again commercial casino counties experienced the poorest growth, while tribal casinos saw the best growth. But the performance gap between the three groups is much smaller.

Data presented in tables 4.5 and 4.6 provide evidence that, in terms of job and income growth, tribal casino counties outperformed both non-casino and commercial casino counties and noncasino counties outper-formed casino counties. One could certainly argue that factors other than casinos produced the differences listed in the tables. In order to disentangle

TABLE 4.5.   Change in county employment, 1995–2002 (%)

	Noncasino	Added Casino in 1993 or 1994	
		Tribal Casino	Commercial Casino
1995–96	2.0	4.8	1.8
1996–97	2.2	4.1	1.9
1997–98	2.5	4.0	1.5
1998–99	1.9	3.6	1.2
1999–2000	2.3	3.2	1.2
2000–2001	0.0	0.9	−0.4
2001–2	−0.1	1.1	−0.6
1995–2002	11.3	23.8	6.7

Source: Authors' calculations based on U.S. Bureau of Labor Statistics and Census Bureau data.

TABLE 4.6.   Change in county per capita income, 1995–2002 (%)

	Noncasino	Added Casino in 1993 or 1994	
		Tribal Casino	Commercial Casino
1995–96	6.0	5.3	4.4
1996–97	4.5	4.0	4.6
1997–98	4.9	5.1	5.1
1998–99	3.2	3.5	2.4
1999–2000	5.0	5.0	5.5
2000–2001	3.6	4.2	3.5
2001–2	1.6	2.3	2.6
1995–2002	32.8	33.3	31.7

Source: Authors' calculations based on U.S. Bureau of Labor Statistics and Census Bureau data.

the impact of casinos from other factors affecting per capita income and employment growth, we apply regression analysis to the data. Equations (4.1), (4.2), and (4.3) list the regression equation against factors hypothesized to affect economic development. Data concerning population, income, and employment for each county were obtained for each county from the U.S. Census Bureau. Such data permit our regression formula to evaluate different parameters and their potential impacts on economic development. We also combed various data sources to determine the first date in which a Class III or commercial casino opened in a particular county. In some cases when actual data were not available, we assumed that a tribal casino opened in the same year as the compact date associated with the operating tribe. Given the long time periods for operation of casinos in Nevada and Atlantic City, we excluded from our analysis all Nevada and New Jersey counties. This permitted a focus on relatively recent additions to the casino market, which would allow a more robust examination of the exogenous impact of the casino as opposed to other county-specific factors.

$$
\begin{aligned}
\text{Emp} = {} & \beta_0 + \beta_1\,\text{PopDen} + \beta_2\,\text{PBlack} + \beta_3\,\text{PO55} + \beta_4\,\text{P2054} \\
& + \beta_5\,\text{PU20} + \beta_6\,\text{NE} + \beta_7\,\text{MA} + \beta_8\,\text{ENC} + \beta_9\,\text{WNC} \\
& + \beta_{10}\,\text{ESC} + \beta_{11}\,\text{WSC} + \beta_{12}\,\text{MT} + \beta_{13}\,\text{Year} \\
& + \beta_{14}\,\text{Casino} + \beta_{15}\,\text{Time} + \beta_{16}\,\text{Time}^2 + \varepsilon. \qquad (4.1)
\end{aligned}
$$

$$
\begin{aligned}
\text{PCapInc} = {} & \beta_0 + \beta_1\,\text{PopDen} + \beta_2\,\text{PBlack} + \beta_3\,\text{PO55} + \beta_4\,\text{P2054} \\
& + \beta_5\,\text{PU20} + \beta_6\,\text{NE} + \beta_7\,\text{MA} + \beta_8\,\text{ENC} + \beta_9\,\text{WNC} \\
& + \beta_{10}\,\text{ESC} + \beta_{11}\,\text{WSC} + \beta_{12}\,\text{MT} + \beta_{13}\,\text{Year} \\
& + \beta_{14}\,\text{Casino} + \beta_{15}\,\text{Time} + \beta_{16}\,\text{Time}^2 + \varepsilon. \qquad (4.2)
\end{aligned}
$$

$$
\begin{aligned}
\text{URate} = {} & \beta_0 + \beta_1\,\text{PopDen} + \beta_2\,\text{PBlack} + \beta_3\,\text{PO55} + \beta_4\,\text{P2054} \\
& + \beta_5\,\text{PU20} + \beta_6\,\text{NE} + \beta_7\,\text{MA} + \beta_8\,\text{ENC} + \beta_9\,\text{WNC} \\
& + \beta_{10}\,\text{ESC} + \beta_{11}\,\text{WSC} + \beta_{12}\,\text{MT} + \beta_{13}\,\text{Year} \\
& + \beta_{14}\,\text{Casino} + \beta_{15}\,\text{Time} + \beta_{16}\,\text{Time}^2 + \varepsilon. \qquad (4.3)
\end{aligned}
$$

The dependent variables Emp, PCapInc, and URate represent the county's level of employment, per capita income, and unemployment rate, respectively. Table 4.7 contains a description of each variable used in the estimation of the three equations. This formula includes data on race and age, which other studies have shown to have a disproportionate impact on economic outcomes within a population.[11] Additionally, instead of using a continuous variable for Year, we use a binary variable for each year of the data except for 1990.

Table 4.8 lists the results from the estimation of equations (4.1), (4.2), and (4.3). As indicated, all casino variables are statistically significant in both estimations. As presented, commercial casinos have a positive impact on per capita income and employment and a negative impact on the county's unemployment rate. Tribal casinos have a positive effect on employment but a negative impact on per capita income and the county's unemployment rate. In all cases the influence of casinos is statistically significant.

However, the impact of a casino on the county differs according to how long the casino has been in operation. For per capita income, the influence rises, reaches a maximum, and then begins to decline. For the county's unemployment rate, the casino's impact also rises, reaches a maximum, and then begins to decline. In other words, the impact of time on each is humped-shaped. For employment, the effect of a casino on employment declines, reaches a minimum, and then begins to increase. That is, the shape of the relationship between employment and time is U-shaped.

Thus, for a county adding a commercial casino (1) per capita income rises with the opening of the casino, reaches a maximum impact in eight years, and then begins to decline; (2) employment increases with the opening of the casino, begins to decline for two years, reaching a minimum, and then begins to grow; and (3) the county's unemployment rate declines with the opening of the casino, grows for four years, and then begins to decline again. For a county adding a tribal casino, the impacts on employment and unemployment rates are the same as those for commercial casino counties. On the other hand, tribal casinos reduce per capita income upon opening. After two years of rising and positive impacts on per capita income, casino operations begin to negatively affect per capita income.

Figure 4.1 profiles per capita income differences between commercial

TABLE 4.7.   Definition of variables used in estimation of equations (4.1, 4.2, 4.3)

Variable	Mnemonic	Description
Employment	Emp	County employment in thousands; Source: U.S. Bureau of Labor Statistics.
Per capita income	PCapInc	County per capita income in thousands; Source: U.S. Bureau of Economic Analysis.
Percent unemployment	Urate	County unemployment rates; Source: U.S. Bureau of Labor Statistics.
Population density	PopDen	County population per square mile; Source: U.S. Census Bureau.
Percent black	PBlack	Percentage of county population that is black; Source: U.S. Census Bureau.
Percent over 55	PO55	Percentage of population over the age of 55; Source: U.S. Census Bureau.
Percent 30–54	P3054	Percentage of population ages 30–54; Source: U.S. Census Bureau.
Percent under 20	PU20	Percentage of population under age 20; Source: U.S. Census Bureau.
New England	NE	A binary variable equal to 1 if county is located in the New England region; equal to 0 otherwise.
Mid-Atlantic	MA	A binary variable equal to 1 if county is located in the Mid-Atlantic region; equal to 0 otherwise.
East North Central	ENC	A binary variable equal to 1 if county is located in the East North Central region; equal to 0 otherwise.
West North Central	WNC	A binary variable equal to 1 if county is located in the West North Central region; equal to 0 otherwise.
East South Central	ESC	A binary variable equal to 1 if county is located in the East South Central region; equal to 0 otherwise.
West South Central	WSC	A binary variable equal to 1 if county is located in the West South Central region; equal to 0 otherwise.
Mountain	MT	A binary variable equal to 1 if county is located in the Mountain region; equal to 0 otherwise.
Year	Year	A binary variable equal to 1 for each year of the sample; equal to 0 otherwise.
Casino	Casino	A binary variable equal to 1 if the county adds a casino; equal to 0 otherwise.
Time	Time	Number of years that casino is in existence; 0 for noncasino counties.
Time^2	Time^2	Time × Time; added to recognize the nonlinear relationship between the length of time a casino is in business and its economic impact.

Note: The New England region includes Connecticut, Maine, Massachusetts, New Hampshire, Rhode Island, and Vermont. The Mid-Atlantic region includes New Jersey, New York, and Pennsylvania. The East North Central region includes Illinois, Indiana, Michigan, Ohio, and Wisconsin. The West North Central region includes Iowa, Kansas, Minnesota, Missouri, Nebraska, North Dakota, and South Dakota. The South Atlantic region includes Delaware, District of Columbia, Florida, Georgia, Maryland, North Carolina, South Carolina, Virginia, and West Virginia. The East South Central region includes Alabama, Kentucky, Mississippi, and Tennessee. The West South Central region includes Arkansas, Louisiana, Oklahoma, and Texas. The Mountain region includes Arizona, Colorado, Idaho, Montana, Nevada, New Mexico, Utah, and Wyoming. The Pacific region includes Alaska, California, Hawaii, Oregon, and Washington.

casino counties and counties without casinos and between tribal casino counties and counties without casinos. For commercial casinos, the difference is negative after fifteen years. For tribal casinos, it is negative throughout the operating life of the casino.

Figure 4.2 profiles employment differences between commercial casino

TABLE 4.8.   Impact of factors on county per capita income and employment

	Per Capita Income		Employment		Unemployment Rate	
	Coefficient	T-value	Coefficient	T-value	Coefficient	T-value
Population density	0.740*	24.166	19.321*	32.951	−0.016	−0.700
Percent black	−5.155*	−11.717	145.946*	17.650	1.241*	3.847
Percent 30–54	16.814*	10.142	33.466	1.777	−8.037*	−5.281
Percent over 55	34.626*	20.696	170.661*	8.999	−3.607*	−2.342
Percent under 20	43.365*	28.955	423.142*	25.620	10.434*	7.385
Mid-Atlantic	1.736*	5.267	64.809*	4.594	−0.080	−0.359
New England	4.116*	8.832	75.563*	3.767	−0.534	−1.697
East North Central	−0.318	−1.397	8.799	0.920	−0.321*	−2.073
West North Central	−1.880*	−8.734	−30.139*	−3.447	−2.566*	−17.173
East South Central	−2.749*	−12.544	−42.922*	−4.526	0.284	1.916
West South Central	−3.205*	−14.135	−22.312*	−2.323	−0.969*	−6.231
Mountain	−1.500*	−5.283	−22.172	−1.859	−0.805*	−4.156
Y91	0.471*	14.504	0.645*	1.962	1.097*	32.354
Y92	1.416*	42.787	1.096*	3.256	1.504*	43.716
Y93	1.883*	55.419	2.076*	5.965	0.976*	27.794
Y94	2.633*	75.039	3.280*	9.062	0.245*	6.794
Y95	3.094*	84.35	4.773*	12.493	−0.015	−0.407
Y96	4.207*	109.528	6.007*	14.885	0.101*	2.609
Y97	5.120*	132.656	7.397*	18.227	−0.311*	−7.999
Y98	6.211*	166.53	9.103*	23.372	−0.683*	−18.029
Y99	6.997*	189.631	10.803*	28.139	−0.955*	−25.418
Y00	8.108*	219.466	11.891*	30.914	−1.210*	−32.166
Y01	8.946*	241.715	11.742*	30.458	−0.594*	−15.764
Y02	9.354*	252.212	11.566*	29.927	−0.034	−0.913
Commercial casino	0.687*	5.148	3.693*	2.702	−0.490*	−3.584
Tribal casino	−0.379*	−4.130	3.426*	3.666	−0.357*	−3.758
Casino × time	0.096*	4.784	−0.909*	−4.500	0.031	1.502
Casino × time × time	−0.006*	−4.878	0.1790*	14.483	−0.004*	−3.369
Constant	−7.964*	−6.449	−126.209*	−8.477	7.591*	6.628
R^2 (%)	95.2		99.5		83.3	

* Indicates that coefficient is statistically significant at .05 level

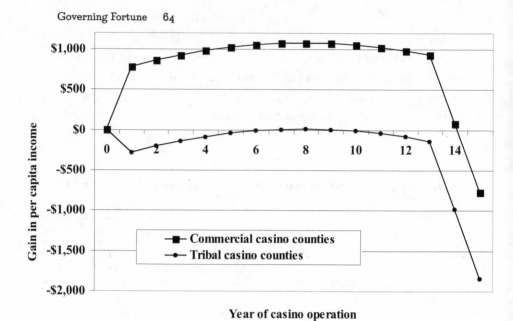

Fig. 4.1. Estimated per capita income gain for casino counties versus noncasino counties

counties and counties without casinos and between tribal casino counties and counties without casinos. For both commercial and tribal casinos, the difference is positive and grows over the life of the casino. The figure shows virtually no difference between the job creation impacts of tribal casinos and commercial casino.

Figure 4.3 tracks unemployment rates for commercial casino counties, tribal casino counties, and noncasino counties. Commercial and tribal casino counties are estimated to have unemployment rates less than counties without casinos for the first fifteen years of operations. Thus in terms of employment impacts, both tribal and commercial casinos create additional job opportunities in the county in which it is located.

Table 4.9 summarizes estimates based on regression results in table 4.8. Column 1 shows the compound annual growth in per capita income from the three groups of counties—commercial casino counties, tribal casino counties, and noncasino counties. Results indicate that noncasino counties grew at a rate exceeding that of the other two groups. Columns 2 and 3 show differences among the three groups for employment and unemployment. In both

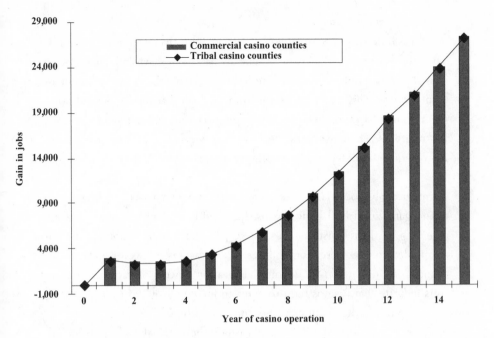

Fig. 4.2. Estimated employment gain for casino counties versus noncasino counties

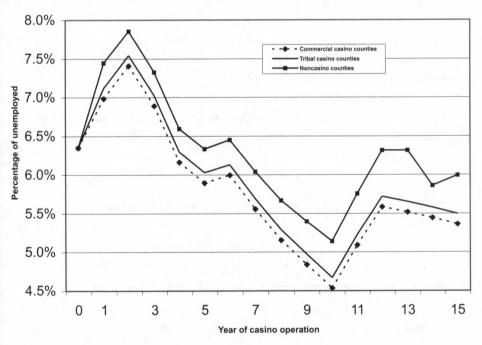

Fig. 4.3. Comparison of county unemployment rates—commercial casino, tribal casino, and noncasino

cases, casino counties performed at a higher level than noncasino counties. Thus results indicate that casinos tend to have a positive influence on job growth and unemployment rates but have a negative impact on per capita income growth. This result may stem from the high share of casino and other entertainment workers who are employed part-time but are included in the job numbers. These workers, because they work fewer hours, earn less. However, we do not test this hypothesis here.

Increasingly, local and state government policymakers are turning to casino gambling to fill budget gaps. In an effort to "sell" expanded casino gambling to their constituencies, these political leaders espouse the economic development creation abilities of the casinos. However, data in this chapter cast doubts on the income-generating powers of casinos. Our results indicate that casinos tend to dampen income growth but increase job opportunities in the counties where they are located.

Regression results indicate that casinos, both tribal and commercial, create substantial job opportunities in terms of new jobs and lower unemployment rates. Furthermore, the gains tend to grow as the casino remains in the county. Contrarily, casinos reduce per capita income, and the reduction gets larger as the casino remains in the county. The addition of part-time casino and entertainment workers due to casino operations may explain this phenomenon.

Additionally, data presented in this chapter and in chapter 3 indicate that casinos have not reduced the relative tax burdens of residents in states with commercial casinos. Data show that taxes, as a share of personal income, ei-

TABLE 4.9.   Change in economic factors after 15 years of casino operation (%)

	Compound Annual Change in Per Capita Income	Compound Annual Change in Employment	Change in Unemployment Rate
Commercial casino counties	3.0	4.2	−1.0
Tribal casino counties	2.7	4.1	−0.9
Noncasino counties	3.2	1.7	−0.4

Source: Estimation from regression models.

ther rose more dramatically or dropped less significantly in states with commercial casinos in comparison to states without commercial casinos. Instead, casinos appeared to produce increases in relative public spending on areas such as education and parks and recreation.

5. Social Costs

Economic development, employment opportunities, and new sources of tax revenues are not the only potential consequences of legalized casino gambling. Concerns about negative social impacts from gambling have long formed a part of the underpinning for criminal proscriptions against it. Policymakers considering whether to change those proscriptions are thus confronted with the question of whether these traditional concerns about social costs are well founded and, if so, whether these costs may exceed any promised benefits.

Evaluations of costs and benefits are part of the legislative process, and social science data form part of the grist for the legislative mill. However, legislators also enjoy political prerogatives, which allow them to make choices that may not always optimize costs and benefits. As one court has noted, "The power [of the legislature] to decide, to be wrong as well as to be right on contestable issues, is both [a] privilege and curse of democracy."[1] Casino gambling presents one of these contestable issues.

Although abundant evidence exists for the proposition that gambling—and more specifically gambling that reaches pathological levels—produces negative social consequences, much of the evidence that provides a direct link between gambling and associated negative consequences involves specific incidents with problem gamblers. Empirical research using sound social science methods has also offered proof on these issues, but that proof is not incontrovertible. Social problems often have multiple causes, and teasing out the extent of contribution by gambling alone has proven to be a daunting task. Given that benefits such as new sources of tax revenue are often more easily measurable than the costs (including hidden substitution effects),[2] industry supporters have seized on the comparative uncertainty surrounding costs as a basis for forging ahead with expanded gambling options.

Nevertheless, the available research supports the proposition that gamblers externalize costs to others. It also supports the likelihood that these costs are substantial. A policy response that neglects these likelihoods is becoming less sustainable as more is learned about gambling effects. The discussion that follows provides an overview of some of the significant research on pathological gambling conditions, as well as important considerations affecting the extension of that research to estimate social costs associated with the gambling industry.

PATHOLOGICAL AND PROBLEM GAMBLING

Social costs from gambling primarily flow from a relatively small segment of the population for whom gambling is not harmless recreation. Much is known about the nature of pathological gambling and its less severe manifestations, sometimes referred to as "problem gambling." The American Psychiatric Association defines pathological gambling in its *Diagnostic and Statistical Manual of Mental Disorders* (DSM-IV) as "persistent and recurrent maladaptive gambling behavior that disrupts personal, family, or vocational pursuits."[3]

According to the DSM-IV, pathological behavior is indicated by five or more of the following conditions: (1) a preoccupation with gambling; (2) a need to gamble increasing amounts in order to achieve desired excitement; (3) repeated unsuccessful efforts to control gambling; (4) restlessness and irritability when attempting to control gambling; (5) using gambling as a means to escape from problems; (6) "chasing" one's losses; (7) lying to conceal the extent of one's gambling; (8) committing illegal acts to finance gambling; (9) jeopardizing relationships (including employment or education) because of gambling; and (10) relying on others to relieve desperate financial situations caused by gambling.[4]

The decision to choose five manifestations as a cutoff for measuring pathology may be conservative, as some experts suggest that four manifestations may be a more appropriate figure.[5] Fewer than five of these behaviors could still produce substantial negative personal and social consequences, and this behavior is often considered under the rubric of "problem gambling."[6] NORC, whose survey on gambling-related social problems was utilized by the National Gambling Impact Study Commission, used the term "at-risk" gambler to define someone who has experienced losses of more than one hundred dollars in a single day and reports only one or two DSM-IV criteria, whereas a "problem gambler" has the same loss experience but reports three or four of these criteria.[7]

Differences in formulating screening tools to identify and diagnose gambling-related behavioral problems account for some variation in research results concerning the number of problem or pathological gamblers.[8] As one study explains: "There is no particular number of symptoms at which true pathological gambling suddenly manifests itself—the designation of pathological gambling is a matter of degree."[9]

The DSM-IV explains that the pathology rarely occurs with the first bet. A course of experience with gambling is required for most people: "There may be years of social gambling followed by an abrupt onset that may be precipitated by greater exposure to gambling or by a stressor."[10] Thus, as gambling opportunities proliferate, it stands to reason that more pathology is likely. The NORC survey indicates that past-year gambling in casinos increased from 10 percent of the population in 1975 to 29 percent by 1998.[11] In contrast, bingo declined from 19 to 6 percent, and horse racing declined from 14 to 7 percent during the same period, suggesting that the marketplace has substituted casino gambling for other games of chance.[12] For 2004, the AGA estimates that 54.1 million Americans visited a casino.[13] This represents about one-fourth of the estimated 2004 adult population, which numbers approximately 212 million.[14]

Pathological gambling is considered a chronic disorder, much like alcoholism. This means that once it develops there is a tendency for recurrence.[15] For this reason, diagnosis of pathological gambling focuses on ascertaining a subject's lifetime experiences, as well as more recent ones. However, lifetime orientations can create problems in estimating the magnitude of the impact of negative gambling-related behaviors in a particular year. For this reason, some studies have included questions about past-year behavior in addition to lifetime time frames.

The causes of pathological gambling are still under investigation. As one study has observed, "Research into the causes of [pathological] gambling is in its infancy compared to research into the causes of other addictive behaviors."[16] Like alcohol dependence, pathological gambling may have an inherited component, as it is more common among people whose parents experience similar pathology.[17] Recent studies have also indicated that brain chemistry affects pathological gambling behavior, including a study in the

Archives of Neurology suggesting that stimulation of dopamine receptors might be responsible for pathological gambling as a complication related to the treatment of Parkinson's disease.[18]

Differences between machine gambling (e.g., slot machines and video lottery terminals) and other forms of gambling may also be reflected in the development of pathological gambling. An empirical study by Breen and Zimmerman indicates that machine gamblers develop problem gambling conditions sooner (1.08 years versus 3.58 years) than their counterparts who gamble in more traditional forms.[19] These researchers note that the differing latency period may be attributable to other factors, such as the convenience and availability of machines. However, the difference also may be due to the stimulus variables provided by gambling machines, including the reinforcement of "small wins," "near misses," and continuous action, which is not prevalent in more traditional gambling forms.[20]

Some research suggests that men tend to experience pathological gambling more than women. The DSM-IV indicates that male problem and pathological gamblers outnumber females by a ratio of 2 to 1.[21] The NORC study shows a similar disparity in 1998, with male pathological and problem gambling at a lifetime rate of 3.7 percent, while only 1.9 percent of females are similarly affected.[22] A nationwide survey conducted from August 1999 to October 2000 by Welte et al. indicated that current-year indications of pathological or problem gambling were in a somewhat closer relationship for males and females, approximately 1.3 to 1.[23] A comparison of the results for the Welte survey and the NORC study for the combined group of problem and pathological gamblers based on current experience is presented in table 5.1.

The DSM-IV also reports that the onset of pathology in males is generally earlier, potentially beginning in adolescence.[24] For this reason, public health authorities have warned against efforts to provide "casino nights" for young people.[25] Although such activities may be well-intentioned efforts to substitute what might be viewed as harmless fun for potential incidents of alcohol abuse, they may ultimately lead to substituting another pathology. Antigambling activists have also seized on this concern in connection with the sale of games and toys with gambling themes.[26]

Racial differences in gambling pathology may also exist. The Welte survey shows that blacks and Hispanics have higher combined rates for problem and pathological gambling than whites.[27] However, the NORC survey produced similar directional results for blacks but lower incidents for Hispanic gamblers. See table 5.1 for comparative results reflecting the past-year experiences of these demographic groups.

White gamblers significantly outnumber those of other races, such that the higher percentage of minority problem gamblers does not necessarily translate into a larger absolute number of problem gamblers from minority communities.

The extent of problem gambling in the United States remains an issue about which experts disagree, in part because of the differing approaches for determining what constitutes a problem gambler. The NORC study concluded that, in 1998, problem and pathological gamblers totaled 1.5 percent of the adult population, or approximately 5.5 million people. An additional 15 million were considered at risk. If those figures are updated to reflect the estimated adult population for 2004 based on U.S. Census Bureau data, the results are approximately 5.7 million problem and pathological gamblers, with an additional 16.3 million at risk. These figures are displayed in table 5.2.

It should be noted that the figures in table 5.2 simply extrapolate the results from a 1998 survey to an updated population. They do not take into account the possibility that additional casino facilities may have increased the manifestation of problem gambling behaviors.

Alternatively, if survey results focusing on casino patrons[28] are applied

TABLE 5.1.   Selected demographic
characteristics of problem and pathological
gamblers (based on past year experiences)

	Welte, et. al. (%)	NORC (%)
Sex:		
Male	4.10	1.70
Female	2.90	.90
Race:		
White	1.80	1.10
Black	7.70	3.20
Hispanic	7.90	0.80
Asian	6.50	N.A.
Native American	10.50	N.A.

N.A. = not available

against the base of estimated casino visitors in 2004, the estimated total for problem and pathological gamblers increases slightly. This methodology also generates a higher proportion of pathological gamblers, who are likely to generate higher social costs. These figures are displayed in table 5.3.

The differing pathology rates between types of casino facilities reflected in the NORC survey data present interesting possibilities for further research to ascertain the basis for the differences. One possibility is that riverboats may involve a greater percentage of local patrons, who visit frequently based on convenient access from their work or home, with relatively fewer tourists traveling to visit them as destination facilities, such as Nevada or Atlantic City casinos.

Using the more recent findings of the Welte study, the total for pathological gamblers grows still larger. The Welte study used two different screens

TABLE 5.2.   Estimated population of problem and pathological gamblers

	NORC Percentage	Estimated 2004 Adult Population	Estimated 2004 Affected Population
Non-gambler	14.40	212,103,606	30,542,919
Low-risk	75.10	212,103,606	159,289,808
At-Risk	7.70	212,103,606	16,331,978
Problem	1.50	212,103,606	3,181,554
Pathological	1.20	212,103,606	2,545,243
Total problem and pathological gamblers:		5,726,797	

Source: National Opinion Research Center data, lifetime survey.

TABLE 5.3.   Estimated problem and pathological gamblers based on NORC surveys of casino patrons applied to 2004 casino visitors

	Riverboats (%)	Tribal (%)	Nevada & Atlantic City Casinos (%)	Average (%)	Casino Visitors 2004 (AGA)	Estimated Population
Non-gambler	0.00	0.00	0.70	0.23	54,100,000	126,233
Low-risk	67.20	73.10	68.10	69.47	54,100,000	37,581,467
At-Risk	15.60	16.40	22.10	18.03	54,100,000	9,756,033
Problem	6.30	6.00	3.40	5.23	54,100,000	2,831,233
Pathological	10.90	4.50	5.40	6.93	54,100,000	3,750,933
Total Problem and Pathological Gamblers			6,582,167			

TABLE 5.4.   Estimated problem and pathological gamblers (Welty)

Methodology	Overall %: (lifetime basis)	Estimated 2004 Adult Population	Estimated Problem & Pathological Gamblers
SOGS (20 factors)	11.50	212,103,606	24,391,915
DIS (10 factors)	4.80	212,103,606	10,180,973

for problem gambling, one of which was based on the ten DSM-IV criteria and the other of which was based on the twenty criteria under the South Oaks Gambling Screen (SOGS) developed by Lesieur and Blume.[29] The results in both cases were higher than the NORC survey, as shown in table 5.4.

As the study explains, "The reason that the SOGS produces higher rates of pathological gambling than the DIS [Diagnostic Interview Schedule from DSM-IV] is that it is easier to obtain five positives from 20 variables than from 10 variables."[30] Nevertheless, even the more conservative definitional approach generates a substantially larger population of problem and pathological gamblers than the previous methodologies, suggesting that one in twenty adults in the United States—or perhaps as many as one in nine—may have a gambling problem. Problem and pathological gamblers may account for up to 15 percent of gambling losses, making them a significant contributor to the industry's profitability.[31]

Despite technical disagreements about measuring the number of problem gamblers, there is general agreement that this pathology generates personal hardship and pain for the individual and also for others. As the National Gambling Impact Study Commission recognized, "All [researchers] seem to agree that pathological gamblers 'engaged in destructive behaviors, they run up large debts, they damage relationships with family and friends, and they kill themselves.'"[32] However, the extent of these costs and related issues involving the causal link between pathology and particular negative outcomes is contested. Herein lies the battleground between industry advocates and detractors.

SOCIAL COST RESEARCH

Research into the social cost impact of introducing a casino encounters several challenges that are often interrelated. First, researchers face the formidable problem of distinguishing between causation and correlation. When one looks at the problems often associated with gambling, such as crime, divorce, bankruptcy, or suicide, it is quite clear that multiple causes may contribute to these problems. It is true that problem gamblers sometimes resort to theft or embezzlement, and significant thefts could cause a business bankruptcy. Debt incurred from excessive gambling could cause marital stress, resulting in personal bankruptcy and possibly divorce or other family-related problems. Complications from divorce spill over into other social problems, which have links to the financial well-being of the former spouses, including unpaid child support, which was estimated at a staggering $95 billion in 2003.[33]

What is not clear in each of these examples is the extent to which some other dysfunctional behavior might also be a contributing, if not intervening, cause of the event. Problem gamblers often share other pathologies, such as alcoholism, that provide additional basis for causation. A significant correlation appears between alcohol abuse and gambling pathology. The Welte study shows that drinkers averaging more than four drinks a day are more than five times as likely to become problem or pathological gamblers than their teetotaling counterparts.[34] This statistic is consistent with previous studies summarized in the National Gambling Impact Study Commission Report.[35]

Nevertheless, free drinks are allowed in several states with commercial casinos. As one court has noted, "[T]he absence of a regulation barring gambling by a drunk patron cannot be considered an oversight or mistake. At the very least the State condones casino patrons drinking while they place bets, and the policy of providing free drinks on request could arguably be said to actively encourage this conduct."[36] The AGA justifies this practice based on customer demands, while adding that "Avid casino players like to be at the top of their game and therefore avoid the consumption of alcohol."[37]

Other disorders, such as emotional or mental health concerns, are also more prevalent in the population of pathological and problem gamblers. The NORC study indicates that problem and pathological gamblers are more than twice as likely to seek mental health treatment than their nongambling or low-risk gambling counterparts.[38] This correlation does not show whether the mental health problem is caused by gambling or whether persons with mental health problems in the first place (or at least a predisposition toward them) are more likely to experience gambling problems. Nevertheless, if either of these conclusions were true, it would present a significant problem for policymakers interested in the public health ramifications of gambling.

Similarly, the NORC study indicates that gamblers generally have higher divorce rates than nongamblers. Approximately 53.5 percent of pathological gamblers, 39.5 percent of problem gamblers, and 36.3 percent of at-risk gamblers had been divorced, as compared with only 18.5 percent of nongamblers and 29.8 percent of those classified as low-risk gamblers.[39] As noted previously with regard to mental health, this data alone is insufficient to show conclusively that divorce occurs on account of gambling as opposed to other problems. However, these significant differences in divorce rates do raise concerns; they do not suggest that expanded gambling is helping to improve these social conditions.

Research also shows that gambling pathologies may vary according to age. Welte et al. showed that problem and pathological gambling prevalence declined significantly in populations over the age of sixty-one.[40] The NORC study similarly showed diminished levels of problem or pathological gambling for those over the age of sixty-five.[41] More recently, researchers examined whether recreational gambling (with problem or pathological gambling specifically included) had a relationship to the health of older adults. Although their research indeed found a positive correlation between the subjective reports of health in the recreational gambling population, correlation also did not necessarily point to causation in this case. As the researchers recognized, there are limits to the conclusions that can be drawn from these results.

> Recreational gambling in older adults may allow for increased socialization, community activity, and travel, which may in turn be reflected in more positive ratings of health. Such an effect may not be evident in younger adults, perhaps because other social or occupational activities take priority. It is also possible that a greater proportion of older, as compared with younger, adults are too sick to gamble and are categorized in the nongambling group, making the older gamblers appear healthier. These sicker older adults might have more limited access to transportation or lack the energy or motivation necessary for specific types of gambling.[42]

The complex sources of causation of many social problems present formidable obstacles in knowing with precision the extent of causation that can be attributed to adding a casino to the environment. Problem gambling conditions may also already exist on account of other gambling sources, including illegal gambling, available prior to the introduction of a casino. Agnostic positions as to causation have academic appeal, and they are often adopted by the industry when it seeks to promote its business.

For example, research has shown that proximity to a casino increases the likelihood for manifestations of problem gambling. Most problem and pathological gamblers live within 50 miles of a casino. Using lifetime experience figures from the NORC study,[43] approximately 4.4 percent of the population within 50 miles of a casino represents problem or pathological gamblers. In contrast, less than half of this proportion lives farther away: approximately 2.1 percent of the population living within 51 to 250 miles of a casino falls into the problem or pathological category, and 2.5 percent of the population living more than 250 miles from a casino is similarly affected. Looking instead at the annual experience figures, the proportion is even more dramatic: approximately 2.4 percent of the population within 50 miles represents problem or pathological gamblers, whereas only 0.9 percent of the population living within 51 to 250 miles and only 0.7 percent living more than 250 miles from a casino are similarly affected.[44] Stated differently, one is about two times as likely to find a problem gambler within 50 miles of a casino.

These findings make sense intuitively, as more convenient access to gambling presents the possibility for more frequent gambling experiences, which in turn could result in the kind of losses associated with problem gambling behavior. Nevertheless, these results were questioned in one recent study, which pointed out that

> it is not possible to determine if (a) the availability of gambling caused this inflated prevalence rate, (b) more people with gambling problems settled in areas closer to major opportunities to gambling, (c) casinos locate in areas that already have a high rate of disordered gambling, or (d) casinos locate in areas with a disproportionately vulnerable population. To understand fully the overall repercussions of gambling on society, a significant research effort is necessary to document the complex interaction among these health and socioeconomic variables, as well as their short- and long-term costs.[45]

Although additional research probably would be helpful, the level of skepticism expressed here borders on the absurd. Policymakers don't have the option of waiting for these questions to be solved with certainty. They must ultimately reach conclusions based on likelihoods rather than scientific precision. To suggest that the industry locates casinos where disordered gambling or particularly vulnerable populations already exist presupposes secret industry knowledge about illegal gambling and/or problem gamblers that is apparently not available to the research community. Alternatively, it presupposes that the industry is very "lucky" in choosing those locations. Neither of these presuppositions is a plausible explanation of the correlation shown here.

The gambling industry often uses this skeptical approach to challenge the findings of research that generates results that are inconvenient for its business goals. It has also been known to engage in dubious uses of statistics to advocate industry-friendly positions. Consider, for example, the AGA's position on bankruptcy, as articulated on its Web site. In support of its position that there is no linkage between casinos and bankruptcy, the AGA cites the following example:

> According to data maintained by the Administrative Office of the U.S. Courts and population statistics from the most recent census (2001), Utah and Tennessee were ranked first and second respectively in 2002 in terms of the number of bankruptcy filings per household. Utah is the only state in the country with absolutely no form of legalized gaming whatsoever, and Tennessee's only gaming is a state-run lottery that is still in the process of coming on-line.[46]

We have also observed industry advocates using this argument in local debates on the issue of expanded gambling.

The fact that high bankruptcy rates exist in Utah and Tennessee, where no legalized casino gambling exists, is entirely consistent with the proposition that bankruptcy is caused by other factors besides excessive gambling losses. But that proposition is hardly contestable. Significantly, this example does not speak at all to the question of whether the introduction of a casino to a jurisdiction has a differential impact over time, which is at the heart of what the industry is questioning here.

Similarly, on the issue of crime, the AGA points to examples where crime rates have dropped in cities with casinos and, in some cases, in cities where casinos have been added.[47] Conversely, it points to increases in crime in locations such as Orlando, where noncasino entertainment is offered.[48] In the case of Atlantic City, which the General Accounting Office (GAO) discussed in some detail as an example of a location where crime rates had increased after casinos opened,[49] the AGA dismissed these results and focused instead on experiences of the past five years, where crime rates have dropped.[50]

The problem for researchers is to ascertain the effects of crime based on the change in conditions attributed to adding casinos instead of to other sources. Crime trends nationally have generally declined. According to the Bureau of Justice Statistics, property crimes have declined substantially during the past three decades.[51] Violent crimes have similarly declined, particularly so in the last decade.[52] However, particular jurisdictions can experience different results based on a number of factors, including employment, economic conditions, and the impact of particular features of the legal system. To the extent that criminals take into account penalties and enforcement efforts, changes in the legal system can also impact crime rates, thus reflecting interjurisdictional competition in setting legal penalties.[53]

The powerful tool of regression analysis is available to evaluate the differential impacts of casinos on a macro level. By looking at casino and noncasino jurisdictions over longer periods of time, and adjusting for other significant differences that appear among these jurisdictions, the impact of casinos on such matters as crime and bankruptcy can be ascertained with reasonable confidence. These results are not free from uncertainty, but they do present powerful evidence that deserves consideration in the policy analysis of casino gaming. Recent research using this methodology has produced strong evidence of a correlation between casinos and crime and between casinos and bankruptcy. Some significant research in these areas is briefly discussed next.

Casinos and Crime

Although several previous studies failed to show a correlation between casinos and crime, a more recent study by the economists Grinols and Mustard took on the task of measuring the externalized costs associated with crime attributed to casino gambling.[54] Grinols and Mustard examined county-level data for the period 1977–96, focusing on data for reported crimes in counties with casinos and in counties without casinos. Their model also accounted for fifty-eight other variables, including demographic factors such as race, sex, and age; unemployment; and personal income.

When one charts the aggregate crime rates for counties with casinos, a decline appears between 1990 and 1996, a time of rapid expansion of casinos. As Grinols and Mustard point out, some researchers claimed that this data suggested that casinos reduced crime. However, a more appropriate measure would focus on the differential experiences between casino and noncasino counties over this period, not a simple evaluation of a trend line. When a more complex analysis is completed, the result is that crime dropped 12 percentage points more in counties without casinos than in the casino counties.

Grinols and Mustard also broke new ground in showing another feature of casinos: the fact that their impacts on crime vary over time after opening. Although crime may drop in the year of opening or in the year or two thereafter, they found statistically significant increases for all crimes except murder. In most cases, these increases occurred after the first two years of operation, reflecting a time lag between opening and the eventual impact on increasing criminal activity.

These results are theoretically consistent with plausible impacts of the casino industry on criminal behavior. As Grinols and Mustard point out, casinos could potentially reduce crime by providing increased wages and positive economic development growth. However, crime would likely increase to the extent that those development opportunities would not be realized or employment growth in other sectors of the economy would be harmed as a result of locating a casino in the jurisdiction. (As discussed in chapter 4, it appears questionable whether these putative benefits from casinos are in fact realized in many jurisdictions.)

In addition to these indirect effects on crime from economic development impacts, Grinols and Mustard also point to the crime experiences of problem and pathological gamblers as a significant factor explaining crime trends in casino counties. The proliferation of casinos decreases the cost of "buying" gambling services, thus increasing consumption by problem gamblers. Some of those gamblers will resort to crimes to pay for this increased consumption. Grinols and Mustard cite studies by the Maryland Department of Health and Mental Hygiene (1990), showing that 62 percent of a Gamblers Anonymous group had committed illegal acts as a result of gambling, and by the noted gambling researcher Dr. Henry Lesieur (1998), showing that 56 percent of those in gambling treatment had engaged in stealing to finance gambling.[55]

A more recent study by the U.S. Department of Justice also appears to confirm a linkage between problem and pathological gambling and crime. The study sampled arrestees in Las Vegas, Nevada, and Des Moines, Iowa. The percentage of problem or pathological gamblers among these arrestees was three to five times higher than that of the general population.[56] Moreover, nearly one-third of the arrestees identified as pathological gamblers admitted to committing robbery in the previous year, and approximately 13 percent had assaulted someone for money.[57]

However, the study also indicated that "pathological gamblers were no more likely to be arrested for property or other white collar crimes (larceny, theft, embezzlement, and fraud) than nongamblers and low-risk and at-risk gamblers. . . . Rather, they were most likely to be arrested for such offenses and probation or parole violations, liquor law violations, trespassing, and other public order offenses."[58] Despite the absence of the property crime link in arrests, it is significant that more than 30 percent admitted to committing robberies in the past year—more than double the percentage for nongambler arrestees.[59] Thus, arrests based on other categories of offenses may mask other criminal behavior—including property-related crimes—for which no arrest was made.

The time lag for crime manifestation in Grinols and Mustard's study may be partially explained by the time period needed for problem gambling behavior to fully manifest itself. However, Grinols and Mustard also suggest another possibility for growing crime rates: perhaps casinos attract visitors who are more prone to commit crime or to be victims of crime.

The AGA points to the theory that higher crime rates around casinos may be linked to higher levels of visitors coming into the area.[60] The theory goes that more visitors create more opportunities for criminals, which ultimately translate into more criminal incidents. Thus, visitors should be counted in computing crime rates, so that per capita figures based on residents are effectively diluted by the increased population of visitors. Grinols and Mustard raise an intriguing counterargument: if more visitors induce more crime, then one should witness higher crime rates whenever there are a lot of visitors to a jurisdiction and not just in cases of casinos. However, cities with large tourist magnets—such as the Mall of America in Bloomington, Minnesota; Disney World in Orlando, Florida; and the country music mecca of Branson, Missouri—are cited as counterexamples where large numbers of visitors did not produce similar crime experiences to their casino-laden counterparts. For example, the Mall of America had 7.7 more visitors than Las Vegas, but its crime rate (as adjusted to take into account visitors per local resident) is less than one-fifteenth of that in Las Vegas.[61]

Examples such as these do not necessarily prove an assertion that the population of casino visitors either causes or attracts more crime. More research is needed to explain these differing crime rates. For example, differences in legal penalties and enforcement priorities can have significant effects on changing crime rates, and these changes are not reflected in bare statistics of criminal convictions in a given period. Displacement of crimes as a result of changing the probability of detection and the applicable sanction is well documented in economic and criminology research.[62] Future research models affecting gambling impacts on crime will also need to take these possibilities into account. However, one additional point also should be noted: to the extent that communities with casinos actually invested more resources into law enforcement after the casino opened, then it is entirely possible that casino impacts on crime are understated rather than overstated.

These correlations between casinos and crime should present significant concerns for policymakers considering the introduction of a casino or for those with casinos operating for a short period within their jurisdictions. The impacts of crime do not only affect the victim and the taxpayers through costs of enforcement and incarceration. Crime may also negatively affect property values and personal income.[63] Investments of significant additional resources may thus be required to address the potential impact of crime on the local community.

After adjustments for other factors, Grinols and Mustard estimate that approximately 8.6 percent of property crimes and 12.6 percent of violent crimes in counties with casinos were due to adding the casino. They translate this into casino-related costs of seventy-five dollars per adult (in 1996 dollars). This means that a casino potentially imposes significant aggregate costs, though as discussed later, the effects of those costs may be diffused among different groups and governmental jurisdiction, thus complicating political decisions in these areas.

Casinos and Bankruptcy

Bankruptcy is another area where casinos may have negative impacts on the surrounding community. As noted previously, the AGA rejects the proposition that casinos can be linked to increased bankruptcy rates. The AGA states in part that "A series of independent government studies conducted during the late 1990s failed to establish a link between casinos and bankruptcy, and statistics support that finding."[64] These include the NORC study, the GAO review of the National Gambling Impact Study Commission Report, and a U.S. Treasury Department study completed in 1999.[65] A closer look at these materials reveals that they indeed fall short of providing conclusive proof of a significant impact of casinos on bankruptcy, but they nevertheless present results that are not favorable to the industry on this question. If the question were framed differently, and the industry were forced to prove conclusively the absence of a link between casinos and bankruptcy, the industry could not meet this standard based on the contents of these studies.

The NORC study examined bankruptcy experiences based on extensive telephone surveys. It found that both problem and pathological gamblers experienced elevated bankruptcy rates as compared with the general population. Pathological gamblers had a bankruptcy rate of 19.2 percent, as compared with 5.5 percent and 4.2 percent for low-risk gamblers and nongamblers, respectively.[66] Although the rate for problem gamblers of 10.7 percent was only "marginally statistically significant,"[67] it was nevertheless used as the basis for estimating the costs that these gamblers imposed on others.

The elevated bankruptcy rates for these populations, which are likely to grow as a result of more convenient access to casinos, suggest a significant impact. To illustrate, assuming 19.2 percent of the 3.75 million estimated pathological gamblers computed in table 5.3 filed for personal bankruptcy, this group alone would produce nearly 720,000 bankruptcy petitions. By comparison, in 2003 there were 1.6 million annual personal bankruptcy filings.[68] Although these petitions would probably not appear in the same year, they still represent a significant pool from which future bankruptcy petitions may come.

The GAO study was also less favorable to the industry than the AGA suggests. First, it reported the NORC study results on bankruptcy experiences from problem and pathological gamblers without questioning them. Although it noted that NORC had also found no significant change in per capita bankruptcy rates in communities where casinos were introduced,[69] those rates were not the source of the social cost estimate that NORC provided to the National Gambling Impact Study Commission.

The GAO study also included a case study of Atlantic City, New Jersey. Here, the GAO observed that Atlantic County (in which Atlantic City is located) showed higher bankruptcy rates than New Jersey or the nation in general for the period 1990–98. In fact, during 1994–98, the Atlantic County rate was double the rate for New Jersey, which approximated the nationwide rate. However, the GAO reported that it was unable to ascertain the basis for that change. The GAO was also unable to ascertain the effects of opening casinos, which occurred in 1978, because county-level data were "not readily obtainable" from the Administrative Office of the United States Courts for that period. The GAO also surveyed officials in government agencies and private industry to ask them about the heightened rate, and their answers were inconclusive.

Rather than provide a ringing endorsement of the proposition that casinos don't cause bankruptcies, the results of the GAO study tip the scale on the side of being concerned about negative consequences more than they allay those concerns. They highlight the need for more research to cover longer time periods associated with our experience with casino gambling.

The Treasury Department study cited by the AGA surveyed the available literature on the relationship between bankruptcy and casinos and engaged in limited empirical analysis of bankruptcy data in certain jurisdictions.[70] In reviewing the available literature, the Treasury Department concluded in part:

While most available studies have pointed toward a connection between gambling and bankruptcy and have found various linkages, none has "proven" that gambling causes bankruptcy. Even among the population of people who went bankrupt because of gambling, there is a question of whether they might, due to a generalized lack of risk aversion, have lost their assets anyway, through other high-risk behaviors.[71]

The Treasury Department thus apparently agrees that some people went bankrupt because of gambling but that gambling was not the only "high-risk behavior" engaged in by these patrons. This is hardly comforting. It is also worth noting that the Treasury Department study agreed that the highest

risk group of gamblers have bankruptcy rates that are roughly two percentage points higher than the rate for occasional gamblers. However, it ultimately dismisses any significance from this difference based on the small population for this group.[72]

The Treasury Department also undertook some of its own empirical research in the form of regression analysis, and it found that gambling effects were inconclusive at the statewide level. However, the study cautions that this analysis was based on a small sample and highly aggregated data.[73] Thus, this failure to find a measurable impact is hardly the last word on the subject.

It is important to put each of these studies into a proper context. First, they were done during a period when there were fewer new casinos opened than we have today. These empirical studies did not take into account the dramatic growth in the number of casinos that has occurred in the past several years since the latest study was completed. Moreover, the time period when new casinos were opened—and thus the opportunities for observation of social costs—was comparatively brief. Interpreting these findings to say "not yet" or "not now" is quite different from interpreting them to mean "not ever." For this reason, more recent studies with a longer time frame of reference deserve greater attention.

Barron, Staten, and Wilshusen recently examined county-level bankruptcy data for the period 1993–97 in counties with commercial casinos, as well as contiguous counties within fifty miles of a casino.[74] They concluded that casinos had a positive and statistically significant impact on increased personal bankruptcy rates. Casinos did not account for the entire increase in bankruptcy filings that occurred nationwide during the 1990s, but their regression analysis showed the likelihood that casinos had some impact on this increase.

We have constructed our own investigation, which operates on an expanded data set covering more years and more observations than the Barron study.[75] We include data from the period 1990–2002 covering both commercial casinos and Class III tribal casinos, which were excluded from the Barron assessment. We focused on time lags between the introduction of the casino and the emergence of bankruptcy experiences. As Grinols and Mustard have demonstrated with casinos and crime, it is conceivable that casino operations may also affect bankruptcy rates differently according to the duration of their operations.

Our data set also focuses on bankruptcy experiences in the county in which the casino is located, and it thus ignores the effects on contiguous counties as identified in the Barron study. This more limited focus probably provides a more conservative measure of bankruptcy impacts, to the extent that it may potentially exclude many gambling patrons of cross-border casinos from the analysis of the casino county and in fact would include them instead in a noncasino county where they reside. Given that a large number of casinos are located along state borders in order to take advantage of trade from noncasino states, this assumption probably understates the differential impact on bankruptcy rates from casinos.

Using a regression analysis that takes into account endogenous factors including population, race, age, personal income, and employment, we examined county-level bankruptcy trends over the period 1990–2002. Focusing on the cohort of counties in which a casino first opened during the relevant period (thus eliminating Nevada and Atlantic County in New Jersey from the mix due to the extended presence of casinos during this period), we then sought to examine the impact of those casinos on bankruptcy rates.

Significantly, we found that the bankruptcy impacts varied according to the duration of operation of casinos within the county. The addition of casinos had a positive and statistically significant impact on individual bankruptcy rates in the first year of operations. Thereafter, casino counties tended to experience bankruptcy rates that were slightly lower than the rate for an equivalent noncasino county. After about the third year, the bankruptcy rate then steadily grew, outpacing the noncasino county in the ninth year of operations, with an increasingly widening gap between them in subsequent years.

Figure 5.1 profiles the estimated bankruptcy rates for casino counties and noncasino counties based on this regression model. Over the twelve-year period, bankruptcy rates in casino counties grew by 180 percent, while bankruptcy rates in noncasino counties grew by only 117 percent. Beginning from a rate of 2.4 bankruptcies per 1,000, the casino county is estimated to grow to 6.7 per 1,000, while a noncasino county would grow to 3.2 per 1,000. For the period of time covered by this analysis, this reflects an increase of more than 2 percent in the annual growth rate for bankruptcy over this period for counties with casinos over their noncasino counterparts.

Although the last word on bankruptcy and casinos has yet to be written,

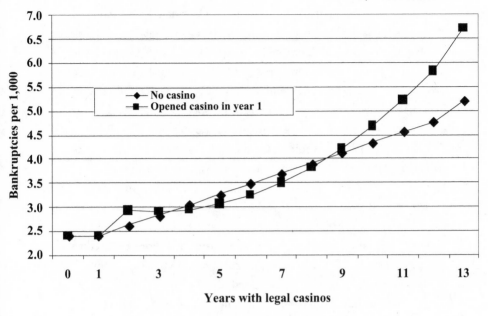

Fig. 5.1. Estimated individual bankruptcy rates—casino versus noncasino county

the available data do suggest that casinos can be linked to bankruptcies. The evidence from surveys of problem gamblers is itself a strong indication that a significant population may be affected by bankruptcy. Even if other behaviors may have contributed to bankruptcy, gambling also appears to be a contributing factor. The empirical evidence of county-level bankruptcy filings provides similarly strong indications that adding a casino has the potential for longer-term manifestations of bankruptcy experiences. As positive economic impacts from employment or tourist patronage fade (as illustrated in chapter 4), the possible negative impact on local populations may then be realized.

ESTIMATING THE INCIDENCE AND MAGNITUDE OF SOCIAL COSTS

Identifying the social problems associated with casino gambling is only part of the process of evaluating the cost side of the ledger for casino gambling. Negative social consequences associated with casino gambling must also be analyzed to determine the incidence of the cost, focusing particularly on those costs that are externalized by the gambler or the industry to others. In addition, estimates of the magnitude of these costs need to be developed.

This process can be dauntingly complex. Consider, for example, the case of a personal bankruptcy triggered by problem gambling. One potential cost involves the debt that is discharged as a consequence of bankruptcy proceedings. Here a creditor has incurred a cost because the debtor's reciprocal promise to repay is effectively nullified by a discharge granted under federal bankruptcy laws.[76] From an economist's perspective, this loss does not necessarily reflect a social cost, as it involves a transfer in which one party (the debtor) is arguably better off by the amount that the other (the creditor) is worse off.[77] Nevertheless, to the extent that the unpaid debt is attributable to losses at the casino, the debtor apparently gambled at the expense of another.

The immediate incidence of this loss appears to fall on the unpaid creditor, but ultimately others may bear this cost. The creditor may address the expected loss in advance by charging its customers more for credit or for the underlying goods or services sold on credit. In this case, some portion of the externalized cost may get passed along to the creditor's customers, which could include both gamblers and nongamblers.

Whether this impact affects local or distant markets might also be considered. For example, a financial institution issuing a credit card with a nationwide customer base could potentially spread this loss over a broader geographical market than the traditional corner store, which generations ago sold goods on personal credit to neighborhood patrons. Changes in bankruptcy laws enacted in April 2005 will potentially enhance protections for these creditors, particularly credit card issuers, from the discharge of indebtedness by problem gamblers. This legislation specifically carves out as nondischargeable any debt to a single creditor over $500 incurred within ninety days of a petition for so-called luxury goods or services.[78] Although this category is not specifically defined, gambling would arguably be included. Further, certain cash advances aggregating over $750 within seventy days of a bankruptcy petition are presumed to be nondischargeable.[79] These provisions could ultimately work against problem gamblers, leaving them with fewer options to discharge their debts. The impact of these provisions on future behavior, and whether that reflects an appropriate policy balance by requiring costs to be internalized by those with pathological conditions, remains to be worked out after this legislation becomes effective.

Bankruptcy also involves other costs, including the transaction costs associated with bankruptcy proceedings. Unlike the costs associated with the debt, these are typically incurred in the jurisdiction where the debtor lives or owns a business. Venue will generally be appropriate in the federal district court where the domicile, residence, principal place of business, or principal assets of the debtor are located.[80] Thus, to the extent that gambling patrons live or own a business in a jurisdiction other than the one in which they regularly gamble, these costs are effectively exported from the casino jurisdiction. A recent study indeed suggests that casinos export bankruptcy costs to the jurisdictions from which they draw visiting patrons.[81]

Some of these transaction costs are jointly paid by the gambler and the creditors, including filing fees, court costs, and the fees paid to legal counsel. Others are borne by taxpayers, who provide funds to support the bankruptcy courts and related judicial machinery administering this area of law. Concepts of variable and fixed costs are potentially relevant here, as the real impact of problem gambling–related bankruptcy is arguably at the margin: Given that bankruptcy has many causes other than gambling, bankruptcy courts and their associated staffs would be needed at some level whether there were casinos or not.

The incidence of costs imposed on taxpayers also raises issues involving jurisdiction. To the extent that federal courts are involved, federal taxes support these activities, thus affecting a diffusion of costs beyond the local region. Other examples of social costs, such as crime-related costs imposed on local law enforcement, may have more direct impacts on local taxpayers. Thus, the type of cost may thus reflect more or less scrutiny from a local taxpayer or politician who is sensitive to the question of who bears the costs and who obtains the benefits.

These issues of incidence are often not addressed in the literature discussing the impact of social costs, which focuses on the bigger picture of the aggregate costs and benefits. However, these issues are potentially relevant to policymakers and legislators, who must consider political interests of their particular constituencies. The impact on one's own constituents, as opposed to the impact on others, creates a powerful incentive for decision making that ignores the impact of costs that may be exported to others. In this sense, the politics of gambling at state and local levels may often violate the Golden Rule, as exports of social costs to another jurisdiction (or to taxpayers accountable to another level of government) are omitted from the total calculus of costs that might otherwise affect decisions about the benefits of gambling.

Estimating the magnitude of these costs presents other significant challenges. First, the statistical base for estimating the contribution of gambling to the social problem must be determined. One approach to this issue focuses on the costs attributed to behaviors associated with problem and/or pathological gamblers. This approach seeks to estimate the marginal contribution of these behaviors to the expected incidence of social costs in populations without problem or pathological gambling experiences. The other approach looks broadly at the results of regression analysis associated with conditions before and after a casino has been added, seeking to ascertain the marginal contribution from all aspects of the casino rather than only from those affected by problem gambling.

Both approaches are subject to the challenges of multiple causation. In other words, some members of these populations could have contributed to these costs regardless of whether legalized casino gambling was present in their community. Estimates that do not separate the impact of other causal factors from that of gambling pathology are subject to challenge. Regression analysis that controls for multiple contributing factors provides a basis to limit the effects from other causes, but the analysis is only as good as the available data.

Data concerning the marginal contribution of problem and/or pathological gamblers have the advantage of being more available and easier to work with than more complex regression models. For example, the NORC study estimated the costs associated with the various social conditions—including lost employment, bankruptcy, criminal justice, divorce, and health issues—from an extensive survey population.[82] By differentiating the experience rates for problem and pathological gamblers over other groups, an estimate of the associated cost can be developed.

However, this estimation method often focuses on incidents per problem or pathological gambler. If a problem or pathological gambler is diagnosed based on lifetime experiences, derivation of an annual estimate of costs is highly uncertain.[83] The NORC survey also queried the population about prior year incidents, which provided a basis for estimating annual impacts on some problems but not on others. More research into the longitudinal patterns of pathological and problem gamblers may yield a more accurate picture of annual costs than this simple methodology.

Grinols has explored this issue thoughtfully and extensively in a recent book, in which he summarizes the results from studies that sought to measure social costs associated with problem and/or pathological gambling.[84] These costs spanned a range of nine different categories, including crime (which included subcategories of costs associated with apprehension and police, adjudication, and incarceration), business and employment costs (including lost productivity, lost time, and unemployment), bankruptcy, suicide, illness, social service costs (including therapy and treatment costs), family costs (associated with divorce and separation), and so-called abused dollars, which refers to money acquired from relatives and friends under false pretenses for use in gambling.[85]

Grinols examined nine studies that computed estimated costs for pathological gamblers. An average of data for studies, adjusted to 2003 dollars, generates an estimated cost per pathological gambler of $10,330.[86] The cost per problem gambler, which was based on three studies examining only a partial listing of costs, was estimated at $2,945.[87] If these costs are applied to estimates of total pathological and problem gamblers developed previously in this chapter, the totals range from $47 billion to $161 billion (see table 5.5). The lower end of this range compares favorably with the lifetime estimates of the NORC study, which was also adopted by the National Gambling Impact Study Commission.

TABLE 5.5.   Estimated aggregate social costs ·

	Grinols Cost Estimate ($)	NORC Patron Survey (table 5.3) ($)	Aggregate Cost ($)
Pathological	10,330	3,750,933	38,747,141,333
Problem	2,945	2,831,233	8,337,982,167
Total			47,085,123,500
	Average Grinols Cost[a]	Welte Study (table 5.4)	
SOGS	6,638	24,391,915	161,901,333,755
DIS	6,638	10,180,973	67,576,208,872

[a]This figure is a simple average of the Grinols cost estimates for problem and pathological gamblers. As referenced in tables 5.2, 5.3, and 5.4 above, the ratio of problem gamblers to pathological gamblers varies in each estimate, with more problem gamblers in one example and more pathological gamblers in two examples. A simple average approximates equal occurrences of each category.

In addition to these aggregate effects on social costs, other costs not listed here may also be relevant. Some of them are inherently personal and difficult to value in monetary terms, such as the pain inflicted on families affected by the problem gambler. Though these kinds of costs are beyond the scope of an economic analysis, they are very real from a human perspective. Problem and pathological gamblers are likely to contribute significantly to casino profits—and government coffers. The NORC study indicated that 15 percent of AGR comes from problem and pathological gamblers.[88] A 1996 study by Grinols and Omorov indicated that a much higher figure was justifiable—perhaps as much as 52 percent.[89] A report prepared by two researchers from the University of Lethbridge on the sources of revenues in Canadian casinos indicated that the proportion of revenue coming from problem gamblers may vary according to the type of game involved. This study, which was based on diary entries for a sample of Canadian gamblers in Ontario, indicated these approximate proportions for different types of gambling. In rank order, the rough proportions are "60% gaming machines; 53% horse racing; 22% casino table games; 22% bingo and raffles; and 19% lotteries."[90]

Given the prevalence of electronic gaming machines in casinos in the United States,[91] the 60 percent estimate for gaming machines suggests that casinos and racinos depend heavily on problem gambling behavior. Even if more conservative measures are used, the revenues from problem gambling are likely to be significant, presenting a dilemma for the industry. It might seem socially responsible to be concerned about problem gamblers. However, getting too concerned might be very bad for business.

As discussed in the chapters that follow, governments have paid comparatively little attention to social costs, and in particular the plight of problem and pathological gamblers, in determining the parameters of the regulatory environment for casino gambling. Instead, they have focused on keeping the industry profitable and using it as a tool for tax collection. The available data on social costs suggest that this is a serious error and that a head-in-the-sand approach of academic agnosticism is no longer a sustainable position for making gambling policies.

6. Regulating Gambling—An Introduction

[T]he power of the State to establish all regulations that are reasonably necessary to secure the health, safety, good order, comfort, or general welfare of the community . . . can neither be abdicated nor bargained away, and is inalienable even by express grant.

> *Atlantic Coast Line R. Co. v. Goldsboro,* 232 U.S. 548, 558 (1914)

[H]e who stirs the devil's broth must needs use a long spoon.

> *Marshall v. Sawyer,* 301 F.2d 639, 648 (9th Cir. 1962)
> (Pope, J., concurring)

In our federal system, regulatory functions are diffused among federal, state, and local governments. In theory, the Founding Fathers designed the federal government with limited powers, thus constraining its ability to encroach upon the governing role of the states. The Tenth Amendment reinforces this design: "The powers not delegated to the United States by the Constitution, nor prohibited by it to the States, are reserved to the States respectively, or to the people."

In practice, however, the federal government's delegated powers have often been exercised rather expansively. In particular, Article I, Section 8, Clause 3 of the United States Constitution grants to Congress the power "[t]o regulate Commerce with foreign Nations, and among the several States, and with the Indian Tribes." Since most activities have some connection with or effect upon commerce, the permissible scope of federal regulation has indeed broadened. Though the Supreme Court has recently expressed some limitations on the scope of the commerce powers,[1] it is difficult to raise a successful constitutional objection to federal legislation regulating (or perhaps even prohibiting) gambling activities under those powers. Alternatively, Congress could also exercise its taxing powers under Article I, Section 8, Clause 1 to regulate or even prohibit gambling.[2] For example, Congress could enact a large federal excise tax on gambling transactions to effectively eliminate legalized gambling by making it uneconomical.

Despite these extensive powers, the federal government has exercised a restrained approach in its oversight of gambling. The states provide most laws involving the regulation of gambling. As political subdivisions of the state, local governments function much like agencies in exercising governmental power, which is effectively derived from the state.[3] Federal policy has generally supported state autonomy over gambling matters, intervening only in limited circumstances to address such matters as interstate aspects of gambling, criminal activities, and gambling conducted by Native American tribes. Federal tax laws specifically applicable to gambling focus primarily on information reporting, and they have only limited effects on the industry's gambling operations.

Significant state regulatory structures affecting commercial casino gambling are discussed in this chapter, followed by more extensive state-specific expositions in chapters 7 and 8. Federal laws regulating gambling, including the peculiar regulatory posture of Native American gaming and the special problems of the Internet, are discussed in chapters 9 through 11.

STATE REGULATION:
WIELDING THE POLICE POWER

A state's authority to regulate (or prohibit) gambling is traditionally associated with so-called police power, which was the subject of some early Supreme Court litigation. In *Stone v. Mississippi,*[4] a corporation challenged the validity of state legislation abrogating its power to conduct a lottery, which the state had previously granted through a corporate charter. The corporation claimed that this legislation impaired contractual rights in violation of the Contracts Clause in Article I, Section 10, Clause 1 of the United States Constitution.[5]

The Court rejected this challenge and confirmed the state's power to regulate gambling, stating in part:

> [Lotteries] are not, in the legal acceptation of the term, *mala in se,* but, as we have just seen, may properly be made *mala prohibita.* They are a species of gambling, and wrong in their influences. They disturb the checks and balances of a well-ordered community. Society built on such a foundation

would almost of necessity bring forth a population of speculators and gamblers, living on the expectation of what, "by the casting of lots, or by lot, chance, or otherwise," might be "awarded" to them from the accumulations of others. Certainly the right to suppress them is governmental, to be exercised at all times by those in power, at their discretion. Any one, therefore, who accepts a lottery charter does so with the implied understanding that the people, in their sovereign capacity, and through their properly constituted agencies, may resume it at any time when the public good shall require, whether it be paid for or not. All that one can get by such a charter is a suspension of certain governmental rights in his favor, subject to withdrawal at will. He has in legal effect nothing more than a license to enjoy the privilege on the terms named for the specified time, unless it be sooner abrogated by the sovereign power of the State. It is a permit, good as against existing laws, but subject to future legislative and constitutional control or withdrawal.[6]

The Court's views reflect the sentiments of the times about gambling; that is, it was not wrong in itself (*mala in se*), though it tended to have negative effects that states could constrain through regulation or prohibition.[7] It is also interesting to note that the Court advanced the belief that lotteries were even more damaging to the social fabric than other forms of gambling and that some government regulation was preferable to none in this area.

> [T]his court said, more than thirty years ago, speaking through Mr. Justice Grier, in *Phalen* v. *Virginia* (8 How. 163, 168), that "experience has shown that the common forms of gambling are comparatively innocuous when placed in contrast with the wide-spread pestilence of lotteries. The former are confined to a few persons and places, but the latter infests the whole community; it enters every dwelling; it reaches every class; it preys upon the hard earnings of the poor; and it plunders the ignorant and simple." Happily, under the influence of restrictive legislation, the evils are not so apparent now; but we very much fear that with the same opportunities of indulgence the same results would be manifested. If lotteries are to be tolerated at all, it is no doubt better that they should be regulated by law, so that the people may be protected as far as possible against the inherent vices of the system; but that they are demoralizing in their effects, no matter how carefully regulated, cannot admit of a doubt.[8]

The police power reflects the ideal of government protecting citizens from one another and, perhaps in some cases, from themselves. For many years, governments have chosen criminal sanctions as the method of exercising the police power to stamp out gambling (particularly in its professional or commercial forms) or at least to constrain its impact on society through deterrent effects. Fraud, cheating, and the economic hardship associated with losing more than a patron could afford, as well as other collateral effects associated with gambling losses, including crime, violence, and strained family relationships, were among the concerns to be addressed. Governments attempted, in general, to reduce these problems by limiting the available opportunities to gamble. Attaching a criminal penalty also reinforced other social values, such as accumulating wealth by earning, saving, and investing for the future rather than by quick gains from beliefs in luck or chance.

However, criminal sanctions provide an imperfect solution to the regulation of gambling. Defects in the statutory scheme, such as incomplete definitions of proscribed forms of gambling, sometimes leave gaps to be exploited.[9] As in other industries, technological changes, including the development of electronic communication media, change the way that business is done; laws must also change to encompass these new technologies.[10] Lawmakers must also take care to adjust the system of criminal penalties to take into account current social conditions and beliefs. A penalty that is judged too harsh will impede prospects for conviction and make enforcement less likely, while a penalty that is seen as too lenient will not deter the proscribed behavior.[11]

Even if lawmakers produce perfectly written statutes, enforcing them is another matter. The fact that gambling is not viewed as *malum in se* may lead to lax enforcement efforts, as officials direct scarce resources toward activities that they believe present more serious social problems. Corrupting influences may also be at work as illicit gambling profits may also find their way to affect the decisions of law enforcement officials.[12] This in turn may create the need for still more laws, and probably federal oversight, to address the problem of state and local corruption.[13]

Even with the most efficient criminal sanctions, some individuals will continue to demand gambling services and will seek out this demand through an underground economy that is beyond the effective reach of governmental authority. Negative collateral effects from gambling still exist in this environment, though they presumably affect fewer patrons.

Of even greater significance to policymakers may be the fact that substantial profits generated in this underground economy are beyond the reach of the government's taxing power. Though governments may tax illicit gains,[14] the collection of such taxes presents a real problem. The prospect of capturing tax and other economic benefits from this underground economy presents a tempting target for those seeking a solution for fiscal needs without the negative political consequences of raising taxes.

Legalization may make illicit alternatives less desirable for both patrons and providers who would prefer to avoid the sanctions and stigma associated with illegal activity. However, it is unlikely to eliminate the underground economy. Regulations impose costs, which increase individual incentives to circumvent the regulatory system. For example, even when options for legalized gambling exist, patrons may continue to choose illegal gaming based on a desire to attain better odds or to avoid tax consequences on winnings.[15]

Thus, criminal sanctions continue to play an important role even in those states that choose the path of legalization. However, such sanctions serve a different function in the legal and social order, in that they tend to protect the state's fiscal interests by channeling behavior away from illegal alternatives and into taxable gambling activities. Their role as a transmitter of social values is compromised by the existence of government-sanctioned outlets for similar behavior.

Legalizing an activity, coupled with the promotion of that activity through advertising, will generally increase the level of that activity that was once prohibited.[16] Some commentators have suggested that legalization may even increase illegal forms of gambling by reducing the stigma associated with gambling.[17] Even if this is not the case, policymakers must recognize that increasing the opportunities for legal gambling activities is likely to exacerbate social problems associated with gambling. As discussed in chapter 5, bankruptcies, crimes, and other negative consequences mean that some of the costs associated with gambling activities may be externalized to others. In an ideal world, a regulatory approach should address these costs and limit their imposition upon others.

STATE REGULATORY STRUCTURES

States with legalized casino gambling have pursued different approaches to licensing and regulating gaming operations, but those approaches share some common features. For the most part, regulatory behavior tends to focus upon the goal of developing public confidence in gaming as a legitimate form of entertainment. Such efforts must overcome years of history and cultural bias: recall that "maintaining a gambling house" was generally considered as a public nuisance to be abated.[18]

To achieve this end, regulations need to address consumer concerns about fraudulent, unfair, or otherwise dangerous practices that potentially affect gaming patrons. Regulators must disassociate criminal elements from state-sanctioned gambling establishments. They must also protect patrons from unscrupulous gaming operators and threats or violence due to gaming losses. Enhancing the legitimacy of the industry will also tend to channel patrons and service providers away from illegal alternatives, which is important for governmental success in capturing the economic benefits that otherwise lurk in the underground economy.

Regulations also must ensure that government-imposed taxes and fees are accurately assessed and collected. Much like owners, governments are concerned about getting their share of the financial rewards generated from a gambling enterprise. Without adequate internal controls and reporting, a cash-based business such as a casino provides a fertile environment for siphoning money back into the underground economy. (The federal government shares this interest with the states. As discussed in chapter 9, it also imposes regulations to prevent money laundering and to protect other fiscal and security interests.)

In many jurisdictions, the regulatory structure also seeks to ensure the economic viability of gaming as an enterprise in the state. States often accomplish this by limiting the supply of gaming licenses, thus preserving what amounts to an oligopolistic status for licensed casinos. This structure tends to ensure that the state will have a reliable flow of tax dollars from an operation with an adequate market share to support a profitable operation, thereby attracting private capital to invest in the casino infrastructure.

Having fewer but larger facilities may also provide other efficiency gains from a regulatory perspective. For example, it is undoubtedly easier to monitor the compliance of fewer larger establishments than many small ones. Moreover, to the extent that the providers are largely made up of publicly traded corporations, additional resources (including government agencies, such as the Securities and Exchange Commission) are available to monitor and regulate the financial responsibility of the industry.

Nevertheless, a structure favoring a limited number of providers also has potential downside risks. The award of a discretionary gambling license increases the possibility that private companies[19] will receive public largess based on their political influences. Though it may be possible to structure licensing decisions in a competitive way to ensure that the public captures a larger portion of the benefits associated with gaming, this is not the dominant approach in jurisdictions with a limited number of licenses.[20]

Finally, government may also seek to address some of the negative consequences of legalized gambling on patrons and their families stemming from excessive gambling losses. Regulations have generally overlooked these consequences on individuals, which are often indirect and hidden, in favor of market competition for the gaming dollar. In part, this regulatory gap may be due to the exigencies of developing an effective business model that will produce the expected revenues promised to constituents. Governments that depend upon tax revenues from gaming operations understandably find it easier to choose a path that maximizes the industry's gains, which may come at the expense of the citizens they are supposed to protect.

Protections for those vulnerable to compulsive gambling behaviors are especially weak, often involving counseling and treatment options that are effective, if at all, after considerable financial and other damage has occurred. The compulsive gambler is thus exposed to ever-expanding opportunities for legal gaming, leaving families and others (including nongamblers) exposed to the attendant social and economic losses from this behavior.

Though a comprehensive state-by-state review of efforts to regulate gambling is beyond the scope of this book, a review of the particular regulatory structures and practices in a few states provides a flavor of different approaches taken and the relative balance achieved between promotion of the industry and protection from its excesses. Nevada's system is well developed and oriented heavily toward the promotion of gambling as a significant part of the state's economy, reflecting its position as an early adopter of legalized gambling as part of the entertainment and tourism industry. As such, it provides a baseline for comparison with approaches taken in other states that have followed Nevada's lead in legalizing casino gambling.

7. Casino Regulation in Nevada

As the leading destination for casino gambling in the United States, Nevada has a long-standing commitment to the gaming industry as an important part of its economy.[1] Nevada has designed a regulatory scheme that links the growth and success of the industry to public trust and confidence in the integrity of the industry and all those who deal with it. As stated in the Gaming Control Act:

> All establishments where gaming is conducted and where gaming devices are operated, and manufacturers, sellers and distributors of certain gaming devices and equipment . . . must therefore be licensed, controlled and assisted to protect the public health, safety, morals, good order and general welfare of the inhabitants of the state, to foster the stability and success of gaming and to preserve the competitive economy and policies of free competition of the State of Nevada.[2]

Because of Nevada's position as the state with the largest casino industry and the longest history of legalized gambling, its regulatory model merits serious attention from those concerned with gaming regulation.

BASIC MECHANISMS OF CONTROL

Nevada pursues its regulatory purposes through two agencies: the Gaming Control Board and the Gaming Commission. The Gaming Commission consists of five members, who are appointed by the governor.[3] In an effort to maintain political neutrality, no more than three members may come from the same political party[4] and no member may currently hold elective office or an official capacity in a political party.[5] In an effort to maintain neutrality from the industry, no member may hold a pecuniary interest in a gaming establishment.[6] The commission has authority to issue gaming licenses and to promulgate regulations affecting the industry.[7]

The Gaming Control Board consists of three members, also appointed by the governor.[8] Like commission members, board members are precluded from holding an elected office or serving as an official in a political party.[9] One member must be a certified public accountant or otherwise qualified to practice public accounting and must also possess expertise in corporate finance, auditing, economics, or gaming.[10] Another member must be selected "with special reference to his training and experience in the fields of investigation, law enforcement, law or gaming."[11]

The board's mission is stated as follows:

> The State Gaming Control Board governs Nevada's gaming industry through strict regulation of all persons, locations, practices, association, and related activities. Through investigations, licensure, and enforcement of laws and regulations we protect the integrity and the stability of the industry and ensure the collection of gaming taxes and fees that are an essential source of State revenue.[12]

An extensive staff, which is organized in six functional divisions, assists the board in carrying out its duties.

The Audit Division, which has a professional staff of more than one hundred employees, audits casinos with more than $3 million in revenue to ensure compliance with applicable gaming laws and proper reporting of gaming revenue.[13] It utilizes traditional audit techniques as part of regular, systematic reviews of casino operations, and it also performs covert operations or other special investigations as needed to detect money laundering, "skimming," or other illegal activities.[14]

Investigative functions are also carried out by two other divisions: the Investigation Division and the Enforcement Division. The Investigation Division carries out background investigations on prospective licensees.[15] The Enforcement Division's responsibilities include investigating suspected criminal activity, monitoring for involvement of organized crime, and checking the backgrounds of prospective employees.[16] The Enforcement Division also recommends to the board persons to be added to the "List of Excluded Persons."[17] As discussed later in the chapter, this list has proved controversial, as it provides a state-sanctioned means for private firms to deny access to specific individuals in an effort to protect the industry's reputation and to further law enforcement efforts.

The Tax and License Division is responsible for collecting all taxes imposed on gambling. It also issues gaming licenses pursuant to the direction of the Gaming Commission, performs compliance reviews for licensees with less than $3 million in gaming revenues, and monitors Indian gaming in Nevada.[18] Gaming taxes and related fees and licenses totaled $819,380,000 in fiscal 2004, representing 19.6 percent of total revenues.[19]

Other divisions are designed to deal with specialized problems. The Corporate Securities Division monitors publicly traded companies and their subsidiaries operating gaming businesses in Nevada.[20] Since the Nevada legislature changed state law to lift restrictions affecting the ability of publicly traded companies to hold gaming licenses, these companies now control approximately three-fourths of gaming revenues in the state.[21] Finally, the Technology Division provides laboratory and field testing for electronic devices and software to ensure their integrity for gaming patrons.[22]

Licensing for casino owners and employees is a central feature of Nevada's regulatory system. It is unlawful for an "owner, lessee, or employee" to carry on any gaming activity without a license.[23] "Restricted" licenses are available to those who choose to operate fewer than fifteen slot machines in an environment that is ancillary to another business, such as in a restaurant or convenience store.[24] Operators and employees of casinos with more than fifteen devices or with table games require an "unrestricted" license.[25]

A prospective licensee bears the burden of proving his or her qualification.[26] The following criteria apply in making licensing decisions:

> An application to receive a license or be found suitable must not be granted unless the commission is satisfied that the applicant is:
> (a) A person of good character, honesty and integrity;
> (b) A person whose prior activities, criminal record, if any, reputation, habits and associations do not pose a threat to the public interest of this state or to the effective regulation and control of gaming or charitable lotteries, or create or enhance the dangers of unsuitable, unfair or illegal practices, methods and activities in the conduct of gaming or charitable lotteries or in the carrying on of the business and financial arrangements incidental thereto; and

(c) In all other respects qualified to be licensed or found suitable consistently with the declared policy of the state.[27]

Operators who apply for a casino license must further establish business competence and experience and prove that adequate financing for the casino operation comes from a "suitable source."[28] Even lenders to casino operations must meet character requirements,[29] and others doing business with the casino may also be subjected to licensing requirements.[30]

Licensing standards serve a public purpose in protecting patrons and others doing business with the casino industry. For example, ensuring the financial wherewithal to meet operational demands tends to ensure that casinos are able to carry out their financial obligations to winning patrons. However, licensing standards also serve another important purpose, which was instrumental in gaining public acceptance for the industry: freedom from association with criminal elements. The Nevada Supreme Court explained this purpose in an early case.

> Throughout this country, then, gambling has necessarily surrounded itself with an aura of crime and corruption. Those in management of this pursuit who have succeeded, have done so not only through a disregard of law, but, in a competitive world, through a superior talent for such disregard and for the corruption of those in public authority.
>
> For gambling to take its place as a lawful enterprise in Nevada it is not enough that this state has named it lawful. We have but offered it the opportunity for lawful existence. The offer is a risky one, not only for the people of this state, but for the entire nation. Organized crime must not be given refuge here through the legitimatizing of one of its principal sources of income. Nevada gambling, if it is to succeed as a lawful enterprise, must be free from the criminal and corruptive taint acquired by gambling beyond our borders. If this is to be accomplished not only must the operation of gambling be carefully controlled, but the character and background of those who would engage in gambling in this state must be carefully scrutinized.[31]

This 1957 opinion was written shortly after an extensive study of organized crime was commissioned by the United States Senate. In 1950, Senator Estes Kefauver, who chaired the Senate Committee to Investigate Organized Crime, delegated to the American Bar Association the responsibility for investigating and evaluating local law enforcement mechanisms and their effectiveness against organized crime.[32] This study, which was issued in 1952, raised important issues concerning the tension between the structurally desirable feature of local law enforcement and control, which is inherent in our federal system, and the deleterious effects of corruption on its effectiveness. If Nevada was to avoid encroachment by federal law enforcement,[33] it was effectively required to demonstrate that its regulatory agencies and its gambling industry were free from the taint of criminal elements.

AGENCY DISCRETION: LICENSING

The Casino Control Act grants extensive discretion to the commission in granting or denying licenses to casino operators and key employees, and that discretion is critical to maintaining the integrity of the industry. The act provides in part: "The commission has full and absolute power and authority to deny any application for any cause it deems reasonable."[34] The act also makes it clear that a license is not a property right but is instead a revocable privilege.[35] Nevada law provides no recourse to judicial review for a prospective licensee whose application is denied.[36] This feature has survived constitutional challenges, leaving the commission with nearly plenary powers over those to whom licenses are granted.

For example, in *State v. Rosenthal,*[37] the Nevada Supreme Court upheld the commission's denial of a license to Frank Rosenthal, who functioned as a key employee of a Las Vegas casino. In support of its decision, the commission had made the following findings about Rosenthal:

> The applicant is a person whose licensing by the State would reflect or tend to reflect discredit upon the State of Nevada by reason of: A) A North Carolina court finding of guilt for conspiracy to bribe an amateur athlete; B) Testimony of Mickey Bruce in Senate subcommittee hearings that applicant attempted to bribe him to throw outcome of 1960 Oregon-Michigan football game; C) Statements by police officers Dardis and Clode to Senate subcommittee and to Florida Racing Commission that applicant admitted he was corrupting public officials in return for protection; D) The applicant's being barred from race tracks and pari-mutual operations in the State of Florida.[38]

In reversing a lower court's finding that the board's decision violated Rosenthal's due process rights, the Nevada Supreme Court treated gambling as a special case suited for the state's exercise of "police powers" outside the scope of federal constitutional protections.

> Gaming as a calling or business is in the same class as the selling of intoxicating liquors in respect to deleterious tendency. The state may regulate or suppress it without interfering with any of those inherent rights of citizenship which it is the object of government to protect and secure.[39]

A legislative decision to leave licensing matters to the discretion of the commission and to provide no resort to judicial review did not offend due process. As a *prospective* licensee, Rosenthal was not deprived of any current property right. Moreover, deference to agency discretion was consistent with the legislature's purpose in regulating legalized gambling. Specialized knowledge was required to effectively regulate the gambling industry,[40] and the qualifications and experience of the commission made it especially well qualified to exercise this discretion.[41]

The commission also serves as the primary decision maker in cases involving revocation or other disciplinary matters affecting licensees. However, judicial review is provided in this context.[42] Unlike the prospective licensee, a holder of an existing license does possess rights that are entitled to due process protections.

AGENCY DISCRETION: BLACKLISTING

The List of Excluded Persons or "Black Book" provides another tool for the state to reinforce its efforts to legitimize the gaming industry. The commission is authorized by statute to create a list of persons "whose presence in the establishment is determined by the board and the commission to pose a threat to the interests of this state or to licensed gaming, or both."[43] The criteria for exclusion include a broad range of activities:

(a) Prior conviction of a crime which is a felony in this state or under the laws of the United States, a crime involving moral turpitude or a violation of the gaming laws of any state;

(b) Violation or conspiracy to violate the provisions of this chapter relating to:

    (1) The failure to disclose an interest in a gaming establishment for which the person must obtain a license; or

    (2) Willful evasion of fees or taxes;

(c) Notorious or unsavory reputation which would adversely affect public confidence and trust that the gaming industry is free from criminal or corruptive elements; or

(d) Written order of a governmental agency which authorizes the exclusion or ejection of the person from an establishment at which gaming . . . is conducted.[44]

Exclusion may not be based on invidious categories, including race, color, creed, national origin or ancestry, or sex.[45] However, the commission need only find one of the permissible enumerated criteria for exclusion in order to support a decision to exclude.[46] The stated criteria allow for exclusion based on information that would be insufficient for a criminal conviction. For example, regulations provide that hearsay evidence—as reflected in reports by federal or state legislative or executive agencies—may be used to establish a "notorious or unsavory reputation" as a basis for exclusion.[47] Associating with illegal sports betting or influencing the outcome of collegiate sporting events is also grounds for exclusion.[48]

The commission's decision is subject to judicial review, but a reviewing court's ability to reverse such a decision is constrained by statute, which limits relief to such circumstances involving a decision that is "unsupported by *any* evidence" or "arbitrary or capricious or otherwise not in accordance with law."[49] The commission is permitted to take punitive measures against any establishment or related individual who "knowingly fails to exclude" a listed person.[50] Listed persons who attempt to enter a casino or otherwise have contact with the industry may be charged with a gross misdemeanor.[51]

The Black Book was initially used to target known members and associates of organized crime, and it was apparently used sparingly during its early years. For example, after existing for more than twenty years, only nine persons were listed in 1987.[52] As of May 2005, thirty-nine persons were listed.[53] Several added to the list in recent years have been included for crimes involving efforts to improperly manipulate electronic gambling devices.[54] Thus, although the origins of the list may have been rooted in protecting the public reputation of the industry, it also protects the casinos from economic losses by providing a centralized means of notice from those with a propensity for electronic theft.[55]

Those selected for inclusion in the Black Book enjoy limited due process rights, which are grounded in the significant reputational interests affected by inclusion.[56] In *Spilotro v. State*,[57] Anthony Spilotro, an organized crime figure who had been placed in the Black Book, unsuccessfully challenged the constitutionality of the Nevada statutes. Among other things, Spilotro alleged that the Nevada scheme violated substantive due process by punishing him for his status or associations. The court rejected this argument, stating in part: "the purpose of the statutes is regulatory, not penal. The exclusionary list is designed not to punish those listed for past bad behavior, but to protect the interests of the State and the licensed gaming industry, by avoiding any potentially significant criminal or corruptive taint and thus maintaining public confidence and trust in the gaming industry."[58] These regulatory purposes also formed the basis for rejecting his argument that inclusion on the list was an unconstitutional bill of attainder, which required a criminal penalty for that status to attach.[59]

The court also rejected challenges based on Spilotro's right to travel, association, and access to public places, which would be affected by inclusion on the list. In particular, it found that no such rights exist for access to casinos.[60] The court found that the rules governing the Black Book were a "reasonable method of achieving a legitimate end of protecting the state's vital gaming industry and thus comply with substantive due process and procedural due process."[61]

Commentators have been critical of the list as a means of regulation, particularly because of the potential impact on economic and associational rights from inclusion, which may be based on evidence that falls short of constitutional sufficiency for a criminal conviction.[62] However, the peculiar nature of casino gambling apparently forms the basis for granting some latitude to the state in choosing the means to accomplish its regulatory purposes.

That latitude is also evident in Nevada's treatment of so-called card counters, who may be excluded from casinos for conduct that does not involve cheating or criminal activity but that instead might threaten the industry's economic well-being. The exclusion of card counters is not expressly sanctioned by state statute; it is the product of a common law rule giving owners of private establishments the right to refuse service to those whom they choose. Although the Gaming Control Act requires that gambling be available to the public, it also specifically allows this "common law right" to continue. The act states that it does not

(a) Abrogate or abridge any common law right of a gaming establishment to exclude any person from gaming activities or eject any person from the premises of the establishment for any reason; or

(b) Prohibit a licensee from establishing minimum wagers for any gambling game or slot machine.[63]

In *Uston v. Hilton Hotels Corporation*,[64] a card counter challenged the legality of a casino's practice of excluding him from the casino, even though his name was not found in the Black Book. Uston had neither cheated nor committed an illegal act; he claimed that his only offense was that he was a "better than average blackjack ('21') player." As the court explained, a "card counter" is "a person that attempts to know every card both in and out of the deck, thereby enhancing his chances of placing a favorable wager."[65] Card counting does not guarantee success, but by evaluating the cards that have been played and by making larger bets as more cards are played (and thus more cards are known), a card counter is able to gain some advantage in assessing the odds affecting a particular hand.[66]

Uston based his claim, in part, on a civil rights statute, 42 U.S.C. § 1983, which requires state action as a predicate. Here, even though his exclusion was not caused by any positive action of a government official or agency, such as the Gaming Control Board or Gaming Commission, Uston alleged "that the actions of the defendants in preventing him from playing the game of '21' were tantamount to state action (1) because of the extent to which the State of Nevada regulates the gaming industry, and (2) because the State of Nevada, charged with the enforcement of the gaming laws, has refused to prohibit the discrimination against card counters."[67]

The court found these arguments to be without merit, stating in part: "Mere state regulation of a private industry in and of itself does not constitute state action. Something more, more in the nature of a substantial and direct state involvement in promoting the challenged activity, must be demonstrated in order to establish state action."[68] In this case, Uston could not show that the state had "to any significant degree promoted or participated in the exclusion of persons suspected by gaming establishments to be

card counters or in Uston's words, 'better than average black jack players.' "[69] The state's inaction—that is, its failure to compel casinos to admit
him because he was not on the List of Excluded Persons—would not give
rise to a cause of action in these circumstances.[70] Having failed to show any
basis for invidious discrimination, Uston was thus left without any legal
recourse under federal law in these circumstances. Moreover, given the specific reservation of the common law right to exclude, it appears that no recourse exists under Nevada state law either.

The *Uston* court is probably correct that no federal civil rights violation
arises from being excluded from a casino because you are perceived to be a
better than average player. Other courts have reached a similar conclusion.[71]
However, the distinction between government action and inaction—that is,
turning a blind eye toward a conspicuous practice—in a pervasively regulated industry is difficult to draw. It is also potentially troublesome from a
political perspective. The fact that state law permits casinos to exclude players considered to be an economic threat reveals the state's interest as a de
facto participant in the gambling business. It also reinforces the state's vital
economic interest in ensuring that casinos are on the winning side of the
gaming equation, even to the detriment of particular citizens.[72]

It strains logic to assert that permitting casinos to adopt exclusionary
practices reinforces consumer confidence in the fairness of the gaming industry. A New Jersey court considering a similar claim by Uston raised these
points.

> The exclusion of persons who can play the licensed games to their advan-
> tage may diminish public confidence in the fairness of casino gaming. To
> the extent persons not counting cards would be mistakenly excluded,
> public confidence might be further diminished. However, the right of the
> casinos to have the rules drawn so as to allow some reasonable profit
> must also be recognized in any realistic assessment. The Commission
> should consider the potentially broad ramifications of excluding card
> counters before it seeks to promulgate such a rule. Fairness and the in-
> tegrity of casino gaming are the touchstones.[73]

Regulators in New Jersey have taken a different approach than Nevada.
Rather than allowing casinos to exclude card counters, New Jersey allows
casinos to take special measures to address the economic threat of card

counters, including reshuffling cards, increasing the number of decks being played, limiting the number of hands that may be played at one time, and lowering betting limits for suspected card counters.[74] However, under either approach, card counters are still not treated the same as other gamblers who lack their skills; the economic interests of the casinos triumph over a skilled player's potential advantage.

CREDIT RULES

Credit is ubiquitous in commerce, and it is commonly understood that granting credit facilitates consumer spending. However, easy access to credit in the emotion-laden environment of a casino also presents the potential for patrons to exacerbate their losses, perhaps to the point of excess. Gaming experts have indicated that credit may account for more than half of the revenues generated in Nevada's larger casinos and that it is an especially critical business practice for casinos that compete for the patronage of foreign gamblers.[75]

Oddly enough, prior to 1983 Nevada followed the common law rule that gambling debts were legally unenforceable.[76] Nevertheless, the industry was apparently quite successful in collecting debts outside the judicial process. Experts in this area estimated a historical collection rate of 95 percent.[77] However, more permissive credit rules in New Jersey, which permitted the enforcement of gambling debts, caused the Nevada gaming industry to seek changes in its laws to ensure that Nevada gamblers would continue to view their debts as valid.[78] The current provision states in part: "A credit instrument accepted on or after June 1, 1983, and the debt that the credit instrument represents are valid and may be enforced by legal process."[79] In order to cut off potential defenses to gambling debts based on compulsive gambling, the statute also provides in part that

> A patron's claim of having a mental or behavioral disorder involving gambling:
> (a) Is not a defense in any action by a licensee or a person acting on behalf of a licensee to enforce a credit instrument or the debt that the credit instrument represents.
> (b) Is not a valid counterclaim to such an action.[80]

Nevada's statutory abrogation of its common law doctrine undoubtedly favors the commercial viability of casinos. The board still regulates a casino's credit practices, including requirements for information gathering to ensure a patron's creditworthiness and to prevent the use of credit as a money-laundering device.[81] It also regulates collection practices to prevent collection abuse.[82] Otherwise, the responsibility for using credit within one's means lies solely with the patron.

While casinos may use the courts to collect debts from their patrons, patrons with claims against casinos for unpaid jackpots or other winnings are required instead to participate in an administrative proceeding before the board or, in cases under five hundred dollars, before a hearing examiner appointed by the board.[83] The statute here essentially provides that, outside of the statutorily prescribed procedures for administrative review, "gaming debts that are not evidenced by a credit instrument are void and unenforceable and do not give rise to any administrative or civil cause of action."[84] After participation in this administrative process, patrons or licensees who are aggrieved by a final decision of the board may petition for judicial review.[85]

Market forces reinforce a casino's interest in paying off jackpots or other winnings, as contrary practices would tend to dry up the market for patrons rather quickly.[86] A casino that fails to pay off a valid jackpot also places its license at risk, which creates an additional disincentive for refusing payment.[87] However, in a rare litigated case where a casino refused to pay, the letter of the law was applied in favor of the casino. This case involved a nineteen-year-old who was lucky enough to win a slot machine jackpot in excess of $1 million. His luck ended, however, when the casino discovered that he was a minor ineligible to gamble under Nevada law.[88] The casino asserted his minority as a contractual defense to payment, claiming that a minor could not form a valid contract under Nevada law. The board agreed with the casino, as did both the Nevada Supreme Court and the Ninth Circuit.[89]

On one hand, this result tends to reinforce government efforts to prevent minors from gambling. By removing the incentive of a large jackpot, a minor might well be deterred from trying to play at all. On the other hand, if undetected minors can win smaller jackpots that do not generate attention from the casino, they might still seek to play despite this ruling. A casino benefits from losses incurred by minors, just as it benefits from the losses of other players.

However, allowing minors to gamble potentially subjects casino operators to disciplinary actions, including fines and the possibility of losing a gaming license.[90] The threat of discipline encourages casino efforts to monitor and exclude minor patrons. That incentive would be strengthened if casinos were also obligated to pay off winnings and to restore losses incurred by minor patrons. This less restrictive approach reflected in current law appears to favor the casino's economic interests.

PROBLEM GAMBLING

Direct efforts to address concerns about the excesses of gambling patrons—including the effects of compulsive gambling—are virtually nonexistent in Nevada. In 1998, the Gaming Control Commission adopted regulations that required its licensees to take some minimal steps toward concerns about problem gambling. First, the regulations require licensees to post information for its patrons.

> Each licensee shall post or provide in conspicuous places in or near gaming and cage areas and cash dispensing machines located in gaming areas written materials concerning the nature and symptoms of problem gambling and the toll-free telephone number of the National Council on Problem Gambling or a similar entity approved by the chairman of the board that provides information and referral services for problem gamblers.[91]

Second, licensees are also required to conduct training programs for their employees about the nature of problem gambling. The purpose of such training appears limited, however, as the regulation specifically provides that "[t]his subsection shall not be construed to require employees of licensees to identify problem gamblers."[92]

Third, certain licensees are required to develop procedures for self-regulation by patrons: "Each licensee that engages in the issuance of credit, check cashing, or the direct mail marketing of gaming opportunities, shall implement a program . . . that allows patrons to self-limit their access to the issuance of credit, check cashing, or direct mail marketing by that licensee."[93]

Public appropriations to treat problem gambling have been nonexistent in Nevada, as this problem has been left in private hands. However, in 2005, Governor Kenny Guinn proposed an appropriation of two hundred thousand dollars over two years to help create a problem gambling program.[94] Although the industry privately funds programs to help problem gamblers, public funding has not previously addressed this issue.[95] Critics point out that the amount of this appropriation pales in relation to the taxes generated from gambling (which, as noted previously, exceed $800 million annually). However, only seventeen states provide some funding for problem gambling.[96] Thus, Nevada's prior funding practices (or lack thereof) do not seem that unusual by this standard.

Although regulations recognize the existence of problem gambling, they do very little to interfere with the business practices of the casinos and the putative freedom of patrons to make their own decisions about how much to lose. Nevada's regulatory approach requires a high level of personal responsibility among gamblers for their own choices. Such an approach is consistent with the business goals of casino operators, particularly when high rollers (so-called whales), who are often from foreign countries, constitute a specific and highly profitable segment among gambling patrons. (As one commentator has quipped, "In Las Vegas, compulsive gambling is defined as 'devoted casino customer.'")[97]

Nevada law provides separate licensing provisions applicable to so-called international gaming salons, which require a minimum of five hundred thousand dollars as a cash deposit or line of credit as a prerequisite to admission[98] and a minimum wager of five hundred dollars.[99] Salon operators must limit admission to those who meet approved financial criteria,[100] which tends to ensure that patrons who participate in this high-stakes environment can afford potentially big losses. Limitations on losses certainly seem incongruous within such an environment. However, patrons with more modest means can undoubtedly still lose more than they can afford without entering an international gaming salon.

The Gaming Commission has taken some steps toward constraining the methods of payment accepted in electronic devices used in gaming, which tend to limit excessive losses by those of more modest means. In 1995, the state legislature adopted a statute that proscribed electronic transfers from a financial institution directly to a gaming device through a credit card.[101] However, the statute was silent as to transfers using debit cards. In May 2003, the Gaming Commission rejected a plan to allow ATM cards in slot machines.[102] The Gaming Control Board recommended further study of the impact of using ATM cards on compulsive gambling, and the commission acquiesced in this recommendation.[103] The commission has also enacted a rule prohibiting the location of an ATM within a designated gaming area of a restricted licensee.[104] Such a restriction might also tend to limit impulse gambling at these locations.

Nevada's casino-friendly rules appear to have been quite effective at developing a successful model for generating economic benefits from the gaming industry. Gaming taxes, which make up nearly 20 percent of state revenues, provide an important source for public funds. Nevada imposes no income taxes on individuals or corporations, but it does have a sales tax, which generates a share of state revenues that is comparable to gaming taxes.[105] Given the substantial dependence on tourism in this economy, it is likely that tourists pay a substantial share of these taxes.

Local taxes in Nevada also appear quite modest. According to one study, a family of four living in Las Vegas and earning $100,000 per year paid an average of $4,217 in state and local taxes, which is well below the national median figure of $8,896.[106] By comparison, that same family in Omaha, Nebraska—a city without legalized casino gambling—paid $8,635.[107] Nevertheless, the tourist-oriented model achieved in Nevada, and particularly in the destination resorts of Las Vegas, has proved difficult to replicate in other venues. Other states have chosen to take slightly different approaches to regulating casinos, which are discussed in the following chapter.

8. Casino Regulation in Other States

Prospects for tourism, economic renewal, and tax relief have provided the impetus for other states beyond Nevada to legalize and regulate casino gambling. New Jersey was the first to pursue this course, approving a constitutional amendment in 1976 to permit casinos in Atlantic City.[1] New Jersey casinos were operational two years later, providing legal competition to the casinos that had long enjoyed an effective monopoly in the United States.

More than a decade later, casino gambling began to expand in the Midwest. Nostalgia for the halcyon days of riverboats and the untamed West provided the model for distinguishing casinos in this region from those in Nevada and New Jersey. In 1989, Iowa became the first midwestern state to legalize riverboat casinos, which policymakers hoped would draw tourists and alleviate economic stagnation in the agricultural and manufacturing sectors of its economy.[2] Other states in the Mississippi River valley, including Illinois, Missouri, Louisiana, and Mississippi, soon followed with riverboat gambling of their own, creating energetic interstate competition for casino patrons.

Land-based operations sprang up in South Dakota, which added limited-stakes casinos in 1989 in the tourist town of Deadwood.[3] Colorado followed suit by enacting laws in 1991 to permit limited gaming in the tourist communities of Cripple Creek, Blackhawk, and Central City.[4] All of these destinations focused on tourist nostalgia for the Old West and further distinguished their brand of gambling by maintaining a limited stakes variety.

Other eastern states decided to cash in on the consumer demand for gambling. Rhode Island, Delaware, and West Virginia added casino-style gambling to their racetracks in an effort to shore up an ailing horse-racing industry. New Mexico added racinos in 1999, and New York followed this trend in 2004.

Pennsylvania also enacted legislation in 2004 that would allow slot machines across the state, with openings expected in 2006.[5] Florida voters likewise paved the way in 2004 by approving a constitutional amendment that would allow slot machines at racetracks in Miami-Dade and Broward Counties.[6] Table 8.1 lists all states with commercial casinos or racinos (i.e., racetrack-based facilities with slot machines or similar games) in 2004, along with associated operations and AGR.

In these states regulatory approaches toward casino gaming share many common features, which borrow heavily from the earlier experiences in Nevada. Licensing is a common central feature of control, and background investigations are a prerequisite to the granting of a casino license. In this sense, licensing provides the important assurance for the public that the casino industry is not tainted by an association with criminal elements.[7] Regulations also affect the fairness of games, the exclusion of minors, and the collection of applicable taxes.[8]

States have also adopted variations from Nevada's regulatory model, as

TABLE 8.1.   Commercial casino/racino operations by state (2004)

	Legalized Year	Opening Year	Number of Operations	2004 AGR Rank	2004 AGR (in millions of dollars)
Colorado	1990	1991	46	11	726
Delaware*	1994	1995	3	12	553
Illinois	1990	1991	9	6	1,718
Indiana	1993	1995	10	5	2,229
Iowa	1989	1991	13	8	1,401
Louisiana	1991	1993	18	4	2,442
Michigan	1996	1999	3	9	1,189
Mississippi	1990	1992	29	3	2,781
Missouri	1993	1994	11	7	1,473
Nevada**	1931	1931	258	1	10,562
New Jersey	1976	1978	12	2	4,807
New Mexico*	1997	1999	5	15	150
New York*	2001	2004	4	14	192
Rhode Island*	1992	1992	2	13	384
South Dakota	1989	1989	36	16	78
West Virginia*	1994	1994	4	10	882

Source: American Gaming Association.

*Racinos Only

**Excludes operations with less than $1 million AGR.

they have sought to adapt gambling to their particular social and economic needs. Variations have commonly involved restricting the location of gambling operations, imposing betting or loss limits, and requiring programs to address concerns about problem gamblers. Channels for distributing government revenues from gaming also differ among the states. Though these revenue features do not directly affect gaming itself, they potentially affect the structure of political support for casino gaming. Given deeply rooted antagonism toward casinos in many communities, these changes have proved highly significant in engendering local support for expanded gaming.

Although a comprehensive review of regulation in all commercial casino states is beyond the scope of this chapter, a brief look at regulatory variation among them provides valuable insight into the nature of this industry and the manner in which states have adapted their legal and economic structures for gambling in their communities. It also provides an interesting backdrop for examining the political forces at work in this environment, including dynamic forces of interstate competition. Regulatory trends seem to be moving in favor of practices that enhance the profitability of the industry, with only modest efforts toward addressing effects of problem gambling.

We begin with New Jersey, the largest of Nevada's land-based casino competitors. We then turn to an extended discussion of Iowa, which provides an interesting case study of how a kinder, gentler form of gambling gave way to more industry-friendly practices in the face of interstate competition for gambling dollars. Two other states with geographical constraints on their casino facilities, Missouri and Mississippi, merit brief discussion for their variations in casino regulation. Finally, we conclude with a look at the tourist model adopted in South Dakota, the smallest of these commercial casino states.

NEW JERSEY

New Jersey's state constitution was amended in 1976 to allow the legislature to authorize "gambling houses or casinos."[9] Among other things, this constitutional amendment limited the scope of legalized gambling to the confines of Atlantic City, a long-standing tourist destination that had fallen into disrepair.[10] New Jersey voters apparently found this constraint acceptable, as they had defeated a previous referendum in 1974 that would have allowed state-owned casinos anywhere in the state with consent from local voters.[11]

This amendment was not based solely on economic development but also on more lofty goals of assisting elderly and disabled citizens with the tax revenues from these enterprises. The amendment specifically required any enabling legislation to restrict the use of revenues from gaming as follows:

> State revenues derived therefrom to be applied solely for the purpose of providing funding for reductions in property taxes, rental, telephone, gas, electric, and municipal utilities charges of eligible senior citizens and disabled residents of the State, and for additional or expanded health services or benefits or transportation services or benefits to eligible senior citizens and disabled residents, in accordance with such formulae as the Legislature shall by law provide.[12]

Targeting casino revenues toward a visible and popular end, rather than merely adding a source of funds for general revenues, might have been helpful in generating popular support for a constitutional change.

In response to this constitutional amendment, the New Jersey legislature adopted the Casino Control Act, which forms the basis for casino regulation. The stated policies and purposes attending the act emphasize the potential for casinos to bring economic development and support to the tourist, resort, and convention industry of the state. However, these policies and purposes also attempted to carve out for New Jersey a different atmosphere for gaming from that in "other jurisdictions" (i.e., Nevada).

> Restricting the issuance of casino licenses to major hotel and convention facilities is designed to assure that the existing nature and tone of the hospitality industry in New Jersey and in Atlantic City is preserved, and that the casino rooms licensed pursuant to the provisions of this act are always offered and maintained as an integral element of such hospitality facilities, rather than as the industry unto themselves that they have become in other jurisdictions.[13]

This goal of linking casino gambling to the hospitality industry in Atlantic City suggests that gambling was originally intended as an ancillary form of entertainment for venturing tourists. However, it is doubtful whether this goal has been realized, as illustrated by a comparison with a sister gaming city—Las Vegas. As of 2000, Atlantic City and Las Vegas both generated approximately $4.3 billion in gaming revenues. However, Las Vegas generated another $4.3 billion in other nongaming revenues, while the comparable amount in Atlantic City was only $0.4 billion—a mere $12 per patron.[14]

The geographical proximity of Atlantic City to other major metropolitan areas, including New York, Philadelphia, and Washington, D.C., has made it a popular destination for commuters. Census data for 2000 indicate that approximately 25 million adults live within 150 miles of the city.[15] Despite comparable figures for Atlantic City and Las Vegas gaming revenues, Atlantic City has fewer than 12,000 hotel rooms, as compared with over 120,000 hotel rooms in Las Vegas.[16] Over 98 percent of visitors to Atlantic City casinos arrive by car or bus.[17]

Restricting casinos to Atlantic City, rather than allowing them throughout the state, potentially served another legislative purpose besides redevelopment: it made access to casino gambling less convenient for New Jersey residents. Restricting casinos to the environs of a coastal city known as a tourist destination would not create easy and ubiquitous access to casino gambling commonly linked to problem gambling behavior.[18] Targeting visitors rather than local patrons creates a more attractive model for gambling, as new dollars are brought into the jurisdiction and consequences from problem gambling are likely to return home with the visitors.

Despite this focus, policymakers eventually realized the New Jersey residents could also be affected by casinos, as well as other forms of gambling available in the state. According to the 2000 census, Atlantic County, in which Atlantic City is located, had about 252,000 residents, and about one-fourth of them were under the age of eighteen.[19] When counties that border Atlantic County are included, the total population balloons to nearly 2.2 million.[20] These New Jersey residents living in close proximity to the casinos in Atlantic City meant local patronage and the potential for problem gambling.

The legislature passed a bill in 2001 to create a mechanism for problem gamblers to exclude themselves voluntarily from a casino.[21] In 2002, this self-exclusion program was expanded to include other gambling venues, including racetracks and off-track betting facilities.[22] The program entails fairly rigorous requirements for participation. An individual seeking exclusion is required to personally appear in state offices located in Atlantic City or Trenton in order to submit a form with pertinent information requesting exclusion for either one year, five years, or a lifetime.[23] The person submitting the request is also required to acknowledge the following statement:

I am voluntarily requesting exclusion from all gaming activities at all New Jersey licensed casinos and simulcasting facilities because I am a problem gambler. I certify that the information that I have provided above is true and accurate, and that I have read and understand and agree to the waiver and release included with this request for self-exclusion. I am aware that my signature below authorizes the Casino Control Commission to direct all New Jersey casino licensees to restrict my gaming activities in accordance with this request and, unless I have requested to be excluded for life, until such time as the Commission removes my name from the self-exclusion list in response to my written request to terminate my voluntary self-exclusion. I am aware and agree that during any period of self-exclusion, I shall not collect any winnings or recover any losses resulting from any gaming activity at all licensed casinos and simulcasting facilities, and that any money or thing of value obtained by me from, or owed to me by, a casino licensee as a result of wagers made by me while on the self-exclusion list shall be subject to forfeiture.[24]

The self-exclusion list is maintained by the Casino Control Commission and distributed to every casino licensee.[25] A photograph of each self-excluded person, as well as a description of that person, is also provided to each licensee for the apparent purpose of aiding in the identification of self-excluded persons who nevertheless attempt to gamble.[26] The identity of those on the list is treated as confidential information, except that it may be disclosed to appropriate casino employees, including those of other licensees in Atlantic City, to assist in enforcement efforts.[27] Licensees bear no liability for disclosure or publication of the identity of members on the list that is not willfully unlawful.[28]

Licensees are required to develop procedures that will ensure that gaming privileges are not extended to self-excluded persons.[29] They must also ensure that credit is not extended to them; that no complimentary goods and services are provided; and that no solicitations, mailings, promotions, or other promotional materials are sent to them.[30] In the event that self-excluded persons do gamble, they are not allowed to collect their winnings or recover their losses.[31] In the event that such persons do collect winnings, they are subject to forfeiture to the commission.[32]

Licensees are statutorily exempt from any liability associated with failing to withhold gaming privileges from a self-excluded person who is allowed to gamble.[33] Although the losses incurred by an excluded person who succeeds in gambling are potentially subject to forfeiture, that possibility occurs only if there was "willful violation" of the self-exclusion regulations.[34] Thus, the economic incentives for vigorous enforcement of the self-exclusion provisions are limited indeed.

These provisions have questionable significance in addressing the concerns of problem gambling. As of January 2003, after more than one year of this program, only 139 people had signed up for self-exclusion, and 10 of these had dropped out, apparently due to the elapse of the one-year period in their exclusion request.[35] Some critics cite a lack of publicity as responsible for the weak response.[36]

This plan also appears vulnerable to other criticism. First, in order to be placed on the self-exclusion list, the patron must admit that he or she is a "problem gambler."[37] Patrons may associate problem gambling with "pathological gambling," which is listed in the DSM-IV.[38] Some people may be deterred from participating in the program because they associate it with admitting to a mental illness or disorder. Moreover, such an admission may be inaccurate for some people, who wish to be excluded before problem gambling behavior has manifested itself. For example, a patron may suffer from depression or manic episodes that lead to gambling behavior that is not considered pathological gambling but might lead to unwanted losses.[39]

Other disorders, such as alcoholism or compulsive shopping, could potentially be assisted from a self-exclusion program. A recovering alcoholic might wish to be excluded from the local pub, and a compulsive shopper might wish to be excluded from the mall.[40] However, popular support for government programs in these areas would appear dubious. Enlisting private business firms to assist adults in monitoring their own behavior is likely to prove unpopular, especially when such assistance is contrary to the firm's economic interests. The ubiquity of opportunities to engage in common activities like shopping or drinking—for example, shopping centers, bars, and liquor stores—also makes it impractical to disseminate information about the affected person so that a business could comply. Moreover, private businesses not accustomed to extensive regulation might resent any requirement that they expend their resources in such a manner.

The comparatively controlled and limited environment of casino gaming establishments makes enforcement of a self-exclusion list plausible in this context. However, as a practical matter, monitoring and excluding patrons may still present a challenge for those who don't utilize players' clubs or electronic payment mechanisms, which provide reliable identification without significant surveillance efforts.

For a protection short of self-exclusion, a patron may also request suspension of credit privileges at a casino.[41] The effect of such a suspension is less significant than exclusion, as it does not affect one's ability to gamble. Such requests may be submitted by mail as well as in person, and they are effective for a minimum of thirty days and thereafter until a request for reinstatement is accepted by the commission.[42] However, the ubiquity of modern credit means that credit can be accessed through other providers, thus allowing a determined patron to gamble excessively if he or she chooses to circumvent the ban on casino credit. Nevertheless, suspending casino credit may erect a barrier to impulsive behavior that could, in some cases, prevent excessive losses.

IOWA

Iowa legalized casino gaming in 1989 by permitting low-stakes riverboat gambling on the Mississippi River and on certain inland waters.[43] One commentator described the regulatory structure that emerged from this legislation as focusing on these six attributes:

> First, that wagering be for low stakes and that no member of the public suffers substantial losses. Second, that proceeds from gaming benefit the public good. Third, that Iowa regulate gaming. Fourth, that gaming be associated with activities that promote tourism. Fifth, that gaming operators contribute to the state economy by hiring Iowa residents and using and promoting Iowa goods. Sixth, that gaming raise tax revenue.[44]

Although most of these attributes may still be found in the current gaming industry in Iowa, competitive pressures have eliminated the "low stakes" requirement and substantially diluted any regulatory orientation toward protecting the public from substantial losses. In this sense, Iowa provides an interesting case study about how well-intentioned regulations eventually fell by the wayside in the pursuit of greater profits for the industry and tax revenues for state and local governments.

The gaming laws enacted in 1989 ensured that any casino gaming operation would be quite different from that which would be found in either Las Vegas or Atlantic City. First, real vessels were required: prospective licensees were required to "develop, and as nearly as practicable, recreate boats that resemble Iowa's riverboat history."[45] Those boats—known as "excursion gambling boats"—had to live up to their name by actually embarking on gambling excursions for a minimum number of days each year.[46] Gambling activities were restricted to no more than 30 percent of the available square footage of an excursion boat.[47] Licensees were also required to ensure that Iowa goods and services were used in operations, and a portion of the boat was required to be reserved "for the promotion and sale of arts, crafts, and gifts native to and made in Iowa."[48]

As in other jurisdictions, minors were prohibited from gambling. However, minority was initially defined at eighteen years old rather than twenty-one.[49] The legislature vacillated on this definition over the next few years, as the age of minority was increased to twenty-one in a bill passed a few days later in 1989.[50] The minimum gambling age was reduced once again to eighteen in 1991[51] and then increased to twenty-one in 1994,[52] where it remains today.[53]

In addition to these regulations affecting the business operations of riverboat casinos, the legislation also provided strict wagering and loss limitations. Casino patrons were allowed to wager a maximum of five dollars per play, with a maximum loss limit of two hundred dollars per excursion.[54] A requirement that all gambling be conducted with tokens or chips, rather than money, made it feasible to enforce these limits.[55] Moreover, during the "excursion season" (April through October)[56] gambling was restricted to such times when the boat actually went on an excursion; in the off-season, the gaming commission established rules for entry and exit that would support the loss limitations.[57] Licensees were also prohibited from lending money to patrons for gambling purposes, thus eliminating a source of credit that could lead to losses beyond what the patron could afford.[58]

This approach geared toward protecting gamblers from excessive losses did not last for long. Building a gaming industry on the excursion boat model presented considerable risks in an environment of mobile facilities and interstate competition. By 1993, three of the five riverboats that had been licensed for the Mississippi River had pulled up anchor and left the state.[59] News reports indicate that one of these boats, the *Dubuque Casino Belle,* was profitable for its first year of operation, but patronage declined as gamblers chose to visit facilities in other states with more liberal betting limits and regulations.[60] Patrons were apparently voting with their feet, and they apparently didn't like the state making decisions about how much or when they could bet.

In 1994, riverboats returned when the Iowa legislature dropped the loss and betting limits and Iowa counties with riverboats approved gaming rules that were friendlier to the business interests of casinos.[61] The legislature responded to pressure from both gambling interests and local government officials by taking several measures that would enhance the competitive position of Iowa boats against competitors in other states, including Illinois. Local governments lobbied for the removal of loss limitations because they wanted additional local revenues from a projected increase in their share of casino profits to address needs imposed by catastrophic flood damage along the Mississippi River valley.[62]

In addition to eliminating the wagering and loss limitation, the 1994 legislation also eased other restrictions. Though riverboat excursions were still required, requirements for a specific duration and limited access by patrons during other times when the boats were docked were eliminated, as they were no longer needed to support the loss limits. Thus, patrons were free to come and go from the boats as they pleased whenever the boats were docked.[63] The availability of slot machines was also expanded from the boats to dog and horse racetracks, which had previously been limited to parimutuel wagering on races.[64] As a protective measure, however, casinos were also prohibited from accepting credit cards for gambling purposes.[65] Later rules would also prohibit any form of electronic dispensing of cash or credit on the gambling floor.[66]

This 1994 legislation did not reflect a situation where the state government imposed its will on local citizens who had previously approved a kinder, gentler form of gambling. The law required local citizens to weigh in on these changes through a referendum process.[67] Thus, the removal of the loss and wagering limitations, as well as the expansion of slot machines into dog- and horse-racing tracks, required the approval of local voters, and such approval was readily given.

Local voting is an important feature of Iowa's regulatory system. The state

racing and gaming commission possesses extensive powers to license and regulate casino gambling on excursion boats.[68] These powers even extend to setting payout levels for authorized games and slot machines.[69] However, the
commission's power to award a license is predicated upon local voter authorization for casino gambling.[70] In the event that a local referendum fails, a license may not be issued and existing licenses may be revoked. Another referendum may not be held again for at least eight years.[71] After approval,
periodic referenda to continue legalized gambling must also occur.[72] Iowa's
history indicates that counties have sometimes rejected legalized gaming
under similar provisions.[73] However, once gaming has become operational,
voters have given overwhelming approval to subsequent referenda.[74]

Another feature of the 1994 legislation was the expansion of slot machines at racetracks. This created two types of casinos in Iowa: racetrack
casinos ("racinos"), which could offer slot machines along with horse or dog
racing but not other games, and excursion gambling boats, which could
offer slot machines and other approved games but no wagering on races.[75]
While the repeal of loss limitations alleviated the financial stress on the
riverboats, the prospect of slot machines at racetracks was designed to improve the financial picture of racing establishments.

The plight of Prairie Meadows, a horse-racing facility financed substantially by bonds issued by Polk County, was apparently an important influence on the decision to expand gambling via slot machines. The original construction of this facility in 1987 was financed by bonds guaranteed by Polk
County, and that guarantee was soon called upon as the track fell short of its
financial projections.[76] Losses mounted in this facility, and the county eventually became the owner of the track in 1993, issuing general obligation
bonds to finance this acquisition.[77]

By the time slot machines had been approved at racetracks in 1994, debt
at Prairie Meadows totaled $89.3 million.[78] Within two years after opening,
this entire debt was repaid.[79] Profits from expanded slot machines thus ex-
tracted Polk County taxpayers from a difficult financial situation without
raising local taxes. However, it made slot machine gambling more accessible
to patrons in the central part of the state, which was not otherwise served
by excursion boats. Moreover, it involved county government as an owner
of a gambling facility (albeit as a landlord)—which was quite different from
the typical role of local governments in other facilities.

Iowa law provides an ownership and tax structure that ensures that local communities obtain some direct benefits from casino revenues. Gaming licenses must be held by a "qualified sponsoring organization,"[80] which is essentially a nonprofit corporation that is eligible for tax-exempt status.[81] The sponsoring organization may contract with another firm to manage the operation, and this firm is also subject to licensure and approval of the gaming commission.[82] Sponsoring organizations are liable for taxes on admissions for each person entering an excursion boat, which are payable to the gaming commission.[83] Cities and counties in which an excursion boat is docked may also impose an admission fee of not more than fifty cents, which is payable to their respective general fund.[84] Licensees must also pay additional assessments to cover licensing costs and other costs of criminal investigations, which are payable to the state's general fund.[85]

The main tax burden on the licensees, however, is the wagering tax. This tax applies on a sliding scale to AGR,[86] ranging from 5 percent on the first $1 million to 10 percent on the next $2 million to 22 percent on amounts over $3 million.[87] Prior to amendment in 2004, a separate, higher tax rate was imposed on AGR at racetrack enclosures, which increased by 2 percent each year, from 22 percent in 1997 to as much as 36 percent in 2004.[88] Racetrack interests successfully challenged this differential tax system in the Iowa Supreme Court, but that ruling was subsequently reversed by the U.S. Supreme Court, which upheld the differential tax rates as a proper legislative classification under the U.S. Constitution.[89] However, the Iowa Supreme Court subsequently persisted in its position that the scheme was unconstitutional, resting its decision on state constitutional grounds.[90] The legislature subsequently changed the differential to make it smaller, limiting the upper level to 24 percent for racetrack enclosures without competing riverboat casinos in the same jurisdiction.[91]

Of this wagering tax, 1 percent is designated to be shared by the city and county government in which the facility is located.[92] One-half of 1 percent (raised from three-tenths of 1 percent in 2004) is designated for a state "gambling treatment fund."[93] The remainder is allocated to the general fund.[94] Thus, most of the gaming tax revenue from casinos finds its way into the central coffers of the state rather than into local government hands.

Of the amounts allocated to the general fund, totals in excess of $60 million are supposed to be dedicated to other state programs designed for the development of recreation, tourism, infrastructure, and schools.[95] For the fiscal year ending June 30, 2003, the state's share of these wagering taxes from riverboats was $120,872,266 and the corresponding amount from racetracks was $57,835,883.[96] Cities and counties reaped a total just short of $10 million, and the gambling treatment program received just under $3 million.[97] Of course, local governments also received additional property taxes and other tax receipts associated with the operation of the gaming business in their locale.[98]

This management structure, which leaves qualified sponsoring organizations in control of gaming, makes it possible for the legislature to impose this additional requirement upon such organizations:

> A qualified sponsoring organization licensed to operate gambling games under this chapter shall distribute the receipts of all gambling games, less reasonable expenses, charges, taxes, fees, and deductions allowed under this chapter, as winnings to players or participants or shall distribute the receipts for educational, civic, public, charitable, patriotic, or religious uses.[99]

A special rule for racetrack operations with debt requires such operations to pay off debt first before engaging in charitable distributions.[100] Racetrack operations may also use receipts from their slot machines to supplement purses paid to dog or horse owners, thus supporting that segment of the racing industry.[101]

Qualified sponsoring organizations are expressly prohibited from making political contributions or other kindred payments.[102] However, this is not to say that they lack the power to affect public opinion about gaming through the distribution of their charitable grants. For example, as of 2002, the Iowa West Foundation, holder of licenses for three casinos in the Council Bluffs area in the far western part of the state, had paid out over $106 million in grants.[103] Through the first half of 2003 alone, it paid out over $7.9 million in grants to cities, counties, and charitable organizations in western Iowa.[104] Such grants are powerful public relations tools, as the libraries, swimming pools, community centers, fire stations, and other highly visible public projects are funded with gaming dollars.

The state also utilizes gaming revenues through other conspicuous programs, which include the Vision Iowa and the Community Attraction and

Tourism (CAT) funds. These funds were established by the legislature in 2000 for the purpose of providing funding for construction projects that support recreation, entertainment, and cultural activities.[105] Both of these funds are administered by a thirteen-member board, who are appointed by the governor.[106] An additional fund for school infrastructure is administered by the Iowa Department of Education.[107]

The Vision Iowa fund receives $15 million annually from wagering tax revenues, while the CAT fund receives $12.5 million.[108] These funds are structured to share the resources generated from wagering taxes throughout the state, including counties and cities without gambling facilities. One-third of the CAT fund revenues are specifically reserved for cities with populations below ten thousand and for the bottom one-third of counties by population.[109] Through these funds, Iowa achieves a redistribution of economic benefits from gambling to counties without gambling facilities—or the population base to support one. Residents of these counties can thus point to a visible community infrastructure improvement—such as a swimming pool, theater, or community center—that would perhaps have been unaffordable without gambling dollars. Such practices would appear to kindle additional political support for gaming in the state.

As for the less visible effects of gambling—namely, the social problems associated with it—the state's primary commitment appears to be the resources committed to the gambling treatment fund. Historically, the legislature had diverted a substantial portion of this fund to other uses, including substance abuse, wellness programs, children's programs, and the Iowa Veterans home.[110] In 2004, the legislature expanded this fund by raising the total cap from commercial casino taxes to $6 million, with an additional $500,000 from the Iowa lottery.[111] This expansion addressed concerns about redirected funds and the level of commitment to gambling treatment, which studies have shown to be quite effective for gamblers who seek it.[112] Redirected funds required cuts in advertising, making it difficult to reach the intended audience of problem gamblers.[113] The head of the state gambling treatment program estimates that twenty thousand Iowans have severe gambling problems, with an additional forty to sixty thousand experiencing problems that could escalate without treatment.[114]

In 2004, Iowa expanded its approach to problem gambling by enacting a self-exclusion provision similar to that used in New Jersey.[115] Prior to this law, the Iowa Gaming Association supported a voluntary self-exclusion provision applicable to people in treatment for problem gambling, but this approach was without the force of law.[116] This law does not specify the process but only requires licensees to come up with such a process. Through its trade organization, the industry came up with an exclusion program that involves an irrevocable, lifetime exclusion from all properties in Iowa.[117] The exclusion form also points out that when signing up for this program "the ultimate responsibility to limit access to any Iowa casino remains mine alone." It also contains an extensive release from any liability associated with a failure to comply with the ban. An excluded gambler must attest to the following statement:

> I will not seek to hold the Casino or any other Iowa casino liable in any way should I continue gambling at any casino despite this exclusion request. I agree to indemnify this Casino and any other casino for any liability the casino may incur relating to this request. Specifically, I, for myself, my family members, heirs, and legal representatives hereby release and forever discharge the Casino and all other Iowa casinos, all of their direct and indirect subsidiaries, their partners, agents, employees, officers, affiliates, directors, successors, and assigns, and those with whom the Casino may lawfully share information regarding this exclusion, including the Iowa Racing and Gaming Commission and any contractor or Internet Services Provider that offers services on the behalf of these entities (collectively, the "Released Parties"), from any and all claims in law or equity that I now have or may have in the future against any or all of

TABLE 8.2.   **Iowa gambling treatment fund expenditures (2001–5 (est.))**[a]

Fiscal Year	Fund Revenue ($)	Program Expenditures ($)	Redirected Funds ($)
FY 2005 (est.)	6,000,000	4,310,000	1,690,000
FY 2004	3,875,436	1,970,428	1,690,000
FY 2003	3,579,350	1,714,479	1,690,000
FY 2002	3,503,005	1,714,443	2,057,298
FY 2001	3,261,636	1,898,762	1,874,750

[a]See Iowa Gambling Treatment Fund: Revenues, Expenses, Redirects at http://www.1800betsoff.org/pdf/revenue_redirect.pdf (accessed May 16, 2005)

the Released Parties arising out of, or by reason of, the performance or
non-performance of this Self-Exclusion Request, or any other matter relating to it, including the release of information contained in this form. I
further agree, in consideration for the Released Parties' efforts to implement my exclusion, to indemnify and hold harmless the Released Parties
to the fullest extent permitted by law for any and all liabilities, judgments, damages, and expenses of any kind, including reasonable attorneys' fees, resulting from or in connection with the performance or non-
performance of this self exclusion request.[118]

The enabling statute provided that "[t]he state and any licensee . . . shall
not be liable to any person for any claim which may arise from this process."
However, this broad release language arguably goes beyond the statute in
providing for indemnification for legal fees, including those which may test
the limits of this liability exclusion.

The Iowa statute focuses on incentives for the gambler rather than on incentives for the casino to enforce the self-exclusion ban. It imposes a sen-
sible requirement that casinos must pay out any winnings by an excluded
person to the gambling treatment fund instead of to the winning patron.[119]
This creates a disincentive for the excluded patron to stray back to the
casino for more betting. However, given the likelihood that players lose over
time, the casino nevertheless benefits from such play to the extent that they
may keep the excluded patron's losses.

Iowa regulations also require disclosure of the average payout percentage
of slot machines.[120] Such disclosure reflects some movement toward regulatory models adopted in other areas, such as tobacco and alcohol, where information and/or warnings of risks are presented as an attempt to ameliorate
harms to citizens from such activities. However, no empirical studies indicate
whether this disclosure is effective at reducing any incidence of problem
gambling behavior. Considerable variation may nevertheless exist among machines grouped together for averaging purposes. Moreover, a casino manager
might advertise low payouts for slot machines with small wagers and high
payout percentages on high-wager machines. In this way, patrons may be
coaxed into betting at higher-value machines, which, over time, might offer
a better return. In doing so, these patrons may be wagering more (and perhaps more than they can afford to lose), thus increasing house profits.

Finally, Iowa's approach to interstate competition also merits discussion. Iowa's casinos in Council Bluffs are within a metropolitan statistical area that spans eight counties, including four counties in the neighboring state of Nebraska with no legalized casino gaming opportunities. Although Nebraska permits noncasino gambling, including a lottery, pari-mutuel betting on horse racing, and keno, casino gambling is prohibited. It is well known that Nebraska residents patronize Council Bluffs casinos, and this fact was highly touted in efforts to legalize casinos in Nebraska funded by an organization known as Keep the Money in Nebraska.[121]

In November 2004, Nebraska voters considered ballot initiatives to provide a legal framework for casino gambling. These legalization initiatives were ultimately defeated, thus allowing Iowa to continue tapping the Nebraska market without in-state competition.[122] However, in anticipation of this vote, the Iowa legislature crafted changes in its gambling laws to strengthen the industry's position in the event of cross-border competition from a Nebraska-based casino. Among other things, this legislation eliminated any requirement that excursion boats must cruise.[123] This would eliminate a competitive disadvantage to land-based facilities, such as those proposed in Nebraska.

In addition, the 2004 legislation included a rather unusual provision allowing expansion through gambling via moored barges in Council Bluffs on "the earlier of July 1, 2007, or the date any form of gambling games, as defined in this chapter, is operational in any state that is contiguous to the county where the licensee is located."[124] Since Nebraska failed to legalize casino gambling, this right to accelerate expansion did not arise. Nevertheless, this legislation signaled the government's resolve to support stiff competition in the face of future legalization efforts across the border.

The Iowa Racing and Gaming Commission approved a significant expansion to a racetrack casino in Council Bluffs early in 2005, as well as other expanded gambling venues in interior Iowa communities in May 2005.[125] Although one of these venues is near Albert Lea, Minnesota, and it may be designed to attract patronage from non-Iowans, others are located in interior counties far from state borders, which would be expected to draw patronage from Iowans. Thus, the cross-border patronage that has been fueling facilities on the eastern and western borders of the state is likely to be displaced by Iowa residents with more convenient access to gambling in nearby communities.

Not only does Iowa compete for patrons from across its borders, but its regulatory structure also attempts to source goods and services for gambling from Iowans as opposed to workers and companies outside the state.

> The [Racing and Gaming] commission shall require that an applicant utilize Iowa resources, goods, and services in the operation of an excursion gambling boat. The commission shall develop standards to assure that a substantial amount of all resources and goods used in the operation of an excursion gambling boat emanate from and are made in Iowa and that a substantial amount of all services and entertainment are provided by Iowans.[126]

Though this patent attempt to discriminate in favor of local goods is of questionable legal validity, it has nevertheless resulted in businesses establishing Iowa offices to service casino customers. This practice keeps more revenue in Iowa communities, but it compounds the political pressures for cross-border competition in Nebraska. Not only are Nebraska patrons losing money in Iowa casinos, but their businesses are also handicapped when it comes to tapping into the economic benefits from the goods and services consumed by that industry. It remains to be seen how long this political tension will continue before Nebraska, too, joins the ranks of commercial casino states.

MISSOURI

Like its neighbor Iowa, Missouri also chose a riverboat model for its casino gaming industry. Missouri voters approved a referendum allowing excursion boat gambling on the Mississippi and Missouri Rivers, subject to loss limitations of five hundred dollars per excursion, in November 1992.[127] During the following year, the legislature enacted a revised version of riverboat gambling, which changed the terms of the referendum in several respects but retained the essential features of riverboat gaming with a loss limitation of five hundred dollars per excursion.[128] The validity of this legislation was quickly challenged; under then applicable provisions of the Missouri Constitution, games of skill were permissible but games of chance were constitutionally prohibited as unlawful lotteries.[129] Since some games conducted aboard excursion boats (including slot machines) could appropriately be classified as games of chance, a portion of the enabling legislation was declared unconstitutional.[130]

This judicial development gave rise to a subsequent referendum in 1994, which allowed such games on excursion boats subject to local voter approval.[131] However, another legal challenge soon emerged, this time based on the definition of where gambling could lawfully occur. The referendum had approved games of chance "only upon the Missouri and Mississippi Rivers," and the plaintiffs claimed that this language affected the validity of gaming licenses issued for gaming facilities located on "artificial spaces" filled with river water but not contiguous to the river. The Missouri Supreme Court agreed that such facilities were not contemplated by the constitutional amendment, thus limiting riverboat gambling in the state to those facilities that are truly on the river or on water contiguous thereto.[132] Given its unique geography, this means that Missouri's casinos will be located near borders with Kansas and Nebraska on the west and Illinois on the east, with a few distributed along the Missouri River, which crosses the northern half of the state.

Despite the competitive pressures of the no-limit gambling adopted in Iowa, Missouri has continued to impose a loss limit of five hundred dollars per person per two-hour excursion period.[133] The Missouri Gaming Commission's annual report points out that Missouri is the only jurisdiction in the world that imposes a loss limitation on its patrons.[134] The commission asserts that this system puts Missouri casinos at a competitive disadvantage to their neighbors in Iowa, Kansas, and Illinois. As the commission explains:

> The reason the loss limit renders Missouri casinos less competitive is that customers do not like it. Those who use Missouri casinos find the loss limit a patronizing intrusion by government into a private business transaction. Perhaps more important to the issue of competitiveness are those who dislike the loss limit so much that they refuse to patronize Missouri casinos, choosing instead to visit casinos in neighboring jurisdictions or to gamble illegally at truck stops and private clubs.[135]

Missouri facilitates this loss limitation system through a requirement for cashless wagering—patrons are required to use tokens or chips, whether in electronic or physical form, for all gambling transactions.[136] Unlike Iowa, Missouri does not require any formal disclosure of payout ratios, but it does impose a limit that no device may pay out at less than an 80 percent rate.[137] Missouri also prohibits casinos from lending to patrons, though credit card or debit card transactions on-site, as well as check cashing, may be permitted.[138]

The Missouri Gaming Commission has also asserted that no evidence exists that the five-hundred-dollar loss limit has effectively curbed problem gambling behavior.[139] A survey of problem gamblers indicates that 90 percent agree with the commission, while about 8 percent believe the loss limit helped them.[140] Although a loss of even five hundred dollars per excursion could easily add up to significant amounts with repeated visits, such a limit may protect against large and significant wagers that could bankrupt either an individual or, if significant enough, perhaps even a casino.

The commission has also reported that fewer than 1 percent of its patrons ever buy in for the full five-hundred-dollar amount, which suggests that most patrons are unaffected by this limit.[141] Nevertheless, the fiscal impact of higher-stakes gamblers is apparently significant. The comparative win per patron (which reflects the average AGR from all patrons) visiting a Missouri casino is substantially lower than its counterpart in Illinois. For example, figures for 2000 indicate that the Missouri patron lost thirty-six dollars versus nearly sixty-seven dollars for riverboat gamblers in Illinois.[142] It thus appears that a small number of patrons may be responsible for a significant portion of casino revenues, and this loss limitation prevents Missouri casinos from capturing revenues from these patrons.

Analysts have predicted that the loss limitation alone results in more than $282 million in lost industry revenues. Moreover, the inability to compete for higher-stakes gamblers means other lost revenues, such as those attributed to facility expansions.[143] Significant political capital is apparently attached to this five-hundred-dollar limit, despite what appears to be a modest effect on the typical gambling patron.

Although the legislature appears steadfast in retaining the five-hundred-dollar limitation, it has taken other steps to enhance industry profitability by keeping it competitive with its cross-border competitors. Legislation passed in 1999 removed an artificial limitation on boarding, which required patrons to queue up for entry at specified times.[144] Patrons complained about this practice, and the legislature overturned this limitation in part to allow Missouri casinos to compete more effectively with Illinois, which had also abandoned this requirement. Though this was probably good for the casino business, it was also good for the state and local tax coffers, as it meant that higher taxes for admission fees could be imposed. Missouri imposes a two-dollar admission tax for each "cruise" period of two hours. With no barriers on entry, a patron who entered the casino a few minutes before the new cruise period and stayed three hours would thus generate three admissions taxes, whereas the previous barrier to entry would have only generated two.[145]

Legislation passed in August 2000 also enhanced industry profitability by allowing so-called vend-to-meter transactions.[146] Prior to this legislation, slot machine players were required to insert tokens for each spin. This caused considerable delay, thus reducing the volume of player wagering and ultimately industry profits. The legislation allowed players to obtain paper credits, which could then be used in slot machines instead of tokens. The commission reported this change as patron friendly: "The benefit to the patron is that they no longer have to expend the physical effort of inserting the token into the slot machine. This benefit is real when you consider it can save the patron from inserting as many as two thousand tokens [i.e., one hundred dollars played in a nickel slot machine] on one transaction."[147]

However, the commission also notes that this significantly increases player wagering and thus state tax revenues: "The average slot play per patron for the six months prior to vend-to-meter was $573 while the average slot play per patron for the last six months of the fiscal year was $679, an increase of 19%. Therefore, the annualized statewide increase in gaming revenue, assuming 22.7 million patrons and a slot hold percentage of 6.4%, is $154 million."[148] Though faster play would also mean faster problems for problem gamblers, this consideration was apparently outweighed by the goal of enhanced revenues.

Missouri has adopted a legal mechanism for voluntary self-exclusion by problem gamblers, similar to that adopted in New Jersey.[149] Individuals who seek self-exclusion are required to state that they are "problem gamblers" as a prerequisite to inclusion on the list of "disassociated persons."[150] Casinos are absolved from any liability associated with their actions in enforcing, or failing to enforce, the terms of membership on the list.[151] However, unlike New Jersey's system, which allows exclusion for periodic terms, Missouri's system requires exclusion for life.[152] The justification for this difference is presumably based on the lifelong nature of pathological gambling conditions. Moreover, listed persons are subjected to a criminal penalty for trespassing if they attempt to enter a casino facility.[153]

Like Iowa, Missouri also maintains a compulsive gamblers fund for gambling treatment, which is funded in part from gaming revenues.[154] The Port Authority of Kansas City also maintains a fund for problem gamblers, which they reportedly plan to use to fund studies of problem gambling and the effectiveness of treatment programs.[155]

The number of gambling facilities licensed in Missouri is a matter of discretion for the Missouri Gaming Commission.[156] It exercises this discretion to ensure that existing markets have the capacity to absorb new facilities without substantially impacting other operations.[157] Thus, industry profitability is a significant consideration in granting new licenses, thus reflecting the state's support for the financial well-being of an industry that contributes substantially to state coffers, albeit at the expense of some of its residents.

Recent commission decisions that have focused on expanding the St. Louis gambling market indicate an increasing focus on gaining revenues from Missouri residents. Jefferson County, which borders the St. Louis metropolitan area on the south along the Mississippi River, was characterized as an "underserved" market. Casinos in the northern part of the city, including suburban St. Charles and Maryland Heights, were drawing patrons from their local communities at two to three times the rate of those who gambled in Jefferson County. Patronage from these local residents would thus presumably increase with another facility, increasing the tax revenues contributed to state coffers.[158]

Licensing is also conditioned upon local approval in the area where the riverboat would be docked or otherwise located.[159] Local government may also submit recommendations to the commission concerning the number and identity of licensees in their area, along with the terms of any local revenue-sharing agreement with a licensee.[160] Although the bulk of gaming taxes is payable to the state,[161] local governments are entitled to 10 percent of gaming taxes plus whatever other amounts they may agree to obtain from licensees.[162] Local governments thus may exercise considerable economic muscle over the benefits they ultimately extract from licensees.

MISSISSIPPI

Mississippi has also pursued legalized casino gaming with a riverboat motif, approving enabling legislation on June 29, 1990.[163] Lotteries are constitutionally proscribed in Mississippi, but the legislature asserted its authority to legislate upon gaming matters notwithstanding this proscription.

The legislature is prohibited from legislating upon lotteries and permitted by virtue of its inherent powers to legislate upon gaming as the occasion arises. The Legislature derives its power to legislate upon gaming or gambling devices from its inherent authority over the morals and policy of the people and such power shall not be considered to conflict with the constitutional prohibition of lotteries.[164]

The Mississippi Gaming Control Act was patterned after the Nevada Gaming Control Act.[165] However, Mississippi's approach differs somewhat from other states in several respects.

First, there is the matter of location. Like its upstream competitors, Mississippi based its gaming industry on a riverboat model—though in its case the riverboat terminology is apparently used rather loosely. Mississippi law limits the sites for legal casino gaming to "vessels" located in the "Mississippi River or navigable waters within any county bordering on the Mississippi River" or in "waters within the State of Mississippi, which lie adjacent to the State of Mississippi south of the three (3) most southern counties in the State of Mississippi."[166] These geographic limits ensure that Mississippi casinos can draw from border states as well as from Gulf Coast counties known to be frequented by tourists. However, any real connection to navigable waters or any significant form of water transportation is quite tenuous.

Although the Mississippi Supreme Court has rejected the Mississippi Gaming Commission's attempt to grant a permit to construct a casino on a manmade waterway, many facilities have nevertheless been approved in manmade waterways.[167] In fact, long canals made it possible to locate facilities very close to Memphis, Tennessee, which permits these facilities to draw customers across state lines.[168] Inland casinos are frequently constructed far from the river by dredging a channel, filling it with floodwater or water pumped in from the river, and floating in a barge.[169]

Moreover, a "vessel" for purposes of this statute need only float on water and be at least 150 feet long.[170] As one commentator has explained, "Although dockside casinos are floating structures, they are not designed or intended to be used in navigation as a means of transportation. This intent is evidenced by the fact that a majority of dockside casinos are permanently moored to land-based structures and lack any means of self-propulsion."[171] As another commentator has noted, "Interestingly, only the gambling equipment needs to float, other parts of the casino can be on dry land. The 'floating' casinos often have more square footage on land than on water. In fact, most of the casinos in Tunica [County] 'look about as seaworthy as Sears Tower.' "[172]

Locating casinos on the river or in coastal areas may tend to constrain the availability of gambling to local citizens by imposing a geographic barrier.[173] At the same time, this approach tends to enhance access by customers from bordering states. However, despite a stated policy against land-based casinos,[174] the industry nevertheless appears to have largely discarded this constraint, insofar as dockside casinos may already resemble their counterparts that are otherwise located on land. The devastating effects of Hurricane Katrina on the coastal areas of Mississippi ultimately produced a change in this policy against land-based casinos in the Biloxi area. Legislation was approved in October 2005 allowing land-based casinos to be constructed within eight hundred feet of the shore in the three most southern counties of Mississippi, thus potentially improving the safety of these casinos in future storms.[175]

Mississippi's approach to local control over granting casino licenses also represents a departure from that of most other states.[176] Mississippi effectively allows gambling in the specified counties bordering the Mississippi River and the Gulf Coast unless local citizens mobilize and petition against legalization. State law requires that a prospective licensee must give notice of intent to apply for a license to the Mississippi Gaming Commission.[177] The prospective licensee is also required to publish this notice for three weeks in a local newspaper in the county where the prospective licensee seeks to do business.[178] Local citizens then have thirty days from the date of the last publication of notice to mobilize a petition drive. If at least fifteen hundred registered voters or twenty percent of the registered voters of the county, whichever is less, sign the petition, then the matter of licensure is put to a local vote.[179] Otherwise, if the petition effort fails, the board of supervisors of that county is required to adopt a resolution effectively authorizing legal gaming in that county.[180] Thus, the default rule favors legalization, and local citizens must undertake a significant effort to prevent that default rule from being implemented.

Of course, the prospective licensee must obtain approval from the Mississippi Gaming Commission for a license, and such approval requires the typical character and fitness requirements.[181] In addition, the site must be approved and environmental permits must be obtained for that particular location.[182] However, the number of licenses is not otherwise limited; the commission may issue a license to any qualified person, without any constraint on the number of licenses based on the need for additional gaming facilities.[183] In contrast, the Iowa Racing and Gaming Commission is specifically authorized to limit the number of gaming licenses.[184] The Missouri Gaming Commission is similarly empowered to determine the number of excursion boat licenses in a given county, although local governments may submit recommendations on this question.[185]

The brisk competition inherent in Mississippi's comparatively laissez-faire attitude toward casino licensing necessarily entails the possibility of winners and losers among casinos, as well as among their patrons. At least two casinos in the state have gone bankrupt and others have consolidated or reorganized.[186] Given that casinos in Atlantic City and Nevada have also filed for bankruptcy from time to time, this unrestricted licensing approach does not appear to have caused significant casino failures. However, the expansion in Mississippi has apparently slowed: in 2005 there were twenty-nine commercial casinos in the state, which is one less than it had in 1997.[187] With statewide gaming revenues of $2.7 billion in 2004, Mississippi only trails behind Nevada and New Jersey in terms of its overall market share for casino gambling.

SOUTH DAKOTA

South Dakota's gambling industry is relatively small, with gross revenues of only $78 million in 2004.[188] Its approach to regulating gambling is also somewhat unique. South Dakota was the first state after New Jersey to legalize casino gambling, with casinos opening in the town of Deadwood on November 1, 1989.[189] Voters in Deadwood approved a measure to allow "limited card games and slot machines" by a vote of 690 to 230, thus bringing casinos to this small town in the Black Hills of western South Dakota.[190]

Deadwood's reputation as a Wild West town that started in the Black Hills gold rush in 1876 provides the base for nostalgic tourism in the area. Modern interest in this town has also been rekindled through the HBO series *Deadwood,* which is set in this historic community.[191] Colorful characters such as Wild Bill Hickok once frequented Deadwood saloons, and tourists are reminded that they can play in the same casino where he was reportedly killed while playing cards.[192] As a historical matter, Deadwood also had a reputation for other vices: in its early days an estimated 90 percent of the female population were prostitutes.[193] However, in keeping with the family tourism tradition common to the Black Hills region, casinos in this area are remarkably family oriented. South Dakota casinos are unique in that minors are allowed on the gaming floor with their parents,[194] though persons under the age of twenty-one are proscribed from playing gambling games.[195]

South Dakota's policies toward gaming reflect the standard reiteration of licensing and regulation as the bedrock of public trust in the integrity of the games and in their freedom from criminal elements.[196] The South Dakota Commission on Gaming is the agency responsible for such regulation, and its actions are similar to those in other jurisdictions, including licensing and inspection of casino facilities and their operators.[197] However, casinos in Deadwood were ushered in based on a very strict limited-stakes model, in which no more than five dollars could be bet at any time.[198] Efforts to raise this amount by referendum in 1993 failed, but in 2000 efforts to raise the limit to one hundred dollars were successful, and this limitation remains in force today.[199] Maximum bets of one hundred dollars may nevertheless generate significant losses for patrons, but such limits also serve to protect the house. Without the possibility of large individual bets, the house removes any threat that a lucky patron might "break the bank" with a winning high-stakes gamble.

South Dakota has also attempted to limit the size of its casinos with a law restricting each licensee to no more than thirty table games and slot machines.[200] However, cooperative efforts by multiple licensees are permitted, which effectively allows several licensees to operate under one roof in what looks like a single casino.[201]

Casino gambling in this town has not become an engine for development as measured by population growth. According to U.S. Census Bureau figures, Deadwood's population has declined by more than 24 percent, from 1,830 in 1990 to only 1,380 in 2000.[202] Main street shops and stores once frequented by tourists have been displaced by casino operations, which have located in historic structures downtown or in newer structures designed to fit the historic Wild West motif.[203] Deadwood's remote location from major population areas coupled with family-oriented tourism make it a difficult choice for a casino market. In an era where major casino operators are building bigger and flashier facilities to attract patrons, the limited size and stakes variety of casino found here is unlikely to generate significant patronage by those seeking a destination for gambling.

Although South Dakota voters were willing to approve the increased betting limits for Deadwood casinos in 2000, it is interesting to note that these same voters narrowly defeated an attempt to remove another form of gambling—video lottery terminals—which is much more widespread. Video lottery terminals resemble slot machines, but they restrict bets to a maximum of two dollars and their payout is restricted to one thousand dollars.[204] These machines can be found throughout South Dakota in bars and taverns, with a maximum of ten machines per establishment.[205]

State law charges the lottery commission with maximizing revenue from these machines, and the state is entitled to half the revenues generated from these machines, all but 0.5 percent of which is to be used for property tax reduction.[206] In fiscal 2004, the property tax reduction fund received over $110 million, which is over one-tenth of the total state revenues of $938 billion.[207] In contrast, the Deadwood casinos generate a total of $78 million in annual gaming revenues, of which less than $12 million is in the form of taxes, which are spent on tourism, county government, and a separate gaming commission fund.[208]

Despite this significant contribution to state coffers, a constitutional amendment to repeal the video lottery failed by a reasonably narrow margin on November 7, 2000.[209] Such narrow approval of a practice that generates such significant state revenues for a popular purpose—property tax reduction—reflects deep public skepticism about gambling in that state. Given the demographics of a state like South Dakota—a small population spread over a large land area, with concentrated populations in cities in the far east (Sioux Falls) and far west (Rapid City)—the practice of restricting casino-style gambling to a limited tourist venue keeps these games beyond the reach of most residents. However, tribal gaming operations are also accessible in nine other venues in the state. As will be discussed in chapter 11, those tribal casinos are, in part, a trade-off that South Dakotans must accept for their limited experiment with casinos in Deadwood. Nevertheless, easy access to the close cousins of slot machines—video lottery terminals—has expanded gambling in the state in a manner that obfuscates somewhat the significance of gambling in that state's economy.

COMMON THEMES

Once gambling expanded into New Jersey, it was only a matter of time before others joined the bandwagon. In fact, it is surprising that it took over a decade for Iowa and the other riverboat states to adopt plans for expanded gambling. States like Iowa and Missouri reflect the well-intentioned beginnings of an expanded gaming industry that was supposed to be different from the commercial norm. Cultural distinctives, including riverboat or Wild West motifs, as well as gambler-friendly limits on betting and losses were initially designed to keep gambling as lighthearted fun. This was undoubtedly part of the early political "selling" of the idea of expanded gambling.

Those distinctives soon gave way to more commercially friendly forms of regulation. The desire to generate more gaming revenues, with resulting profits for business and taxes for government, gave way to regulations that promoted more efficient means to extract revenues from patrons. Mississippi's rules regarding vessels show the lengths to which legal definitions can be stretched in order to facilitate expanded play, particularly if that means the ability to attract valuable cross-border patronage. Interstate competition plays a significant role as these states also court more lucrative forms of play to attract cross-border patronage. In doing so, however, their own citizens appear to be an increasingly large source of patronage.

South Dakota, in contrast, continues to have only a tiny casino industry, as continuing restrictions tend to stunt further investment and growth. South Dakota's lottery—particularly through the prevalence of video lottery terminals—suggests competition from another state-supported form of gambling, which further limits the potential for casino growth in that jurisdiction. Lottery competition is also being felt in other states, including Iowa, which has issued a moratorium on new touch-screen lottery terminals, a close cousin to slot machines, in convenience stores and other businesses.[210] This moratorium is based in part on concerns about problem gambling (including access by minors) and in part on the competitive impact with Iowa's casino industry.

As will be discussed in later chapters, electronic gambling has proved to be an instrument for growth in the gaming industry, and this appetite for electronic forms of competition may present additional pressures on the states. The federal government's role in assisting the states with gambling enforcement is discussed in chapter 9. The particular threats presented by the Internet are explored in chapter 10.

9. Regulating Gambling: The Federal Government's Role

The federal government has traditionally considered gambling to be a matter of public morality or social welfare that should be left to the purview of the states. Though federal laws and regulations addressing national concerns about money laundering, tax evasion, and organized crime may affect casino operations, the extent of federal interference in the business of legalized gambling within the United States has historically been quite limited. For the most part, federal laws can be viewed as supporting and reinforcing the framework for regulation developed by each state rather than imposing a consistent and coherent national policy. The federal government has sometimes intervened to address cross-border conflicts, which arise on account of the limited jurisdictional reach of the enforcement powers of the states; otherwise, it has been remarkably restrained in this area.

Deference to state sovereignty presents both social and political advantages. It allows social policies to be developed by government officials who are presumably attuned to local values and politically accountable to the citizens most affected by their decisions. It also allows for policy experimentation, which has been touted as one of the strengths of our political system. As U.S. Supreme Court justice Louis Brandeis once said, "It is one of the happy incidents of the Federal system that a single courageous state may, if its citizens choose, serve as a laboratory; and try novel social and economic experiments without risk to the rest of the country."[1]

However, technological developments have made it increasingly difficult to constrain the effects of any "gambling experiment" within a state's geographical borders. Effective transportation systems, coupled with the proliferation of gambling establishments, have put gambling opportunities within easy reach of a substantial portion of the population in the United States. These features heighten prospects for interstate competition for gambling patrons, which creates special pressures on state and local governments in close proximity to jurisdictions with legalized gambling.

Potentially even more significant are developments in communications technologies that have made it possible to expand gambling operations without regard to geographical borders. Telephone, wireless, and Internet technologies make it possible for gambling operations to be located remotely from their patrons. The prospects of revenue flows to unregulated (and untaxed) providers outside the state raise both fiscal and public welfare concerns for state governments, which are difficult to address given limitations on their enforcement jurisdiction.

The Internet has elevated the locus for these concerns to the international arena. By allowing patron relationships to develop in a virtual environment, without the need for local agents or facilities, the Internet presents the possibility for casinos and their patrons to bypass traditional law enforcement methods. The enforcement of federal criminal proscriptions to constrain the growth of gambling, to control its effects, and to preserve revenue sources for the states emerges as a potentially significant federal function in this changing environment.

The discussion in this chapter provides an overview of significant federal laws that currently constrain or affect gambling activities. Constitutional questions also lurk here, as the Commerce Clause and the First Amendment may constrain the states from doing what they wish to do. Even international trade agreements may constrain government authority in this area. The particular problems of Internet gambling are addressed in some detail in chapter 10. Tribal gaming, which presents a different policy approach involving federal intrusion on state sovereignty in favor of tribal sovereignty, is discussed in chapter 11.

A CASE STUDY IN FEDERAL POLICY: COMPETITION IN STATE LOTTERIES

In understanding the current posture of federal-state relations with regard to gambling activities, it is important to recognize that cross-border impacts from gambling are not only a recent phenomenon. Federal government efforts to address interstate and international aspects of gambling—and to exercise restraint in doing so—have a long pedigree in our nation's history. However, government intervention in this context is rooted primarily in concerns about state welfare and revenue rather than in any national interests in uniform treatment of the subject of gambling. Moreover, that intervention occurs in the shadow of important constitutional structures, including the Commerce Clause, that are designed to shape the contours of government authority over commercial activities.

The cross-border effects of state lotteries provided one of the earliest demands for federal regulation of gambling issues. Current federal laws in this area are rooted in an 1895 statute[2] that the Supreme Court upheld against a constitutional challenge in *Champion v. Ames*.[3] Champion had been indicted for conspiracy to transport lottery tickets across state lines. The tickets in question were issued by the Pan-American Lottery Company, which held a monthly drawing in Asuncion, Paraguay.[4] Champion argued that the statute criminalizing his conduct exceeded Congress's powers under the Commerce Clause. The Court disagreed, explaining in part:

> Congress . . . does not assume to interfere with traffic or commerce in lottery tickets carried on exclusively within the limits of any state, but has in view only commerce of that kind among the several states. It has not assumed to interfere with the completely internal affairs of any state, and has only legislated in respect of a matter which concerns the people of the United States. . . . In legislating upon the subject of the traffic in lottery tickets, as carried on through interstate commerce, Congress only supplemented the action of those states—perhaps all of them— which, for the protection of the public morals, prohibit the drawing of lotteries, as well as the sale or circulation of lottery tickets, within their respective limits. It said, in effect, that it would not permit the declared policy of the states, which sought to protect their people against the mischiefs of the lottery business, to be overthrown or disregarded by the agency of interstate commerce. We should hesitate long before adjudging that an evil of such appalling character, carried on through interstate commerce, cannot be met and crushed by the only power competent to that end.[5]

Congress thus chose to limit the scope of its regulation to purely interstate or, in the case of importation, international activities. It did not impose restrictions on the states, even though it may well have thought that such restrictions were advisable based on the Court's moral characterization of lotteries.[6]

This restrained approach proved inadequate to the task of suppressing interstate activities in carrying out a lottery business. In *Francis v. United States,*[7] decided the same day as *Champion v. Ames,* the Court set aside a conviction under this same statute in the case of agents who transported slips of paper representing chances in a game known as "policy."[8] In this case, the lottery drawing was held in Ohio, but the lottery company had agents in other states, including Kentucky, where the defendants resided. After selling tickets, the agents made duplicate slips of paper indicating the numbers the customer had chosen, which were then transported to Ohio to assist the company in determining the identity of the winner.

Though this practice seemingly circumvented the intent of the federal statute upheld in *Champion v. Ames,* the Supreme Court gave a strict interpretation to that statute, holding that the agents' conduct was outside the confined scope of its criminal prohibition. The agents were not transporting lottery tickets themselves, only slips of paper representing the numbers chosen on the tickets. The tickets sold to customers did not leave the state, and the slips were not equivalent to the tickets because the lottery prize would ultimately not be awarded without the original ticket.[9] Such an interpretation made it possible for schemes like this one to operate so long as local law did not prohibit them.

The statutory gap exposed in *Francis* would soon reemerge in the late twentieth century when private firms sought to use electronic means to transport lottery information across state lines. Sensing that profits could be made through trafficking in lottery tickets from different states, entrepreneurs sought to use computer technology to communicate lottery information between out-of-state patrons who wanted lottery tickets and purchasing agents located within the state sponsoring the lottery. Conveniently for these firms, the Court's decision in *Francis* remained good law and the applicable federal statute was essentially unchanged: no tickets were being transported across state lines, only intangible signals from one computer to another.[10]

In response to this practice affecting state lotteries, Pennsylvania adopted a criminal proscription against selling lottery tickets from another state.[11] In *Pic-A-State v. Pennsylvania,*[12] a Pennsylvania firm carrying on a business in facilitating the sale of out-of-state lottery tickets challenged the validity of this state law under the dormant Commerce Clause. The firm's argument was simple and elegant: (1) lottery tickets were objects of commerce, and their sale in interstate commerce was a proper matter for federal regulation; (2) Congress had not prohibited this method of commercial exchange; (3) Pennsylvania citizens can legally purchase Pennsylvania lottery tickets, thereby reflecting state policy that lotteries are not unlawful; and (4) the Pennsylvania statute proscribing the sale of tickets from another state facially discriminates against interstate commerce and is presumptively invalid.[13]

The federal district court substantially agreed with this argument, finding in part that Congress had not given the states a free pass from Commerce Clause constraints.

> [W]hile [Congress] has legislated to facilitate the operation of legal state lotteries, it has never characterized as worthy of protection a state's right to choose to allow its citizens to play only its own state-sponsored lottery. Its emphasis has been on protecting the states that choose to prohibit lotteries. Thus, whatever the authority of an individual state to authorize a state lottery or to allow no lotteries at all, that state's authority remains bound by the dormant Commerce Clause just as it is in other subject areas.[14]

Applying a heightened level of scrutiny, the court proceeded to examine whether the state's purposes behind this facially discriminatory act "could be as well served by nondiscriminatory means."[15] Here, the state's concerns, which included risk of fraud from these agencies and (probably more important) the loss of revenues to the Pennsylvania lottery and its preferred programs of caring for elderly citizens, were insufficient to support the statute. According to the court, Pennsylvania could regulate the ticket agencies much like it regulated its own lottery sellers; it could also impose taxes on sales of such tickets to make up for lost revenues.[16] Thus, it struck down the Pennsylvania statute as unconstitutional.

The state appealed to the U.S. Court of Appeals for the Third Circuit, and during the pending appeal, Congress passed the Violent Crime Control and Law Enforcement Act of 1994.[17] Despite the seemingly inapplicable title of this law, it included a provision that effectively made the conduct of a business like that of Pic-A-State a federal crime, unless participating lottery states enacted a compact for interstate sales.[18] According to the Third Circuit, Congress's intervention here impacted the Commerce Clause analysis applicable to the Pennsylvania statute: "Where Congress has proscribed certain interstate commerce, Congress has determined that that commerce is not in the national interest. Where such a determination has been made by Congress, it does not offend the purpose of the Commerce Clause for states to discriminate or burden that commerce."[19]

Here, Congress had not preempted the field of lottery ticket sales. Instead, it had carefully crafted this provision to support state regulatory efforts, including the allowance of interstate sales with the support of an interstate compact.[20] In these circumstances, the Pennsylvania statute complements, rather than conflicts with, the federal criminal statute.[21] As a result, the state statute remained valid and was not preempted by the federal provision.[22]

Pic-A-State raised one final constitutional challenge, which the Third Circuit also rejected. In *Pic-A-State PA, Inc. v. Reno*,[23] Pic-A-State argued (much like Champion had done years before) that Congress's enactment of the federal criminal ban against selling interstate lottery tickets exceeded its power under the Commerce Clause. Adding a modern twist to the Champion case, however, Pic-A-State argued that Congress's regulation in this area presupposed that lotteries were "evils" to be constrained and that this was no longer true in light of the legalization of lotteries in over thirty states.[24] It also argued that Congress's choice constituted an irrational restraint of trade.[25]

The Third Circuit wasted little time in disposing of these arguments and by doing so reaffirmed the propriety of the protective role undertaken by Congress in these circumstances. Here, the putative status of lotteries as "evils" was irrelevant to the court, as long as there was some rational basis for the legislation. Loss of state revenue to out-of-state competition, coupled with the need to protect state sovereignty over such matters, was a sufficient basis for upholding the act under a rational basis standard.[26] The court noted: "Although many states have legalized lotteries, some have not. Congress could rationally decide to legislate in support of the policies of nonlottery states by placing the regulation of lotteries within the discretion of each state and prohibiting out-of-state interference."[27]

In further support of the rational basis for congressional action, the court also stated:

In the context of the one-hundred year history of [18 U.S.C.] § 1301 and the Federal regulation of lotteries, Congress could rationally conclude the need for an amendment to close a loophole created by advances in technology unforeseeable at the time the statute was originally drafted. Congress believed that since the sale of lottery tickets across state lines was illegal, the sale of interests in tickets across state lines by computer should be illegal as well. We believe the Commerce Clause requires no more indication of rationality for us to uphold the statutory scheme adopted by Congress.[28]

This brief saga affecting the cross-border conflicts in connection with the sale of lottery tickets provides some important lessons for understanding the unusual regulatory environment being cultivated here. In response to consumer demand, commercial interests spawned innovation that pushed the limits of existing state laws. Instead of adopting a singular national policy, Congress continued to leave the status of gambling through lotteries in the hands of the states. Rather than resolving the issue itself, Congress provided a default rule that protected state interests but also allowed a different result to be achieved through state cooperation.

What is particularly unusual here is that instead of encouraging robust competition among the states offering lotteries, Congress chose to protect state fiscal interests by effectively restraining trade. To the extent that gambling is viewed as merely another form of commerce, such a protectionist approach would probably not be tolerated. For example, the states would surely not be allowed to preclude their merchants from selling apples grown elsewhere if domestic apples were available. Thus, despite modern attempts to characterize gambling as merely another form of entertainment, Congress clearly viewed it differently than other commercial ventures.[29]

In part, this special treatment may reflect the close relationship between commercial gambling establishments and the taxes that they pay to state governments. State governments obtain considerable revenues from gaming taxes; competition threatens this revenue stream. Whether this relationship is a sufficient justification for different treatment is debatable. Other industries might also provide important contributions to the tax rolls if they are protected from competition. Nevertheless, the difference remains.

FEDERAL CRIMINAL SANCTIONS AFFECTING GAMBLING ENTERPRISES

Federal criminal statutes applicable to gambling other than lotteries reflect a similarly restrained approach that is sensitive to state interests. Instead of imposing a uniform federal standard, these laws generally define proscribed activities in relation to the legal status of the activity within the affected states. Moreover, their application is generally limited to activities with interstate and international effects, where the independent enforcement actions of the states are likely to be ineffective.

By erecting barriers to cross-border gaming operations, these laws serve multiple purposes. They protect the viability of state revenue streams obtained from legalized operations by making the detection and prosecution of illegal activities more likely. They support the policies of states that have chosen to follow the path of prohibiting gambling within their borders. They also assist the federal government in its efforts to stamp out organized crime, a problem that often involves interjurisdictional dimensions.

Significant federal statutes that potentially affect cross-border gambling operations include the Wire Act,[30] the Interstate Transportation of Paraphernalia Act,[31] and the Travel Act.[32] These three laws were originally enacted in 1961 as part of anticrime legislation; only limited amendments have occurred since that time. A provision of more recent vintage, the Professional and Amateur Sports Protection Act,[33] was enacted in 1992. Highlights from each of these laws are explored in the next sections.

The Wire Act (18 U.S.C. § 1084) and Related Legislation

The Wire Act was enacted in 1961 as part of a package of legislation proposed by Attorney General Robert F. Kennedy to address concerns connected with gambling and organized crime.[34] The Wire Act provides in part:

> Whoever being engaged in the business of betting or wagering knowingly uses a wire communication facility for the transmission in interstate or foreign commerce of bets or wagers or information assisting in the placing of bets or wagers on any sporting event or contest, or for the transmission of a wire communication which entitled the recipient to receive money or credit as a result of bets or wagers, or for information assisting

in the placing of bets or wagers, shall be fined . . . or imprisoned not more than two years, or both.[35]

According to the legislative history, this new law was designed "to assist the various States . . . in the enforcement of their laws pertaining to gambling, bookmaking, and like offenses and to aid in the suppression of organized gambling activities."[36] Government officials were particularly concerned that modern gambling operations were using telephone and other electronic means to facilitate illegal gambling activities that primarily benefited organized crime.[37]

Conduct proscribed by this statute is limited to that of persons "engaged in the business of betting or wagering." The scope of activity that rises to the level of being in the business of betting or wagering has proved controversial. For example, in *Pic-A-State,* the federal district court agreed that the Wire Act did not apply to the lottery ticket vendor, as it was not engaged in the business of wagering or betting because "they set no odds, accept no wagers and distribute no risks."[38] Both the Eighth and Ninth Circuits have held that placing bets on behalf of others is not a requirement for conviction; a person wagering for his own account could potentially be included.[39] On the other hand, the act has been interpreted as not reaching a bettor who regularly placed bets with a friend in the business of gambling.[40] In one case, even betting between eight hundred and one thousand dollars per day, three or four times per week, was held insufficient to be engaged in the business of betting or wagering.[41]

Despite this uncertainty, it is plain that the Wire Act was not designed to reach the casual gambler; such activities would be punished, if at all, under state law. Unlike other regulatory efforts, there is no intent here to preempt state law and occupy the field. The act specifically provides that "[n]othing in this section shall create immunity for criminal prosecution under any laws of any State."[42] On the other hand, federal prosecution could also occur without the necessity for state cooperation, a desirable feature when local law enforcement was corrupted or otherwise unable (such as through a lack of resources or through jurisdictional conflicts) to step in and enforce local gambling laws.

The act is also careful to preserve the rights of states to allow legalized gambling. Subsection (b) provides in part: "Nothing in this section shall be construed to prevent . . . the transmission of information assisting in the placing of bets or wagers on a sporting event or contest from a State or foreign country where betting on that sporting event or contest is legal into a State or foreign country in which such betting is legal."[43] At the time this legislation was enacted, Nevada was the only state where remote betting was legal. As explained in the legislative history,

> [T]he transmission of gambling information on a horserace from a State where betting on that horserace is legal to a State where betting on the same horserace is legal is not within the prohibitions of the bill. Since Nevada is the only State which has legalized offtrack betting, this exemption will only be applicable to it. For example, in New York State pari-mutuel betting at a racetrack is authorized by State law. Only in Nevada is it lawful to make and accept bets on the race held in the State of New York where pari-mutuel betting at a racetrack is authorized by law. Therefore, the exemption will permit the transmission of information assisting in the placing of bets and wagers from New York to Nevada. On the other hand, it is unlawful to make and accept bets in New York State on a race being run in Nevada. Therefore, the transmission of information assisting in the placing of bets and wagers from Nevada to New York would be contrary to the provisions of the bill.[44]

Legality in both states is a prerequisite for protection under this exception, and courts have held that proof of violation of a state statute is not a predicate to prosecution under the Wire Act.[45] States thus maintain a prerogative to legalize the use of interstate communications in connections with gambling, but they have not taken this route. Typical provisions limit legal gambling to situations of in-person contacts, thus keeping the effects (and profits) of such activities within the state where the bet is placed.[46]

Two other statutes originally enacted in 1961 addressed the related problems of interstate travel to facilitate unlawful gambling and the transportation of gambling paraphernalia. The Travel Act[47] provides a federal criminal penalty (including fines and imprisonment for up to five years) on the following persons:

> whoever travels in interstate or foreign commerce or uses the mail or any facility in interstate or foreign commerce, with intent to—

(1) distribute the proceeds of any unlawful activity; or . . .

(2) otherwise promote, manage, establish, carry on, or facilitate the promotion, management, establishment, or carrying on, of any unlawful activity.[48]

For this purpose, "unlawful activity" includes "gambling . . . offenses in violation of the laws of the State in which they are committed or of the United States."[49] The scope of the Travel Act extends to interstate activities, though the mere fact that people cross state lines to participate in gambling that might violate local law has been held to be outside the scope of this provision.[50]

The Interstate Transportation of Paraphernalia Act[51] addresses a related problem of transporting items used in illegal gambling activities. The act provides in part:

Whoever, except a common carrier in the usual course of its business, knowingly carries or sends in interstate or foreign commerce any record, paraphernalia, ticket, certificate, bills, slip, token, paper, writing, or other device used, or to be used, or adapted, devised, or designed for use in (a) bookmaking; or (b) wagering pools with respect to a sporting event; or (c) in a numbers, policy, bolita, or similar game shall be fined under this title or imprisoned for not more than five years or both.[52]

Like the Travel Act, this act also contains exceptions for items involved in a state where gambling is legal.[53] Manufacturers of gaming devices are also subject to additional rules that require them to register with the attorney general prior to manufacturing gaming devices and that provide criminal sanctions on the interstate transportation of such devices without proper registration and record keeping.[54] In this way, federal law supports state efforts to prevent illegal gambling, while also providing a means for federal intervention to combat organized crime.

The Professional and Amateur Sports Protection Act

Though the Wire Act specifically includes "bets or wagers on any sporting event or contest" within its scope, it also contains a specific exemption for state-sponsored gambling. In 1991, some members of Congress became intensely interested in issues surrounding gambling on sporting events. However, unlike previous legislation that was motivated by a desire to bolster law enforcement efforts in the battle against illegal gambling operations run by organized crime, the legislation that would emerge would instead be motivated primarily by concerns about the proliferation of state-sponsored forms of legalized gambling. In breaking with its tradition of legislating to support state discretion on legalized gambling, Congress enacted legislation that partially banned state-sponsored sports betting, effective January 1, 1993.

Sports have enjoyed a special role in American culture. As the legislative history to the Professional and Amateur Sports Protection Act[55] points out, "Sports are national institutions, and Congress has recognized a distinct federal interest in protecting sports from corruption."[56] As early as 1964, Congress had expressed this interest by making it a federal crime to attempt to influence a sporting contest by bribery.[57] The reported cases under this antibribery law primarily involve offenses relating to horse racing,[58] which was a more common form of legalized gambling at the time the law was enacted. Illegal betting on other sports also existed long before this provision was enacted, though state law provided the basis for criminal proscription.[59]

Concerns about the corrupting effects of gambling on important American values tied to sports formed a part of the basis for further legislation in this area. The legislative history to the Sports Protection Act quotes Paul Tagliabue, commissioner of the National Football League, in part:

> Sports gambling threatens the character of team sports. Our games embody our very finest traditions and values. They stand for clean, healthy competition. They stand for teamwork. And they stand for success through preparation and honest effort. With legalized sports gambling, our games instead will come to represent the fast buck, the quick fix, the desire to get something for nothing. The spread of legalized sports gambling would change forever—and for the worse—what our games stand for and the way they are perceived.[60]

In particular, concerns were expressed about the effects of gambling on young people, in terms of both the erosion of core values and the contribution to problem gambling behaviors. The legislative history continues:

> The committee is especially concerned about the potential effect of legalized sports gambling on America's youth. Beyond impairing the values sports represent to our young people, new technologies are being con-

sidered that, while designed to make gambling more convenient for adults, also would make gambling more convenient for children. . . . Youngsters would inevitably find sports gambling schemes that utilize these new technologies to be highly seductive.

Teenage gambling-related problems are increasing. Of the approximately 8 million compulsive sports gamblers in America, 1 million of them are under 20. Teenagers gamble on sports, lotteries and card games. *Governments should not be in the business of encouraging people, especially young people, to gamble.*[61]

It is significant to note that in this situation congressional concern was focused on the impact of legalized gambling rather than illegal forms. In fact, the interstate competition for gambling provided the basis for intervention.

Sports gambling is a national problem. The harms it inflicts are felt beyond the borders of those states that sanction it. The moral erosion it produces cannot be limited geographically. Once a state legalizes sports gambling, it will be extremely difficult for other states to resist the lure. The current pressures in such places as New Jersey and Florida to institute casino-style sports gambling illustrate the point. Without Federal legislation, sports gambling is likely to spread on a piecemeal basis and ultimately develop an irreversible momentum.[62]

Although federal interference in this context would undoubtedly affect the states' ability to raise revenues by expanding legalized gambling options, the majority did not find that to be a persuasive basis for rejecting the bill: "The answer to state budgetary problems should not be to increase the number of lottery players or sports bettors, regardless of the worthiness of the cause. The committee believes the risk to the reputation of our Nation's most popular pastimes, professional and amateur sporting events, is not worth it."[63]

Moreover, the Senate Judiciary Committee believed that the legalization of sports gambling would, in many cases, potentially lead to more social costs. The committee report quoted the commissioner of baseball, Francis T. Vincent Jr., in part: "once the moral status of sports betting has been redefined by legalization . . . many new gamblers will be created, some of whom inevitably will seek to move beyond lotteries to wagers with higher stakes and more serious consequences."[64] Thus, sports gambling was effectively analogized to a "gateway drug," with potentially deleterious moral and social consequences.

Despite these articulated concerns about the moral fabric, the Sports Protection Act did not go as far to repair it as logic might have dictated. In recognition of the political realities, the act contained a "grandfather provision" that prevented retroactive application to Oregon, Delaware, and Nevada, which had already instituted sports-related lotteries. The legislative history is particularly solicitous of Nevada's interests, stating in part that the committee had no "desire to threaten the economy of Nevada, which over many decades has come to depend on legalized private gambling, including sports gambling, as an essential industry."[65] Thus, it would appear, the youth in these jurisdictions would have to gain the values taught by fair competition in sport through some other means.

Republican senator Charles Grassley submitted a minority report that took the majority to task for this legislation. First, he found that it substantially intruded into states' rights by constraining them from raising revenues through expanded gambling options. The Reagan Justice Department agreed with Grassley on this point in opposing the bill.[66] Second, and perhaps more trenchant in effect, Senator Grassley pointed out that the bill would effectively grant a federal monopoly to the three states affected by the grandfather provision. He also pointed out the perverse effects that such grandfathering would have on the purported moral values advanced by the majority. Leveling a charge specifically at the professional sports leagues, who helped support the bill, he stated in part: "If the professional sports leagues were truly concerned about the risk of 'fixed' games, the integrity of professional sports, and the protections of their alleged trademarks, they would be seeking to prohibit this $1.8 billion head-to-head sports wagering industry in Nevada."[67] He further pointed out that the sports leagues benefited from this interest in sports wagering, as evidenced by the fact that Jimmy "The Greek" Snyder offered wagering advice in National Football League pregame shows and that virtually every major newspaper printed "point spreads" and similar wagering advice.[68]

Senator Grassley also took issue with another fundamental belief of the majority: that making sports betting illegal would prevent the growth of gambling. To the contrary, Senator Grassley suggested that "the principal beneficiar[ies] will be organized crime and the local bookie."[69] In the majority's view, legalization leads to greater demand for both legalized and illegal gambling. On the illegal side, the majority cited testimony from an FBI agent to the effect that "illegal entrepreneurs can always 'outmarket' their legitimate counterparts, offering credit, better odds, higher payout, and, most important, tax-free winnings."[70]

It remains to be proved empirically whether Senator Grassley or the majority was correct on this point. However, the economic rationale expressed by the majority seems hard to contradict. Anecdotal evidence of betting in the United Kingdom suggests that gambling has indeed proliferated there once it was legalized. On most any block in London, betting shops can be found. Betting lingo has found its way into the language of the popular culture, reflecting a ubiquity of gambling that is in stark contrast to the United States today,[71] though this may not always be so.

Sports betting is also common on college campuses today. The National Collegiate Athletic Association (NCAA) announced that FBI agents would be meeting with all thirty-two teams in the collegiate basketball championships in 2006 (compared to only the final four teams in 2005) due to results from a study showing widespread gambling among college athletes.[72] According to this study, which the NCAA completed in 2003 through a survey of twenty-one thousand student athletes, gambling among college athletes was common, despite NCAA rules to the contrary. Approximately 35 percent of male athletes and 20 percent of female athletes reported wagering on a sporting event in the past year, which is in direct violation of NCAA rules.[73] Though such wagering might include comparatively innocuous behavior, such as participation in a sports pool for an unrelated sport, the study indicated that about 2 percent of men's football and basketball athletes had been asked to affect the outcome of a game.[74] One percent of football players and 0.5 percent of men's basketball players admitted to accepting money to play poorly.[75] Less than 5 percent of male athletes and less than 0.5 percent of female athletes were categorized as problem or pathological gamblers.[76] Nevertheless, these results suggest that gambling is a growing problem on campuses and that sports gambling may already be affecting the integrity of athletic competitions.

OTHER FEDERAL REGULATIONS: TAX AND MONEY LAUNDERING RULES

In addition to federal criminal proscriptions that affect the scope and extent of legalized gambling operations, other federal laws can also affect casino operations. Though a complete review of every form of federal regulation is beyond the scope of this text, two areas merit particular attention: tax and money laundering rules.

Taxing Gambling Businesses

It has been said that "the power to tax is the power to destroy."[77] Tax policy undoubtedly has a regulatory dimension, as the Supreme Court has explained:

> The lawmaker may, in light of the "public policy or interest served," make the assessment heavy if the lawmaker wants to discourage the activity; or it may make the levy slight if a bounty is to be bestowed; or the lawmaker may make a substantial levy to keep entrepreneurs from exploiting a semipublic cause for their own personal aggrandizement.[78]

Although Congress has the power to impose taxes that would effectively destroy the economic viability of gambling businesses, it has chosen not to do so.[79] Apart from a limited exception for certain federal excise taxes, Congress has chosen not to burden gambling businesses with significant tax assessments that differ from those applicable to other trades or businesses. Instead, this power has been left to the states, which have exercised this power with alacrity.

Section 4401 of the Internal Revenue Code imposes a federal excise tax on persons in the business of accepting wagers, but this tax has little economic significance for state-authorized gambling businesses. First, the code defines wagers in a very restrictive manner:

> The term "wager" means—
>   (A) any wager with respect to a sports event or a contest placed with a person engaged in the business of accepting such wagers,
>   (B) any wager placed in a wagering pool with respect to a sports event or a contest, if such pool is conducted for profit, and
>   (C) any wager placed in a lottery conducted for profit.[80]

The term *lottery* is further restricted to exclude any game in which wagers are placed and prizes are determined and paid out in the presence of those playing the game.[81] Specific exemptions also exist for wagers placed in parimutuel enterprises licensed under state law, any coin-operated devices, and state-conducted lotteries.[82] Thus, the typical table games and slot machines played at a casino would be outside the scope of this tax.

Second, even if a wager would fall within the applicable definition, as in the case of sports betting, the tax rate on legal wagers is only 0.25 percent of the wager.[83] An annual tax of fifty dollars is also imposed on persons accepting wagers under these provisions that are not otherwise exempt.[84] Thus, the tax burden, if any, on legal operations from this federal excise tax would be quite modest.[85]

Illegal operations are subject to a higher tax rate of 2 percent and an annual tax of five hundred dollars.[86] Prior to amendment in 1974, the rate of this federal excise tax was 10 percent.[87] The 1974 amendments also responded to the Supreme Court's ruling in *Marchetti v. United States,*[88] which held that registration requirements associated with this excise tax as applied to taxpayers involved in illegal gambling activity violated their Fifth Amendment right against self-incrimination. Under current law, strict limitations on disclosure to law enforcement agencies apply to cure these Fifth Amendment infirmities.[89]

A significant tax on wagers, as opposed to taxes on winnings, would undoubtedly cut into the house's margin on gambling and potentially make the business of gambling uneconomical. For example, in some table games such as blackjack, a skilled player may allow a house advantage of less than 1 percent.[90] If even a 2 percent wagering tax was imposed on the casino, the game would produce virtually certain losses for the house in the long run if payouts remained the same. The only way to change such a result would be to change the rules so as to increase the house advantage or reduce payouts, which would effectively shift the incidence of that tax to the players. This may channel demand for legal gambling activities to illegal ones, or it may simply depress the demand altogether given the increase in costs.

Taxing Gamblers

Income tax rules affecting the treatment of a gambler's winnings and losses can also affect the economics of gambling transactions and thus indirectly affect the demand for legalized gambling. For federal income tax purposes, winning bets generate gross income, which may in turn generate income tax liability. As a technical matter, the amount of gross income is the excess of the winning payout over the amount of the wager; the portion of that payout that represents the initial wager should be treated as a nontaxable return of capital.[91] However, few gamblers have only winning bets during a taxable year. Losing bets may be deductible against gambling winnings, thus reducing taxable income, but, as explained later, such deductions are subject to restrictions that potentially limit their effectiveness. As a result, the government can be viewed as a partner of the winning gambler, but the losing gambler is an orphan.

Since 1934, the Internal Revenue Code has imposed a special limitation on the deductibility of gambling losses: "Losses from wagering transactions shall be allowed only to the extent of the gains from such transactions."[92] In contrast, taxpayers engaged in other business or profit-seeking activities are potentially allowed to deduct losses from one business activity against gross income from other business activities; moreover, excess losses may be carried to other tax years.[93]

This limitation on the deductibility of gambling losses reflects the policy judgment that gambling activities are different from other business or profit-seeking ventures. As the Supreme Court observed in a 1987 tax case,

> Federal and state legislation and court decisions, perhaps understandably, until recently have not been noticeably favorable to gambling endeavors and even have been reluctant to treat gambling on a parity with more "legitimate" means of making a living.[94]

The differential treatment accorded to gambling transactions may reflect vestiges of moral disapproval, and commentators have criticized aspects of the current tax structure on this basis.[95]

However, the differential treatment of gambling is not without some rational basis. Though gambling may entail profit-seeking motivations, gambling is primarily a pleasure-seeking activity in which patrons tolerate losses as the price of entertainment. Though some people may gamble with sufficient continuity and regularity to establish that their primary motivation in gambling is to seek income or profit, this is the exceptional case. In reality, the odds of most games are stacked against the gambler, leaving few opportunities to exploit specialized knowledge or skill to overcome the house advantage. (Poker may represent one of the few games in which the skilled competitor maintains an advantage over other players.) Further, the legislative history suggests that Congress was also concerned about the practices of gamblers who would report their losses but fail to report their winnings; such a practice is negated by the rule limiting the deduction of losses.[96]

The gambler who earns (or attempts to earn) his or her livelihood through gambling is allowed to deduct gambling losses (including related expenses) directly against his or her winnings, but only to the extent thereof.[97] Unlike the professional trader of stocks or securities, the professional gambler is not allowed tax benefits for losses in excess of gambling winnings.[98] This is perhaps a concession to congressional doubt about the validity of a profit motivation in this context but also perhaps a judgment about the comparative value of the gambler's contribution to the social good. A speculative day trader in stocks, whom some would consider to be engaged in a similar activity to the gambler, at least provides liquidity in the capital markets; the gambler can make no similar claim.

For those who engage in gambling primarily for pleasure (albeit also motivated by the hope for profit), losses are subject to the same special restriction as professional gamblers; that is, they cannot be used to offset income from sources other than gambling. However, they are also subject to a further restriction on their deductibility: unlike professionals, who can deduct losses directly against their winnings and are taxed (if at all) only on the net result, a casual gambler is required to treat gambling losses as an itemized deduction.[99] Among other things, this rule can cause hardships for taxpayers seeking tax benefits based on limitations imposed on adjusted gross income. For example, the tax court recently ruled that a low-income taxpayer appropriately lost a portion of her earned income credit due to gambling winnings, even though such winnings were offset entirely by losses that were allowed as an itemized deduction.[100] A middle-class taxpayer with significant gambling activity may also find that he or she is ineligible to obtain such benefits as the child tax credit, deductions for certain retirement contributions, and tuition payments to pursue higher education.[101] These effects tend to undermine the purposes that are otherwise intended by these social welfare provisions that are built into the tax code, and that denial occurs regardless of whether the taxpayer experiences true economic gains commensurate with reportable winnings.

Moreover, all gambling taxpayers must meet a burden of proof in substantiating their loss deductions. In Revenue Procedure 77-29,[102] the Internal Revenue Service set forth guidelines for the proof required to document gambling losses. These guidelines state in part:

> An accurate diary or similar record regularly maintained by the taxpayer, supplemented by verifiable documentation will usually be acceptable evidence for substantiation of wagering winnings and losses. In general, the diary should contain at least the following information:
>
> 1) Date and type of specific wager or wagering activity;
> 2) Name of gambling establishment;
> 3) Address or location of gambling establishment;
> 4) Name(s) of other person(s) (if any) present with taxpayer at gambling establishment; and
> 5) Amount(s) won or lost.[103]

In addition, the procedure suggests:

> Where possible, the diary and available documentation generated with the placement and settlement of a wager should be further supported by other documentation of the taxpayer's wagering activity or visit to a gambling establishment. Such documentation includes, but is not limited to, hotel bills, airline tickets, gasoline credit cards, canceled checks, credit records, bank deposits, and bank withdrawals.[104]

These substantiation requirements have been characterized as being more stringent than those imposed on taxpayers in other contexts.[105] To the extent that the gambler is unable to meet the burden of proof, any tax benefits from losses are effectively denied. Few gamblers keep sufficient records to satisfy this burden, thus exposing them to potential liability on audit.

It is a familiar rule of tax law that deductions are matters of legislative grace and that taxpayers have the burden of establishing the right to a deduction before they are allowed to reduce their tax liability.[106] It would be possible for Congress to design a tax system that would tax winning bets but treat losing bets as nondeductible personal consumption expenditures. Although the current system may indeed work this harsh result on gamblers who do not itemize deductions or who cannot meet the burden of proof, better treatment is possible for those who can comply.

In fact, the deductions available to gamblers may actually work out better than the result obtained for taxpayers engaged in so-called hobby activities, which lack the requisite profit motivation to be considered a trade or business. Section 183 of the code disallows deductions incurred in connection with such to the extent that those deductions exceed the gross income generated from that activity. Moreover, these deductions are allowable only as itemized deductions, which in this case are subject to a "floor" or limitation based on 2 percent of adjusted gross income.[107] Gambling losses are not subject to this 2 percent "floor," and casual gamblers are thus in a better situation than the hobbyist involved in other pursuits where pleasure, rather than profit, is the dominant motivation.

Tax rules affecting gambling winnings and losses potentially affect the odds associated with positive economic outcomes from gambling. As the effective tax rates increase, the expected value of any positive economic outcome decreases. To illustrate, consider the recent case of the gambler who decided to sell all his worldly goods and bet the proceeds on a single spin of a roulette wheel in Las Vegas.[108] The typical roulette wheel in the United States consists of thirty-eight numbered slots, containing the numbers 1–36, 0, and 00.[109] Only numbers 1–36 are colored red or black, and a bet on either red or black produces a payout of "even money" or double the amount bet. In these circumstances, a bet on either red or black produces a winning probability of 47.37 percent and a losing probability of 52.63 percent, reflecting a house advantage of 5.26 percent.[110]

Assuming a stake of $100,000 was wagered on red, the gambler could potentially double his money if he won. However, the expected value of the bet would be $94,740, reflecting a deduction for the house advantage:

$$\frac{\text{Probability}}{.4737} \times \frac{\text{Payout (pretax)}}{\$200,000} = \frac{\text{Expected Value}}{\$94,740}.$$

Thus, pure logic would not support this wager; the gambler is already starting out with a disadvantage to the house. He must believe he will be "lucky" in order to proceed with this bet.

Just how lucky he must be depends on the probability assigned to winning bets. It is interesting to note that this gambler staked all his wealth on a bet with a relatively high probability, nearly even odds. Had he chosen instead to bet on a single number, the odds against him would be much higher (37 to 1, or about 2.63 percent), but that bet would have produced a much higher payout (35 to 1 instead of 2 to 1) if it was successful. Nevertheless, the house advantage on this bet is still 5.26 percent, despite the fact that there is a greater potential for gain.[111] Thus, the expected value of the wager is similar in each case. Presumably, this gambler chose a less risky alternative because of the comparatively high probability of walking away with nothing.

This analysis ignores the effect of taxes imposed on winnings, which could significantly lower the true value of the expected payout. If this gambler is successful in betting red, his $200,000 payout will consist of $100,000 of return of capital and $100,000 of taxable income. Assuming for illustration purposes an average income tax rate of 20 percent, the after-tax value of the payout is $180,000, not $200,000. As a result, the expected value of the bet is really $85,266, not $94,740:

$$\frac{\text{Probability}}{.4737} \times \frac{\text{Payout (after tax)}}{\$180,000} = \frac{\text{Expected Value}}{\$85,266}.$$

Thus, the outcome is even less attractive from the gambler's perspective when the government's share of the winning bet ("government's advantage") is also added to the house advantage.

Whether tax considerations actually change behavior in a particular case would, of course, depend on the gambler. It is doubtful that the gambler who risks all on one spin is acting on pure reason. Few recreational gamblers probably understand or consider the tax consequences of their behavior. For example, the lower-income taxpayer with gambling losses probably does not consider the loss of her eligibility for the earned income credit as she considers the consequences of gambling winnings and losses.[112] Nevertheless, whether the gambler is engaged in a single wager or repeated transactions, these tax rules can have a real effect on the expected value of winning. The gambler has to be much luckier than the odds might otherwise indicate in order to come out ahead when tax effects are considered. Few gamblers probably understand this phenomenon, or they learn about it when it is too late and a tax deficiency is proposed.

Of course, taxpayer compliance with these rules is another consideration; tax avoidance undoubtedly occurs in the context of many gambling transactions. The house advantage in casino games means that the predicted results for casino gamblers who bet regularly will, as a general matter, experience net losses from gambling activities, giving little tax significance to the population when viewed as a whole. However, relatively large jackpots from progressive slot machines, bingo, or lotteries present the possibility that some gamblers may indeed have significant tax liability in a given tax year because their winnings exceed their losses—or more particularly the losses that they are able to prove. These taxpayers face the greatest risk of discovery in the event they improperly report their tax liability, as the code imposes financial reporting requirements on gambling businesses that are designed to identify such taxpayers to the government.

Section 6041 of the code generally imposes an information-reporting requirement on taxpayers engaged in a trade or business who make payments totaling six hundred dollars or more in "rent, salaries, wages, premiums, annuities, compensations, remunerations, emoluments, or other fixed or determinable gains, profits, and income."[113] This general rule applies to table game winnings.[114] However, some gambling activities are subject to more specific regulations, which require a casino to collect information and report payments of twelve hundred dollars or more from a bingo game or slot machine play, without regard to the amount wagered.[115] These regulations also require reporting for winnings of fifteen hundred dollars or more from a keno game, but this amount is reduced by the amount wagered in that game.[116]

Information reports provide an audit trail for the Internal Revenue Service to track down gamblers with potential tax liability. In some cases, an audit also produces evidence that the taxpayer failed to report not only winnings reported on the Form W-2G but also other winnings that were not subject to these reporting requirements. Losses, on the other hand, are not subject to similar reporting requirements. As a result, in a system in which the proof of winnings is assisted by the casino and the proof of losses is left to the taxpayer's own devices, a taxpayer may be unable to overcome the assessment of a deficiency, along with possible penalties.[117]

In addition to the reporting requirements, casinos may also be subject to income tax withholding requirements on certain winnings.[118] These withholding requirements impose additional administrative burdens on casinos and other gambling businesses when more significant payouts are involved. Like the information reporting requirements, these rules ensure that winners have an additional incentive for filing a return: they may ultimately get their withheld taxes back if they can prove sufficient losses were incurred to offset those large winnings. These rules also help to constrain the illegal practice known as "ten percenting"—paying another patron a percentage of winnings (often 10 percent) in order to provide false identity information to avoid tax compliance.[119] However, these withholding rules are not foolproof, as withholding is not required in all cases.[120] Only a system of purely electronic wagering, with a record of wins and losses, would ensure that all these transactions are properly reported.

MONEY LAUNDERING

The tax reporting and withholding rules previously described impose an administrative burden on casinos and other gambling businesses. In effect, casinos are legally required to assist in the enforcement of the income tax laws affecting their patrons. Rules governing the disclosure of large cash transactions also assist the government in the enforcement of tax laws, but their primary purposes involve detection and prevention of money laundering activities.

The term *money laundering* refers to the process by which criminal enterprises seek to mask the origins of cash generated through unlawful activities by associating it with legitimate sources.[121] Though money laundering enforcement efforts previously focused on domestic criminal enterprises (including drug trafficking), efforts to detect and suppress international terrorist organizations have gained attention in recent years.

Congressional findings in connection with anti–money laundering legislation passed in 2002 reflect an increasing concern about the impact of money laundering on the world economy and the particular threats raised by international actors. The following findings were revealed:

(1) money laundering, estimated by the International Monetary Fund to amount to between 2 and 5 percent of global gross domestic product, which is at least $600,000,000,000 annually, provides the financial fuel that permits transnational criminal enterprises to conduct and expand their operations to the detriment of the safety and security of American citizens;

(2) money laundering, and the defects in financial transparency on

which money launderers rely, are critical to the financing of global terrorism and the provision of funds for terrorist attacks;

(3) money launderers subvert legitimate financial mechanisms and banking relationships by using them as protective covering for the movement of criminal proceeds and the financing of crime and terrorism, and, by so doing, can threaten the safety of United States citizens and undermine the integrity of United States financial institutions and of the global financial and trading systems upon which prosperity and growth depend.[122]

Current law imposes reporting requirements on businesses that receive large cash deposits, in order to address these international and domestic threats from money laundering activity. These reporting requirements emanate from two different sources: the Bank Secrecy Act[123] and the Internal Revenue Code.[124]

Section 6050I of the Internal Revenue Code generally requires a person engaged in a trade or business who receives cash of more than ten thousand dollars in a single transaction, or two or more related transactions, to file a Form 8300 with the Internal Revenue Service.[125] Attempts to "structure" transactions by dividing them into smaller components that fall below the ten-thousand-dollar limit are prohibited.[126] Moreover, "cash" is defined to potentially include cashier's checks, money orders, traveler's checks, and similar instruments if the recipient "knows that such instrument is being used in an attempt to avoid the reporting of the transaction."[127]

Certain businesses may be exempt from reporting under section 6050I, including financial institutions that are subject to similar reporting requirements under the Bank Secrecy Act.[128] Casinos with gross annual gaming revenues over $1 million are within the scope of the Bank Secrecy Act and thus potentially fit this exemption.[129] However, exemption is discretionary and is granted on a case-by-case basis.[130] The Internal Revenue Service has specifically ruled that Class III Indian Casinos are within the scope of this exemption.[131] Small casinos—that is, those with annual gaming revenue of less than $1 million—are required to report under section 6050I.[132] Moreover, all casinos are required to report cash receipts in excess of ten thousand dollars in connection with nongaming businesses, including entertainment, shops, and hotels.[133]

Under the Bank Secrecy Act, casinos are obligated to report cash transactions over ten thousand dollars in connection with a broad range of transactions involving cash in or cash out. Cash-in transactions include

(A) Purchases of chips, tokens, and plaques;

(B) Front money deposits;

(C) Safekeeping deposits;

(D) Payments on any form of credit, including markers and counter checks;

(E) Bets of currency;

(F) Currency received by a casino for transmittal of funds through wire transfer for a customer;

(G) Purchases of a casino's check; and

(H) Exchanges of currency for currency, including foreign currency.[134]

Cash-out transactions include

(A) Redemptions of chips, tokens, and plaques;

(B) Front money withdrawals;

(C) Safekeeping withdrawals;

(D) Advances on any form of credit, including markers and counter checks;

(E) Payments on bets, including slot jackpots;

(F) Payments by a casino to a customer based on receipt of funds through wire transfer for credit to a customer;

(G) Cashing of checks or other negotiable instruments;

(H) Exchanges of currency for currency, including foreign currency; and

(I) Reimbursements for customers' travel and entertainment expenses by the casino.[135]

Verification of the identity of the person for whom the reportable cash is received is required,[136] thus providing a paper trail for law enforcement officials to follow.

A specialized agency within the Treasury Department, the Financial Crimes Enforcement Network (known as FinCEN), issued regulations in 2002 to prescribe additional requirements for casinos in connection with the reporting of so-called suspicious transactions. It explained the enhanced focus on casino enterprises as follows:

[T]hese actions to expand the obligations of casinos reflect the continuing determination not only that casinos are vulnerable to manipulation by money launderers and tax evaders but, more generally, that gaming establishments provide their customers with a financial product—gaming—and as a corollary offer a broad array of financial services, such as customer deposit or credit accounts, facilities for transmitting and receiving funds transfers directly from other institutions, and check cashing and currency exchange services, that are similar to those offered by depository institutions and other financial firms.[137]

Perhaps even more significant is the fact that money launderers are believed to be efficient actors: "Money launderers will move their operations to institutions in which their chances of successful evasion of enforcement and regulatory efforts are the highest."[138]

The regulations prescribe the following standards that trigger a reporting obligation for a suspicious transaction:

A transaction requires reporting under the terms of this section if it is conducted or attempted by, at, or through a casino, and involves or aggregates at least $5,000 in funds or other assets, and the casino knows, suspects, or has reason to suspect that the transaction (or a pattern of transactions of which the transaction is a part):

(i)   Involves funds derived from illegal activity or is intended or conducted in order to hide or disguise funds or assets derived from illegal activity (including, without limitation, the ownership, nature, source, location, or control of such funds or assets) as part of a plan to violate or evade any federal law or regulation or to avoid any transaction reporting requirement under federal law or regulation;

(ii)   Is designed, whether through structuring or other means, to evade any requirements of this part or of any other regulations promulgated under the Bank Secrecy Act. . . .;

(iii)   Has no business or apparent lawful purpose or is not the sort in which the particular customer would normally be expected to engage, and the casino knows of no reasonable explanation for the transaction after examining the available facts, including the background and possible purpose of the transaction; or

(iv)   Involves use of the casino to facilitate criminal activity.[139]

These standards are subject to criticism for their imprecision. Commentators expressed concerns about the difficulties of determining when a transaction is suspicious.[140] However, FinCEN retained this generalized approach, which is rooted in a fundamental belief in the advantages of experienced industry participants over government officials:

> [T]he employees and officers of those institutions are often more likely than government officials to have a sense as to which transactions appear to lack commercial justification (or in the case of gaming establishments, transactions that appear to lack a reasonable relationship to legitimate wagering activities) or that otherwise cannot be explained as constituting a legitimate use of the casino's financial services.[141]

In addition to the financial reporting rules, casinos are also subject to a complementary requirement to develop a monitoring program that evaluates customer activities for risks associated with money laundering.[142] As further explained in the preamble to the regulations:

> FinCEN wishes to emphasize that the rule is not intended to require casinos mechanically to review every transaction that exceeds the reporting threshold. Rather, it is intended that casinos, like every type of financial institution to which the suspicious transaction reporting rules of 31 CFR part 103 apply, will evaluate customer activity and relationships for money laundering risks, and design a suspicious transaction monitoring program that is appropriate for the particular casino in light of such risks. In other words, it is expected that casinos will follow a risk-based approach in monitoring for suspicious transactions, and will report all detected suspicious transactions that involve $5,000 or more in funds or other assets. A well-implemented anti-money laundering compliance program should reinforce a casino's efforts in detecting suspicious activity. In addition, casinos are encouraged to report on a voluntary basis detected suspicious transactions that fall below the $5,000 reporting threshold, such as the submission by a customer of an identification document that the casino suspects is false or altered, in the course of a transaction that triggers an identification requirement under the Bank Secrecy Act or other law.[143]

Compliance with the Bank Secrecy Act regulations is potentially costly to casinos. Estimated burdens published in the *Federal Register* in 2002 indicate that the currency transaction reporting requirement alone would affect 550 casinos, requiring 237,000 responses annually and a total of 94,800 human hours.[144] The suspicious transaction reporting requirements were thought to have a more limited impact, in that existing casino business practices already involve monitoring customers' information and thus may be amenable to being adapted to meet the requirements of those rules.[145]

These regulations may well contribute to enhanced enforcement efforts, but it is important to recognize that they have inherent limitations. Short of requiring all casino transactions to be conducted through electronic means, coupled with rigorous identity verification requirements for casino players, gaps will remain in this system designed for detection. Such a comprehensive, electronic-based system would be considered threatening to many gamblers, who would prefer that their activities remain private and out of the range of government supervision.

The suspicious transaction rules are particularly vulnerable to skepticism about their effectiveness. Although they do provide a legal means for cooperative activity by casinos, such cooperation is hardly in their economic interests, as it potentially involves the loss of a valuable customer. Casinos benefit from gathering information about their customers and their betting preferences, but learning "too much" might trigger a reporting obligation. It would be interesting to learn whether these regulations will ultimately have any impact on the information that casinos gather for their own business purposes, as well as whether they will make a positive contribution toward law enforcement efforts. Such information is likely to be kept as a trade secret by casinos, however, which will make sure it does not reach the light of day.

FIRST AMENDMENT CONSTRAINTS ON REGULATION OF CASINO ADVERTISING

One other topic merits attention in this chapter: the impact of the First Amendment on the regulation of commercial speech involving gambling businesses. State and local governments have occasionally sought to impose restrictions on advertising for gambling businesses, such as banning local advertising of casinos in an attempt to curb gambling by local citizens, while at the same time choosing to permit advertising in venues targeted toward tourists.[146] Although such restrictions might arguably serve a valid public interest in constraining social costs arising from local patrons, they constrain the commercial interests of the casino as well as the interests of those who might wish to hear that speech.

Interstate commerce issues also lurk here. Some forms of advertising, such as billboards and signs, may have a distinctly local impact, but others are less easily tied to particular geographic regions. Broadcast media are perhaps the most difficult to constrain, as their signals may reach well beyond the borders of a particular state. Congress weighed in on these conflicting interests by imposing a ban on radio and television broadcast advertising of information for any "lottery, gift enterprise, or similar scheme,"[147] terminology that has been interpreted to include casinos.[148] However, that ban has been weakened through statutory exceptions, including those allowing advertising for state-run lotteries and charitable gaming.[149] What was left of the ban was weakened even further by the Supreme Court's efforts to strengthen the protections available to commercial speech.[150]

This complex area has been the subject of extensive academic commentary, which will not be exhaustively explored in this context.[151] However, a brief discussion of several gambling-related cases that reached the Supreme Court is helpful in understanding the changing parameters of regulation of commercial speech and its effects on the regulation of casino advertising.

In *Posadas de Puerto Rico Associates v. Tourism Company of Puerto Rico,*[152] the operator of a Puerto Rican casino challenged government regulations that constrained the casino's ability to advertise. Puerto Rico had legalized casino-style gambling in 1948 for the purpose of generating tourism and enhancing the tax revenues available to the government.[153] The enabling legislation also imposed restrictions on casino advertising. In particular, section 8 provided that "[n]o gambling room shall be permitted to advertise or otherwise offer their facilities to the public of Puerto Rico."[154] Section 7 granted regulatory powers to a public corporation, which would implement these advertising restrictions.[155]

Regulations promulgated under section 7 essentially allowed casinos to advertise in venues that would be available primarily to tourists but prohibited advertising in venues that would target local Puerto Rican residents. For example, an advertisement in the *New York Times,* which might reach a local subscriber, would be permitted. However, advertising in local media would be restricted as to the content of casino gaming that could be included.[156] Although the effectiveness of these restrictions is disputable, their articulated purpose was to protect local residents from media exposure to the "experiment" of casino gambling, while at the same time allowing the casinos to fulfill their goals of promoting tourism.[157]

The Supreme Court noted that purely commercial speech was involved, and thus it invoked the so-called *Central Hudson* test:

> Under *Central Hudson*, commercial speech receives a limited form of First Amendment protection so long as it concerns a lawful activity and is not misleading or fraudulent. Once it is determined that the First Amendment applies to the particular kind of commercial speech at issue, then the speech may be restricted only if the government's interest in doing so is substantial, the restrictions directly advance the government's asserted interest, and the restrictions are no more extensive than necessary to serve that interest.[158]

Here, both residents and tourists could gamble legally, and affected advertising was neither misleading nor fraudulent. Thus, the analysis turned on the latter three elements of this test, which require the Court to consider the weight of the governmental interest and the fit between that interest and the means chosen to advance it.

First, the Court found that substantial government interests were present. The government's brief alleged legislative concerns that "[e]xcessive casino gambling among local residents . . . would produce serious harmful effects on the health, safety and welfare of the Puerto Rican citizens, such as the disruption of moral and cultural patterns, the increase in local crime, the fostering of prostitution, the development of corruption, and the infiltration of organized crime."[159] As the Court noted, "These are some of the very same concerns . . . that have motivated the vast majority of the 50 States to prohibit casino gambling. We have no difficulty in concluding that the Puerto Rico legislature's interest in the health, safety, and welfare of its citizens constitutes a 'substantial' governmental interest."[160]

The Court also found that the regulations directly advanced the government's interest in reducing the risks to the public associated with casino gambling. Even though other forms of gambling (such as cockfighting, horse racing, and lotteries) could be advertised locally, the Court deferred to the legislative judgment that particular harms associated with casino gambling could be singled out for protection.[161]

Finally, the Court found that the measure was not more extensive than necessary to serve the government's interest. The Court rejected an approach that would respond to social problems through allowing more speech rather than through constraining commercial speech. According to the Court, this was a matter to be reserved for the legislature.[162] The greater power to ban gambling included a lesser power of regulating commercial speech associated with gambling. As the Court explained,

> [I]t is precisely *because* the government could have enacted a wholesale prohibition of the underlying conduct that it is permissible for the government to take the less intrusive step of allowing the conduct, but reducing the demand through restrictions on advertising. It would surely be a Pyrrhic victory for casino owners such as appellant to gain recognition of a First Amendment right to advertise their casinos to the residents of Puerto Rico, only to thereby force the legislature into banning casino gambling by residents altogether. It would just as surely be a strange constitutional doctrine which would concede to the legislature the authority to totally ban a product or activity, but deny to the legislature the authority to forbid the stimulation of demand for the product or activity through advertising on behalf of those who would profit from such increased demand. Legislative regulation of products or activities deemed harmful, such as cigarettes, alcoholic beverages, and prostitution, has varied from outright prohibition on the one hand, see, *e.g.,* Cal. Penal Code Ann. § 647(b) (West Supp.1986) (prohibiting soliciting or engaging in act of prostitution), to legalization of the product or activity with restrictions on stimulation of its demand on the other hand, see, *e.g.,* Nev.Rev.Stat. §§ 244.345(1), (8) (1986) (authorizing licensing of houses of prostitution except in counties with more than 250,000 population), §§ 201.430, 201.440 (prohibiting advertising of houses of prostitution "[i]n any public theater, on the public streets of any city or town, or on any public highway," or "in [a] place of business"). To rule out the latter, intermediate kind of response would require more than we find in the First Amendment.[163]

This dimension of the Court's analysis granted significant government power over commercial speech involving "vices" that nevertheless had legal status. In *United States v. Edge Broadcasting Company,*[164] the Court considered whether a Federal Communications Commission ban on lottery advertising in broadcast media satisfied the First Amendment. A radio station that was located in North Carolina (where the lottery was illegal) but that nevertheless reached customers in Virginia (where the lottery was legal) challenged this ban as violating its rights to commercial speech.

Although the government argued that the principle stated in *Posadas* that "the greater power to prohibit gambling necessarily includes the lesser power to ban its advertisement" should control the outcome here, the Court nevertheless required a full *Central Hudson* analysis.[165] However, the Court also recognized that "the activity underlying the relevant advertising—gambling—implicates no constitutionally protected right; rather, it falls into a category of 'vice' activity that could be and frequently has been, banned altogether."[166] The Court ultimately found that the requirements of *Central Hudson* were met and that the ban was appropriate to meet the substantial governmental interest in balancing the policies of states that prohibit lotteries against those that do not. As in *Posadas,* the Court in *Edge Broadcasting* was willing to defer to the legislative judgment about the validity of its policies rather than relying on the approach of answering commercial speech that hinders a government policy with counter-speech.[167]

This deferential approach to the legislature in matters involving "vice" would soon be abandoned, however, as the Court took a different tack toward commercial speech that refused to countenance a judgment that any legal activity could be characterized as "vice." In *44 Liquormart, Inc. v. Rhode Island,*[168] which involved a state ban on price advertising for liquor by state-licensed retailers, the Court explained that the deferential approach articulated in *Posadas* was an aberration that would no longer be followed. According to the Court, First Amendment jurisprudence was designed to embrace a skeptical view of outright bans of truthful commercial speech.

> Precisely because bans against truthful, nonmisleading commercial speech rarely seek to protect consumers from either deception or over-reaching, they usually rest solely on the offensive assumption that the public will respond "irrationally" to the truth. The First Amendment directs us to be especially skeptical of regulations that seek to keep people in the dark for what the government perceives to be their own good.[169]

Based on this view, deference to the legislature on matters of suppressing commercial speech was inappropriate.

Because the 5-to-4 decision in *Posadas* marked such a sharp break from our prior precedent, and because it concerned a constitutional question about which this Court is the final arbiter, we decline to give force to its highly deferential approach. Instead, in keeping with our prior holdings, we conclude that a state legislature does not have the broad discretion to suppress truthful, nonmisleading information for paternalistic purposes that the *Posadas* majority was willing to tolerate.[170]

Moreover, the Court also rejected reliance on the "greater includes the lesser" principle as a basis for supporting government regulation of commercial speech.

Although we do not dispute the proposition that greater powers include lesser ones, we fail to see how that syllogism requires the conclusion that the State's power to regulate commercial *activity* is "greater" than its power to ban truthful, nonmisleading commercial *speech*. Contrary to the assumption made in *Posadas,* we think it quite clear that banning speech may sometimes prove far more intrusive than banning conduct. As a venerable proverb teaches, it may prove more injurious to prevent people from teaching others how to fish than to prevent fish from being sold. Similarly, a local ordinance banning bicycle lessons may curtail freedom far more than one that prohibits bicycle riding within city limits. In short, we reject the assumption that words are necessarily less vital to freedom than actions, or that logic somehow proves that the power to prohibit an activity is necessarily "greater" than the power to suppress speech about it.[171]

In a further retreat from its prior precedent in *Edge Broadcasting,* the Court also rejected the concept of a special class of commercial speech accompanying "vice" activities.

[T]he scope of any "vice" exception to the protection afforded by the First Amendment would be difficult, if not impossible, to define. Almost any product that poses some threat to public health or public morals might reasonably be characterized by a state legislature as relating to "vice activity." Such characterization, however, is anomalous when applied to products such as alcoholic beverages, lottery tickets, or playing cards, that may be lawfully purchased on the open market. The recognition of such an exception would also have the unfortunate consequence of either allowing state legislatures to justify censorship by the simple expedient of placing the "vice" label on selected lawful activities, or requiring the federal courts to establish a federal common law of vice. For these reasons, a "vice" label that is unaccompanied by a corresponding prohibition against the commercial behavior at issue fails to provide a principled justification for the regulation of commercial speech about that activity.[172]

Thus, the Court apparently takes an increasingly agnostic view about the moral dangers associated with activities that the legislature chooses to make legal and removes legislative prerogatives with regard to banning speech in these areas.

The significance of this change in approach for commercial speech involving gambling was further evidenced in the Court's 1999 decision in *Greater New Orleans Broadcasting Association, Inc. v. United States,*[173] which involved the application of regulations under 18 U.S.C.A. § 1304 to prohibit certain types of advertising for private legal casino operations via television media. Unlike the radio advertising in *Edge Broadcasting,* which occurred through a radio station located in a state in which the advertised gambling was illegal, the television stations involved in this case were located in Louisiana, where private casino gambling was legal. However, their signals potentially reached into states such as Texas and Arkansas, where private casino gambling was not legal.[174]

The government alleged that substantial interests were at stake, including familiar assertions about the social costs of commercial casino gambling.

> Underlying Congress' statutory scheme, the Solicitor General contends, is the judgment that gambling contributes to corruption and organized crime; underwrites bribery, narcotics trafficking, and other illegal conduct; imposes a regressive tax on the poor; and "offers a false but sometimes irresistible hope of financial advancement." With respect to casino gambling, the Solicitor General states that many of the associated social costs stem from "pathological" or "compulsive" gambling by approximately 3 million Americans, whose behavior is primarily associated with "continuous play" games, such as slot machines. He also observes that compulsive gambling has grown along with the expansion of legalized gambling nationwide, leading to billions of dollars in economic costs; injury and loss to these gamblers as well as their families, communities, and government; and street, white-collar, and organized crime.[175]

Although the Court grudgingly recognized that these interests could indeed be substantial, it also noted that federal policies in this area had changed substantially since the enactment of 18 U.S.C. § 1304 in 1975. Numerous exceptions had been appended to the broadcast ban, and the federal policy expressed in the Indian Gaming Regulatory Act had also effectively promoted casino gambling.[176] These inconsistencies proved to create a fatal flaw in the government's case. As the Court explained,

> The operation of § 1304 and its attendant regulatory regime is so pierced by exemptions and inconsistencies that the Government cannot hope to exonerate it. Under current law, a broadcaster may not carry advertising about privately operated commercial casino gambling, regardless of the location of the station or the casino. On the other hand, advertisements for tribal casino gambling authorized by state compacts—whether operated by the tribe or by a private party pursuant to a management contract—are subject to no such broadcast ban, even if the broadcaster is located in, or broadcasts to, a jurisdiction with the strictest of antigambling policies. Government-operated, nonprofit, and "occasional and ancillary" commercial casinos are likewise exempt.[177]

Since these exempt forms of casino gambling would presumably present the same kinds of social costs as private casino gambling, the government could not meet its burden. Moreover, the Court also suggested that other means could be used to address these social concerns that would not burden commercial speech.

> Ironically, the most significant difference identified by the Government between tribal and other classes of casino gambling is that the former is "heavily regulated." If such direct regulation provides a basis for believing that the social costs of gambling in tribal casinos are sufficiently mitigated to make their advertising tolerable, one would have thought that Congress might have at least experimented with comparable regulation before abridging the speech rights of federally unregulated casinos. While Congress' failure to institute such direct regulation of private casino gambling does not necessarily compromise the constitutionality of § 1304, it does undermine the asserted justifications for the restriction before us. There surely are practical and nonspeech-related forms of reg-

ulation—including a prohibition or supervision of gambling on credit; limitations on the use of cash machines on casino premises; controls on admissions; pot or betting limits; location restrictions; and licensing requirements—that could more directly and effectively alleviate some of the social costs of casino gambling.[178]

Congress's failure to require more restrictive forms of federal regulation thus proved inconsistent with the overall goals articulated in the restriction on casino advertising. The concern raised in *Posadas* as a reason for granting legislative deference, that is, that government might otherwise have to restrict the people's freedom to *do* the activity, was now embraced as a preferable one to restricting commercial speech about the activity.

As a result of the Supreme Court's change in views about the scope of First Amendment protections for commercial speech, it appears that policymakers will be unable to impose substantial restrictions on casino advertising in connection with decisions to regulate the gaming industry. Appropriate time, place, and manner restrictions (such as keeping casino ads from public schools or other environs targeted to minors) may well continue to be upheld under the *Central Hudson* analysis. Challenges to false or misleading speech may also be sustained, though misleading speech can be difficult to define. For example, would an advertisement inviting debtors to win their way out of financial worries by coming to the casino be acceptable commercial speech? As casino markets become more saturated and thus more competitive, more of these issues are likely to be presented.[179]

Whether the Court's change in approach is desirable from a policy perspective is a matter for debate. On one hand, the idea that consumers should have access to information that is neither false nor misleading appeals to our belief in reason and rational discernment. However, cultural matters of sensibility are also at stake, which are not easily dismissed. For example, would the Court be willing to apply its rationale to allow constant media bombardment to the type of services and prices available in connection with the legal prostitution services (which are allowed in some Nevada counties)? The real extent to which the courts are willing to reject the concept of "vice" for all activities that are legally permitted remains to be seen. A more culturally sensitive alternative of toleration without permitting commercial enterprises to flout cultural norms appears outside the realm of possibility under this approach.

To the extent that advertising for casino gaming has a negative impact on other cultural values, such as work, saving, and temperance, those values will apparently have to be addressed through counter-speech. Alternatively, to the extent that empirical research demonstrates a connection between advertising and problem gambling behavior, counter-speech might be needed. Whether the legislature will require the casino industry to fund such speech and whether they have the power to do so are issues that may be presented in the future; the tobacco industry currently faces similar issues that may provide some indication of future trends. (Those issues are discussed further in chapter 12.)

In the meantime, however, it is quite clear that protections for commercial speech do not extend to advertising unlawful activities.[180] The current illegality of Internet gambling in the United States means that targeting advertisers becomes a legitimate tool for enforcing antigambling laws, a topic discussed in the following chapter.

10. The Internet: Gambling's New Frontier

The technologies that have made the Internet so attractive to other commercial ventures have also attracted the gaming industry. Although the diffused and geographically ambiguous nature of the Internet makes it difficult to assess its economic impact, analysts at the General Accounting Office have estimated that more than $4 billion was wagered on the Internet in 2003.[1] The recent phenomenal growth of online poker, which is estimated to have grown from less than $100 million in 2002 to more than $1 billion in 2004, suggests continued expansion in online markets.[2] Some sources estimate online patron losses at $12 billion for 2005.[3]

The economic potential for Internet gambling may also be revealed through an indirect measure—the amount that online casinos have paid to promote their sites to potential patrons. Prior to federal government efforts to restrict Internet advertising, paid listings in commonly used search engines reflected competitive bids by commercial gaming interests, thus providing an indication of the commercial value placed on certain terms. As of April 2004, the top bid for the word *casino* as a paid placement on sites such as Yahoo! and Google was $14.97 per "click-through."[4] This appears to be a significant investment for the privilege of accessing a potential customer, who ultimately may not choose to wager on the site. However, one online gambling firm headquartered in Gibraltar, PartyGaming PLC, disclosed profits of $350 million on $600 million in revenues in 2004, suggesting that this kind of online advertising spending is not irrational.[5] As of August 2005, PartyGaming PLC had a market capitalization of 6.55 billion British pounds—more than that of British Airways.[6]

Growth in this industry has been substantial. In 1997, as few as thirty Web sites apparently offered online gambling.[7] Seven years later, several thousand sites offered some form of gaming services.[8] As many as seventy-six different jurisdictions may be offering some form of government license for Internet gambling.[9] The ubiquity of the Internet coupled with jurisdictional constraints on the efficacy of federal and state laws make the Internet a particularly challenging environment to regulate. The nature of that challenge and some potential means for dealing with it are discussed in the sections that follow.

THE BUSINESS MODEL FOR INTERNET GAMBLING

Internet gambling creates the possibility of reaping economic benefits without a significant investment in a physical plant or employee base. Unlike their traditional counterparts, Internet casino operations do not require extensive investments in lavish, customer-friendly facilities. Their secure servers can be located in inconspicuous buildings in remote locales; physical access and the creature comforts are not a consideration in the world of virtual gaming. Construction and maintenance of facilities require significant up-front investments for traditional casino operations, which create barriers to entry and significant ongoing cost, particularly in competitive tourist markets. For example, it has been reported that the failure of Trump-owned casinos in Atlantic City to make renovations and improvements put them at a competitive disadvantage to other newer casinos.[10]

Internet operations also do not require extensive employee staffing to serve the needs of their customers. Employees who run the games, such as dealers and croupiers, are instead replaced by computerized versions for online patrons. The pit boss and the supervisory personnel who are otherwise employed to watch over these employees are also unnecessary, as computer algorithms are designed to ensure against human foibles that might otherwise cheat the house of its advantage. Computer technologists and programmers thus substitute for other forms of human employment, providing a productivity advantage and likely reduction of overhead costs.

Both virtual and traditional casino operations share the common need for advertising to attract customers. First Amendment protections for commercial speech permit a broad range of advertising targeted at potential patrons for legal operations. Print and broadcast media frequently tout opportunities to gamble at legal casino operations, and thus media companies benefit indirectly from this enhanced demand for advertising. Even though advertisements may cross state lines into jurisdictions that do not permit casino gambling, state regulation or censorship of such advertising is likely to be unsuccessful as long as the casino's operation is legal and the advertising is not false or misleading.[11]

Though Internet gambling operations have also used traditional media,[12] most use the Internet as their primary medium to reach customers. Internet providers and users face a practical problem in finding one another, and search engines have been developed to address this problem. Search engines potentially provide access to available content without special costs or charges to the indexed sites, but the crowded marketplace has made this process somewhat cumbersome. The search term *casino* provides millions of "hits" on a typical search engine. The industry has therefore had to resort to more costly methods of targeting potential customers.

As previously noted, pay-for-listing services in major search engines provide one approach to distinguish an Internet casino from its competition. In a typical pay-for-listing arrangement, competitors submit bids to search engine providers for the privilege of a preeminent listing in search results associated with specified key words. These bids commit the site to pay the host a stated amount per click-through to the bidder's site. Unlike ads in broadcast or print media, where an approximation of the number of potential readers or listeners may be available but actual contact with the ad is unknown, click-through measurements provide a reasonably accurate indication of actual consumer interest.

However, a click-through does not necessarily consummate a customer relationship. Thus, the online casino continues to bear some risk. Assuming a rate of $14.97 per click-through, the casino would pay $14,970 to the advertiser for each thousand click-throughs. In order for that casino to be profitable, click-throughs would have to generate player relationships that would generate gaming losses to cover this customer acquisition cost plus other operational costs. Thus, for example, average losses of one hundred dollars per account would require a response rate of at least 150 customers per thousand click-throughs or 15 percent, in order to cover the advertising cost. As losses or response rates increase above these levels, profitability may be possible.

Predicting profitability based on the willingness to pay customer acquisition costs in an online business is hazardous, as many online firms that fit this profile failed during early phases of e-commerce applications on the Internet. However, regardless of whether these ads are profitable for the online casinos, they provide revenue to the online advertiser. In 2004, Yahoo! Inc. experienced record profits, which it attributed in part to online advertising.[13] While it is uncertain how much revenue it generated from casinos, the trend toward online advertising generally presents a picture of unrelenting growth. Reported earnings for 2005 indicate that online advertising generated $1.32 billion for Yahoo!—a 39 percent increase over 2004.[14]

In addition to paid placements, online casinos have a variety of other means to reach their Internet customers. Links to casinos through other Web sites provide another option for reaching casino customers. In these relationships, the online casino may offer the owner of a referring Web site a portion of the revenues or net winnings generated through their patrons.[15] In this manner, the online casino may acquire customers without a significant up-front payment, as in the case of a paid placement in a search engine. Of course, such an arrangement may pose other risks, including the monitoring and enforcement of the payment terms, which would be left to the site owners.

"Pop-up" advertising has also become a popular means for online casinos to advertise on the Internet. Despite annoying many Internet users to the point of developing blocking software as a means of self-help, they are apparently effective in attracting customers by matching and cross-selling similar content-based interests. For example, online gaming sites sometimes utilize adult entertainment themes to build upon the affinity of patrons for sex and gambling—not unlike their counterparts in Las Vegas who match sexually charged entertainment productions with their gambling operations. Pop-up ads for online casinos have even been reported to be found on a Web site designed to help compulsive gamblers.[16] Though this pop-up ad would undoubtedly reach the type of customer an online casino longs for (at least from an economic perspective), the placement certainly raises questions about social responsibility and the obligations that government may impose on gambling operators for the good of the public.

Licensing issues affect online casinos much like they affect their traditional counterparts. However, differences in the potential customer base of an online casino, as well as differences in the business model, affect the scope and impact of licensing decisions. The online gambling industry is currently located outside of the United States, and the economic interests of foreign governments hosting these operations are often at odds with the interests of the country from which patrons are likely to come. As one analyst has pointed out,

> The Internet gambling industry can be an attractive source of export earnings, with minimal infrastructure requirements. Additionally, the social cost of gambling is exported as the consequences of gambling addiction and problem gambling are bourne by the community in which the gambler lives. This can be an attractive proposition for those countries providing the access to online gambling and a troubling one for those supplying the gamblers.[17]

Licensing officials in jurisdictions with traditional casinos have some incentives to examine the operational impacts on local populations when determining the conditions for licensing. These concerns about community effects also provide incentives for casino operators to behave responsibly, to the extent that they depend on government cooperation for the purpose of renewing those licenses. Internet operations designed to attract foreign patrons have diminished interests in these areas. For example, it is doubtful that Internet operations will make any significant contributions toward social costs or community betterment affecting their patrons. Even cooperative advertising efforts to warn about problem gambling behaviors among online patrons would not be expected. In the current online environment, such efforts are simply not good for business.[18]

A NEED FOR REGULATION?

Gambling patrons also have economic interests that are integral to their participation in the online marketplace. The extent to which government regulation plays a role in ensuring patron security is an interesting, yet undeveloped, question. With traditional casinos, regulation provides an indication that games are being played fairly and that the casino is financially capable of paying off a winning bet. Other physical cues of reliability may also be available, such as the ability to watch dealers perform their tasks and to witness other patrons winning jackpots. In a traditional casino, not only do these cues indicate that the patron is getting his or her money's worth, but they also contribute to an atmosphere of excitement that may loosen a patron's purse strings.

Similar physical cues are generally unavailable online, as players are relegated to a private, computer-based experience. However, sophisticated online players may also access other sources of information. Here, the Internet's capacity for efficient information sharing may provide additional indications about the reliability of an online casino, which might even be used as a substitute for government regulation. Online patrons can share information in user groups, which provide an informal basis for comparing anecdotal Internet gambling experiences. For example, message boards at sites such as Winneronline.com provide a means for disgruntled players to share their concerns about nonpayment for a winning account.[19] Public relations representatives from online casinos have also been known to frequent such boards to address the problems raised by patrons.

Online patrons may also be able to access sites that are specifically devoted to sharing information about online casino payouts. Independent accounting firms such as PricewaterhouseCoopers provide audit services to casinos. This public attestation function is designed to bolster marketplace reliance on a secure and fair online gaming experience.[20] Web sites may also rank online casinos based on their payout rates.[21] However, it is up to the patron to determine whether these rates are accurate. Assuming disclosures are accurate, then the online player may even have an advantage over players in traditional casinos, which often do not advertise these rates.

Sports-betting sites avoid some concerns about fairness because the standards for winning and losing are readily available and accessible to patrons from reliable third-party sources. Thus, the online sports bettor need only concern himself or herself with the viability of the enterprise with whom the bet is placed; concerns about whether the electronic deck is stacked or the roulette wheel is rigged are not relevant, thus providing another level of security to the player. This added security, coupled with pervasive popular interest in sports and the belief that superior sports knowledge may provide an advantage, perhaps helps to account for the popularity of online sports betting.

Online patrons who rely on information-based monitoring are placing trust in private sources rather than in government-backed regulators. Given the information transparency that is possible in the online marketplace and the availability of private attestation functions, it is a fair question to ask whether government regulation would truly add to the reliability of online games. However, in the event of the financial failure of an online gambling firm, the player relying on private ordering principles would be well advised to be diversified. The prospects of pursuing claims in foreign courts may well prove daunting to most players, who would likely choose to cut their losses and move on.

The psychological profile of the online gambler is likely to involve a significant risk-taking component, which may limit the practical impact of inquiries into the nature and extent of government protections. Despite the potential risks, some gamblers seem intent on using online casinos without regard to their local legal status or to whether an effective means of government regulation and oversight exists among the many nations that permit some form of online gaming.

FEDERAL GOVERNMENT EFFORTS TO CONTROL ONLINE GAMBLING

Congress's tepid efforts to control sports betting in the Professional and Amateur Sports Protection Act, discussed in chapter 9, suggest the possibility that the federal government may possess a similarly limited commitment to preventing online gambling. Though critics have raised concerns about the protection of minors in the online forum, the increased social costs from online gambling, and even psychological harms from the potentially addictive character of video-based gambling activities, a comprehensive legislative solution has not been forthcoming.

This legislative failure may be attributed, in part, to the difficulty of enforcing what laws we currently have against online gambling. Even assuming that legislative goals can be identified, implementing legislation in an environment with jurisdictional as well as technological complexity presents formidable challenges.

THE FEDERAL GOVERNMENT STRIKES: PROSECUTION OF JAY COHEN

One of the most visible prosecution efforts affecting an international Internet gaming enterprise involves the case of *United States v. Cohen*.[22] This case has garnered significant international attention because of the application of U.S. laws to an individual conducting a business that is legally operating in a foreign country. In 1996, Jay Cohen left his position as a market maker at a San Francisco firm that traded in options and derivatives for an alternative risk-driven career as an international bookmaker. He became the president of the World Sports Exchange (WSE), a firm that began a sports-betting operation in the tiny Caribbean nation of Antigua and Barbuda.

Antigua and Barbuda are two small Caribbean islands with a combined population of about seventy thousand residents. According to the CIA's *World Factbook,* only about five thousand residents had Internet access as of 2001,[23] but that figure doubled to ten thousand in 2002, the latest year for which estimates are available.[24] Despite apparently limited Internet usage among Antigua natives, the island has nevertheless become a haven for Internet gaming firms. In 2001, the Antiguan government established a Free Trade and Processing Zone, which created a regulatory and tax structure that proved attractive for other firms interested in offering Internet gaming services. However, the WSE was ahead of the curve in choosing to begin its operations in Antigua before these incentives were enacted. The fact that gambling was legal in Antigua and that Antigua was also connected to the United States by an undersea fiber-optic cable (thus assuring Internet connectivity even during a hurricane) probably influenced its locational decision.[25]

WSE targeted customers in the United States by advertising in various media, including radio, newspaper, television, and the Internet. Customers who responded could set up accounts to bet with WSE via telephone or Internet. After depositing at least three hundred dollars via wire transfer into an account located in Antigua, the customer was allowed to instruct WSE to make bets on sporting events using those funds. Average accounts ran from one thousand to three thousand dollars, though some deposited as much as thirty thousand dollars.[26] WSE profited from a 10 percent commission on each wager.[27]

The prospects of Internet-based sports wagering proved attractive in the marketplace, as WSE had over sixteen hundred customers after its first year of operation. A *Wall Street Journal* story in April 1997 examined Cohen's new business venture, providing readers with an explanation of the business and a Web site address for potential customers and curiosity seekers to find out more.[28] Customers responded with gusto, including many from the United States. By November 1998, WSE had received over sixty thousand telephone calls from the United States.[29]

Unfortunately for Cohen, the media attention that proved so good for business also attracted the attention of law enforcement authorities. FBI agents in New York opened accounts and placed bets with WSE both by phone and by Internet.[30] On the basis of these contacts, Cohen was arrested and indicted for offenses in violation of the Wire Act, 18 U.S.C. § 1084(a). In particular, Cohen was charged with "(1) transmission in interstate or foreign commerce of bets or wagers; (2) transmission of a wire communication which entitles the recipient to receive money or credit as a result of bets or wagers, and (3) information assisting in the placement of bets or wagers."[31] He was ultimately convicted and sentenced to twenty-one months in prison.

Enforcement of laws against Internet gaming involves more than discovering and proving the elements of a crime. The government must establish personal jurisdiction over the defendant in order to exact a criminal punishment, and Jay Cohen squarely presented this problem. Although he was a U.S. citizen, the government could not reach him as long as he resided in Antigua. Instead of remaining in Antigua and evading the risk of prosecution, Cohen chose to surrender himself to authorities and to challenge the underlying basis for a violation of the Wire Act.

Unfortunately for Cohen, his challenge to the application of the Wire Act proved unsuccessful. Among other things, Cohen argued that he was entitled to protection under a safe harbor provision in the Wire Act, which provided in part that

> [n]othing in this section shall be construed to prevent the transmission in interstate or foreign commerce of information for use in news reporting of sporting events or contests, or for the transmission of information assisting in the placing of bets or wagers on a sporting event or contest from a State or foreign country where betting on that sporting event or contest is legal into a State or foreign country in which such betting is legal.[32]

Cohen argued that customers were only transmitting information and that the bet or wager was actually placed in Antigua.[33] However, the court found that the customers were indeed placing bets from the United States.[34] The trial judge's instruction to the jury explicitly referenced either telephone or Internet transmissions as being within the scope of the Wire Act.[35] Moreover, it was quite clear that such betting was illegal under New York law, and that provided a sufficient basis to find that he was not within the scope of the safe harbor.

Cohen's case also clarified that using telephone or Internet connections to transmit betting information could result in a violation of the Wire Act. Though Cohen had argued that he did not transmit information but merely received it, the court was unpersuaded.

> Cohen established two forms of wire facilities, internet and telephone, which he marketed to the public for the express purpose of transmitting bets and betting information. Cohen subsequently received such transmissions from customers, and, in turn, sent such transmissions back to those customers in various forms, including in the form of acceptances and confirmation. No matter what spin he puts on "transmission," his conduct violated the statute.[36]

Cohen was one of fourteen people indicted by federal prosecutors for offshore online gambling operations.[37] However, his case became a celebrated cause for the offshore betting community. Cohen petitioned the U.S. Supreme Court for review, and that petition was supported by the Antiguan government, which filed an amicus brief in support of Cohen's petition. Moreover, as discussed subsequently, the Antiguan government also chose to use the U.S. government's position in this case as a basis for challenging U.S. compliance with its treaty obligations involving international trade, which remains an ongoing dispute.

Though Cohen's case is significant, the language of the Wire Act may nevertheless impose limits on the federal law enforcement efforts directed toward Internet gambling. The operative provision of the Wire Act, 18 U.S.C. § 1084(a), states in relevant part:

> Whoever being engaged in the business of betting or wagering knowingly uses a wire communication facility for the transmission in interstate or foreign commerce of bets or wagers or information assisting in the placing of bets or wagers on any sporting event or contest, or for the transmission of a wire communication which entitles the recipient to receive money or credit as a result of bets or wagers, or for information assisting in the placing of bets or wagers, shall be fined under this title or imprisoned not more than two years, or both.[38]

First, the language of the Wire Act suggests that only those engaged in the business of placing bets are affected. It does not address the casual gambler, who might utilize the Internet to engage in online casino gambling.[39] Targeting casual gambling behavior on a large scale may be an unwise use of limited federal prosecution resources. However, the potential for federal enforcement of laws against Internet gambling may well deter some patrons from the activity. Any deterrent effect is nullified if the public knows that no basis for prosecution exists.[40]

Second, the scope of the Wire Act may be further limited by its reference to wagers "on any sporting event or contest." The Fifth Circuit has recently concluded that the Wire Act does not apply to casino gaming on the Internet because such wagering does not involve a "sporting event or contest."[41] The Fifth Circuit agreed with the rationale of the federal district court, which found that a "plain reading of the statutory language" supported by the legislative history required this result.[42]

However, this reading is contestable. The language "on any sporting event or contest" modifies the first appearance of "bets or wagers" in section 1084(a), but "bets or wagers" appears two more times in that statute without the limiting language. While it is true that the legislative history, which extends back to 1961, focused on sports betting, this predates the advent of the Internet and its potential to bring other kinds of gambling to remote bettors. A New York state court has agreed that the Wire Act does apply to online casino gaming, based in part on the broader purpose of preventing unlawful gambling.[43]

Members of Congress have recognized this potential deficiency in the language of the Wire Act, but proposed legislation to amend it has failed.[44] A failure to adopt an amendment does not necessarily mean that Congress approves of Internet casinos. The scope and extent of the current version of the Wire Act may yet be tested in other jurisdictions. As discussed subsequently, the Justice Department has used the threat of prosecution under "aiding and abetting" theories to address ancillary business participation in Internet casino gambling. Nevertheless, it is true that the current language does present some uncertainty and that Congress has yet to pass a comprehensive legal solution.

The international gaming community remains very concerned about the prospects of prosecution for Internet wagering activities such as those in *Cohen*. An amicus curiae brief in support of Cohen's petition for certiorari in the U.S. Supreme Court filed by the Antiguan government stated in part:

> The Second Circuit's decision would criminalize not only the activities of American citizens in Antigua, but also activities of non-American citizens engaged in the betting or wagering business from Antigua, suppliers for that business, and even Antiguan governmental officials not protected by the doctrine of Sovereign Immunity.
>
> Should the petition for certiorari not be granted and the present decision be allowed to stand, it would have a very negative impact on the Antiguan economy and hamper the country's efforts to create strong regulatory controls over all interactive wagering.[45]

Since the Supreme Court denied certiorari in this case, it remains to be seen whether the ultimate impact on Antigua will be as negative as predicted. As discussed subsequently, the World Trade Organization (WTO) proceedings involving Antigua provided one way for this nation to strike back against U.S. policy using trade laws. First, however, we look at what tools lie in the law enforcement arsenals of the states.

THE STATES STRIKE: INTERNET ENFORCEMENT EFFORTS

State laws may also affect the legality of Internet betting operations. Like their federal counterpart, state governments also face jurisdictional constraints. Finding an appropriate nexus between the criminal activity and the state is typically not the problem, but enforcing a judgment over the operator of an offending Web site may present an insurmountable practical barrier to effective legal governance. As a result, there are few reported cases in which state governments seek to prosecute Internet gaming operations.

People v. World Interactive Gaming Corporation[46] is a notable case in this area because of the state's ability to overcome those jurisdictional limitations. The World Interactive Gaming Corporation (WIGC) was incorporated in Delaware but maintained an office in New York. Through a wholly owned Antiguan subsidiary, Golden Chips Casino, Inc. (GCC), WIGC operated an Internet casino pursuant to a license from the Antiguan government. GCC promoted this casino on the Internet and through advertising in a national gambling magazine, and New York residents viewed these ads. Like its sports-betting counterpart, the WSE, the GCC required its Internet casino users to wire funds to an Antiguan bank account, from which bets would ultimately be made.

In June 1998, the attorney general's office downloaded gambling software from GCC's Antiguan Web site, and the following month they began placing bets. The GCC software asked users to enter their permanent address. If the user reported an address in a state that permitted land-based gambling, such as Nevada, the software granted permission for the user to gamble in virtual games, which included slot machines, roulette, and blackjack. If the user reported an address in New York, where land-based casino gambling was illegal, permission was not granted. However, New York users who were denied access could easily circumvent this restriction by changing the registration to Nevada, since the software did not monitor actual locations.

On the basis of this activity, the attorney general sought an injunction against WIGC to prevent it from "running any aspect of their Internet gambling business within the State of New York." WIGC challenged this action on jurisdictional grounds, but this challenge failed. WIGC managed this business from its offices in New York. It made administrative decisions and did computer research for the business in New York. It also worked with a New York–based design firm, Imajix Studios, to design graphics for the Web site. Even if its offices had not been in New York, these systematic and purposeful contacts with the state would have been sufficient to satisfy jurisdictional requirements.[47]

As for its subsidiary, GCC, personal jurisdiction would ordinarily be more difficult to establish. If GCC were treated as a separate legal entity, the state would be required to show that it had sufficient contacts with New York to support jurisdiction. However, in this case, such a showing was obviated by the court's determination that GCC's corporate form would not be respected on the ground that it was a "mere agent, department, or alter ego" of WIGC.[48] Here, WIGC "completely dominated" its subsidiary. The GCC Web site had been "purchased" by WIGC, which also provided administration services. GCC's top employees were hired by, and reported to, WIGC. Work on the servers that hosted the Web site was also done pursuant to contracts with service providers that were maintained by WIGC.

Thus, WIGC not only ignored corporate formalities but also provided support for the gaming operations of its subsidiary to an extent that it could be categorized as an agent of that subsidiary. It was relatively easy to find that WIGC was guilty of promoting gambling in violation of New York law. In fact, the court noted that violation of New York law had even occurred before any New York resident wagered on the GCC Web site, to the extent that their conduct in creating and soliciting patronage for unlawful games "materially aids [unlawful] gambling activity."[49] The fact that Internet gaming was legal in Antigua was not a defense, as these activities occurred in New York.

A similar case was also presented in Minnesota during the early years of Internet casinos. In *State v. Granite Gate Resorts, Inc.,*[50] the attorney general filed a complaint against a Nevada corporation and its principal officer, alleging that these defendants engaged in deceptive trade practices, false advertising, and consumer fraud based on designing and hosting an advertisement for an online wagering service based in Belize. Although the corporation and officer were both domiciled in Nevada, the state of Minnesota asserted jurisdiction based on the nature and extent of Internet contacts with Minnesota residents. The company's Web site advertised an online wagering service that was soon to become operational as "a legal way to bet on sporting events from anywhere in the world."[51] In addition, it explained how to subscribe to the service and provided a form to enroll on a mailing list and a toll-free number for Internet users to contact them. At least one Minnesota resident became part of the mailing list, and computers in Minnesota contacted the Web site several hundred times.

The Minnesota Court of Appeals concluded that the state had jurisdiction in these circumstances. Based on the quantity and quality of the contacts with the state through the Web site and the strong interests of the state in enforcing its consumer protection laws and regulating gambling, the court found that the jurisdictional threshold had been met. This meant that the state could proceed, imposing injunctive relief as well as civil penalties against the foreign corporation and its officer.

Other courts have similarly found personal jurisdiction over an online gambling operation based on contacts with state residents on interactive Web sites.[52] Though a purely passive Web site might not pass muster under current case law dealing with Internet jurisdiction, the typical casino gaming site would indeed have engaged in contracts with state residents over the Internet and in doing so would repeatedly transmit computer information to that jurisdiction. These activities would generally be sufficient to support a finding of personal jurisdiction, thus potentially subjecting the Internet casino to legally enforceable judgments.

The potential extent of jurisdictional reach is also illustrated in *Alitalia-*

Linee Aeree Italiane v. Casinoalitalia.com,[53] a case involving a trademark infringement claim against an Internet casino. Alitalia Airlines, an Italian corporation, brought suit in a federal district court in Virginia against an Internet casino operator based in the Dominican Republic. Alitalia alleged that the Internet casino had infringed its trademark as a result of the use of its corporate name in its Web site. Alitalia claimed that such usage created a false impression that the airline was supporting online gambling. It also claimed that such usage further tarnished its mark because the word *casino* meant *brothel* in Italian, thus suggesting to Italian-speaking users that Alitalia may be in another tawdry business.

At the heart of the case was the basis for personal jurisdiction in a Virginia court. Other than operating the Web site, which did indeed reach five Virginia customers, the defendant corporation had no other contacts with Virginia, as its operations were based entirely in the Dominican Republic. Nevertheless, the court found that these limited contacts were sufficient to provide personal jurisdiction over the site: "Defendant's contacts with these residents are sufficient to put the defendant on notice that it is purposefully directing its activities at Virginia, and that it should therefore foresee being haled into court in this forum."[54]

Though states may well have a legal foundation for pursuing online casinos that violate state gambling laws, such efforts are nevertheless likely to be fruitless in many cases. In the *Granite Gate Resorts* and *World Interactive Gaming* cases, the defendants were both incorporated in the United States. Thus, a valid judgment could potentially be enforced against assets and persons located in the United States through other courts with jurisdiction over those assets and persons. However, a well-advised Internet casino operator could easily avoid the mistakes that were made in those cases by incorporating in a foreign jurisdiction and maintaining operational control outside of the United States. The fact that there are no more recent reported cases involving state attorneys general seeking relief from domestic Internet casino operations suggests that the Internet gaming marketplace has indeed learned these simple lessons and has avoided similar mistakes.

In a case like *Alitalia,* the defendant was located in the Dominican Republic and apparently limited its base of operations accordingly. Enforcement of any judgment that affected operations in a foreign country would ordinarily require cooperation from a foreign government, which would have the power to compel the defendant to comply. Absent a treaty provision to aid in that enforcement, the chances of success would be doubtful. Thus, the domestic judgment would effectively have no impact on a foreign corporation operating an Internet casino site, as long as that corporation and its operators stayed outside of the jurisdiction of the United States.

ANTICYBERSQUATTING CONSUMER PROTECTION ACT: IN REM THEORY

Alitalia involved a somewhat unusual situation because the applicable federal statute forming the basis for relief, the Anticybersquatting Consumer Protection Act (ACPA), provides that if the plaintiff cannot get personal jurisdiction over the owner of that domain name, it could bring suit under a theory of in rem jurisdiction (i.e., jurisdiction based on the location of the property—the domain name) in a federal district court where the domain name is registered.[55] Although this kind of suit would not be effective for monetary damages, it could provide relief in the form of either cancellation or transfer of ownership of the infringing domain name.[56] Since the entity that controlled the registration of that Web site, Network Solutions, was a corporation domiciled in Virginia,[57] this relief would be effective without any concerns about enforcing a judgment in the Dominican Republic.

Although the ACPA is narrowly tailored to address the problems of trademark infringement, its approach of dealing with trademark infringement could potentially provide a framework for addressing Internet casino gaming enforcement. If Congress wished to impose a significant barrier to Internet gambling, it could enact a similar provision that would allow an in rem action against the offending Web site operating the online casino. Alternatively, to the extent that personal jurisdiction is proper based on contacts with domestic gamblers, a court might award a remedy of canceling or transferring the ownership of an offending domain name. Thus, state or federal government officials could effectively wrestle away control of Web sites that violate federal or state gambling laws through doing business with U.S. customers.

Current technology does permit Web sites to block access to patrons with Internet addresses in a particular country. Such technology is becoming increasingly important in addressing problems of content that may violate local laws, as was recently litigated in connection with challenges by the French government to Internet content offered by Yahoo! involving Nazi materials.[58] Such an approach might also provide an effective means to address a gaming operation that unlawfully does business with patrons within the United States, failing to implement good-faith efforts to block access to patrons in countries where Internet gaming is illegal.

Of course, there are significant political barriers to this approach. The Internet community would probably become apoplectic over a single nation's attempt to wrestle away control over Web sites based on the location of domain name registrars within their own jurisdiction. Such an approach has some intuitive appeal as a means of restoring domestic sovereignty over the scope of legal conduct in the gaming area, but this means of enforcement may also have unintended consequences. Internet domain name registrars might simply choose to locate in other countries that do not share a concern about the violation of domestic gambling laws in the United States. For example, a registrar could locate in a jurisdiction friendly to Internet gambling and register domain names for Internet casinos under its own geographical domain name system, thus foiling any attempts to affect their ownership via court judgments from the United States. An international treaty may be required in order to deal effectively with the enforcement issues presented by Internet casino operations.

TARGETING ADVERTISING AND FINANCE

Although government actors may directly challenge Internet gambling operations, the viability of Internet gambling operations may also be affected by indirect efforts. Legal challenges to the mechanisms for Internet payments and to advertising and support structures have made it more difficult to manage and operate a viable Internet gambling operation. In the long run, these efforts may prove most effective in reducing, though not eliminating, Internet gambling.

As discussed previously, advertising is a critical part of the business model for Internet gambling. Firms that provide advertising, whether in the form of paid placements on search engines, banner ads, or other more traditional forms, thus participate indirectly in the lucre of the Internet gambling industry, even though such gambling may not be legal in a particular jurisdiction. Although First Amendment protections extend to commercial speech, such protections do not extend to speech that facilitates the violation of federal or state laws.[59]

Federal prosecutors reportedly convened a grand jury investigation of Internet gambling that resulted in the issuance of subpoenas to broadcasters, publishers, and Web sites that advertise for offshore operations.[60] Prosecutors alleged that advertisers were "aiding and abetting" the violation of antigambling laws. Using a similar theory, federal marshals seized $3.2 million from Discovery Communications, a television and media company that owns the Travel Channel. These funds were payment for thirty-second commercials to be run in a six-month period during broadcasts of the World Poker Tour for ParadisePoker.com, an online poker site.[61]

Although the legal foundation for these tactics is far from certain, the potential for adverse legal ramifications has apparently affected major advertisers. Internet search engines Yahoo!, Google, and Lycos have agreed to stop running advertising for online casinos,[62] although Yahoo! indicated that it would continue to run these ads in markets outside of the United States. Major broadcasters such as Clear Channel Communications and Infinity Broadcasting have also stopped taking online gambling ads. Electronic Arts, an online video game provider, has followed suit, citing the potential for future "policy and legal" problems for the company.[63] Such actions are likely to make it more difficult for Internet gambling enterprises to reach their customers. However, determined patrons will probably be undeterred and will find other ways to access these sites through foreign sites providing links and advertising.

Legal challenges affecting the financing of Internet gambling activities may also threaten the growth of Internet gambling firms. Understanding the nature of a credit card transaction is an important prerequisite to understanding how payments are made and the allocation of payment risks under various payment mechanisms.

A credit card transaction typically involves several intermediaries between the merchant (casino) and the cardholder (patron).[64] Card associations, such as Visa and Mastercard, make a branded product available for issuance by financial institutions and provide rules for members of the association that affect the terms of card use as well as the payment rights and obligations of participating members.

Financial institutions such as banks issue credit cards to their customers, thus initiating a credit relationship with the cardholder. They may set credit limits based on credit information that the customer provides, and they may perform the billing and collection services for the cardholder, though often this role is outsourced to a third-party processor. The issuing institution thus makes money by extending credit and earning interest on any unpaid balances. It also makes money through sharing in the fees generated from merchants who receive payments through the customer's cards. Its primary risk derives from cardholders who default—a risk that can be managed by using credit filters and raising interest rates on unpaid balances.

Financial institutions may also be involved in the capacity of enrolling merchants to participate in the card payment service. These institutions, known as "acquiring banks," are effectively extending credit to the merchants. Merchants agree to receive payment from customers through means of the credit card and to process payment information through an established protocol. Merchants submit customer requests for credit through an extensive computer network to a processor, which in turn contacts the issuing bank for a determination of whether to approve credit for the customer. The merchant then sends records of its approved transactions to the acquirer, which in turn credits the merchant's account for the total amount of billings less an allowance based on a negotiated discount.

This discount from the merchant is intended to cover the expenses associated with payment and collection from the issuing bank, as well as other processing costs. Those expenses may be significant, particularly if the merchant is involved in a business where customers ultimately express dissatisfaction and dispute the charges. Gambling and pornography are notorious businesses for dissatisfied customers, particularly when an unsuspecting spouse has found out about secret online exploits. To the extent that a merchant engages in fraud or otherwise fails to deliver a product or service purchased with a credit card, a charge-back process occurs, which ultimately may reach the merchant. Herein lies an important dimension of risk for the acquiring financial institution: some merchants close their shops and flee the jurisdiction, leaving the acquirer to ultimately bear the loss.

This system generally works very well for consumers, who can effectively purchase with greater confidence by using the delay in time between purchase and payment on their account to their advantage. This time delay allows the customer to determine whether a merchant has held up his or her end of the bargain, to withhold payment, and to dispute the transaction under the card association rules. Merchants also benefit from this system, to the extent that it facilitates payment and increases sales opportunities.

Though other forms of payment may exist for a remote seller, such as wire transfers, checks, or money orders, each alternative form has its drawbacks. Wire transfers can result in fairly quick transfers of cash, but once that cash is gone, the advantage is clearly on the side of the transferee. Thus, a customer with doubts about the integrity of the merchant would probably be hesitant to use this method. Moreover, wire transfers are typically relatively expensive, making them unsuitable for frequent small consumer transactions.

Checks and money orders may be less expensive to process, but they may also involve considerable delay. There are also payment risks to consider. From the customer's perspective, a money order involves an immediate monetary outlay. A check may allow time for a stop payment order, though such an effort is certainly not as consumer friendly as under the dispute provisions of the credit card. Merchants also face payment risks, which are rooted in the creditworthiness of the customer. Though the merchant may compensate by waiting to deliver until a check has cleared, this entails further delay and hinders sales growth. A credit card, on the other hand, gives the customer the luxury of delayed evaluation of the transaction to ensure that the merchant is delivering what was promised, coupled with the speed and assurances of creditworthiness that the merchant desires.

The credit card industry is well acquainted with the risks associated with illicit operations, particularly those involving pornography or gambling. Acquiring financial institutions in the United States that seek Internet-based merchants typically include provisions that shun operations dealing in pornography or online gambling.[65] Offshore gambling operations that use credit cards often must establish relationships with foreign acquiring banks, which thus assume the credit risks associated with charge-backs and other defaults by merchants in the online gambling business.[66] The online payment service PayPal, which is sometimes used in lieu of credit card payments, includes provisions in its online user agreement that specifically preclude its use in connection with gambling and adult-oriented businesses.[67]

In addition to the risk of charge-backs, the possibility of legal liability on account of aiding and abetting an illegal operation is also presented. This concern is illustrated by recent litigation in which cardholders with Internet gambling losses brought a class action lawsuit against Mastercard, Visa, and the banks that issued their credit cards.[68] These plaintiffs alleged that the credit card companies and banks were part of a "worldwide gambling enterprise" with unnamed Internet casinos. By extending credit for gamblers and collecting on those debts, credit card companies had allegedly facilitated a criminal enterprise that violated federal and state criminal gambling laws. In particular, the plaintiffs alleged that such conduct constituted racketeering and unlawful collection of debt, which entitled them to civil remedies under the Racketeer Influenced and Corrupt Organizations Act (RICO).[69]

A claim of racketeering under RICO requires a showing of at least two predicate criminal acts based on either state or federal law.[70] Here, the plaintiffs alleged violations of the Wire Act, as well as violations of other federal provisions addressing mail and wire fraud. However, the court rejected these claims based on federal law. With regard to the Wire Act, the court limited its application to sports betting—conduct that was not pleaded in this case.[71] As for the fraud violations, it found that the plaintiffs failed to plead any fraudulent representations by the defendants in connection with any gambling activity.[72]

The plaintiffs also claimed that the defendants' conduct violated a Kansas criminal statute proscribing commercial gambling. The court ultimately considered two elements of that statute, which involved, "[f]or gain, becoming a custodian of anything of value bet or offered to be bet" and "[s]etting up for use or collecting the proceeds of any gambling device."[73] In this context, the particulars of Internet gambling worked in favor of the defendants, as the court found that the credit card companies did not violate these provisions.

In a typical transaction, the plaintiffs used their credit cards to purchase credits from the Internet casino prior to gambling. The credits are maintained in an account with the Internet casino, and the patron can access these credits for the purpose of placing bets. Losses are deducted from the account, but winnings are credited to the account. However, any net winnings are not credited to the patron's credit card but instead are paid by alternate mechanisms.[74]

Under these facts, the district court found that the extension of credit to the cardholder, in the form of purchasing credits, had occurred before any illegal gambling had occurred: "It is a temporal impossibility for the defendants to have completed their transaction with the plaintiff before he gambled and to then be prosecuted for collecting the proceeds of a gambling device, which can only take place after some form of gambling is completed."[75] Although an opinion of the Kansas attorney general found that placing bets from a computer in Kansas to an online casino would violate Kansas law, the court limited the scope of the legal violation to the activities of the plaintiffs and the online casinos, not to the activity of extending credit to the cardholder.[76] The Fifth Circuit agreed, noting that it was also impossible to "take custody" of a bet if the transaction with the credit card companies occurred before any bet was placed.[77]

Oddly, the facts in this case indicated that the ultimate charge on the cardholder's account did depend on the losses accrued. For example, one of the named plaintiffs, Thompson, had purchased $1,510 in credits using his Mastercard; he lost everything.[78] Bradley, the other named plaintiff, had purchased $16,445 in gambling credits, but his credit card billing statements showed only $7,048 in purchases at the casino.[79] This difference between purchases and billings suggests the possibility that the net result after winnings and losses was ultimately charged to his credit card. Otherwise, one would expect to see the charge of only $16,445 on his monthly statement. This also suggests that the amount ultimately paid by the cardholder to the issuing bank was determined after his gaming transactions had been completed. Though there were no net winnings, it strains credibility to believe that every transaction under the account was a losing transaction and that he lost only half the value of the account with no wins to offset those losses. No explanation of this factual discrepancy appears in the case.

The court's restrictive approach toward finding any violation of the Wire Act and applicable Kansas law helped to ensure that the credit card industry avoided significant financial liability as a result of Internet gambling losses in this case. Though the entire amount at stake is not stated in this litigation, two of the plaintiffs named in the litigation had lost several thousand dollars. Those similarly situated might number in the thousands, presenting substantial claims had this litigation been successful.

Even though the plaintiffs in this matter did not achieve a legal victory, the case nevertheless sent a strong cautionary message to the credit card industry. If the gamblers had been located in a state with more comprehensive antigambling laws, or if violations of the Wire Act could be clearly proven through involvement with Internet-based sports betting, it is plausible that a credit card company and the issuing bank could indeed face liability under RICO. Moreover, the concept of "aiding and abetting" violation of state laws through extending credit might lend itself to other plaintiffs seeking to establish liability, particularly when the identity of the Internet casino and the involvement in illegal gambling are known to those involved in processing these payments.[80] The Web site maintained by the Kansas attorney general stated in part in 2004:

> [P]ersons or organizations who knowingly assist Internet gambling organizations in any unlawful activity may themselves be held liable for that unlawful activity. Thus, for example, Internet access providers and credit card companies that continue to provide services to gambling organizations after notice that the activities of the organizations are illegal would be subject to accomplice liability.[81]

Legislation to cut off the mechanisms for funding Internet gambling has been before Congress but has not yet been brought to a final vote. The Internet Gambling Funding Prohibition Act was reported out of the Senate Committee on Banking, Housing, and Urban Affairs on October 27, 2003, which unanimously recommended passage. As explained in the committee report:

> The bill would prohibit gambling businesses from accepting credit cards, checks, or other bank instruments from gamblers who bet over the Internet. To accomplish this purpose, the bill would require designated payment systems to establish policies and procedures designed to identify and prevent transactions in connection with Internet gambling. Most financial institutions have some capacity to identify and block restricted transactions for the purposes of compliance with other laws, such as those relating to U.S. economic sanctions programs and money laundering prevention. Some participants in these payment networks have already voluntarily established policies to prohibit these types of transactions. Thus, it is anticipated that the costs of compliance imposed by this bill would be small. In addition, to the extent that individual gamblers will be precluded from using bank instruments, financial entities may experience some cost savings as they will be less likely to have gamblers defaulting on debts incurred.[82]

Although this bill was never enacted into law, the industry is apparently taking the concerns raised by the bill into account.

THE INTERNATIONAL GAMING INDUSTRY STRIKES BACK: WTO CHALLENGE

Further complexity in the international dimensions of Internet gambling arose in 2003, when the government of the Caribbean nation of Antigua and Barbuda brought a complaint against the United States before the WTO, arguing that the United States had unfairly discriminated against the online gambling services offered by Antiguan firms. Antigua claimed that the United States was in violation of the General Agreement on Trade in Services (GATS). In particular, Antigua claimed:

> The central, regional or local authorities of the United States allow numerous operators of United States origin to offer all types of gambling and betting services in the United States (sometimes via exclusive rights or monopolistic structures). There appears to be no possibility for foreign operators, however, to obtain an authorization to supply gambling and betting services from outside the United States.[83]

Antigua submitted an extensive list of federal and state statutes, as well as other legal sources, including attorney general opinions and cases such as *United States v. Cohen* and *World Interactive Gaming,* discussed previously.[84] It claimed that these sources together operated as "measures" that completely prohibited the remote provision of gambling services by a foreign operator. They further alleged that this prohibition violated obligations under GATS, to which the United States was a signatory nation.

The United States' initial response to these claims involved rather interesting legal posturing. Among other things, the United States' request for a preliminary ruling from the WTO panel contended that, as a technical matter, some of the authorities cited by the Antiguans were technically not measures at all, since they did not constitute legal instruments with functional lives of their own.[85] Thus, for example, a state attorney general opinion or an opinion of courts inferior to the U.S. Supreme Court was arguably not sufficient to serve as a measure under this standard.

More significant, however, was the United States' position that Antigua's bare citation of state and federal laws applicable in the United States, even if they were "measures," failed to meet its burden of proof in showing that these laws and regulations effected a "total prohibition" in violation of the

GATS obligations. Here, the United States used the complexity of its laws involving Internet gambling to its advantage; Antigua would be forced to explain how those laws created such a total ban. The United States asserted that "Antigua must not be permitted to hide behind the excuse that U.S. law is supposedly too complex and opaque; Antigua and its two outside law firms are certainly capable of identifying and attempting to establish a prima facie case as to specific measures if they choose to do so."[86]

This was an obligation that Antigua did not readily embrace. As it pointed out, the state of law in the United States was a matter of "significant debate within the United States legal community."[87] Moreover, Antigua recognized that it was caught on the horns of a dilemma.

> If [Antigua] were to have listed the Wire Act only there is little doubt that, at the stage when the United States needed to implement any recommendations and rulings resulting from this dispute, the United States would have taken the position that it needed only to disapply or adapt the Wire Act and could continue to apply other laws because these would have been outside the terms of reference of the Panel. This concern has been vindicated by the fact that the United States now adopts a very similar formalistic and obstructive approach in the Request.[88]

Thus, Antigua sought a more comprehensive solution based on the totality of effect of U.S. laws.

The Antiguan challenge also addressed the heart of the GATS treaty obligation: should gambling services be included within the scope of free trade commitments regarding "entertainment services (including theater, live bands and circus services)" and "other recreational services (except sporting)"?[89] The United States argued that remote gambling services were outside the scope of the ordinary meaning of these two terms. In fact, the exception of "sporting" could be viewed as an express elimination of gambling from the scope of this term, to the extent that the *Merriam-Webster's Collegiate Dictionary* defines *sporting* in part in relation to gambling.[90]

This position offered by the United States was arguably inconsistent with the dominant marketing practices of casino gaming operations in the United States. The gaming industry promotes its operations as involving entertainment and/or recreation. For example, the AGA's annual reports describe gambling in the same category as other entertainment options.[91]

Other countries, including eight European members of the WTO, specifically excluded gambling from this listing of services; the United States did not. Whether in hindsight the United States should have been expected to invoke a specific exclusion raises a provocative question: Was the cultural transformation of gambling from vice to entertainment sufficiently complete to hold the United States to a broader dimension for these terms? The United States devoted much of its submission to the historical, moral, religious, and practical justifications for treating gambling as a different matter than other services. On the other hand, Antigua argued about the nature and extent of gambling practices in the United States, which are indeed substantial.

Even if Antigua were to be sustained on this argument, however, the United States raised still other challenges for Antigua's position. Article XVII of GATS provides a basic rule according the same national treatment to domestic and foreign suppliers of scheduled services:

> In the sectors described in its Schedule, and subject to any conditions and qualifications set out therein, each Member shall accord to services and service suppliers of any other Member, in respect of all measures affecting the supply of services, treatment no less favourable than that it accords to its own like services and service suppliers.

Thus, to the extent that Antigua could show that the United States had adopted measures affecting the supply of "remote" gambling (i.e., accessible via the Internet or via telephone), were those measures effectively treating a foreign supplier differently from a domestic one? This question hinged on the extent to which Internet gambling was indeed the same as other forms of land-based gambling. If it was indeed a different product and both domestic and foreign providers are subject to the same restrictions on such remotely provided services, then Antigua would not have a viable claim.

The differences between remote gambling services and other gambling activities were briefly discussed in the first written submission of the United States, but still more extensive attention was directed to this issue in a second submission.[92] This submission went into considerable detail about operational and consumer characteristics, as well as the regulatory characteristics, which merit a distinction between remote and in-person gambling activities.

As for operational and consumer characteristics, the United States cited reports by consultants (including Bear Stearns) to the effect that Internet operations have different customers than land-based operations. In part, Internet customers choose this form of gambling because they want "the ability to indulge in gambling in seclusion without the stigma or effort required to go to a public gambling facility."[93] They also differ in psychological perceptions, including the motivation to gamble, physiological experiences, and socialization.[94] Thus, consumers perceive Internet gaming differently from in-person gambling experiences.

From a regulatory perspective, the United States also took the position that remotely provided gambling presents more significant threats than land-based operations in terms of organized crime, money laundering, and fraud.[95] Antigua attempted to address these issues through its own regulatory framework. However, such matters touching on national security would undoubtedly concern policymakers in the United States, who would not be content to entrust them to a foreign government, even a friendly one.

The public health dimension of online gambling also received attention from both sides. Though Antigua attempted to show that online gambling is no more addictive than other forms of gambling, the United States pointed to uncertainties about health effects posed by online play. For example, it cited the American Psychiatric Association's concerns about the dangers posed by the solitary nature of Internet gambling and the prospects of lengthy, uninterrupted play. However, even if Internet gambling was less addictive, the sheer potential magnitude of gambling in every location with an Internet connection raises the prospect of "an enormous growth in the opportunity for gambling and, consequently, for gambling addiction."[96]

Public health effects on minors posed a related threat. Whereas in-person contacts with casino gambling present many opportunities to detect and eliminate underage gambling, the online environment provides the possibility for minors to play online. The United States cited examples of child-oriented games licensed by the Antiguan government, which included "cartoon-like design, and childish iconography."[97] It also presented evidence that requiring identification through a credit card or debit card was not an effective means of preventing access by minors. Based on 1999 data, approximately 28 percent of minors between the ages of sixteen and twenty-two had at least one major credit card, and these figures were likely to understate current cardholders on account of extensive marketing efforts directed toward college students under the age of twenty-one.[98]

Finally, the United States also raised other arguments based on another provision of GATS, Article XIV, which provides several general exceptions.

> Subject to the requirement that such measures are not applied in a manner which would constitute a means of arbitrary or unjustifiable discrimination between countries where like conditions prevail, or a disguised restriction on trade in services, nothing in this Agreement shall be construed to prevent the adoption or enforcement by any Member of measures:
>
> (a) necessary to protect public morals or to maintain public order;
>
> (b) necessary to protect human, animal or plant life or health;
>
> (c) necessary to secure compliance with laws or regulations which are not inconsistent with the provisions of this Agreement including those relating to:
>
> > i. the prevention of deceptive or fraudulent practices or to deal with the effects of a default on services contracts; . . .
> >
> > ii. safety.

Given the extensive history of U.S. laws directed toward protecting the public morals and public order and the concerns about public health and safety raised by online gambling, the United States also alleged that, if it was found to have generally prohibited remote gambling, it should be allowed to do so within the scope of these exceptions. The fact that remote access allowed gambling into uncontrolled settings that are particularly accessible to children raised a significant concern about public order and public morals.[99] Moreover, the uncertain controls over offshore funds also "could pose a risk to national security from terror and/or criminal organizations."[100]

The WTO dispute resolution panel released its 273-page report on November 10, 2004,[101] but a confidential draft released to the parties reached major news media as early as March 2004.[102] The decision was generally unfavorable to the United States, though it failed to address some of the more interesting policy dimensions outlined previously. Instead, it focused on more narrow legal grounds and arcane matters of treaty interpretation. The panel found that the United States had indeed made commitments under Article XIV of GATS with regard to gambling, though it may well have done so inadvertently.[103] It also found that U.S. laws (including both federal and state provisions) failed to accord services of Antigua a position no less favorable than that allowed to domestic providers.[104] Oddly, the panel acknowledged that these laws "are designed so as to protect public morals or maintain public order," but it enigmatically concluded that the United States had failed to meet its burden to show that its laws "are necessary to protect public morals and/or public order."[105] Moreover, the United States had failed to show that its enforcement efforts were consistent with the requirements of its treaty obligations.[106] In particular, the panel pointed to off-track betting operations allowed for horse racing as allowing remote gambling via telephone or Internet.[107] The panel thus recommended that the United States make conforming changes in its laws.[108]

This result sent immediate tremors throughout the gaming industry, which wondered whether international competition through the Internet would soon become available in the United States.[109] The ruling also raised questions about unintended consequences of trade agreements, including state sovereignty over gambling within their borders. It is doubtful that most Americans would consider their state and local laws to be superseded by an international treaty obligation, over which their state legislators and governors would have no say whatsoever. Despite the considerable merits of global trade, the attempt to treat gambling as any other entertainment service arguably pushed beyond the current cultural sensibilities of most Americans, as well as threatened to undermine traditional regulatory structures for gambling.

Antigua's jubilation over the ruling proved short-lived, as the United States filed notice of appeal on January 7, 2005.[110] Antigua also appealed certain elements of the decision, and third-party submissions were also filed by other nations, including the European Community and Japan, which both supported the proposition that the United States had indeed made a commitment for free trade in gambling services.[111] The Appellate Body issued its decision on April 7, 2005, and this decision substantially pared back any impact of the panel decision.

First, the Appellate Body focused only on federal laws, ruling that Antigua had failed to make the prima facie case showing that state laws were inconsistent with GATS treaty obligations.[112] The Appellate Body found, however, that Antigua had made a prima facie case for inconsistency with regard to the federal Wire Act, the Travel Act, and the Illegal Gambling Business Act.[113] It also agreed with the panel that the United States had made a commitment with regard to trade in gambling under GATS.[114]

As for the applicable federal laws, the Appellate Body agreed with the panel that these laws implicated public morals and public order, but it reversed its decision that these laws were not "necessary to protect public morals or to maintain public order." The Appellate Body explained that the "necessary" requirement involves a balance between the effectiveness of the measures in accomplishing domestic ends and the restrictive impact of the measure on international trade.[115] As a general matter, the United States had the burden to put forth evidence of these public purposes, and Antigua as respondent had the burden to show a reasonably available means to these ends that does not restrain trade.[116]

In this context, the Appellate Body found that the United States had indeed shown a prima facie case that these measures were necessary, noting that the panel had also recognized the close connection between these laws and important societal interests. Antigua's alternative, on the other hand, consisted solely in proposed consultations with the United States, which the Appellate Body found to be insufficient as an alternative means of addressing these interests.[117]

Despite these rulings favoring the United States, the Appellate Body also found that the United States had potentially discriminated against foreign gaming service suppliers in one respect: it appeared to allow off-track betting on horse racing in certain situations, pursuant to the Interstate Horseracing Act.[118] Thus, despite a failure to show enforcement discrimination favoring domestic suppliers over foreign suppliers with regard to the Wire Act, Travel Act, and Interstate Gambling Business Act, the Interstate Horseracing Act presented a potential problem.

The manner of bringing U.S. law into conformity with GATS in this situation continues to be the subject of negotiations between the United States and Antigua. An arbitrator was appointed to help resolve the dispute.[119] It appears that the United States will not take the position of opening up the Internet freely to gambling interests. However, the manner of enforcing domestic laws against Internet gambling remains an important issue.

The WTO dispute highlights the need for careful attention to international agreements in the quest for solutions to conflicts arising from the use of the Internet. Cultural differences about the role of gambling in society undoubtedly deserve greater attention in specific treaty negotiations; the current approach of Antigua and the WTO apparently disregards these significant concerns in seeking to enter markets in the United States by a side door left open by trade negotiators. It also remains to be seen whether the concerns raised about public health, public morals (particularly of youth), public safety, and national security will provide a sufficient impetus for federal legislation that will clearly and comprehensively address the legal status of online wagering activity. So far, these concerns have resulted in much bluster but no concrete actions from lawmakers.

Threats of enforcement of existing laws against Internet gambling, even though not completely successful in all venues, have undoubtedly curtailed the industry's growth online, as well as the behavior of industry actors. For example, a recent convention of online casino operators chose to meet in Toronto rather than in the United States, based on fears about arrest if they entered the United States.[120] The controversial efforts to seize cash from otherwise legitimate enterprises engaged in advertising will also get the attention of liability-conscious executives, making it more difficult for the industry to promote itself via traditional advertising media. However, patrons have still managed to find Internet businesses and to gamble. Reports of the recent public stock offering by PartyGaming PLC, a Gibraltar-based firm that has studiously avoided legal contacts with the United States, indicate that 90 percent of its $600 million in annual revenues come from American gamblers.[121]

Though law enforcement may send symbolic messages to this industry, the Internet is clearly not within its complete control. Internet gambling will remain an alternative outlet to those who choose to evade regulatory efforts in land-based casinos. This frontier will be hard to tame.

II. Tribal Gaming

Indian tribes occupy an unusual legal status in our federal system. On one hand, tribes possess a limited sovereignty consistent with their status as "domestic dependent nations."[1] This limited sovereignty means that tribal governments have some inherent powers, including powers of self-government, which are akin to those of a separate government entity.[2] This status serves as a barrier to state and local governmental interference with many aspects of tribal government. For example, states may not tax Indian lands, and the jurisdictional reach of their criminal and regulatory laws is constrained by principles of tribal sovereignty and self-governance.

On the other hand, their dependent status makes Indian tribes subject to the federal government's power, without particular representation in that government as allowed to the states. Congress's power over Indian affairs has been characterized as "plenary and exclusive," and this power is rooted primarily in the Indian Commerce Clause of the U.S. Constitution.[3] The Treaty Clause technically grants authority to the executive branch, but it has also been viewed as a source of legislative power in this area.[4] Congress in 1871 authorized no further treaties with Indian tribes, but already extant treaties were not affected by this rule. Thus some matters of tribal governance fall under the authority of treaty obligations rather than other federal statutes.[5]

The policies of the federal government toward the Indian tribes have vacillated over time. As the Supreme Court recently explained,

> Congress has in fact authorized at different times very different Indian policies (some with beneficial results but many with tragic consequences). Congressional policy, for example, initially favored "Indian re-

moval," then "assimilation" and the break-up of tribal lands, then protection of the tribal land base (interrupted by a movement toward greater state involvement and "termination" of recognized tribes); and it now seeks greater tribal autonomy within the framework of a "government-to-government relationship" with federal agencies.[6]

Tribes have not always benefited from their treatment at the hands of the federal government. Many of them have effectively disbanded, as their ability to pass on their cultural traditions and to maintain a sustainable economic way of life has been jeopardized by the encroachment of modern cultural and economic practices. However, some of the tribes that have survived have seized upon the popular interest in gambling as a means to provide economic development. Some tribes have been able to parlay their unique legal status into a preferred position in the gaming marketplace, where they have successfully attracted non-Indian patrons and their financial resources.

This path toward gambling put tribal governments on a collision course with the states in which tribal lands are located. Despite the fact that states had traditionally exercised authority over the legal status of gambling within their borders, tribes contended that gambling activities fell within the realm preserved for tribal sovereignty. Efforts of the Department of the Interior to bolster tribal self-determination and government through gaming fueled this conflict with the states, and the Supreme Court took up this issue in the seminal case of *California v. Cabazon Band of Mission Indians.*[7]

In *Cabazon Band,* Indian tribes with reservations in Riverside County, California, sought a declaratory judgment to the effect that neither state nor county government had any authority to enforce its gambling laws on reservation lands. The tribes had been offering card games and high-stakes bingo primarily to non-Indian patrons from surrounding communities who came to the reservation to gamble. The tribes had conducted these games pursuant to an ordinance approved by the secretary of the interior, which granted authority to operate the games and to use the revenues generated from them to improve the health, education, and welfare of tribal members. The games provided the sole source of income for the tribes, and they provided the major source of tribal employment.

The state of California and Riverside County intervened for the purpose of asserting that the tribes' practices violated state and local laws. Bingo was allowed in California, but it was limited to the context of charitable gaming. Among other things, California law required that operators of charitable bingo games must limit the stakes to $250 and that those operating the games must be unpaid workers. The tribes failed to comply with either of these requirements, and they challenged the state's power to impose them on games conducted on their reservations.

California's authority over criminal acts committed on the reservation was rooted in a specific grant from Congress, which extended criminal jurisdiction to offenses committed by or against Indians within all Indian country within the state.[8] However, Congress had not granted general civil regulatory authority over matters on Indian lands.[9] The character of the applicable state laws affecting gambling was thus at the heart of this litigation: Was the state seeking to enforce a criminal proscription (appropriate), or was it seeking to enforce civil regulatory provisions (not appropriate)? Drawing a bright line between these two categories is difficult, as enforcement of civil regulations might well involve a threat of criminal prosecution.

The Court's analysis ultimately focused on whether the rules are prohibitory or regulatory in nature—a balancing determination with somewhat mystical dimensions. On one hand, California limited bingo games to charitable operations; it had banned commercial gambling operations, in part because of concerns about attracting organized crime.[10] It also imposed limits on the prizes, which the tribes did not do.

On the other hand, California had also allowed gambling in other forms, including horse racing and card games, and it promoted gambling through its own state lottery. Bingo games were open to the public. California law imposed no express limit on the number of games that could be played or the amount that a participant could spend.[11] This general policy toward allowing and even promoting gambling apparently influenced the Court's decision that the law at issue was regulatory and thus not applicable in the tribal context.[12] Though high-stakes bingo may well attract organized crime, such matters were left to the province of federal prosecution under the Organized Crime Control Act.[13] However, the Court suggested that this concern was more theoretical than actual, as it noted the absence of a single federal prosecution connected with more than one hundred Indian bingo operations at that time.[14]

Rather than prosecuting gaming operations, the federal government had been encouraging them. President Reagan stated in 1983, "It is important to the concept of self-government that tribes reduce their dependence on federal funds by providing a greater percentage to the cost of their self-government."[15] The Department of the Interior had chosen gambling as a means of fostering employment and economic development within the tribes, and allowing state regulation would effectively hinder this important federal policy.[16]

The result in *Cabazon Band* caused considerable consternation in states with Indian lands. The Court's analysis greatly expanded the likelihood that tribal gambling operations could be developed without regard to competing economic and regulatory considerations of the states. On the economic side, the expansion of tribal gambling undoubtedly competes with state-sponsored gaming activities, which generate revenues for the public fisc. Under generally applicable principles of state taxation, Indian gaming would not generate those tax revenues.[17] Further, absent a framework for federal regulation of Indian gaming, legitimate concerns may also be raised about the involvement of criminal elements in this cash-oriented business.[18]

Protective interests of the state may also be presented: though gaming may well help to achieve federal goals in fostering economic development for tribes without other significant natural resources, this policy choice would also affect non-Indians, who are likely to be the primary patrons of those gambling establishments. As the dissent in *Cabazon Band* pointed out:

> [The tribes] and the Secretary of the Interior may well be correct, in the abstract, that gambling facilities are a sensible way to generate revenues that are badly needed by reservation Indians. But the decision to adopt, to reject, or to define the precise contours of such a course of action, and thereby to set aside the substantial public policy concerns of a sovereign State, should be made by the Congress of the United States. It should not be made by this Court, by the temporary occupant of the Office of the Secretary of the Interior, or by non-Indian entrepreneurs who are experts in gambling management but not necessarily dedicated to serving the future well-being of Indian tribes.[19]

Congress soon weighed in on these issues by enacting the Indian Gaming Regulatory Act (IGRA) of 1988. The IGRA addresses the extent to which the goals of tribal self-determination and self-sufficiency through Indian gaming should be balanced against state interests affecting the availability of gambling within their borders. Its stable legal foundation for tribal gambling has been responsible for considerable growth in tribal casino operations, including the applications of numerous groups to reestablish their tribal status in order to profit from offering casino gambling services.

OVERVIEW OF THE IGRA

The stated purposes of the IGRA, as set forth in the act itself, are as follows:

(1) to provide a statutory basis for the operation of gaming by Indian tribes as a means of promoting tribal economic development, self-sufficiency, and strong tribal government;

(2) to provide a statutory basis for the regulation of gaming by an Indian tribe adequate to shield it from organized crime and other corrupting influences, to ensure that the Indian tribe is the primary beneficiary of the gaming operation, and to assure that gaming is conducted fairly and honestly by the operator and the players; and

(3) to declare that the establishment of independent regulatory authority for gaming on Indian lands, the establishment of Federal standards for gaming on Indian lands, and the establishment of a National Indian Gaming Commission are necessary to meet congressional concerns regarding gaming and to protect such gaming as a means of generating tribal revenue.[20]

Toward these ends, the IGRA establishes a regulatory structure that is based on three different categories of gaming activity. Class I gaming is exclusively within the jurisdiction of the Indian tribe.[21] This category includes "social games solely for prizes of minimal value or traditional forms of Indian gaming engaged in by individuals as a part of, or in connection with, tribal ceremonies or celebrations."[22] These games have no real potential for commercial profit, and they would be unlikely to affect any competing state interests.

Class II gaming is subject to oversight by the National Indian Gaming Commission. This category includes games such as bingo and certain card games that are otherwise allowed by the state.[23] Slot machines are specifically excluded from Class II games.[24] Class II games can be economically significant, and they may only be carried on within states that permit such gaming "for any purpose by any person, organization or entity."[25] Thus, a state that adopts a public policy prohibiting gambling altogether may effectively enforce that policy on Indian lands within the state. However, a state that offers gaming privileges to others may not deny that privilege to tribes within its borders. This provision thus reflects an attempt to accommodate legitimate state concerns about the effects of gambling on its citizens while preventing discrimination against Indian operations.

Class II gaming operations require the approval of the chairman of the National Indian Gaming Commission, which is subject to several important conditions.[26] One of these conditions requires that the construction, maintenance, and operation of the gaming facility must adequately protect the environment and public health and safety. Although the tribe must comply with federal environmental laws, compliance with state or local building and safety codes is not necessarily required.

This application of local zoning or building codes was recently litigated in *Cayuga Indian Nation of New York v. Village of Union Springs.*[27] In 2004, a federal district court held that a tribe's construction of a gambling facility on reservation lands it had recently acquired from non-Indians was not subject to state or local zoning or building codes. The fact that non-Indians would be the primary patrons of the facility did not change this result. Thus, based on this decision, the particular parameters for satisfying the standard of public health and safety appear to be within the discretion of the tribe, subject to oversight by federal officials. However, late in 2005 this result was overturned on the basis of the U.S. Supreme Court's decision in *City of Sherrill v. Oneida Nation,*[28] which rejected the proposition that acquisition of land by a tribe restored aboriginal title and thus tribal sovereignty as a protection from local regulation. On the authority of *City of Sherrill,* the district court removed an injunction barring enforcement of zoning and building codes on the affected property.[29] Nevertheless, the application of zoning rules or building codes on historical reservation property would continue to present issues not resolved by this decision.

The rest of these conditions imposed on Class II gaming operations are designed to ensure the financial integrity of the operation and to safeguard benefits to tribal members. The Indian tribe must have the sole proprietary interest in the activity, or it must contract with a service provider that will meet similarly stringent operational standards. The net revenues from tribal gaming must be used for specified purposes, which include funding tribal government operations or programs, supporting the general welfare of the tribe and its members, promoting economic development, donating to charities, and supporting operations of local government agencies.[30]

The tribal operation is also subject to annual audits, which must extend to all contracts for supplies, services (other than legal or accounting), or concessions involving contract amounts in excess of twenty-five thousand dollars. These audits must be provided to the commission. In addition, the commission is empowered to engage in continuous monitoring, inspection, and oversight of the tribal operation.[31] Such financial oversight presumably addresses concerns about corruption and other criminal activities being funded with gaming revenues.

Along these same lines, the tribe must provide a monitoring system that ensures that background investigations are conducted on management and key employees of the gaming operation. These employees must meet licensing standards that ensure that "any person whose prior activities, criminal record, if any, or reputation, habits and associations pose a threat to the public interest or to the effective regulation of gaming, or create or enhance the dangers of unsuitable, unfair, or illegal practices and methods and activities in the conduct of gaming shall not be eligible for employment."[32]

The act recognizes the potential for these operations to generate sufficient income to the tribe that may even allow for per capita distributions of profits to tribal members.[33] However, such distributions may only be made if the commission is satisfied that the tribe has an adequate plan to support tribal government and economic development and that such plan has been adequately funded.[34] Moreover, the act expressly states that such distributions are subject to federal income taxation in the hands of the recipients.[35]

Though Class II gaming is subject to active monitoring and inspection by the National Indian Gaming Commission, the act also provides a means for tribes to minimize the commission's involvement and to engage in self-regulation. Tribes that have engaged in continuous operations of a Class II facility for at least one year may petition for the right of self-regulation. Such a petition requires showing that the tribe essentially has a clean record of operating fairly and honestly, that it has adequate systems for financial and operational integrity, and that it is fiscally sound.[36]

If the petition is granted, the tribal operation is still subject to the annual auditing requirement and must submit the results of such an audit to the commission. However, the tribe is otherwise exempt from the active intervention by the commission. In this way, the act provides a means for greater independence and self-government of the tribe with regard to gaming operations, while at the same time providing a limited means for the commission to identify and address problems through the annual audit.

The third category of gaming under the IGRA—Class III—encompasses all other forms of gambling not included in Classes I or II.[37] Thus, the traditional casino table games and slot machines—which are among the most lucrative forms of gambling available—are within this class. Not only are these activities economically significant, but they also present some of the greatest regulatory challenges.[38]

Much like Class II gaming, Class III gaming requires a tribal ordinance within a state that "permits such gaming for any purpose by any person, organization, or entity."[39] However, it also requires a tribal-state compact, which must be negotiated with the state and approved by the secretary of the interior.[40] The compact provisions may include the following subjects:

(i)   the application of the criminal and civil laws and regulations of the Indian tribe or the State that are directly related to, and necessary for, the licensing and regulation of such activity;

(ii)   the allocation of criminal and civil jurisdiction between the State and the Indian tribe necessary for the enforcement of such laws and regulations;

(iii)   the assessment by the State of such activities in such amounts as are necessary to defray the costs of regulating such activity;

(iv)   taxation by the Indian tribe of such activity in amounts comparable to amounts assessed by the State for comparable activities;

(v)   remedies for breach of contract;

(vi)   standards for the operation of such activity and maintenance of the gaming facility, including licensing; and

(vii)   any other subjects that are directly related to the operation of gaming activities.[41]

Thus, the IGRA gives considerable latitude to state governments in the negotiation of regulatory limits on gambling. For example, Arizona's model compact contains limits on the financial services available in gaming facilities, including restricting the location of ATM machines near gaming devices, prohibiting acceptance of electronic benefit transfer cards from welfare programs, and prohibiting the extension of credit by the casino.[42] Guidance about such matters as notices for persons with problem gambling, prohibitions on advertising aimed at minors, and self-exclusion programs for problem gamblers is also part of the compact process in Arizona.[43] States that prohibit certain types of Class III games may also extend those prohibitions to the tribal casino and may thus refuse to negotiate on such matters.[44] However, the fact that the state restricts Class III games to charitable purposes, even though embedded as a constitutional restriction, has been ruled an insufficient basis for restricting tribal gaming pursuant to a compact with the state.[45]

Though the states may negotiate over regulation of Class III gaming, it is significant to note that the IGRA provisions delineating the content of tribal-state compacts impose limits on taxes and fees that may be imposed on the sponsoring tribes. States may lawfully negotiate for financial assessments against the tribes, but paragraph (iii) permits this only "in such amounts as are necessary to defray the costs of regulating such activity." Paragraph (iv) allows taxation "by" the Indian tribe, but it does not permit taxation "of" the Indian tribe. This taxing issue is significant and merits further discussion.

TAXES AND TRIBAL CASINOS

State taxing power over tribes has long been subject to significant restraints, which protect the tribes from incursions by competing state and local government powers. Tribal members have been held to be exempt from state taxation on their income or property so long as it is sufficiently connected to reservation lands.[46] Limited incursions of this exemption from state taxation have been permitted at the pleasure of Congress. As the Supreme Court has stated:

> In keeping with its plenary authority over Indian affairs, Congress can authorize the imposition of state taxes on Indian tribes and individual Indians. It has not done so often, and the Court consistently has held that it will find the Indians' exemption from state taxes lifted only when Congress has made its intention to do so unmistakably clear.[47]

However, the Court has also recently imposed a limit on the property tax exemption associated with tribal lands when those lands were brought into the reservation through purchase.[48] This decision struck a balance in favor of the state and local tax base, as well as regulatory requirements applicable to activities on such lands, when such lands had been subject to state and local government sovereignty prior to acquisition. However, it does not speak to the issue of gaming taxes, which are highly significant for casino operations.

The IGRA is quite clear on the point that compacts are not to be used as a means of expanding the taxing powers of state and local government:

> Except for any assessments that may be agreed to under paragraph (3)(C)(iii) of this subsection, nothing in this section shall be interpreted as conferring upon a State or any of its political subdivisions authority to impose any tax, fee, charge, or other assessment upon an Indian tribe or upon any other person or entity authorized by an Indian tribe to engage in a class III activity. No State may refuse to enter into the [compact] negotiations . . . based upon the lack of authority in such State, or its political subdivisions, to impose such a tax, fee, charge, or other assessment.[49]

Elsewhere, the IGRA also provides that an attempt to impose any direct taxes on the tribe would be considered evidence of bad faith on the part of the state.[50]

Nevertheless, several states have obtained payments from tribes that appear to circumvent these provisions. Instead of characterizing these payments as taxes, they are treated as fees in exchange for the state's grant of exclusive rights to offer Class III gaming activities. Thus, to the extent that a state has sufficient tribal interests in operating casino facilities, it can effectively reap economic benefits for the state treasury by granting exclusive rights. This same opportunity is not available to states with both commercial and tribal facilities, as the state tax limitations will ordinarily apply in that situation.

California is one state in which an exclusive right is granted for tribal gambling. The preamble to the model compact adopted in California states in part:

> The exclusive rights that Indian tribes in California, including the Tribe, will enjoy under this Compact create a unique opportunity for the Tribe to operate its Gaming Facility in an economic environment free of competition from the Class III gaming referred to in Section 4.0 of this Compact on non-Indian lands in California. The parties are mindful that this

unique environment is of great economic value to the Tribe and the fact that income from Gaming Devices represents a substantial portion of the tribes' gaming revenues. In consideration for the exclusive rights enjoyed by the tribes, and in further consideration for the State's willingness to enter into this Compact, the tribes have agreed to provide to the State, on a sovereign-to-sovereign basis, a portion of its revenue from Gaming Devices.[51]

Under the California system, payments from tribal operations include both license fees and an assessment based on a stated percentage of net gaming revenues. License fees from gaming devices, which begin at $900 per device for 351 licensed devices per operation and increase to as much as $4,350 per device for operations with 1,251–2,000 licensed devices, are paid into a Revenue Sharing Trust Fund.[52] This fund is used to distribute revenues from gaming tribes to other tribes without gaming operations. Its progressive structure ensures that those tribes that are the most successful at gaming operations bear more of the burden for supporting other tribes that may lack a suitable geographic location to profit from a gaming operation.[53]

In addition, a percentage of the "net win" from establishments with more than 200 gaming devices is also paid over to a Special Distribution Fund. This percentage also reflects a progressive rate structure:

Terminals	Percentage
First 200	0%
Next 300	7%
Next 500	10%
Over 1,000	13%[54]

This Special Distribution Fund is subject to appropriations by the legislature for various purposes, including gambling addiction programs, grants to state and local government agencies affected by tribal gambling, regulatory costs, and "any other purposes specified by the Legislature."[55]

Arizona's model compact for tribal gaming similarly extracts a tribal contribution to the state in exchange for exclusivity rights. Its model compact provides as follows:

In consideration for the substantial exclusivity covenants by the State . . . the Tribe shall contribute for the benefit of the public a percentage of the

Tribe's Class III Net Win for each fiscal year of the Gaming Facility Operator as follows:

(1) One percent (1%) of the first twenty-five million dollars ($25,000,000.00);

(2) Three percent (3%) of the next fifty million dollars ($50,000,000.00);

(3) Six percent (6%) of the next twenty-five million dollars ($25,000,000.00); and

(4) Eight percent (8%) of Class III Net Win in excess of one hundred million dollars ($100,000,000.00).[56]

In the event that those exclusive rights are abrogated, the tribal contribution is substantially reduced, presumably to comply with the IGRA provisions limiting the state's taxing powers.[57] Of these total funds, 88 percent are allocated to the Arizona Benefits Fund, which is used to cover regulatory costs, problem gambling programs, education, trauma and emergency services, wildlife conservation, and tourism.[58] The other 12 percent of the funds are allocated to a separate fund that is used to help cities, towns, and counties fund "government services that benefit the general public, including public safety, mitigation of impacts of gaming, and promotion of commerce and economic development."[59]

Connecticut, home to the world's largest casino, has also granted exclusive rights to tribal operations, for which it extracts a payment of 25 percent of gross slot machine revenues from casinos operated on Indian lands by two tribes, the Mashantucket Pequot and the Mohegan.[60] This amount increases to 30 percent of gross revenues in the event that the total contribution from each of the two tribes falls below $80 million.[61] The tribes' "memorandum of understanding" with the state ensures that the obligation to make these payments to the state ends if the exclusive right is terminated by state law.[62] Revenues from tribal gaming are part of the state's general fund and are thus not subject to targeted spending requirements.[63]

Michigan had initially assessed additional fees against tribal operations, but it was forced to stop collecting those fees when commercial casinos obtained the right to offer gaming services in Detroit.[64] Pursuant to a compact with the state, the tribes were obligated to pay over 8 percent of their net win from electronic casino games as long as they held the "exclusive right to operate" those kinds of games in the state. Subsequent to that compact, the people of Michigan passed an initiative known as the Michigan Gaming Control and Revenue Act, which authorized up to three casino licenses in Detroit. The Sixth Circuit concluded that the exclusivity condition would end when a license was issued to a nontribal holder by the Michigan Gaming Control Board.[65]

Some commentators have argued that the payments to states in exchange for exclusive gambling rights are inconsistent with the IGRA.[66] However, the Ninth Circuit has recently upheld the California provisions in a tribal challenge that they were inconsistent with the IGRA. In a case entitled *In re Indian Gaming Cases*,[67] the tribe alleged that the financial assessments in the California compact violated the terms of the IGRA and showed a lack of good faith on the part of the state.

The tribe alleged that the Revenue Sharing Trust Fund, which was used to share revenues with nongaming tribes, constituted an unlawful tax that went beyond the scope of "assessments" allowed to defray the cost of regulating tribal gaming.[68] However, the Ninth Circuit rejected this claim, finding instead that the Revenue Sharing Trust Fund advances the congressional goals in the IGRA by "creating a mechanism whereby *all* of California's tribes—not just those fortunate enough to have land located in populous or accessible areas—can benefit from Class III gaming activities in the State."[69] Even if the fund contributions were "demanded" (as opposed to negotiated), and even if it was considered a "direct tax" on the tribes, the court was not concerned about this type of tax. According to the court, the IGRA does not convert any attempt to tax into conclusive proof of a lack of good faith: "the good faith inquiry is nuanced and fact-specific, and is not amenable to bright-line rules."[70] The fact that the fund actually originated in a tribal proposal and that it was adopted by all other tribes was also helpful in supporting its validity.

As for the Special Distribution Fund, the court had no trouble in finding that "all of the purposes to which money can be put are directly related to tribal gaming."[71] Even the fact that distributions could be made "for any other purposes specified by the legislature" was thought to be limited by the interpretational principle of *ejusdem generis*, meaning that it is limited to similar gambling-related purposes as set forth in the other examples of appropriate spending targets.[72] The fact that the state gave the tribe exclusivity rights bolstered the court's view that these kinds of payments were not contrary to the IGRA: "We do not find it inimical to the purpose or design of the IGRA for the State, under these circumstances, to ask for a reasonable share of tribal gaming revenues for the specific purposes identified in the SDF provision."[73] Unlike a situation where the state was using tax assessments to protect other gaming enterprises from competition by tribal casinos, here the state was granting a valuable exclusive right to operate free from other market forces.[74] Apparently, the court viewed some compensation for this right to be an appropriate action by the state, which was distinguishable from a more generalized exaction in the form of a tax assessment.

This case indicates that compacts may effectively impose payment obligations that look like taxes on the tribal operations, despite the strong language against taxation in the IGRA. However, the peculiar context of this case merits some caution before extending its result to all exclusivity arrangements. First, this case involved a single tribe's complaint about a compact system that approximately sixty other tribes had accepted. The potential to upset the entire regulatory structure affecting such a diverse group of tribal, state, and local government actors undoubtedly weighed heavily on the side of sustaining these practices, particularly when the vast majority of tribes had no objection to the practice.

Second, the California funds had limited purposes that closely related to ensuring tribal welfare and ameliorating ancillary negative effects of casino operations. As the court pointed out, the California compact

> differs in this respect from the revenue sharing provisions found in Tribal State compacts entered into by the States of Connecticut, New Mexico, and New York, for example. In those states, revenue derived from tribal gaming goes into the States' general funds. The legality of such compacts is not before us, and we intimate no view on the question.[75]

The fact that a state does not specifically earmark funds obtained from tribal gaming sources should not be dispositive of the validity of such assessments, but this case leaves open the possibility of a different result.

The constraint of state taxing powers raises some interesting political issues, which will need to be resolved in the near future. Non-Indian citizens have often been supportive of Indian gaming, in part because they want the option to participate in gaming activities that might otherwise be unavailable to them. For example, in both Arizona and California, Indian tribes have used public initiatives to legalize Indian gaming, which might otherwise not have occurred if the matter was left in the hands of their government officials. Local opposition based on concerns about spillover effects of casino operations on a local neighborhood is typically insufficient to impact gambling policy at the state level, where the enabling compacts are made. Tribal gaming operations have also grown in their political influence, as they have considerable resources to distribute in favor of candidates who will support their businesses.[76]

However, opposition to Indian gaming may be growing. The tax-favored status of tribal gaming operations played an important role in the 2003 California gubernatorial recall election. One journalist recounted the following ad sponsored by Arnold Schwarzenegger's campaign:

> "Their casinos make billions, yet they pay no taxes and virtually nothing to the state," pronounced Arnold Schwarzenegger in one of his campaign ads. "It's time the Indians pay their fair share. All the other major candidates take their money and pander to them." He stares into the camera. He shakes his head slowly back and forth. He squints hard. "I don't play that game."[77]

Despite tribal gifts of $8.2 million to his Democratic opponent, Lieutenant Governor Cruz Bustamonte, and $2.5 million to his competing Republican candidate, Tom McClintock, Schwarzenegger ultimately triumphed. It remains to be seen whether he will be successful in renegotiating the financial terms in which tribes are allowed to carry on Class III gaming to make them more favorable to the State.

Although California's fiscal crisis may be easing, there are other reasons to support a modification of the tax burdens imposed on Indian casinos. State and local governments are likely to incur ancillary social costs associated with casino operations that will exceed the direct costs of regulation allowed to be recovered under the IGRA. It is arguably appropriate to require casino operations to internalize those costs through payments to state and local governments. States with exclusivity agreements can address these issues indirectly through requiring revenue-sharing provisions in their compacts. However, states without exclusivity arrangements lack this option, as they are subject to the more stringent tax prohibitions of the IGRA.

States that legalize casino gambling for commercial enterprises are thus

disadvantaged in their dealings with tribal operations. To the extent that patrons substitute play in a tribal operation instead of a commercial casino,
revenues from direct taxes imposed on commercial casinos are lost. Moreover, enhancements to the state and local tax base from adding commercial
casinos are largely unavailable for tribal casinos.[78] Their effective exemption
from direct taxes on net gaming receipts, property taxes on facilities, and
sales taxes on food and beverage operations clearly limits any tax contribution to the local community.

Tribal gaming operations may nevertheless generate some benefits for
the local economy. For example, casinos may provide employment opportunities for non-Indians. They may also purchase goods and services from
local businesses. However, these benefits may be offset by displacements in
spending on local establishments, as local patrons spend their money in the
casino instead of in other local businesses. Although it is difficult to gauge
the magnitude of these competing economic flows, the disadvantage for
local governments on the tax side of the ledger as compared with a similar
commercial casino operation is quite clear.[79]

The tribal advantage inherent in this arrangement was an intentional feature of the IGRA. It was originally designed as an indirect means of delivering economic benefits to a group that has historically suffered from poverty
and unemployment. However, generalizations about Indian tribes, as well as
other ethnic or racial groups, can be hazardous.

Tribal membership is not limited to the poor and unemployed, and that
remains true after a tribe is granted the valuable right to open a casino. For
example, the Cabazon band in California, which initiated the Supreme Court
case that is credited with generating the IGRA, has only fifty members,[80] yet
it operates a casino facility that attracts 1.5 million visitors annually and contains nearly two thousand slot machines.[81] Similarly, the Chippewa tribe of
Michigan is reported to hold a portfolio of $1.2 billion, giving each tribal
member a net worth of more than $400,000. Adult tribal members receive
$52,000 per year and children receive $13,000 per year from casino profits,
without a requirement for meaningful work or participation in the enterprise.[82] Although these tribes may once have needed support in addressing
poverty and unemployment, it is difficult to argue that a continuing economic advantage in a regulated industry is still needed in this case.

Aggregate tribal benefits from gaming are not necessarily transmitted to individual members of a tribe. Only about one-fourth of tribes engage in some form of per capita payments to tribal members.[83] The rest of the tribes purport to devote their revenues to services for tribal members, economic and community development, and charitable purposes. Questions have been raised about the effectiveness of tribal governance and disclosure concerning how gaming revenues are spent. A series of articles in the *Detroit News* in 2001 covered disputes that arose in the Sault Ste. Marie Chippewa tribe over the management of tribal wealth generated from its casino operations.[84] Tribal sovereignty means that tribal remedies may not meet the expectations of those who are accustomed to the political structures, due process, and legal remedies accessible outside the tribal context.

Efforts to share the benefits reaped from casino gaming with nongaming tribes, such as the California system discussed previously, have been quite limited in scope. Poverty and unemployment continue to be a problem in Indian communities, and many of them continue to be left out of the bonanza granted through Indian gaming. Most have no real opportunities to benefit from gambling because their geographic location gives them no access to a sufficient market of non-Indian patrons. Creating the prospects of extraordinary wealth for a few well-placed tribes through government-imposed advantages makes for dubious policy, which is likely to be reexamined if gambling continues to proliferate.

ENFORCING THE COMPACT PROCESS: PROBLEMS OF STATE SOVEREIGN IMMUNITY

The compact requirement in the IGRA provides a somewhat unusual approach toward resolving some of the practical and political problems involved in offering Class III gaming. Courts have described the compact approach as being rooted in the need for an appropriate regulatory system for Class III gambling; the absence of federal or tribal regulatory systems requires reliance on state models.[85] Since Class III games may only be held on tribal lands within states that have legalized those games, and then only to the extent that particular games are legal, the state would be expected to have regulatory systems in place for such games. However, it should be noted that the IGRA does not rule out the prospect of concurrent regulation by the tribes, provided that it is not inconsistent with or less stringent than the state regulatory requirements.[86]

The compact approach potentially has desirable political effects, to the extent that it requires a dialogue between the state and the tribe. Some have referred to this as an example of "cooperative federalism," to the extent that competing interests of federal, state, and tribal governments can be addressed through the compact.[87] In theory, this might produce amicable and effective solutions to problems presented by locating a tribal casino within the state. However, such solutions depend on good faith cooperation; human beings do not always behave that way, particularly when something as complex and controversial as gambling is involved.

The IGRA anticipates that tribal and state authorities may not reach agreement, and it provides for federal court jurisdiction over disputes initiated by the Indian tribes arising from a failure to enter into compact negotiations or to conduct negotiations in good faith.[88] However, these provisions have only limited effectiveness because the Supreme Court has held that Congress was not empowered to abrogate the sovereign immunity that the states enjoy in this context under the Eleventh Amendment.[89] Thus, a state may raise sovereign immunity as a defense against an action initiated by a tribe, thus bypassing the federal court's authority as a mechanism for enforcement.

In light of this legal development, the secretary of the interior promulgated regulations that deal with the possibility that a state may elect not to negotiate a compact and assert sovereign immunity in federal court.[90] The regulations state the following process:

An Indian tribe may ask the Secretary to issue Class III gaming procedures when the following steps have taken place:

(a) The Indian tribe submitted a written request to the State to enter into negotiations to establish a Tribal-State compact governing the conduct of Class III gaming activities;

(b) The State and the Indian tribe failed to negotiate a compact 180 days after the State received the Indian tribe's request;

(c) The Indian tribe initiated a cause of action in Federal district court against the State alleging that the State did not respond, or did not respond in good faith, to the request of the Indian tribe to negotiate such a compact;

(d) The State raised an Eleventh Amendment defense to the tribal action; and

(e) The Federal district court dismissed the action due to the State's sovereign immunity under the Eleventh Amendment.[91]

If a state raises sovereign immunity as a bar to litigation, these regulations provide a means for tribes to go directly to the secretary to seek permission regarding Class III gambling. The secretary must request a proposal from the state and may order mediation if the parties cannot reach agreement on which proposal to accept.[92] The secretary may ultimately either adopt the mediator's proposal or provide his or her own procedures consistent with the IGRA for Class III gaming to go forward.[93] This process has recently been invoked by the Kickapoo Traditional Tribe of Texas, but the state of Texas initiated litigation to block it, which was ultimately unsuccessful.[94]

It should be noted that tribes have sometimes chosen to act without a compact in place. For example, in California, a number of tribes had decided to engage in Class III gaming without a compact; then-Governor Wilson refused to negotiate for a compact until the tribes ceased these operations. As one court noted, "Because IGRA grants the federal government exclusive jurisdiction to prosecute any violations of State gambling laws in Indian country, the State's refusal to engage in negotiations was one of the few forms of leverage it possessed to force tribes to comply with IGRA's compacting requirement."[95] In Nebraska, which had not authorized Class III gaming, federal officials also had to intervene to enjoin tribal operations that violated state law and occurred outside of the IGRA provisions.[96] States and the tribes thus share a dependency on federal officials in this area.

THE SCOPE OF "INDIAN LANDS"

Indian gaming governed by the IGRA is restricted to that conducted on "Indian lands,"[97] a term that includes

(A) all lands within the limits of any Indian reservation; and
(B) any lands title to which is either held in trust by the United States for the benefit of any Indian tribe or individual or held by any Indian tribe or individual subject to restriction by the United States against alienation and over which an Indian tribe exercises governmental power.[98]

The parameters of these Indian lands are somewhat malleable to the extent that a tribe may acquire new lands that are held in trust for its benefit. The IGRA contemplates this possibility, and it imposes significant limits on the extension of gaming to trust lands acquired after October 17, 1988.

The legislative history speaks to the scope of tribal lands as follows:

> Gaming on newly acquired tribal lands outside of reservations is not generally permitted unless the Secretary determines that gaming would be in the tribe's best interest and would not be detrimental to the local community and the Governor of the affected State concurs in that determination.[99]

Although these limits are designed to protect the interests of local communities that could be affected by the construction of a casino facility, those protections have sometimes proved illusory.

New trust lands eligible for gaming are generally limited to parcels meeting certain requirements. For tribes with existing reservations, the IGRA provides that gaming could be conducted on newly acquired trust lands within or contiguous to the boundaries of that reservation.[100] This permits a limited geographical expansion of the country in which gaming is permitted, but such expansion is anchored to the locus of the reservation. Thus, this provision would generally prevent a tribe occupying a remote, rural reservation from reaching an urban population center conducive to supporting a gaming operation.

For tribes with no reservation lands as of October 17, 1988, a different rule was provided, depending on the location of the trust lands acquired for their benefit. If the land was acquired in Oklahoma, gaming would be permitted if that land was within the tribe's former reservation or contiguous to other land held in trust for the tribe.[101] If the land was outside of Oklahoma, gaming would be allowed on lands within the boundaries of the tribe's "last recognized reservation within the State or States within which such Indian tribe is presently located."[102] These rules similarly constrict the possibility of expanding gaming by tribes that do not have a reservation but wish to participate in a casino operation.

The IGRA nevertheless contains some exceptions to these restrictive rules to accommodate the potential for Indian gaming on other trust lands. The secretary of the interior is given discretion to allow Indian gaming if these conditions are met:

> the Secretary, after consultation with the Indian tribe and appropriate State and local officials, including officials of other nearby Indian tribes, determines that a gaming establishment on newly acquired lands would

be in the best interest of the Indian tribe and its members, and would not be detrimental to the surrounding community, but only if the Governor of the State in which the gaming activity is to be conducted concurs in the Secretary's determination.[103]

This provision is designed to provide political protection for local communities potentially affected by casinos on newly acquired trust lands. The secretary is required to find that a casino "would not be detrimental" to the local community before he or she can permit gaming to occur. Local officials are entitled to consult with the secretary, thus providing input about any concerns that might make a casino undesirable for their community. The governor also has veto power, thus providing additional assurance that federal officials who are largely immune from local political accountability do not inappropriately dismiss local concerns in favor of the tribe.

Other exceptions to the general prohibitions on expanding tribal gaming include

> Lands . . . taken into trust as part of—
>   (i)   a settlement of a land claim,
>   (ii) the initial reservation of an Indian tribe acknowledged by the Secretary under the Federal acknowledgment process, or
>   (iii) the restoration of lands for an Indian tribe that is restored to Federal recognition.[104]

The secretary may create new reservations, as well as restore lands to tribes that had previously lost their status through termination procedures adopted in the mid-1950s. However, that process occurs without the benefit of the political protections for local communities that may be affected. The process of restoration has generated bitter disputes between tribes, the federal government, and state and local governments, which have resulted in litigation.

A recent case that illustrates this conflict is *City of Roseville v. Norton*,[105] in which two cities in California and a local nonprofit organization known as Cities for Safer Communities (together referred to as "Cities") challenged the scope of the restoration exception outlined previously. In 1994, Congress passed legislation restoring tribal status to the Auburn Indian band, which had had no federally recognized existence since 1967, when Congress terminated its forty-acre reservation, distributed the lands in fee title to individuals, and terminated federal trust responsibilities over the tribe.[106] The 1994 legislation restored the tribe's status and authorized the secretary of the interior to take land back into trust to serve as a reservation for the approximately 247 members of the tribe. The Auburns did not seek to reacquire their original reservation, which was held in fee title by individuals (including non-Indians). Instead, they sought to acquire a 49.21-acre parcel of land for the purpose of constructing a casino.[107]

This location was apparently valuable for several reasons. It was close to the large population base of the Sacramento area. It was also located on the route to Reno, Nevada, a popular commercial casino destination approximately one hundred miles away. Experts had predicted that this location would be highly profitable, as it had the potential to capture a significant portion of the patronage that might otherwise go across the border to the casinos in Reno.

From the Cities' perspective, this location was objectionable. They claimed that the casino would create adverse impacts on their communities from crime, interference with planned residential developments, and interference with the family-oriented nature of the area.[108] They also argued that the Bureau of Indian Affairs was not legally authorized to proceed with the acquisition without a determination that the proposed gaming activity "would not be detrimental to the surrounding communities" and the consent of the governor.

In response, the Bureau of Indian Affairs took the position that the land was exempt from the finding of no community detriment, since this was within the exception for "restoration of lands" under the IGRA. It was also thus exempt from any requirement of consent from the governor. The bureau nevertheless treated this acquisition as a "discretionary" acquisition, which did require the balancing of the interests of the tribe against potential land use conflicts associated with the acquisition. However, this balancing of interests fell on the side of the tribe, thus allowing the approval of the acquisition.[109]

The district court dismissed the Cities' claims, and the District of Columbia Circuit Court of Appeals was ultimately called upon to decide the question of whether this land would be considered to be a part of a "restoration of lands," even though it was never a part of the Auburns' original reservation. In a lengthy analysis, the court of appeals agreed that the word *restoration* could encompass either of the interpretations sought by the parties. Thus, "neither side can prevail by quoting the dictionary."[110] However, when considering the purposes of the IGRA and the act restoring the Auburn tribe, the balance moved against the Cities' claims. Here, treating this acquisition as a "restoration of lands compensates the Tribe not only for what it lost by the act of termination, but also for opportunities lost in the interim."[111] A broader approach toward restoration was also deemed to be more consistent with the purposes of the IGRA to promote tribal economic development and self-sufficiency.[112] Moreover, it was also consistent with the purpose of the legislation restoring the Auburn tribes, which did not limit the selection of a reservation to particular lands but gave discretion to the secretary.[113]

This case suggests the possibility that tribal casino operations could be placed in many locations that have not traditionally been considered to be Indian lands and in fact were never characterized in this way. The Bureau of Indian Affairs is thus given extensive powers that effectively bypass the statutory protections granted to local governments in other contexts. In this case, the planned casino did turn out to be among the most successful in the country, with more than 3 million visitors and estimated profits of more than $300 million during its first calendar year of operations.[114]

However, traffic problems associated with that facility have been considerable. News reports indicated that cars were backed up for miles when the casino opened.[115] Those disruptions may have subsided somewhat as "opening day" has passed. Placer County, which was not a party to the litigation against the tribe, entered into a memorandum of understanding with the tribe in which the tribe agreed to pay traffic mitigation fees of $4.8 million and to make certain road improvements.[116] However, the Cities have obtained nothing. The extent of other concerns raised by the Cities remains to be seen, but they remain closed out of any governing process associated with an enterprise that could have a significant effect on their communities.

Even without a formal restoration act, as was the case in *City of Roseville*, the IGRA provisions on Indian lands may present other disputes over the expansion of Indian gaming. A particularly interesting case involves the Wyandotte tribe of Oklahoma, which sought to expand some two hundred miles into Kansas for the purpose of opening a casino. Faced with "meager financial resources and the dim prospects for gaming on its Oklahoma reservation,"[117] the Wyandottes acquired property adjoining an Indian cemetery in Kansas City, Kansas, and submitted an application to the secretary of the interior to take this land into trust for the purpose of developing and operating a casino on the land.[118]

The cemetery had once been part of lands acquired by the Wyandottes from the Delaware Nation of Indians in 1843.[119] Pursuant to an 1855 treaty, the Wyandottes agreed to dissolve the tribe, accept U.S. citizenship, and cede their lands to the United States. However, the cemetery was specifically singled out to be "permanently reserved and appropriated" as a burial ground.[120] Approximately two hundred Wyandottes chose not to accept citizenship, and Congress reconstituted this group as the Wyandotte tribe in 1867. This reconstituted tribe settled in Oklahoma. The Wyandottes were again terminated in 1956, but their status was restored in 1978. In 1984, Congress appropriated money to satisfy judgments obtained by the tribe for lands they had ceded to the United States; these funds were to be used to purchase lands that would be held in trust for their benefit.[121] These lands surrounding the cemetery were purported to be such lands.

The status of the cemetery as a reservation was very important to the Wyandotte's plan. If the cemetery was considered to be a Wyandotte reservation, the tribe could conduct gaming without the need for consultation with local government or approval from the governor of Kansas. The land would be considered "contiguous" to reservation land and thus outside the scope of these provisions involving the approval of state and local government. If these trust lands were not deemed contiguous, they would fall within the category of lands acquired after 1988, which would be subject to these provisions. Given the opposition of the governor, who was joined by other tribes operating competing casino facilities in pursing this litigation, such approval would not be forthcoming and the Wyandottes' plan would be thwarted.

Although the Tenth Circuit Court of Appeals held that the cemetery was not to be considered a "reservation," Congress enacted legislation that cast doubt on this result. Section 134 of Public Law 107-63 clarifies that the secretary of the interior has discretionary authority to determine whether land qualifies as a reservation.[122] For a brief period, the Wyandottes did indeed open a casino with Class II games on their acquired land. However, the National Indian Gaming Commission intervened and shut down the casino in early 2004, citing its view that the casino site did not meet the definition of "tribal land" under the IGRA.

The tribe's distant connection to the state of Kansas, where other local tribes do enjoy gambling privileges, undoubtedly put it in a more difficult political position than it might otherwise have occupied as a local tribe with roots in the community. The governor and the attorney general focused significant attention on the Wyandottes' operation, and they publicly announced their efforts to work with the National Indian Gaming Commission to stop it.[123]

It should be noted that a similar claim for Indian lands has been made based on a cemetery adjoining the campus of the University of California at Chico.[124] The state of California refused to negotiate a compact with the tribe, since the tribe had no land other than the cemetery. The tribe sued to compel negotiations, but the federal district court rejected that claim, stating in part:

> It is hard to believe that the Tribe really wants to negotiate to build a gambling casino on their burial ground, but that is what they argue. At oral argument, the Tribe's counsel admitted that the Tribe hopes to use lands outside the former Chico Rancheria, the subject of a pending fee-to-trust application, for a gaming facility. Thus, use of the cemetery parcel seems to be merely a pretense to force the State into negotiations in an attempt to forestall any delay in installing a future gaming facility on the land outside the former Chico Rancheria.[125]

More of these issues are likely to emerge as more tribes are recognized and Indian lands are restored. It is understandable that tribes will want to locate casino facilities near urban population centers, where they have the greatest prospects for success. The extraordinary potential for wealth generation in the right location certainly creates an incentive to pursue these opportunities through any legal means. However, the injection of gaming facilities into urban areas without the support of state and local governments and appropriate political mechanisms to address the externalities accompanying such facilities is problematic. Taken to the extreme, such efforts could prove to become catalysts for significant rethinking of the scope and extent of Indian gaming: the goose that lays the golden eggs may well be unintentionally devoured as a result of controversial extensions of gaming without substantial local political support.

THE LIMITS OF CLASS II GAMING:
WHAT IS A SLOT MACHINE?

A final issue with a potentially significant consequence to Indian casino operations involves the borderline between Class II and Class III gaming. The
IGRA specifically restricts slot machines to Class III gaming jurisdictions.
Though slot machines have long been a part of successful Las Vegas–style casinos, their popularity with consumers and casino operators has increased over
time. Technological improvements, including not only more lights and "bells
and whistles" but also appearances by famous personalities through audio and
video features, have increased the extent of their play.[126] Horse-racing facilities have scrambled to add slot machines, thus transforming into so-called racinos on account of the revenue-enhancing potential of slot machine play.

Despite their apparent popularity, slot machines have also been described
as the "crack cocaine of gambling" by antigambling activists.[127] Sophisticated
electronic features are designed to create conditions that are conducive to
continuous, repetitive play—conditions that also have a potential to manifest problem gambling behaviors.[128] Lured by the possibility of very high
(though very rare) payouts, coupled with intermittent smaller rewards,
players have been known to continue for hours. With a slot machine designed around a standard of six seconds between plays, the typical player
betting two dollars per play is wagering up to twelve hundred dollars per
hour.[129] Even with a relatively high average payout of 90 percent, this translates to gross profits of more than one hundred dollars per hour. The wealth-
generating potential from these machines for the casino operator, particularly with thousands of them on the floors of large casinos, is enormous.

The electronic features that make slot machine play so attractive to patrons have not escaped the notice of tribes operating Class II facilities, which
rely on more traditional games such as bingo and pull-tabs. The IGRA
specifically contemplates the possibility that "electronic aids" might be used
to assist players in these kinds of games.[130] However, recent decisions by the
Eighth Circuit and the Tenth Circuit Court of Appeals illustrate the technological blurring of the differences between electronic aids and slot machines. This blurring has potentially significant legal consequences for the
nature and extent of Indian gaming.

In *Seneca-Cayuga Tribe of Oklahoma v. National Indian Gaming Commission,*[131] the Tenth Circuit addressed the issue of whether "The Magical Irish Instant Bingo Dispenser System (the Machine)" constituted a slot machine, which would thus fall under the Class III gaming regulation system. The Machine dispenses paper pull-tabs from a roll containing up to seventy-five hundred individual tabs. When a player inserts money into the Machine and presses a button marked "DISPENSE," the Machine cuts a pull-tab card and dispenses it into a tray for the player to receive. The Machine is also capable of scanning a bar code on the tab, which displays the contents of the paper tab on a video screen viewed by the player. If the tab is a winner, the player takes the tab to a clerk, who confirms the win and pays out the appropriate prize.

As the court noted, "The game played with the Machine can be a high-stakes, high-speed affair. A winning ticket pays up to $1,199.00 per one-dollar play. When working properly, the Machine completes one play every seven seconds."[132] Thus, the Machine presumably helped to make a comparatively mundane game of pull-tabs more visually exciting. It would also make play more frequent and regimented, potentially enhancing the profitability for the operator.

The Tenth Circuit faced the issue of whether the Machine was essentially an electronic aid to playing pull-tabs, which were allowed as Class II devices, or whether, as argued by the government, the game was essentially an "electromechanical facsimile version of slots," which would thus constitute a Class III device.[133] The Machine was functionally similar to another device known as the "Lucky Tab II," which the District of Columbia Circuit had previously held to be an authorized Class II technologic aid. The Tenth Circuit essentially agreed. In evaluating the Machine, the court observed that the player was still essentially playing a pull-tab game.

> Although a pull-tabs player may opt to view the video display regarding the contents of the paper pull-tabs, players of the Machine must still manually peel back the top layer of the pull-tab to confirm victory, and it is that tab presented for visual inspection to a gaming hall clerk that entitles players to winnings. We thus reject the argument that the game played with the Machine is slots: although we acknowledge some superficial similarities between the two, pull-tabs, even when sped up, placed under lights, and depicted with a spinning machine on the side, is still pull-tabs.[134]

The Lucky Tab II machine was also the subject of litigation in *United States v. Santee Sioux Tribe of Nebraska*,[135] in which the federal government sought to enjoin a tribe from using the machines in its Class II facility. Here, too, Eighth Circuit followed the District of Columbia Circuit in finding that the machine merely facilitates the playing of paper pull-tabs.

> While this case presents a close call, we think the better view is that operation of the Lucky Tab II machines does not change the fundamental fact that the player receives a traditional paper pull-tab from a machine, and whether he or she decides to pull the tab or not, must present that card to the cashier to redeem winnings.[136]

As for the argument that the machines were facsimiles of slot machines, the court noted: "These machines may look and sound like slot machines, but they cannot make change, accumulate credits, or pay out winnings. Thus, they are not exact copies (the commonly understood definition of a facsimile) of a slot machine."[137]

The U.S. government filed a petition of certiorari for review of both of these cases, but the Supreme Court denied these petitions.[138] The states of California, Alabama, Connecticut, Texas, Minnesota, Nebraska, Nevada, South Dakota, and Texas—which all have within their borders Indian tribes that currently operate gaming facilities or may seek to do so in the future—submitted an amicus brief in support of the petition. These states claimed that ruling that the devices were technologic aids rather than slot machines "threatens substantially to undermine the only means available for States to ensure adequate regulation of slot-machine gambling conducted on Indian lands, vis., the negotiated tribal-state compact."[139]

The states argued that when slot machines are subject to the compact requirement as a Class III game, the states may exercise considerable control or oversight over the regulation of gambling. Moreover, in states like California, the compact not only limits the number of slot machines but also subjects those machines to license fees. Moreover, the Class III facilities must also comply with revenue-sharing requirements, which are not applicable to Class II operations. To the extent that these restrictions can be circumvented, the protections of the IGRA are made ineffective. As the states point out:

By virtue of the Tenth Circuit's decision, the Tribes' ability entirely to circumvent IGRA's negotiation obligations with respect to slot machines is merely a function of human creative ability to design slot machines that—in the case of pull-tab devices, for example—permit push-button "play" of a coded strip-roll of paper "pull-tabs," providing a visual and auditory display of the outcome represented by bells and the aligning of reels of a virtual "one-armed bandit." From the player's point of view— and, therefore, from the perspective of a need for negotiated compact treatment—these so-called "technologic aids" are indistinguishable in any meaningful sense from any other slot machine along the casino wall.[140]

Although the Supreme Court was apparently not persuaded of the need for its intervention, the significance of this controversy has not been lost on the National Indian Gaming Commission. On January 21, 2004, the commission announced the formation of a Class II Game Classification Standards Advisory Committee to provide more definitive technical standards and regulations for the parameters of Class II games. Representatives were named on March 8, 2004, approximately one week after the Supreme Court's denial of certiorari in the Eighth and Tenth Circuit cases. It remains to be seen whether the committee will indeed promulgate more restrictive rules on electronic aids. If they fail to do so, this may present another case in which aggressive and technically correct legal positions expose fundamental political flaws in the regulatory system, which in turn will generate more restrictive rules. Detailed draft regulations were released in March 2005, though final regulations have not been promulgated.[141]

TRIBAL POLITICAL INFLUENCE

As shown previously, tribes enjoy a privileged status under current law. It is not surprising that tribal governments have been active in political efforts designed to maintain their privileged status. The recent controversies surrounding the indictment and guilty plea of the lobbyist Jack Abramoff, whose clients included several Indian tribes with gaming operations, have brought these efforts to light.

The total amount spent by tribes to influence legislation at both state and federal levels is difficult to ascertain. This difficulty is partly attributable to the fact that funds may be channeled to grass roots organizations that do not engage in lobbying government representatives but instead provide other services. These kinds of expenditures are outside the scope of election law reporting. Expenditures at the state and local levels are also difficult to track, as they are also outside the scope of federal election laws. However, federal expenditures provide a window of insight on the political influence of tribes, which merits some attention.

The Center for Responsive Politics, which operates opensecrets.org, a Web site examining the political expenditures on behalf of various industries, provides some insight into the magnitude and direction for political contributions of the Indian gaming industry. Data compiled from reports to the Federal Election Commission show that the Indian gaming industry contributed an estimated $7.3 million in the 2004 election cycle.[142] Most of the industry contributions (approximately 68 percent, or $4.8 million) went to Democratic candidates.

Although $7.3 million may seem significant, this total is dwarfed by other industries. For example, defense contractors, which are highly connected to and dependent upon actions in the political world, spent over $15 million.[143] Pharmaceutical firms spent about $18 million.[144] The commercial gambling industry spent about $11 million.[145] All totaled, House and Senate candidates received over $1 billion in 2004.[146] Thus, the contributions of any particular industry look small indeed in relation to this massive total. Nevertheless, it is interesting to note some of the particular matters that invoked tribal lobbying and political efforts. For examples we need to look no further than some of Abramoff's clients.

One issue that focused tribal concerns on federal legislation involved the federal tax treatment of tribal governments. The Mississippi band of Choctaw Indians was one of Abramoff's clients with interests in this area. The Choctaws have extensive business holdings in Mississippi and other parts of the Southeast, extending into Mexico. Their Web site lists Choctaw enterprises in manufacturing, retail, service, and tourism as providing more than eight thousand jobs, making them one of the top ten employers in Mississippi.[147] Although the tribe touts manufacturing as the basis for its economic success, it cites the Silver Star Casino as "the largest and most profitable Choctaw Enterprise to date."[148]

The growing influence and profitability of tribal casinos were drawing attention from commercial casino competitors, which did not enjoy the tax-exempt status of Indian tribes on similar enterprises. As a result, the tax-exempt status of tribal governments was at risk of being legislatively overturned. Tribal governments mobilized in opposition to this legislation. Jack Abramoff's close connections to antitax groups, which were particularly influential in Congress during this period, proved useful in helping to defeat this legislation, which Abramoff characterized as another attempt to raise taxes.[149]

In the process of representing the Choctaws, however, Abramoff apparently exacted funds from the Choctaws through related enterprises engaged in grass roots lobbying, which made payments to Abramoff that were not disclosed to the Choctaws.[150] The tribe asserts that they have cooperated with the Justice Department's investigation and that they have reached a settlement with Abramoff's former law firm that resolves their claims for past misdoings while he was associated with the firm.[151]

Abramoff's political influence was also deployed by tribal governments to protect their casino enterprises from incursion by other tribes. The Tigua tribe's Speaking Rock Casino located near El Paso, Texas, which borders neighboring Louisiana, was the target of a lawsuit filed in 1999 by Texas attorney general John Cornyn (now a U.S. senator).[152] This suit sought to enjoin the tribe from continuing casino-style gambling on its reservation, which the state contended was in violation of Texas and federal law. The federal district court ruled in favor of the state, and the facility was enjoined from operating casino games otherwise prohibited to Texas citizens in 2002.[153]

The political intrigue surrounding this case is rooted in the tenuous status of tribal gaming in the hands of federal and state authorities. The tribe had its status restored pursuant to federal legislation, and the ability to pursue gambling on the reservation was a matter that was specifically addressed in the restoration bill. State and federal officials were consulted in this process, and the federal restoration act for the tribe ultimately tied the fate of gambling to Texas law.[154] The broader IGRA was held not to abrogate this provision, which was effectively considered a compact with the state of Texas.[155]

Since the fate of the tribe's gambling operations, as well as the employment of casino workers, was at stake in this litigation, it was theoretically possible to resolve the matter through changing Texas law. The tribe was reported to employ 785 people at the casino, with a payroll of $14 million.[156] Thus, intense local interests were affected.

Of course, not everyone would line up with the interests of the Tiguas and their employees on this matter. Neighboring casinos in Louisiana, also run by Native Americans, would stand to gain from the elimination of a cross-border competitor. In particular, the Coushatta tribe of Louisiana, which operated the Coushatta Casino Resort in nearby Kinder, Louisiana, reportedly utilized Abramoff's services on this matter.[157]

Grass roots political interests against expanding gambling would become a valuable tool in ensuring against a political solution favoring another Texas casino. Ralph Reed, former executive director of the Christian Coalition, was hired by Michael Scanlon, an Abramoff associate, and his firm was reportedly paid more than $4 million to engage in opposition to Texas casino expansion.[158] Though Reed, who was staunchly antigambling in his beliefs, refused to take money from casino-owning tribes, the use of an intermediary here apparently hid the source of this spending. In response to an extensive public relations campaign by the Tiguas against the efforts of Attorney General Cornyn, Reed promised to send fifty pastors as "moral support" for Cornyn.[159] Reed, who is a candidate for lieutenant governor in Georgia, has subsequently claimed not to have known about any connection between tribal contributions and his political work against expanded casinos.[160]

The Tiguas were apparently also unaware of Abramoff's efforts against them in the Texas legislature. Those efforts did not stop Abramoff from subsequently being retained by the Tiguas for the purpose of lobbying Congress in order to change the undesirable judicial outcome. However, the Tiguas reportedly had trouble paying their retainer. According to a report in the *Weekly Standard,* Abramoff proposed an "elder legacy plan," which involved taking out life insurance policies on older tribal members, with the proceeds being paid to Abramoff on their demise. The tribe rejected this plan.[161]

Political contributions by the Tiguas to individual representatives, including Ohio congressman Bob Ney, have been the subject of continuing interest as this saga continues to unfold.[162] Representative Ney resigned his post as chairman of the House Administration Committee in early 2006, for the apparent purpose of avoiding "distraction" from his committee work as a result of Abramoff-related investigations.[163]

The Coushatta tribe and the Choctaws of Mississippi also apparently involved Abramoff in lobbying against casino competition in Louisiana from a neighboring tribe, the Jena Choctaw. An e-mail by Abramoff to Italia Federici, head of a Republican environmental advocacy group called the Council of Republicans for Environmental Advocacy (CREA), stated in part:

> There is a tribe in Mississippi and Louisiana called the Jena Choctaw. They are a federally recognized tribe and trying to get a gambling compact in Mississippi and/or Louisiana. The Jens are also trying to get land put into trust (ostensibly for "economic development", but really for gambling). This is totally horrible for both the Choctaw in Mississippi and the Coushatta. The Interior Department BIA has sent a letter out (I will fax this to you right now at the [blank] number) soliciting local input, as if they are going to do this !! [W]e have to squash this very, very hard and fast.[164]

It should be noted that the CREA hosted social events at which Interior Secretary Gale Norton and other Department of the Interior officials were invited guests.[165] The tribes were solicited to participate in this organization as "trustees" through contributions of fifty thousand dollars.[166] This apparently provided at least the perception of acquiring greater access to these officials.

In each of these examples, tribal political influence was brought to bear on issues that were important to them. Their involvement appears no different from that of other business enterprises seeking to defend business turf or to extend favorable tax preferences. The criminal information against Abramoff suggests that tribes were indeed victims of Abramoff to the extent that their funds may have been channeled to organizations that benefited Abramoff without their knowledge. However, their intentions to obtain benefits from those expenditures—just as other enterprises benefit from lobbying expenditures—were also clear.

In addition to these specific payments to lobbyists, tribes also made significant political contributions to individual candidates through Abramoff and his associates. According to a recent investigation compiled by the *Washington Post,* Abramoff, members of his lobbying team, and tribal associates contributed over $4 million to individual politicians during the period 1999–2004.[167] The possibility that these contributions may have caused specific legislative actions is a matter worthy of investigation.

It is important to recognize that the special status enjoyed by the tribes provides particularly enticing circumstances for lobbying activity. Whenever a business activity or economic benefit is held at the pleasure of government to the exclusion of others, competing interests will have incentives to remove those benefits. Political activists thus enjoy a position that lends itself to the extraction of tribute to preserve the status quo. As illustrated in the previous discussion, purveyors of government influence may play both sides of the political fence, leaving the tribes caught in the middle. When fueled by the considerable cash profits of a successful tribal gaming operation, the influence of tribes on politics is a force to be reckoned with. Citizens also need to be watchful about such expenditures at the state and local level, particularly in jurisdictions affected by tribal casino operations.

12. Governing Fortune in a Changing World

As legal and geographic barriers have crumbled, casino patrons have experienced unprecedented opportunities to pursue the whims of fortune. Traditional legal proscriptions against professional gaming houses have been transformed into components of a regulatory structure that supports a large commercial industry. Instead of struggling to suppress the demand for gambling, governments have chosen to exploit it by channeling patrons toward state-approved providers that can capture tax revenues and provide legitimate employment opportunities.

Expanded gambling has also exposed dimensions of human weakness that otherwise might have remained latent. There is still much to learn about the nature and extent of problem gambling, but the extant data suggest that its dimensions are significant. The National Council on Problem Gambling estimates that 3 million adults in the United States meet criteria for pathological gambling each year, with another 2–3 percent (6–9 million) experiencing serious problems due to gambling.[1] As discussed in chapter 5, these figures may be conservative. Problem and pathological gamblers are a significant source of revenues for casino operations.

Problem gambling behavior affects nongamblers as well as gamblers. Our own research has found that opening a casino produces a significant increase in personal bankruptcy rates over time.[2] Each bankruptcy translates into losses for creditors, and the associated costs they incur are likely to be passed along to others. Other researchers have identified a correlation between casino gambling and crime. Some have estimated that criminal activity associated with casinos exacts aggregate costs that outweigh any countervailing aggregate economic benefits.[3]

Children and families are also apt to suffer from problem gambling behavior. Gambling spouses may incur debt secretly and impose legal responsibility for those gambling-related debts on a nongambling spouse. In some cases, gambling losses may mean that child support goes unpaid, potentially impacting dependent children and adding further strain to the social safety net. As of 2003, nationwide arrearages in child support totaled over $95 billion—a stunningly large number that has been growing over time.[4]

News accounts commonly report these negative consequences, including embezzlement from employers or clients, family discord and divorce, and even suicide as a result of excessive gambling losses.[5] More stories probably lie below the surface, as family-related problems involving human weakness tend to be hidden in order to avoid embarrassment. Industry advocates may continue to challenge the certainty of scientific proof about a connection between gambling and social costs, but as time goes on that position becomes harder to maintain. It is evident that the costs are not zero and that they are likely to be significant.

In this environment, government officials may experience tension between their desire to raise revenue from this industry and their traditional responsibilities to protect the public welfare. Personal freedom is a powerful political ideal, and some people connect the pursuit of gambling with the pursuit of happiness. However, even libertarian principles recognize the need to internalize costs from such pursuits. In this final chapter, we look further at the political and legal environment with an eye toward the future of industry regulation.

If legalized gambling persists in some jurisdictions (as it is likely to do), the paradigm for regulation needs to change to address the reality of externalized social costs. The current system may seem highly resistant to change, but that resistance may be softening. We suggest one possibility for change that may provide a suitable compromise between freedom and responsibility. It involves wrapping new technology around an old idea with deep historical roots: licensing gamblers.

THE CURRENT POLITICAL MILIEU

Policymakers have given surprisingly little attention to social costs in formulating casino gambling policies. In fact, the successful expansion of the industry has been achieved in significant part by ignoring them. Industry proponents have achieved political success by exploiting the fact that costs associated with the gambling industry are diffused and difficult to measure, whereas benefits (such as tax revenues) are tangible and quantifiable.[6] Casino promoters have adopted the strategy of shifting the burden of proof on social costs to their opposition, while at the same time touting the casino as a tonic for economic vitality, a politically attractive source for tax revenues from a voluntary and popular activity, and a vanguard of individual liberty.

Although casino promoters have achieved success with this approach, it has played best in times of economic difficulty. In those situations, social risk taking may seem to be a viable step on the path to prosperity. Government officials thus view the easy money offered by the casinos as a preferable alternative to offer to their constituents, particularly when other alternatives may be based on less popular options involving sweat, tears, and toil. In modern times, such alternatives are hardly the stuff of which political success is made.

Signs of change may nevertheless be on the horizon. Citizens have continued to scrutinize the collateral effects of casinos on economic and social structures. Grass roots political efforts have proven remarkably effective against coordinated and well-funded efforts from commercial casino forces. Even the industry itself appears to be willing to take greater steps to address problem gambling.

An apt example occurred in November 2004, when a majority of Nebraska voters rejected statewide initiatives to legalize casinos. Two separate initiatives were on the ballot—one sponsored by the legislature and the other sponsored by a coalition of pro-gaming interests (including prospective casino investors) known as Keep the Money in Nebraska.[7] Both initiatives sought to establish legal casinos in Nebraska to compete with facilities in neighboring states, particularly those in Council Bluffs, Iowa, which shares a border with Nebraska on the Missouri River across from Omaha, Nebraska's most populous city. Although competition between these two plans may have contributed to electoral division within pro-gambling forces, thus weakening their prospects for success, grass roots political opposition from a group known as Gambling with the Good Life[8] was also instrumental in this outcome.

Though reportedly outspent by twenty to one,[9] Gambling with the Good Life successfully mobilized voters, particularly those interested in the social costs associated with gambling. They used connections with local churches and civic groups to spread their message, which emphasized the deleterious effects of problem gambling as a counterweight to the putative economic benefits associated with expanded gambling. The leader of this group, Pat Loontjer, a housewife, volunteered her time and mobilized many other volunteers to do the same. She was also supported by visible public figures, including congressman and former University of Nebraska football coach Tom Osborne and "Oracle of Omaha" Warren Buffet, who helped spread a message favoring work and saving over the ephemeral riches associated with gambling. Some businesses, including restauranteurs concerned about displacement effects of casino spending, also joined in such efforts. With little spending in the mass media, Loontjer spearheaded a grass roots campaign based on people-to-people contact, town meetings, and yard signs spreading word of individual support.

In contrast, Keep the Money in Nebraska focused heavily on mass media advertising that emphasized the economic drain from Nebraska residents' gambling across the river in Iowa. Images of millions of dollars floating across the bridge linking Omaha to Council Bluffs casinos flooded the airwaves. When questioned about social costs, the pro-casino spokespersons took an aggressive position that such costs had not been proven. They chose instead to emphasize the economic benefits, including jobs and taxes, that legalized gambling could deliver if Nebraskans gambled at home.

After the election, Keep the Money in Nebraska continued to advocate for legal change in state casino policy. However, their position seems to recognize social costs as part of the gambling equation. Their Web site states in part:

> Nebraska continues to have the vast majority of its citizens frequent bordering casinos, extensive participation in sports book, an eruption of illegal machines in private clubs and out state bars, and rapid expansion of Internet gaming. *Between 3% and 5% of our population already has a gaming related behavior disorder.* That figure is very comparable to states with full fledged casino gaming. We have most all of the downsides of expanded gaming and simply none of the upsides. There is a silver lining in all this. We have the opportunity to focus on the best possible way to minimize the downside and deal with it in a socially responsible manner in the new petition language.[10]

To recognize that a significant percentage of the population has a gambling-related disorder seems a significant concession. It remains to be seen how any new initiative they intend to sponsor will address problem gambling issues. Discussion of new initiatives to legalize casino gambling for the ballot in November 2006 suggests that the issue will not go away quietly.[11]

Local citizens also rejected initiatives for slot machines in Miami-Dade County, Florida, in 2005, after a statewide initiative was approved. The approval process for this initiative illustrates the difficulty of including social costs into the economic calculus associated with new gambling legislation. Florida law requires that constitutional amendments proposed through citizen initiatives must include "an analysis and financial impact statement to be placed on the ballot of the estimated increase or decrease in any revenues or costs to state or local governments resulting from the proposed initiative."[12] An initial attempt to include a reference to costs associated with "problem gambling" in this statement was opposed by the attorney general.[13] The Florida Supreme Court resolved this issue in the government's favor. The following language ultimately appeared on the ballot:

> This amendment alone has no fiscal impact on government. If slot machines are authorized in Miami-Dade or Broward counties, governmental costs associated with additional gambling will increase by an unknown amount and local sales tax-related revenues will be reduced by $5 million to $8 million annually. If the Legislature also chooses to tax slot machine revenues, state tax revenues from Miami-Dade and Broward counties combined would range from $200 million to $500 million annually.[14]

Thus, although the initiative recognized the potential for governmental costs to increase, the only quantifiable costs involved foregone sales tax revenues to local government, which are quite modest in relation to the direct taxes that the state would gain from expanded gambling.

After gaining narrow approval for this initiative in a statewide election in November 2004, local voters were then required to give further approval to expanded gambling. Broward County voters approved the measure, but Miami-Dade voters apparently changed their minds and voted against it in March 2005, despite giving 57 percent approval the previous November. Broward County has experienced further delays in the installation of slot machines. Enabling legislation was delayed, as the legislature was unable to agree on regulatory details. Further litigation may ultimately be required to resolve these issues.[15]

In July 2004, Pennsylvania approved a measure to allow up to sixty-one thousand slot machines across the state.[16] Neighboring Maryland, despite threats that these machines could draw patrons across state lines, is holding fast against expanded gambling. Pro-gambling interests in Maryland spent more than $2.3 million on lobbying efforts during the 2004 legislative session, which is not insubstantial in relation to the total estimated spending on all issues of $30 million the prior year.[17] One commentator analogized the interstate competition to an "arms race" between states competing for gambling patrons.[18] If so, a "peace movement" may well be at work, as resistance to slot machines in Maryland has been going on for three years. Though lobbyist spending there remains large, it has declined, reflecting the possible concession to the political will against expanding the industry.[19]

These recent examples show that public resistance to gambling remains a force to be reckoned with. Citizens continue to be skeptical about the economic and social dimensions of gambling. Sometimes regional interest groups like Gambling with the Good Life help in the dissemination of academic research that is problematic for the industry, which otherwise might be relegated to the ivory tower. Other organizations, including the National Coalition Against Legalized Gambling and the National Coalition Against Expanded Gambling, have also disseminated this research, reaching community activists and thus supporting grass roots resistance efforts. Religious convictions may also be playing an important role in the actions of many gambling opponents, and this force continues to be influential in American politics.

Skepticism about the benefits of gambling may also be rooted in personal experiences. The proliferation of gambling has produced shared experiences with problem gambling, which may be spread interpersonally. Claims of tax relief may also ring hollow, as neighbors in gambling states are still likely to complain about their high taxes. Personal stories should not be underestimated as an animating force behind a resistance to expanded gambling. This kind of information has the potential to overcome the influence of corporately funded mass media efforts to communicate a more positive message. Moreover, in states with populist traditions (like Nebraska), voters may already have a skeptical predisposition toward positions advanced by well-heeled corporate sources.

In some areas of the country, gambling markets are also maturing. Although early casino adopters found it easy to tap into consumer demand, particularly from patrons living in bordering states that restricted legal casinos, later adopters have found a more competitive marketplace. The proverbial "low-hanging fruit" has been picked, and competition for gaming dollars is intensifying. One effect of this competition is that the industry must spend more and more to create an attractive gambling environment. The recent experience of Trump Hotels and Casino Resorts in Atlantic City provides anecdotal evidence of this trend: after restructuring under federal bankruptcy protection, it will invest heavily to refurbish the facility to compete with other newer properties in Atlantic City.[20] In Las Vegas, the new Wynn Las Vegas hotel has reportedly cost $2.7 billion to construct—topping a previous billion-dollar expenditure on the Bellagio as the most expensive new property in the city.[21] As previously discussed, the capital markets have also expressed skepticism about the future profitability trends for this competitive industry.[22]

The political nirvana of tourist-based gambling, in which a casino does attract new dollars to the local economy, has proved exceedingly difficult to achieve. Las Vegas is unusual in this respect, as it remains an important tourist destination even for those with local gambling options. A recent Zogby survey has even reportedly shown that a majority of New Jersey residents would prefer to gamble in Las Vegas over Atlantic City.[23] However, without significant market differentiation (such as through special amenities or other tourist attractions, which Las Vegas can readily offer), it seems unlikely that patrons interested in gambling will travel elsewhere for that purpose. As a result, casino revenues (and associated taxes) in many locations are likely to come increasingly from local patrons at their "hometown" casino.

Local patronage still generates gambling taxes from willing participants, which might be viewed as politically preferable to increasing forced exactions from the general population. However, local citizens (including those who do not participate in gambling at all) may also bear some hidden costs. Increased reliance on local patronage also spells trouble for any prospects of turning the casino into a positive force working for economic development. In contrast to losses from their nonresident counterparts, wagering losses from local patrons may displace other local consumption instead of bringing in new dollars to the local economy. Moreover, the typical taxing structures that redistribute public gambling revenues ensure that a portion of gambling losses will be transferred outside of the local economy. Prospects for significant local benefits from gambling become more remote as nonresident patrons are removed from the mix.[24] The associated social costs of these problem gamblers also remain localized instead of being exported to other jurisdictions where nonresidents return.

Although the political and economic forces discussed previously may provide a basis for constraining the expansion of gambling (or at least slowing that growth), jurisdictions with existing casino facilities face other difficulties. To the extent that government officials take steps to address the costs of problem gambling, they face the prospects of a corresponding decline in government revenues from gambling taxes—at least in the short run. Moreover, in an environment of interstate competition (which potentially extends internationally through the Internet), designing and implementing a more restrictive regulatory system proves daunting. Creating a competitive disadvantage with facilities in neighboring jurisdictions may not seem like a prudent business choice in an environment where interstate competition— a casino "arms race"—is under way.

Once casinos become established, inertial forces tend to ensure their continuity. Significant past investments in infrastructure and jobs, as well as government reliance on revenues from the industry, encourage preservation of the status quo. Moreover, the practical reality of reliable campaign contributions cannot be ignored. An industry with cash to spend whose existence is at the pleasure of the state or local government has a powerful incentive to continue giving to support that status.[25] Growing economic and political clout provides a basis for skepticism and suspicion about the degree of scrutiny that elected officials are willing to turn upon the industry and its effects on the larger society, even if social costs are being imposed.

Recent events in Iowa illustrate this basis for skepticism. In 2004, the Iowa legislature required a study of socioeconomic effects from gambling, which was to be completed prior to a vote on expanding casino gambling in that state.[26] However, it appropriated only ninety thousand dollars to complete this research[27]—quite a modest expenditure in relation to the more than $200 million in gambling taxes contributed annually to state coffers. The legislature also expected this work to be done in a compressed time frame of approximately five months. Such constraints on time and resources raise the question of how much the legislators really wanted to learn about the impact of casinos in their state.

Further intrigue also surrounds this study. A legislative committee initially selected Per-Mar Security, a firm from Davenport, Iowa, to perform this research. In doing so, it passed over proposals from academics, including those from two state universities. Per-Mar Security later withdrew from the engagement after local media reported that it had economic ties to the industry, as it had sold security equipment and provided services to an Iowa casino.[28] Legislators, some of whom also received campaign contributions from this firm, claimed not to know of this apparent conflict of interest.[29]

An academic group from the University of Northern Iowa was ultimately chosen to complete the study, but only after a considerable delay. Moreover, the state persisted in approving an $85 million expansion of a casino in Council Bluffs without the benefit of any results from the study.[30] Such expansion in the face of uncertainty about the nature and extent of social costs provides an additional source of skepticism about the extent to which the public good is being considered by those who regulate the industry.

The current regulatory system has worked effectively during a phase where growing the industry and enhancing its profitability have served both government and industry interests. However, it falls short of an ideal system, which would sort out those with problem gambling behaviors who impose costs on others while allowing other patrons to exercise freedom in pursuing their own conception of the good.

Self-selection has not proven effective as a means for exclusion, as those with gambling problems often don't respond until after they have experienced significant losses—and likely imposed costs on others. Moreover, self-exclusion mechanisms ultimately depend on the gambler's own initiatives, which have been known to be faulty. One patron reported gambling over eighty times after she enrolled in an exclusion program; prior to enrollment she had lost over four hundred thousand dollars in personal savings and incurred thousands more in debt.[31]

Technology may now provide an unprecedented means to identify problem gamblers and to help them control their tendencies. To civil libertarians, technology may pose a threat that conjures up the image of "Big Brother" intruding directly on their personal pleasure seeking. However, one Internet firm has adopted a software-based solution to monitor gambling patterns and to warn those who may be venturing into problem areas, including reckless betting behavior. These patrons are contacted by an employee described as a "recovering gambling addict" and counseled to seek help.[32] This practice seems contrary to the short-term economic interests of the casino, which would presumably benefit from high levels of consumption at all times.

However, such behavior is not uncommon in other business environments. For example, drinking establishments have been known to cut off customers who have overindulged. In part, they may do so for altruistic and noble reasons, such as genuine personal concern for their customer. But the threat of liability may also encourage this behavior as a self-interested means to reduce the risk of exposure to penalties or civil claims through the legal system. In the casino industry, where the fate of the industry may lie in the hands of government officials moved by political winds, it may also be prudent to consider these longer-term interests.

LITIGATION THREATS TO THE GAMBLING INDUSTRY: SOME RECENT CASES

As more information becomes known about the nature and extent of problem gambling, evidence of indifference to these problems, or of the knowing design of casino environs to take advantage of human weaknesses, could well shift legal and political winds against the industry. When government officials are unwilling to impose changes through regulatory channels, litigation can serve as a catalyst for change. The possibility that casino patrons or those harmed by problem gambling behavior may pursue claims against casinos or their affiliated suppliers lurks in the background as a potential future threat to the industry.

Those who find such a threat implausible should consider recent legal actions against the tobacco industry. Following complaints brought by individuals, state attorneys general and eventually the federal government sought redress for harms and costs associated with adverse public health effects associated with the industry. The fact that the industry was specially taxed and that the government carefully regulated the sale of its products was apparently an insufficient basis to stop these actions from going forward and producing large cash settlements. Government can be a fickle business partner when it becomes advantageous to do so.[33]

As for private claims, class action lawsuits can present a formidable threat for any industry. Given the extensive costs to litigate and the prevalence of the so-called American Rule in requiring each party to bear his or her own attorney's fees, an individual plaintiff with a small or even modest-sized claim for damages would not choose to incur the transaction costs necessary to obtain redress. Attorneys working on a contingent fee basis could become interested, however, in the event that multiple claims could be joined together, thus allowing the potential for aggregate recoveries to justify the substantial litigation costs.

In *Poulos v. Caesars World, Inc.,*[34] the Ninth Circuit considered whether casino patrons could maintain a class action lawsuit seeking damages from the casino industry. The plaintiffs had lost money playing video poker and electronic slot machines. They brought a civil RICO claim alleging that the casinos had "engaged in a course of fraudulent and misleading acts and omissions intended to induce people to play their video poker and electronic slot machines based on a false belief concerning how those machines actually operate, as well as the extent to which there is actually an opportunity to win on any given play."[35]

With regard to video poker, the plaintiffs claimed that the electronic version of the game did not replicate a random deal from a conventional deck of cards. The computerized version was, instead, more predictable for the house, thus giving the house a greater advantage than in a conventional game.[36] They similarly claimed that the electronic slot machines were designed to appear similar to their mechanical counterparts, but their results were also based on computer programming that did not match the odds from mechanical devices. In addition, they claimed that casinos could also program the electronic versions to generate "near misses" for patrons, thus manipulating players by inducing them to believe they had just missed a jackpot and otherwise inflating the perceived chances of winning.[37]

Unfortunately for the plaintiffs, the court found that their claims were not suitable for class certification because of problems with individual proof of causation. In a civil RICO claim, the plaintiffs must show that a defendant's conduct proximately caused the injury.[38] For example, a slot machine player might meet this burden by showing

> that the Casinos' failure to inform players that the electronic slot machines operate differently than their mechanical counterparts affected

her decision to play, or that she was influenced by the fact that electronic slot machines look like traditional slot machines. In turn, this would require her to establish that she was aware of how the mechanical slot machines operated, was unaware that the electronic slot machines operated differently than those machines, and was motivated to play the electronic slot machine based on her knowledge of these factors.[39]

Alternatively, a video poker player might show the causal link between the casino's conduct and her losses by establishing

> that she was an ace player in the traditional table poker game and played the video poker game, at least in part, because she was misled into believing that the video poker and table poker games functioned similarly and offered the same odds. It is not enough to say "I played the games and I lost money" or "I didn't make any money."[40]

People gamble for many different reasons, and not every potential member of the class would be expected to be able to prove causation in this manner. As the court observed:

> [T]here may be no single, logical explanation for gambling—it may be an addiction, a form of escape, a casual endeavor, a hobby, a risk-taking money venture, or scores of other things. The vast array of knowledge and expectations that players bring to the machines ensures that the "value" of gambling differs greatly from player to player, with some people playing for entertainment value or for any number of other reasons as much as to win. [41]

Although the court recognized that some securities cases had been allowed to proceed as class actions without a similar showing of reliance and causation, it distinguished those cases as involving claims based entirely on omissions. In this case, the plaintiffs alleged affirmative mislabeling and specific acts on the part of the casino defendants.[42] Thus, their class certification was denied.

The law firm of Lionel, Sawyer, and Collins, which represented casino industry defendants in this case, issued a statement that this case caused "a collective sigh of relief around the globe as the casinos and manufacturers locally, nationally, and internationally were able to rid themselves of what would have been a time-consuming, multibillion dollar lawsuit."[43] The plaintiffs' attorneys in this case vowed to fight on with individual cases, though the damages threat to the industry posed by these cases is undoubtedly less significant than if a class had been certified.

Other class action efforts on a state level have also proven unsuccessful. In *Kraft v. Detroit Entertainment, LLC,*[44] the Michigan Court of Appeals dismissed a class action lawsuit based on the Michigan Consumer Protection Act and common law claims of fraud and unjust enrichment. In this case, class members asserted that the slot machines they played were deceptive in that they misrepresented the chances of winning a large payoff by failing to disclose that the machines were programmed to stop more frequently on spaces with lower valued payoffs. The expansive regulatory system applicable to gambling was held to preempt all state law claims against the casino, thus providing extensive protection for the industry from legal liability. In essence, redress for the failure to disclose was limited to that which might be provided by the casino regulators, and the courts would not intervene.

Problem gamblers have also sought to recover on an individual basis for substantial losses flowing from their gambling behavior. In *Merrill v. Trump Indiana, Inc.,*[45] a compulsive gambler brought suit in federal court seeking $6 million in damages from a riverboat casino. The gambler, Mark Merrill, was at the time of the litigation serving time in a federal prison in Florida for robbing banks, an activity he traced to the need to cover substantial gambling losses at the defendant casino. As the court wryly noted, "Mr. Merrill, by his own admission, is a compulsive gambler. Like East and West, this is a twain that should never meet. But it did."[46]

Merrill alleged that he had requested that the casino evict him if he should ever show up to gamble. The casino's failure to do so formed the basis for his complaint. Merrill asserted both contract and tort theories under Indiana law, but the district court dismissed all of them. On appeal, Merrill focused solely on his tort claims—that is, that the casino had violated a duty of care or engaged in willful and wanton misconduct by allowing Merrill to gamble.

For the source of this duty of care, Merrill first focused on regulations promulgated by the Indiana Gaming Commission that required casinos to maintain an eviction list. However, these regulations were not enacted until 2000—after Merrill had incurred his losses. Even if the law had applied to

Merrill, the court refused to create a private cause of action from the regulation. A violation of the regulation might get the casino in trouble with the commission, but that did not necessarily form a basis for recovery by an individual.[47]

Merrill also sought to develop a common law basis for a duty, but the court similarly rebuffed this theory. Though a duty of care exists where the safety of a casino patron was at issue, those problems were not presented here. The court found that the closest analogy under common law was the duty of care that a tavern owner had to protect its patrons. Although Indiana law might allow a third party to recover for injuries caused by an intoxicated patron, that patron could not recover from his own injuries.[48] Here, the court assumed that the same rule would apply to a compulsive gambler. As for Merrill's claim of willful and wanton conduct, the court rejected it on the basis that no facts were presented that could lead a jury to find such misconduct by the casino. Thus, Merrill was out of luck; his case was dismissed.

Though the court's approach in *Merrill* appears to limit gambler claims based on their own losses, the analogy between casinos and tavern owners presents the potential for future claims by third parties injured by compulsive gamblers. For example, in Merrill's case, a bank from whom Merrill had stolen could have brought a claim against the casino on this theory. Suits like these face practical barriers, including the difficulty of proving a linkage between their losses and the casino's breach of a putative duty. Behavior such as bank robbery is subject to explanation by other intervening causes, including psychological and moral defects unrelated to gambling. Negligence on the part of claimants may also bar recovery, to the extent that they failed to prudently guard their own property to protect it from loss.

Nevertheless, common law theories such as this one present the potential for third parties to recover externalized costs from the industry. As with the tobacco industry, some commentators have suggested that the gaming industry may be subject to lawsuits to recover social costs imposed by pathological gambling behaviors on state and local governments.[49] Though such lawsuits have not yet materialized in the United States, growing evidence of the existence of connections between gambling and social costs may well be cause for concern.

The industry may find that government support is built on financial rewards; loyalty can change to the extent that financial rewards can be obtained through other means. The tobacco industry certainly discovered this truth. After years of paying extraordinary taxes on tobacco products and adapting to government requirements to warn potential customers, it has faced lawsuits by both the federal government and state attorneys general for billions more on account of perceived harms associated with the legal use of their product. Given the long-term manifestation period of public health effects from smoking, proactive changes by the tobacco industry proved too little too late. The gaming industry may find itself in a more favorable position, with the hope that changes in its practices could have more immediate positive effects.

CHANGING THE REGULATORY PARADIGM: A LICENSE TO GAMBLE?

Allowing people to make their own choices—and to suffer the consequences for them—is a politically attractive option. If gambling is just another form of entertainment, then perhaps society ought to be indifferent as to whether people want to spend their money playing coin-operated slot machines or video games. However, a closer inspection suggests that these activities may actually be quite different.

Unlike other forms of entertainment, gambling lacks well-defined boundaries for consumption. Although it is possible to overindulge in any activity, gambling involves spending as a form of recreation that can result in losing a fortune in a few moments. Gambling losses also appear to have an inverse relationship to normal consumption patterns: one is unlikely to believe that enjoyment increases as you lose more money. Moreover, the potential for addictive behavior that the bells and whistles of electronic slot machines and similar devices can induce may raise still other concerns, which are not present in most other forms of entertainment.

Our legal and moral traditions recognize that it is entirely appropriate to constrain behavior that imposes costs on others without their consent. The well-being of children also weighs heavily on the side of government reinforcement of individual responsibility versus the more abstract pursuit of the good. In particular, the potential for government intervention to regulate the demand side of gambling, rather than the supply side, merits some attention.

Licensing is an important component of the current regulatory structure. However, licensing focuses primarily on providers of gambling services rather than patrons. Licenses are required to operate a casino, and licensing requirements also extend to casino employees, who must undergo background checks and maintain a safe distance from those suspected of criminal enterprises. Licensing is intended to eliminate connections between casinos and criminal enterprises and to ensure that the state gets its share of the lucre generated from patrons. In many states, licenses also limit the supply of gambling services available to the public, which is likely to have positive effects on casino profits for existing licensees. In contrast, the demand side remains remarkably free, with the notable exception of proscriptions against gambling by minors.

A licensing requirement for gambling patrons would not be inconsistent with restrictions on other activities that potentially impact the community. Driving a car, owning a handgun (in many jurisdictions), and operating a restaurant all involve licensing functions that balance competing demands of personal liberty and public welfare. Moreover, such a concept is not entirely novel. Patron-based regulations extend all the way back to the Nevada frontier. An 1877 Nevada law prohibited gambling by debtors and persons with wives and dependent children.[50] Family members were given the power to inform gambling proprietors of ineligibility, and a misdemeanor criminal sanction was imposed on those who won money from ineligible gamblers.[51]

This law reflects the policy judgment that a bachelor miner could wager his silver with little impact on the economic health of others but that the person with debt or other support obligations could not. It is unclear whether this Nevada law significantly affected the incidence of gambling losses. However, in this era of rugged individualism, the apparent consciousness about the impact of gambling on the social order is remarkable. Instead of shifting social costs to others through government programs or legal structures (such as liberal bankruptcy laws), this approach seeks to reinforce individual responsibility to curtail those costs in the first place. At the same time, it preserves freedom for those with the capacity to bear these costs themselves.

Categorical restrictions on access to privileges such as gambling may be politically controversial, but the constitutional prerogative to impose restrictions on access to gambling is beyond serious question. Gambling is not a fundamental right.[52] As a result, the state can choose to regulate it by imposing conditions on access that are rationally related to legitimate state interests.[53] This should allow rather broad discretion in segmenting the patron market if the government wished to do so, provided that these categories were tailored toward achieving viable policy objectives.

Some categories would be more easily defensible than others. Relatively noncontroversial candidates for exclusion might include those receiving public assistance or those behind on child support payments. Each of these categories would appear able to withstand the applicable rational relationship analysis. When viewed in economic terms, a wager virtually always has a negative expected value equal to the house advantage. In the long run, gambling losses are likely, and those losses potentially displace dollars that might otherwise be used for beneficial purposes, such as support or maintenance of oneself or a minor child. When the state is advancing funds to assist individuals with those needs, restricting the ability to gamble seems appropriately connected to the desired end.

Another possible category might include those who have recently demonstrated financial irresponsibility through filing a bankruptcy petition. A discharge in bankruptcy allows the debtor to impose costs involuntarily upon unpaid creditors.[54] However, it is unclear whether this classification could be sustained under current law, which prohibits state discrimination against a debtor in matters of licensing based solely on the status of filing a petition in bankruptcy.[55] Section 525 of Title II of the U.S. Code is designed to reinforce the "fresh start" purposes of the Bankruptcy Code. The legislative history explains in part:

> The prohibition does not extend so far as to prohibit examination of the factors surrounding the bankruptcy, the imposition of financial responsibility rules if they are not imposed only on former bankrupts, or the examination of prospective financial condition or managerial ability. The purpose of the section is to prevent an automatic reaction against an individual for availing himself of the protection of the bankruptcy laws. Most bankruptcies are caused by circumstances beyond the debtor's control. To penalize a debtor by discriminatory treatment as a result is unfair and undoes the beneficial effects of the bankruptcy laws. However, in those cases where the causes of a bankruptcy are intimately connected with the license, grant, or employment in question, an examination into

the circumstances surrounding the bankruptcy will permit governmental units to pursue appropriate regulatory policies and take appropriate action without running afoul of bankruptcy policy.[56]

A federal bankruptcy court interpreted this provision in a case involving a debtor licensed as a horse trainer under Maryland racing law who challenged the loss of his horse training license after filing a bankruptcy petition. In these circumstances, the bankruptcy court found that it was appropriate for the state to impose a financial responsibility requirement and that such requirement was imposed on all trainers whether bankrupt or not. The court made it clear that enforcement was not a penalty for past irresponsibility but instead was focused prospectively on subsequent behavior.

> [The financial responsibility requirement] does not *per se* preclude one from obtaining a horse trainer's license because of impoverishment. There is no requirement in the rule that one must enjoy a certain position of wealth in order to qualify. Second, there is a subtle but important distinction between requiring a debtor to make good on outstanding debts (which are dischargeable in bankruptcy) as opposed to requiring licensees to demonstrate their *prospective* financial responsibility as a condition for the granting or renewal of licenses. This rule does not *per se* require the debtor to satisfy his outstanding judgments. Third, the prohibition against financial irresponsibility, in conjunction with the others enumerated above, is reasonably related to the protection and promotion of the horse racing industry in Maryland.[57]

The debtor in question had substantial gambling debts, as well as unpaid debts for feed and horses incurred while engaged in the business of being a trainer. Thus there was ample evidence apart from the bankruptcy petition itself to question his prospective financial responsibility.

If events unrelated to gambling, such as illness or lost employment, are the cause of bankruptcy, then excluding all bankrupt debtors from the privilege of gambling is potentially overbroad. If no future obligation exists to creditors, excluding the debtor from gambling arguably appears more like a penalty for past misbehavior than one protecting future social interests.

However, it should be noted that recent revisions to the bankruptcy laws have modified the extent to which a "fresh start" is available to debtors. Section

707 of the Bankruptcy Code imposes a new requirement on debtors with certain minimum levels of income to make payments to creditors out of a portion of their current disposable income.[58] Query whether restricting gambling privileges for these debtors would satisfy legitimate state interests by supporting the future obligation of repayment.

More dubious classifications might involve income testing, in an attempt to limit gambling to those who could "afford" to lose. Casino gambling in Great Britain was once limited to social clubs, which could define their own parameters for membership.[59] Limiting access to the comparatively wealthy presumably had some limiting effect on personal hardship from problem gambling behaviors. A recent proposal for casino gambling in Singapore imposes barriers to play by low-income residents in an effort to reduce social costs but to attract revenues from tourists. This proposal is meeting political opposition. After all, the rich may also have creditors, and even the poor have dreams to get "lucky."

An income cutoff as suggested in Singapore is both over- and underinclusive. If a person with modest income chooses to spend money on gambling and if that spending does not breach obligations to others, there is no rational basis to exclude him or her from pursuing an activity that the government otherwise defines as recreation. Whether one can gamble without externalizing the costs is hardly dependent solely on income, as wealthy gamblers may also have considerable debt, which is perhaps even larger in magnitude. As one commentator has written about the Singapore proposal:

> The casino doorman will ask: "Tell me your background first. . . . You are a well-known, but shady, businessman with three companies on the verge of bankruptcy? . . . In you go sir. The blackjack tables are to your left." "And you sir? . . . You've been a hard-working, taxi driver for 15 years? . . . Piss off, you peasant."[60]

Those with histories of problem gambling present a similar dilemma in crafting the limits for state action to protect citizens from their own bad choices. If harm to others becomes the touchstone for intervention, then a license might be used for the limited purpose of assisting those who wish help. For example, those seeking treatment could voluntarily surrender their licenses, thus providing a more robust approach to self-exclusion than the lists used in some states, which provide no real penalties for a casino's failure to exclude a listed member. Alternatively, the fact that a license provides a more robust means of tracking patronage could itself provide a means for intervention before losses mounted. This approach is used in the Netherlands, where casino staff members will approach patrons when their visits go up suddenly or when their visits exceed fifteen times per month.[61]

Licensing also offers the potential to internalize other costs within the gambling community. For example, whether one holds a license to gamble could be included on a credit report, allowing creditors to segment their customers and to make sophisticated pricing decisions based on differences in perceived risks. Losses associated with the gaming segment (such as in the form of a credit card default) could thus be shared among other gamblers rather than indirectly imposed on nongamblers. The insurance industry's treatment of smokers provides an apt example of this kind of segmented structuring to permit individual freedom while requiring participants to internalize the costs of the activity.

Of course, there are enormous practical barriers to a licensing program. In order to be effective, licensing would require greater dependence on electronic identification and gaming practices. The industry is already moving in this direction, as player's club programs become ubiquitous. Missouri casinos require that patrons register to enter a casino, a practice that is used to limit gaming purchases (and thus, indirectly, losses) during each gambling session. Electronic slot machines and even video lottery terminals could be programmed to comply with the goal of licensing. Tax reporting and money laundering concerns could also be addressed in this approach, if the political will can be mustered to address these concerns.

However, some other barriers must also be overcome. The interstate dimensions of modern casino gaming erect one such barrier, as licensing requirements in one state could be circumvented by patrons who choose to travel to a bordering state without such requirements. The experiences of Iowa and Illinois in the early 1990s showed the difficulty of imposing gambling restrictions in the form of loss limits, as riverboats floated elsewhere to pursue more lucrative markets without limitations on profit.[62] Patrons also followed, as they chose the kind of experience they wanted—which was free from limits on betting and losses. Tribal casinos would also create a knotty problem for a state-based scheme, as a tribal facility could provide a readily accessible alternative to the state-licensed casino imposing a licensing requirement.

Federal law could also be used to overcome these problems of interstate competition, but a federal role does not come without difficulty. Privacy advocates may well become apoplectic over the idea of a government licensing program of this magnitude, which would require databases to be maintained at state or federal levels to include those with licensing privileges and those who are barred from obtaining licenses. However, privacy is but one of the many competing values that are impacted in this arena. As recent terrorism threats have indicated, many citizens are willing to trade privacy for security. Such trade-offs may also be politically acceptable here, when doing so means reinforcing freedom for gamblers and nongamblers alike.

A federal scheme would also have to address a formidable future threat—that of circumventing government regulation through the Internet. Absent a comprehensive treaty dealing with Internet gambling providers, a regulatory scheme based on licensing could potentially be circumvented. However, this threat must be kept in perspective. Like drug addicts, gambling addicts may well pursue their addictions in realms that are not safe. But relegating their pursuits to unregulated markets undoubtedly deters some people from this behavior.

Although licensing would not avoid all of the social costs associated with legalized gambling, this concept has the potential to reduce those costs while at the same time safeguarding liberty for those who wish to gamble and can do so responsibly. From a political perspective, it is hard to argue for personal freedom when doing so involves the use of public funds devoted to the welfare of families and children or when personal obligations for child support go unpaid. If those kinds of gamblers are contributing substantially to industry coffers such that removing them threatens the industry's viability, then perhaps this industry should not be operating.

This book has shown that there are no easy solutions to the problems presented by casino gambling. The costs and benefits of legalized gambling each present elements that cannot easily be quantified. The dilemma can be illustrated by an encounter that one of us had recently with two gamblers. Both worked as nurses and had families to support. One of them had been to a casino before work that morning, where she reported losing four hundred dollars. She was visibly depressed, and she commented that she always seemed to lose when she needed the money the most. The other went occasionally with friends and wagered a total of fifty dollars "until it was gone," and she reported having a fabulous time.

Policymakers considering the expansion of legalized gambling should recognize that the responsible gambler probably represents the majority of the gambling population. They engage in an activity that apparently gives them pleasure and seems harmless enough. However, for the minority who lose more than they can afford, creating convenient access to gambling creates a significant potential for harm, not only to themselves but also to others. Although definitive answers to important questions, such as how much industry revenue comes from problem gamblers, have not been resolved, the available data suggest that this minority of the gambling population is providing a significant portion of the revenue. This presents a dilemma for jurisdictions where local gamblers are the primary source of patronage.

As Nelson Rose, a prominent academic commentator, observed more than a decade ago, "Throughout history, every society that has allowed casinos to cater to local customers has eventually outlawed gambling."[63] Professor Rose predicted a future crackdown on gambling to the extent that local populations become the source for gambling dollars.[64] This prediction has not yet come true in many jurisdictions. However, it may explain the reticence to expand gambling in other jurisdictions, where policymakers are not content to look solely at the positive side of the ledger.

In jurisdictions with significant gambling investments, the prospects of returning to a regime of criminal proscription are remote. As in the ancient myth, the contents of Pandora's box could not be returned once they had been released into the world. However, it should be remembered that this box also contained hope. If casino gambling is to persist, then regulators must address the serious problems it creates, even if that means that casino profits and state tax revenues suffer as a result. Informed citizens will be indispensable in ensuring that government officials are held accountable in this area. Continued attention from the academic community in addressing the critical questions presented by legalized casino gambling will play a vital role in sorting out the truth and bringing it to light. Governing fortune is hard work.

NOTES

CHAPTER 1

1. *See* THE DEVELOPMENT OF THE LAW OF GAMBLING: 1776–1976 at 3–4 (1977) [hereinafter DEVELOPMENT OF THE LAW OF GAMBLING]. This study was commissioned by the National Institute of Law Enforcement and Criminal Justice, Law Enforcement Assistance Administration of the United States Department of Justice, under the Omnibus Crime Control and Safe Streets Act of 1968. Much of the historical material in this chapter is drawn from this extensive and thorough work.

2. *Id.* at 4–5.

3. *See id.* at 5–7.

4. *See id.* at 6–7.

5. *See id.* at 7–13.

6. *See id.* at 12.

7. *Id.* at 12.

8. *Id.* at 13–16. The titles are instructive. The Statute of Charles II (1664) was entitled "An Act against deceitful, disorderly, and excessive gaming," *id.* at 13, while the Statue of Anne (1710) was entitled "An Act for the better preventing of excessive and deceitful gaming," *id.* at 15.

9. *Id.* at 16–17. Half the damage award would go to the plaintiff, the rest to the poor. Id. at 17. It is uncertain how the poor's share was actually administered. At this time, ten pounds was not an insubstantial sum, as it represented more than two hundred times the daily wages of common laborer (i.e., one shilling). *See id.* at 17 n.41.

10. *Id.* at 18.

11. *See id.* at 33.

12. *See id.* at 30.

13. *See id.*

14. *See id.* at 41.

15. *See id.* at 41–42.

16. *See id.* at 43.

17. *Id.* at 48.

18. *See id.* at 127–33.

19. *See id.* at 132.

20. *See id.* at 46–47.

21. *See id.* at 242–44.

22. *See id.* at 243.

23. *Id.*

24. *See* Ronald L. Rychlak, *The Introduction of Casino Gambling: Policy and Law,* 64 MISS. L.J. 291, 299–301 (1995).

25. *See id.* It should be noted that Harvard, Yale, and Princeton were also religiously affiliated institutions.

26. *See* DEVELOPMENT OF THE LAW OF GAMBLING, *supra* note 1, at 72.

27. *See id.* at 65–72.

28. *See id.* at 64–65.

29. Irwin v. Williar, 110 U.S. 499, 510 (1885).

30. Harvey v. Merrill, 150 Mass. 1, 11, 22 N.E. 49, 52 (1889) ("It is now settled here that contracts which are void at common law, because they are against public policy, like contracts which are prohibited by statute, are illegal as well as void. They are prohibited by law, because they are considered vicious, and it is not necessary that a penalty be imposed in order to render them illegal.").

31. *See* W. PAGE KEETON ET AL., PROSSER AND KEETON ON THE LAW OF TORTS 683–84 (5th ed. 1984).

32. *See, e.g.,* DEVELOPMENTS IN THE LAW OF GAMBLING, *supra* note 1, at 68 ("General social disruption was thought to be another byproduct of the tavern scene.").

33. BLACK'S LAW DICTIONARY 1208 (5th ed. 1979).

34. Commonwealth v. Burns, 27 Ky. 177, 1830 WL 1856 (1830).

35. O'Blennis v. State, 12 Mo. 311, 1848 WL 4097 (1848). Faro was a fast-paced card game with a low house advantage and was frequently played on the frontier. For a description of this game, see <http://www.greedyhog-gambling.com/docs/faro-the-frontier-favorite.shtml> (visited May 23, 2006). The author of this Web site speculates that the demise of faro was attributable to such factors as a low house edge (less than 2 percent) and widespread cheating. *See id.*

36. State v. Smith, 10 Tenn. 272, 1829 WL 501 (1829).

37. *Id.*

38. *See* DEVELOPMENT OF THE LAW OF GAMBLING, *supra* note 1, at 377–79. Concepts of Jacksonian democracy were thought to play an important foundational role in enacting these prohibitions.

39. *See id.* at 382.

40. *See id* at 380, 384, 389.

41. *See id.* at 381–82.

42. *See id.* at 387–89.

43. *See id.* at 388.

44. *See id.*

45. *See id.*

46. *Id.* at 403–6.

47. *Id.* at 407.

48. *Id.* at 410–12.

49. *Id.* at 411 n.93 (quoting a portion of a legislative committee report on the 1869 legalization act).

50. *Id.* at 416 n.6.

51. *Id* at 416 n.7. This regulation would be repealed in 1905. *See id.* at 426 n.41.

52. *Id.* at 416 n.8.

53. *See id.*

54. *Id.* at 417.

55. 1874 WL 3931, at 3 (Nev.).

56. State v. Overton, 1881 WL 4088, at 6–7 (Nev.).

57. DEVELOPMENT OF THE LAW OF GAMBLING, *supra* note 1, at 427.

58. *See id.* at 428–32.

59. *See id* at 432–41.

60. This is not to say that gambling was unavailable elsewhere. New Orleans was also well-known as a city that tolerated gambling, despite *de jure* criminalization. *See generally id.* at 286.

61. *See id.* at 362, 263–69.

62. *See id.* at 362.

63. *See id.* at 346, 364, 402.

64. *See id.* at 364.

65. *See, e.g.,* LaTour v. Louisiana, 778 So. 2d 557, 562–64 (La. 2004) (tracing the history of the transformation of gambling from vice to economic development tool in Louisiana).

66. *See* North American Association of State and Provincial Lotteries, *Fiscal Years 2002, 2003, and 2004 Lottery Sales and Profits,* available at <http://www.naspl.org/sales&profits.html>.

67. *See id.* The impact of video lottery terminals appears significant. In contrast to North Dakota, neighboring South Dakota had per capita lottery spending of $874.24. South Dakota has video lottery terminals; North Dakota does not.

68. *See id.*

69. Tax issues are addressed in greater detail in chapter 3.

70. *See* AMERICAN GAMING ASSOCIATION, STATE OF THE STATES 2 (2005), available at <http://www.americangaming.org/assets/files/uploads/2005_State_of_the_States.pdf>.

71. *See* ALAN MEISTER, INDIAN GAMING INDUSTRY REPORT 1 (2004) (estimating 2003 data); American Gaming Association, *Gaming Revenue: Current-Year Data* (August 2004), available at <http://www.americangaming.org/Industry/factsheets/statistics_detail.cfv?id=7>.

72. *See* American Gaming Association, *States with Gaming* (May 2005), available at <http://www.americangaming.org/Industry/factsheets/general_info_detail.cfv?id=15>.

73. *See* American Gaming Association, *Gaming Revenues: Current-Year Data* (August 2004), available at <http://www.americangaming.org/Industry/factsheets/statistics_detail.cfv?id=7>, which estimates the total at $72.87 billion. However, this includes lottery winnings of only $19.93 billion instead of the broader total of approximately $48 billion in lottery spending. If all lottery spending is included, the total would be approximately $30 billion higher.

74. *See* AMERICAN GAMING ASSOCIATION, STATE OF THE STATES 4 (2004) available at <http://www.americangaming.org/assets/files/uploads/2004_Survey_for_web.pdf>. The AGA shows only commercial casino spending in its comparison.

75. For an excellent historical and cultural analysis of the concept of luck in America, see JACKSON LEARS, SOMETHING FOR NOTHING (2003).

76. *See generally* GAO, IMPACT OF GAMBLING: ECONOMIC EFFECTS MORE MEASURABLE THAN SOCIAL EFFECTS (GGD-00-78, April 27, 2000), available at <http://www.gao.gov/new.items/gg00078.pdf>. The putative benefits and costs associated with gambling are discussed at greater length in chapters 3–5.

77. NATIONAL GAMBLING IMPACT STUDY COMMISSION REPORT at 47 (1999).

CHAPTER 2

1. These developments are chronicled in greater detail in chapter 8.

2. *See* AMERICAN GAMING ASSOCIATION, STATE OF THE STATES 5 (2002), available at <http://www.americangaming.org/assets/files/AGA_survey_2002.pdf>.

3. *See* AMERICAN GAMING ASSOCIATION, STATE OF THE STATES 2 (2005), available at <http://www.americangaming.org/assets/files/uploads/2005_State_of_the_States.pdf>.

4. *See id.*

5. *See* ALAN MEISTER, INDIAN GAMING INDUSTRY REPORT (2005–6).

6. *See id.*

7. *See id.*

8. See chapter 8 for more details on this legislation.

9. See chapter 8 for discussion of recent developments in Iowa that may expand casinos in interior locations.

10. AGR represents the gross gambling revenues minus winnings paid to the gambler.

11. Revenue per visitor in Missouri may be understated, however, due to the

fact that the Missouri system for regulation involves a five-hundred-dollar loss limit per "excursion." *See generally* MISSOURI GAMING COMMISSION, ANNUAL REPORT 2003, at <http://www.mgc.dps.mo.gov/annual%20reports/2003/annual2003.html>. If multiple excursions per visitor are taken into account, the AGR per patron is comparable to that in Iowa and Louisiana. Missouri's regulatory system is discussed in greater detail in chapter 8.

12. 480 U.S. 202 (1987).

13. A detailed discussion of the development of tribal gaming and its regulatory environment is provided in chapter 11.

14. 25 U.S.C. §§ 2701–2721.

15. *See* 25 U.S.C. § 2702.

16. All tribal casino data in this chapter come from MEISTER, INDIAN GAMING INDUSTRY REPORT (2005–6).

17. *See* Fitzgerald v. Racing Ass'n of Central Iowa, 675 N.W.2d 1, cert. denied 541 U.S. 1086 (2004). *See also id.,* 539 U.S. 103 (2003) (holding that the Iowa scheme satisfied federal constitutional constraints).

18. This estimate comes from Yahoo.com or <http://finance.yahoo.com>.

19. Diamonds (DIA) and Spyders (SPY) are shares of stock that are composed of a portion of the Dow 30 industrial companies and the S&P 500 companies, respectively.

20. Only firms from table 2.8 with available financial statements are listed.

21. Christiansen Capital Advisors promotion spending <http://news.mainetoday.com/indepth/gambling/030502blom.shtml> (accessed May 27, 2006). Harrah's promotion <http://brokopp.casinocitytimes.com/articles/678.html> (accessed May 27, 2006). Grand Victoria Casino <http://www.grandvictoria elgin.com/property/press1.php?UID=53> (accessed May 27, 2006). Majestic Star promotion spending <http://info.detnews.com/casino/newdetails.cfm?column=grochowski&myrec=109> (accessed May 27, 2006). Caesars in Tunica promotion spending <http://www.tunica-ms.com/events.htm> (accessed May 27, 2006).

CHAPTER 3

1. *See* Cherokee Nation v. Georgia, 30 U.S. (Pet.) 1, 20 (1831).

2. *See* ALAN MEISTER, CASINO CITY'S INDIAN GAMING INDUSTRY REPORT, 28 (2005–2006).

3. Wisconsin state officials confirmed that this statement was indeed correct. *See Milwaukee Journal-Sentinel,* June 23, 2005, at <http://www.jsonline.com/news/state/jun05/335634.asp>.

4. <http://www.schwarzenegger.com/news.asp>.

5. <http://news.findlaw.com/scripts/printer_friendly.pl?page=/prnewswire/20050622/22jun20051730.html>.

6. <http://www.coloradogaming.com>.

7. <http://www.illinoiscasinogaming.org/industry_resources.htm>.

8. <http://www.in.gov/gaming>.

9. <http://www.state.ia.us/irgc>.

10. <http://www.dps.state.la.us/lgcb>.

11. See chapter 8 for further details.

12. "The day-to-day operating expenses of the MGCB are paid for by the An-nual State Services Fee (this fee is not related to the casinos' gaming revenues). Each year, $2 million of this $25 million Fee goes toward compulsive gambling pro-grams, administered by Michigan Department of Community Health. No single casino's share shall exceed 1/3 of the total Annual State Services Fee Adjusted an-nually by Detroit Consumer Price Index." See Michigan Gaming Control Board, at <http://www.michigan.gov/mgcb/0,1607_120_1395_1469_7138_11436_,00 .html> (accessed May 26, 2006).

13. "The entire State Wagering Tax (8.1% of the casinos' Net Win) is deposited into the School Aid Fund for statewide K–12 classroom education. The City Wager-ing Tax (9.9% of the casinos' Net Win) may be used by the City of Detroit for hiring, training, and deployment of street patrol officers; neighborhood and downtown eco-nomic development programs designed to create local jobs; public safety programs such as emergency medical services, fire department programs, and street lighting; anti-gang and youth development programs; other programs that are designed to contribute to the improvement of the quality of life in the City; relief to the tax-payers of the City from one or more taxes or fees imposed by the City; capital improvements costs; and road repairs and improvements." See Michigan Gaming Control Board, at <http://www.michigan.gov/mgcb/0,1607,7-120-7863_15534 _F,00.html> (accessed May 30, 2006).

14. See Iowa Racing and Gaming Commission, yearly reports, at <http://www .state.ia.us/irgc>.

15. Nevada is not considered, since ten of the sixteen counties in the state have casinos and the casinos had been in existence for many more decades than casinos in other states.

CHAPTER 4

1. Thomas A. Garrett, *Casino Gaming and Local Employment Trends*, 86 Fed. Re-serve Bank of St. Louis Rev. Len. 9–22 (2004).

2. Thomas Garrett & Mark Nichols, Do Casinos Export Bankruptcy? (Federal Reserve Bank of St. Louis Working Paper No. 2005-19A, 2005), available at <http://research.stlouisfed.org/wp/2005/2005-019.pdf>.

3. Ernest Goss & Edward A. Morse, The Impact of Casino Gambling on Personal Bankruptcy Rates (1990–2002) (August 25, 2005, Social Science Re-search Network Working Paper), <http://ssrn.com/abstract=801185>.

4. S. Cornell, J. Kalt, M. Krepps, and J. Taylor, *American Indian Gaming Policy*

and Its Socio-Economic Effects. A Report to the National Gambling Impact Study Commission (Economic Resource Group, Inc. July 31, 1998).

5. Jonathon Taylor & Joseph Kalt, *American Indians on Reservations: A Databook of Socioeconomic Change Between the 1990 and 2000 Census* (Harvard Project on American Indian Economic Development, January 2005).

6. Ernie Goss, *The Economic Impact of an Omaha, Nebraska Casino.* Research report prepared for the Greater Omaha Chamber of Commerce, 2002, available at <http://www.outlook-economic.com/ResearchAndNews/Research/gambling.pdf>.

7. These losses result from the expectation that 13.7 percent of Omaha casino patrons will come from Nebraska outside of metropolitan Omaha. This results in reduced spending for the non-Omaha portion of Nebraska.

8. Data on tribal casino employment are not available on a consistent and timely basis. Consequently only commercial casino employment data are presented.

9. AMERICAN GAMING ASSOCIATION, 2004 REPORT, at <http://www.americangaming.org/assets/files/2004_survey_for_web.pdf>.

10. In this case, state employment is compared to national employment. Thus LQ equals the percent of state employment in leisure and hospitality divided by the percent of national employment in leisure and hospitality. See chapter 3 for a discussion of LQs.

11. See TERESA A. SULLIVAN, ELIZABETH WARREN, & JAY LAWRENCE WEST-BROOK, THE FRAGILE MIDDLE CLASS (Yale 2000). Data from studies in 1991 and 1997, which are both within the period analyzed here, suggest that bankruptcy filings are higher in demographic groups with people between the ages of twenty-five and fifty-four. *See id.* at 38–41. A 1991 study also indicated that African American racial groups had a higher proportion of bankrupt debtors in relation to population as compared with other ethnic groups. *See id.* at 41–50.

CHAPTER 5

1. *See* National Paint & Coatings Ass'n v. City of Chicago, 45 F.3d 1124, 1127 (7th Cir. 1995).

2. *See generally* GAO, IMPACT OF GAMBLING: ECONOMIC EFFECTS MORE MEASURABLE THAN SOCIAL EFFECTS (GAO/GGD-00-78, April 27, 2000), available at <http://www.gao.gov/new.items/gg00078.pdf> [Hereinafter GAO Study].

3. AMERICAN PSYCHIATRIC ASSOCIATION, DIAGNOSTIC AND STATISTICAL MANUAL OF MENTAL DISORDERS 615 (4th ed. 1994) [hereinafter DSM].

4. *See id.* at 618.

5. *See* NATIONAL OPINION RESEARCH CENTER, GAMBLING IMPACT AND BEHAVIOR STUDY at 16, 20 (1999) (Report to the National Gambling Impact Study Commission) [hereinafter NORC Study].

6. *See, e.g.,* NATIONAL GAMBLING IMPACT STUDY COMMISSION REPORT at 4-1

(1999); Howard J. Shaffer & David A. Korn, *Gambling and Related Mental Disorders: A Public Health Analysis,* 23 ANN. REV. OF PUB. HEALTH 171, 174 (2002) ("subclinical or problem gambling is a milder form of pathological gambling") [hereinafter Shaffer & Korn (2002)].

7. *See* NORC Study, *supra* note 5, at 21.

8. *See id; see also* John Welte et al., *Alcohol and Gambling Pathology among U.S. Adults: Prevalence, Demographic Patterns and Comorbidity,* J. STUD. ALCOHOL 706–7 (September 2001) [hereinafter Welte Study].

9. Welte Study, *supra* note 8, at 708.

10. *See* DSM, *supra* note 3, at 617.

11. *See* NORC Study, *supra* note 5, at 7.

12. *See id.*

13. AMERICAN GAMING ASSOCIATION, STATE OF THE STATES 3 (2005), at <http://www.americangaming.org/assets/files/uploads/2005_state_of_the_states.pdf>.

14. *See* Population Division, U.S. Census Bureau, Table 1: Annual Estimates of the Population by Sex and Five-year Age Groups for the United States: April 1, 2000 to July 1, 2004 (NC-EST2004-01, Release Date June 9, 2005). This total includes all population ages twenty and over. This may overstate the population slightly to the extent that adults under age twenty-one are not permitted to gamble legally in casinos.

15. *See* NORC Study, *supra* note 5, at 21.

16. *See* Carlo C. DeClemente, Marilyn Story, & Kenneth Murray, *On a Roll: The Process of Initiation and Cessation of Problem Gambling Among Adolescents,* 16 J. GAMBLING STUD. 289, 294 (2000).

17. *See* DSM, *supra* note 3, at 617.

18. *See* M. Leann Dodd, Kevin J. Klos, et al., *Pathological Gambling Caused By Drugs Used to Treat Parkinson Disease,* 62 ARCHIVES OF NEUROLOGY (2005), available at <http://archneur.ama-assn.org/cgi/content/full/62.9.noc50009v1> (accessed July 13, 2005).

19. *See* Robert B. Breen & Mark Zimmerman, *Rapid Onset of Pathological Gambling in Machine Gamblers,* 18 J. GAMBLING STUD. 31 (2002).

20. *See id.* at 40–41.

21. *See* DSM, *supra* note 3, at 616–17.

22. *See* NORC Study, *supra* note 5, at 26, table 7.

23. *See* Welte Study, *supra* note 8, at 709.

24. *See* DSM, *supra* note 3, at 616.

25. *See* Iowa Department of Public Health, *Healthy Iowans 2010,* chap. 20, p. 10 (January 2000), available at <http://www.idph.state.ia.us>.

26. *See* National Coalition Against Legalized Gambling, *Addicts R' Us' Games Invade Children's Shelves,* 3 BET'S OFF BULLETIN (January 2005).

27. *See* Welte Study, *supra* note 8, at 706, 707.

28. *See* NORC Study, *supra* note 5, at 26, table a.

29. *See* H. R. Lesieur and S. B. Blume, *The South Oaks Gambling Screen (SOGS): A New Instrument for the Identification of Pathological Gamblers,* 144 AMER. J. OF PSYCHOL. 1184 (1987).

30. *See* Welte Study, *supra* note 8, at 708.

31. *See* NORC Study, *supra* note 5, at 33–34.

32. *See* NATIONAL GAMBLING IMPACT STUDY COMMISSION REPORT at 4-1 (1999) (quoting National Research Council, *Pathological Gambling: A Critical Review* [April 1, 1999], Exec-2).

33. *See* United States Department of Health and Human Services, Office of Child Support Enforcement, Table 11: Total Amount of Arrearages Due FY 2003, available at <http://www.acf.hhs.gov/programs/cse/pubs/2004/reports/preliminary _data/table_11.html> (accessed June 3, 2005).

34. Welte Study, *supra* note 8, at 710.

35. *See* NATIONAL GAMBLING IMPACT STUDY COMMISSION REPORT at 4-7, table 4-3 (1999).

36. *See* Tose v. Greate Bay Hotel and Casino, Inc., 819 F.Supp. 1312, 1320 (D. N.J. 1993) (discussing New Jersey alcohol regulation in casinos).

37. *See* American Gaming Association, *Casino Alcohol Policies,* at <http://www .americangaming.org/Industry/factsheets/issues_detail.cfv?id=31> (last visited July 23, 2005).

38. *See* NORC Study, *supra* note 5, at 29–30.

39. *See id.* at 49.

40. *See* Welte Study, *supra* note 8, at 709.

41. *See* NORC Study, *supra* note 5, at 27.

42. Rani A. Desai et al., *Health Correlates of Recreational Gambling in Older Adults,* 161 AM. J. PSYCHIATRY 1672–79 (September 2004).

43. *See* NORC Study, *supra* note 5, at 27.

44. *See id.*

45. *See* Shaffer & Korn (2002), *supra* note 6, at 177.

46. *See* American Gaming Association, *Bankruptcy Fact Sheet,* available at <http://www.americangaming.org/Industry/factsheets/issues_detail.cfv?id=2> (last visited July 23, 2005).

47. *See* American Gaming Association, *Crime Fact Sheet,* available at <http:// www.americangaming.org/industry/factsheets/issues_detail.cfv?id=23> (last visited July 25, 2005).

48. *See id.*

49. *See* GAO Study, *supra* note 2, at 35–42 (discussing the example of Atlantic City).

50. *See* American Gaming Association, *Industry Information,* available at

<http://www.americangaming.org/industry/faq_detail.cfv?id=63> (last visited July 25, 2005).

51. *See* United States Department of Justice, Office of Justice Programs, *Bureau of Justice Statistics* (showing property crime rates from 1973 to 2003), available at <http://www.ojp.usdoj.gov/bjs/glance/house2.htm> (last visited July 25, 2005).

52. *See id.* at <http://www.ojp.usdoj.gov/bjs/glance/cv2.htm>.

53. *See generally* Doran Teichman, *The Market for Criminal Justice: Federalism, Crime Control, and Jurisdictional Competition,* 103 MICH. L. REV. 1831 (2005).

54. Earl L. Grinols & David B. Mustard, *Casinos, Crime, and Community Costs,* 88 REV. ECON. & STAT. 28 (2006).

55. *See id.* These studies are also referenced in the NORC Study, *supra* note 5, at page 47.

56. *See* United States Department of Justice, Office of Justice Programs, *National Institute of Justice, Gambling and Crime Among Arrestees: Exploring the Link* (July 2004), at <http://www.nijrs.gov/pdffiles1/nij/203197.pdf> (last visited May 15, 2006).

57. *See id.*

58. *See id.*

59. *See id.*

60. *See* American Gaming Association, *supra* note 50.

61. *See* GRINOLS, *supra* note 53, at 32.

62. *See generally* Teichman, *supra* note 53, at 1831, 1839–49.

63. *See id.* at 1838.

64. *See* American Gaming Association, *Industry Information,* at <http://www .americangaming.org/industry/faq_detail.cfv?id=62> (last accessed July 25, 2005).

65. *See id.*

66. *See* NORC Study, *supra* note 5, at 46. It should be noted that other studies have also claimed that pathological or compulsive gamblers had a bankruptcy rate of approximately 20 percent. *See* Department of the Treasury, *A Study of the Interaction of Gambling and Bankruptcy* at 43 (July 1999). SMR Research claims 20 percent of compulsive gamblers were forced to file bankruptcy; interviews with bankruptcy lawyers indicated that 10–20 percent were bankrupt due to gambling debts; *id.* at 45 (University of Minnesota Medical School study of pathological gambling treatment patients showed 21 percent had declared bankruptcy); *id.* at 45–56 (Abt Associates, Inc., study indicated 20 percent rate for comparable population of pathological gamblers).

67. *See* NORC Study, *supra* note 5, at 46.

68. *See* Administrative Office of the United States Courts, Table 5A (U.S. Bankruptcy Courts Business And Nonbusiness Bankruptcy County Cases Commenced, By Chapter Of The Bankruptcy Code, During The Twelve Month Period Ended Dec. 31, 2003).

69. *See* GAO Study, *supra* note 2, at 21.

70. *See* Department of the Treasury, *supra* note 64.

71. *See id.* at 47.

72. *See id.* at 64.

73. *See id.* at 54.

74. John M. Barron, Michael E. Staten, & Stephanie M. Wilshusen, *The Impact of Casino Gambling on Personal Bankruptcy Filing Rates,* 20 CONTEMP. ECON. POL'Y 440–55 (2002).

75. ERNEST GOSS & EDWARD A. MORSE, THE IMPACT OF CASINO GAMBLING ON PERSONAL BANKRUPTCY RATES (1990–2002) (August 25, 2005, Social Science Research Network Working Paper), <http://ssrn.com/abstract=801185>.

76. *See* 11 U.S.C. § 727(a) (providing conditions for discharge in bankruptcy).

77. *See* NORC Study, *supra* note 5, at 45; *see also* EARL L. GRINOLS, GAMBLING IN AMERICA 134 (2004) (explaining this principle in connection with the analogous issue of theft losses).

78. *See* Pub. L. 109-9 at § 310 (amending 11 U.S.C. § 523).

79. *See id.*

80. 28 U.S.C. § 1408(a).

81. *See* THOMAS GARRETT & MARK NICHOLS, DO CASINOS EXPORT BANKRUPTCY? (Federal Reserve Bank of St. Louis Working Paper No. 2005-19A, 2005), available at <http://research.stlouisfed.org/wp/2005/2005-019.pdf>.

82. *See generally* NORC Study, *supra* note 5, at 38–60.

83. *See id.* at 52–53.

84. *See generally* GRINOLS, *supra* note 77, at 167–73.

85. *See id.* at 172–73 (table 7.1). Grinols also included a category for government regulatory costs, but none of the other studies included data on this issue.

86. *See id.*

87. *See id.* at 174 (table 7.2).

88. NORC Study, *supra* note 5, at 40.

89. E. L. Grinols & J. D. Omorov, *Development or Dreamfield Delusions? Assessing Casino Gambling's Costs and Benefits,* 16 J.L. & COMM. 58–60 (1996).

90. *See* Robert Williams & Robert Wood, *The Demographic Sources of Ontario Gaming Revenue* at 42 (Ontario Problem Gambling Research Center, June 23, 2004).

91. In Missouri casinos, where slot machine revenues are tracked separately from table games, slot machines typically generate the vast majority of AGR. The largest of these casinos, Harrah's in Maryland Heights, showed slot machine AGR of $263.573 million, more than 87 percent of total AGR of $300.775 million in 2004–5. These results are not atypical for other casinos in this jurisdiction. See MISSOURI GAMING COMMISSION, ANNUAL REPORT 2005, at the appendix, available at <http://www.mgc.dps.mo.gov/annual%20reports/2005/apx.pdf>.

CHAPTER 6

1. *See, e.g.*, United States v. Morrison, 529 U.S. 598 (2000) (finding the federal Violence Against Women Act was beyond Congress's Commerce Clause authority); United States v. Lopez, 514 U.S. 549 (1995) (finding that the Gun-Free School Zones Act of 1990 exceeded Congress's Commerce Clause authority). In *Lopez,* the Court identified three broad categories of activities that are within the scope of modern Commerce Clause authority: regulating use of the channels of interstate commerce; regulating and protecting instrumentalities of interstate commerce or persons or things in interstate commerce (including threats from intrastate activities); and regulating activities that have a "substantial relation" to interstate commerce. *See id.* at 558–59.

2. *See, e.g.*, United States v. Hallmark, 911 F.2d 399, 401 (10th Cir. 1990) ("Congress may, in any case, regulate or prohibit wagering activities pursuant to its enumerated powers; to do so by means of a tax would not violate the Constitution.") A Tenth Amendment argument against allowing federal taxation of wagering was considered "meritless."

3. *See* Hunter v. City of Pittsburgh, 207 U.S. 161 (1907).

4. 101 U.S. 814 (1879).

5. This provision states in part: "No State shall . . . pass any . . . Law impairing the Obligation of Contracts."

6. *Id.* at 821.

7. This conclusion follows from the fact that state governments and others had long utilized lotteries to fund worthy projects. As the Court explained, "We are aware that formerly, when the sources of public revenue were fewer than now, they were used in some or all of the States, and even in the District of Columbia, to raise money for the erection of public buildings, making public improvements, and not [i]nfrequently for educational and religious purposes." *Id.* at 818.

8. *Id.*

9. Such problems were confronted by the American Bar Association's Commission on Organized Crime as it evaluated the scope of state laws in the early 1950s. *See* Paul Bauman & Rufus King, *A Critical Analysis of the Gambling Laws*, *in* II ORGANIZED CRIME AND LAW ENFORCEMENT 74–76 (Morris Ploscowe, ed., 1952). This commission ultimately developed the Model Anti-Gambling Act to address these concerns.

10. For example, coverage of the Wire Act and its extension to Internet gaming, as discussed in chapter 10, provides an interesting modern example of this phenomenon.

11. *See* Bauman & King, *supra* note 9, at 75.

12. *See, e.g.*, United States v. Allen, 10 F.3d 405 (7th Cir. 1993) (prosecution of sheriff's department investigator for bribery arising from FBI sting operation involving illegal gambling operation in Indiana). A similar problem exists in other

criminal enterprises, such as the distribution of illicit drugs. *See, e.g.,* Eric Luna, *Drug Exceptionalism,* 47 VILL. L. Rev. 753, 796 (2002).

13. *See generally* Steven C. Yarborough, *The Hobbs Act in the Nineties: Confusion or Clarification of the Quid Pro Quo Standard in Extortion Cases Involving Public Officials,* 31 TULSA L.J. 781 (1996) (discussing the Hobbs Act as a means to prosecute corruption); Adam A. Kurland, *The Guarantee Clause as a Basis for Federal Prosecutions of State and Local Officials,* 64 S. CAL. L. REV. 367, 373 n.21 (1989) (citing federal legislation applicable to state and local corruption from gambling).

14. *See, e.g.,* United States v. Sullivan, 274 U.S. 259 (1927) (bootlegger's income was subject to tax despite being derived from illegal activity); James v. United States, 366 U.S. 213 (1961) (embezzled funds are held taxable).

15. *See, e.g.,* Alan Feuer, *7 Accused of Operating a Lucrative Citywide Betting Ring,* N.Y. TIMES, July 29, 2004, at <http://www.nytimes.com/2004/07/29/nyregion/29numbers.html> (accessed July 29, 2004) (referring to policy rackets in New York as "shadow Lotto" for those who want better odds and tax-free winnings); Suk Tom, *Illegal Gambling? Iowans Find Ways to Bet on It,* DES MOINES REGISTER, April 5, 2003, at 1B (2003 WL 6703144) (discussing similar attractions of illegal gambling to Iowans, despite legal outlets).

16. *See, e.g.,* Ronald L. Rychlak, *The Introduction of Casino Gambling: Public Policy and the Law,* 64 MISS. L.J. 291, 335–36 (1995) (noting that legalization encourages new gamblers to play, which in turn creates new potential problem gamblers).

17. *See, e.g.,* Theresa A. Gabaldon & John Law, *With a Tulip, in the South Seas: Gambling and the Regulation of Euphoric Market Transactions,* 26 J. CORP. L. 225, 260 (2001); Rychlak, *supra* note 16, at 349.

18. *See* W. Page Keeton et al., PROSSER AND KEETON ON THE LAW OF TORTS 683–84 (5th ed. 1984) (discussed in chapter 1).

19. Indian tribes may also benefit from government treatment. See chapter 11.

20. *See generally* Stephanie A. Martz, *Note, Legalized Gambling and Public Corruption: Removing the Incentive to Act Corruptly, or, Teaching an Old Dog New Tricks,* 13 J.L. & POL. 453 (1997).

CHAPTER 7

1. Nevada's Gaming Control Act states this commitment in part: "The gaming industry is vitally important to the economy of the state and the general welfare of the inhabitants." Nev. Rev. Stat. Ann. § 463.0129(a).

2. *Id.* § 463.0129(d).

3. *Id.* §§ 463.022, .024.

4. *Id.* § 463.023 (4).

5. *See id.* § 463.023(2).

6. *See id.* § 463.023(3).

7. *See, e.g., id.* § 463.150.

8. *Id.* §§ 463.030, .050.

9. *Id.* § 463.040(2).

10. *See id.* at § 463.040(5).

11. *Id.* at § 464.040(6).

12. <http://gaming.state.nv.us/about_board.htm>.

13. <http://gaming.state.nv.us/documents/pdf/audit_div_overview.pdf>.

14. *See id.*

15. *See* <http://gaming.state.nv.us/about_board.htm>.

16. *See id.*

17. *See id.*

18. *See id.*

19. *See* State of Nevada, *Citizen's Assets* (2004), available at <http://controller.nv.gov/CAFR_pdf_files/PopularReport01.pdf> (accessed May 3, 2005). Monthly fees imposed on holders of nonrestricted revenues, which are tied to the level of gross gaming revenues, are a substantial source of these taxes. Fees range from 3 percent for amounts under $50,000 per month to 6.25 percent for amounts in excess of $134,000 per month. *See* Nev. Rev. Stat. § 463.370(1). As discussed in chapter 5, these tax rates are modest in comparison to other gaming states. This potentially allows operators to invest more heavily in entertainment or other accoutrements designed to attract patrons.

20. *See id.*

21. *See* Lionel, Sawyer & Collins, Nevada Gaming Law 27 (3d ed. 2000).

22. *See* <http://gaming.state.nv.gov/about_board.htm#tech> (visited May 22, 2006).

23. *See* Nev. Rev. Stat. Ann. § 463.0152.

24. *See id.* § 463.161.

25. *See id.*

26. *See id.* § 463.170(1).

27. *See id.* § 463.170(2).

28. *See id.* § 463.170(3).

29. *See id.*

30. *See id.* § 463.167.

31. Nevada Tax Commission v. Hicks, 310 P.2d 852, 854 (Nev. 1957). *See also* Kraft v. Jacka, 669 F.Supp. 333, 337 (D. Nev. 1987) ("The members of the State Gaming Control Board and the Nevada Gaming Commission are charged with the awesome responsibility of regulating the gaming industry in Nevada and keeping undesirable elements out of the gaming industry.").

32. *See* 1 Organized Crime and Law Enforcement xvii–xxvi (Morris Poscowe, ed. 1952) (introduction by Senator Estes Kefauver).

33. The nature and extent of federal regulation of gambling are discussed in chapter 9.

34. Nev. Rev. Stat. § 463.220(7).

35. *Id.* § 463.129(2).

36. *Id.* at § 463.318(2) ("Judicial review is not available for actions, decisions and orders of the commission relating to the denial of a license or to limited or conditional licenses."). However, exceptions may exist for *ultra vires* acts of the commission or for decisions influenced by corruption, as suggested in Cohen v. State, 930 P.2d 125 (Nev. 1997). *See also* LIONEL, SAWYER & COLLINS, *supra* note 21, at 96. A remedy in federal court might be available in the event that a board's decision was based on racial animus or other criteria violating federal civil rights. Cf. Kaft v. Jacka, 669 F.Supp. 333 (D. Nev. 1987) (rejecting claim based on 42 U.S.C. § 1985 due to failure to show racial or other class-based "invidious discriminatory animus"), aff'd, 872 F.2d 862 (9th Cir. 1989), overruled on other grounds, Dennis v. Higgins, 498 U.S. 439 (1991).

37. 559 P.2d 830 (Nev. 1977).

38. *Id.* at 833 (quoting the commission report).

39. *Id.* (quoting State ex. rel. Grimes v. Board, 1 P.2d 570, 572 (Nev. 1931)).

40. *See id.* at 833.

41. *See id.* at 834.

42. *See, e.g.,* Nev. Rev. Stat. Ann. § 463.310(8).

43. *Id.* § 463.151.

44. *Id.* § 463.151(3).

45. *Id.* § 463.151(4).

46. *See* State v. Rosenthal, 819 P.2d 1296, 1299 (Nev. 1991).

47. NGR § 28.010(3).

48. Id. § 28.010(4).

49. Nev. Rev. Stat. Ann. § 463.317(3); *see also* Rosenthal, *supra* note 46, 819 P.2d at 1299.

50. Nev. Rev. Stat. Ann. § 463.154.

51. *Id.* § 463.156.

52. *See* Michael W. Bowers & A. Costandina Titus, *Nevada's Black Book: The Constitutionality of Exclusion Lists in Casino Gaming Regulation,* 9 WHITTIER L. REV. 313, 318 (1987).

53. <http://gaming.state.nv.us/loep_main.htm> (visited May 3, 2005). As of January 2006, only thirteen were listed.

54. *See, e.g.,* Brendan Riley, *Convicted Slot Cheat Added to Nevada's "Black Book,"* at <http://www.lasvegassun.com/sunbin/stories/nevada/2003/feb/20/022010167 .html> (discussing addition of Tommy Glenn Carmichael despite his attempts to use his cheating skills to improve slot machine security by inventing an "anti-cheating" device).

55. The Gaming Control Board also publishes a "most wanted list" on its Web site, which consists of those wanted in connection with casino-related crimes. *See*

<http://gaming.nv.gov/wanted_main.htm> (visited January 14, 2006). A list of those denied or found unsuitable for gaming licenses is also published, presumably for the benefit of those considering hiring these individuals or otherwise involving them in casino-related enterprises. *See* <http://gaming.nv.gov/unsuitable.htm> (visited January 14, 2006).

56. *See* Thomas v. Bible, 694 F.Supp. 750, 760–61 (D. Nev. 1988). *See also* Nev. Rev. Stat. Ann. §§ 463.152 (notice requirements) and .153 (hearing requirements). The statutorily prescribed right to notice and a hearing does not attach until after a name is placed on the list. *See* Thomas v. Bible, 694 F.Supp. at 759. However, in Spilotro v. State, 661 P.2d 467 (1983), the facts suggest that a hearing was granted before inclusion. *See id.* at 468–69.

57. 661 P.2d 467 (1983).

58. *Id.* at 470.

59. *See id.*

60. *See id.* at 471.

61. *Id.* at 472. Spilotro is followed in Rosenthal, *supra* note 46, 819 P.2d at 1300.

62. *See, e.g.,* Bowers & Titus, *supra* note 52, 313.

63. Nev. Rev. Stat. Ann. 463.0129(3).

64. 448 F.Supp. 116 (D. Nev. 1978).

65. *Id.* at 118 n.1.

66. *See also* Doug Grant, Inc. v. Greate Bay Casino Corp., 273 F.3d 173 (3d Cir. 2000) (discussing card-counting strategies).

67. Uston, *supra* note 64, 448 F.Supp. at 118.

68. *Id.* (citation omitted).

69. *Id.*

70. *See id.*

71. *See, e.g.,* Brooks v. Chicago Downs Ass'n, Inc., 791 F.2d 512 (7th Cir. 1986) (applying common law rule of exclusion in favor of Illinois racetrack in efforts to exclude "expert handicappers" from betting on horse races).

72. *Cf.* Marshall v. Sawyer, 301 F.2d 639, 648 (9th Cir. 1962) (Pope, J., concurring) ("True the gambling casinos are operated by individuals or corporations under state license, but in a very real sense, and in essence, the State of Nevada itself is in the gambling business, and its continued maintenance of that institution is vital to the State's life and its economy.").

73. Uston v. Resorts International Hotels, Inc., 445 A.2d 370, 376 (N.J. 1982).

74. *See* Campione v. Adamar of New Jersey, Inc., 714 A.2d 299, 306–8 (N.J. 1998), for an overview of the history of the countermeasure regulations issued after *Uston.*

75. *See* Lionel, Sawyer & Collins, *supra* note 21, 256.

76. *See, e.g.,* State Gaming Control Board v. Breen, 661 P.2d 1309, 1311 (Nev. 1983); Sea Air Support, Inc. v. Herrmann, 613 P.2d 413 (Nev. 1980).

77. *See* Lionel, Sawyer & Collins, *supra* note 21, at 260.

78. *See id.*

79. Nev. Rev. Stat. § 463.368(1).

80. *Id.* § 463.368(6).

81. *See* Lionel, Sawyer & Collins, *supra* note 21, at 265–70. Money laundering is a federal offense. See chapter 9.

82. *See id.* at 270.

83. *See* Nev. Rev. Stat. § 463.361–.366.

84. *See id.* at 463.361(1).

85. *See id.* at 463.366.

86. Anecdotal evidence indicates that concerns about the reliability of games and the payoff of jackpots may deter some players from gambling via the Internet. See chapter 10.

87. *See* Nev. Rev. Stat. § 463.1405(3) (allowing revocation or suspension of "any cause deemed reasonable by the commission").

88. *See id.* § 463.350.

89. For a history of this action, *see* Erickson v. Desert Palace, Inc., 962 F.2d 694, 694–96 (9th Cir. 1991); Lionel, Sawyer & Collins, *supra* note 21, at 321–23.

90. *See* Nev. Rev. Stat. § 468.350.

91. NGC Regulation 5.170(2).

92. *Id. at* 5.170(3).

93. *Id.* at 5.170(4).

94. Elizabeth White, *Nevada Proposes Helping Problem Gamblers for the First Time,* Las Vegas Sun, February 19, 2005.

95. *See id.*

96. *See id.*

97. *See* John L. Smith, *Bennett's Bottom Line on Gambling out of Line in More Than One Way,* Las Vegas Rev.-J., May 7, 2003, available at <http://www.reviewjournal.com/lvrj_home/2003/May-07-Wed-2003/news/21266047.html> (last visited May 3, 2005).

98. *See* NGR 5.200(2)(f).

99. *Id.* at 5.200(3)(f).

100. *See id.* at 5.200(3)(i).

101. *See* Nev. Rev. Stat. § 463.3557. This provision was amended in 2002 to allow a transfer to an "interactive gaming system" if the commission promulgated regulations that authorized interactive gaming. *See id.* However, no such regulations have been forthcoming.

102. *See* Liz Benston, *Gaming Panel Shelves ATM Slots,* Las Vegas Sun, May 23, 2001 (2003 WL 7821332).

103. *See id.*

104. N.G.Reg. 3.015(8).

105. *See* State of Nevada, *supra* note 19.

106. *See* U.S. Census Bureau, Statistical Abstract of the United States: 2002 (122d ed.), Table 433, Estimated State and Local Taxes Paid by a Family of Four in Selected Cities: 2000.

107. *See id.*

CHAPTER 8

1. *See* N.J. Const. Art. 4, § 7, 2.D.

2. *See, e.g.,* Cabot et al., eds., International Casino Law 59 (1991).

3. S.D. Stat. 42-7B-1 (1989).

4. Colo. Legis. S.B. 91-149 (June 4, 1991).

5. 2004 Pa. Legis. Serv. Act. 2004-91 (H.B. 2330) (July 6, 2004). This legislation was fueled by promises of property tax relief coupled with benefits for tourism and an ailing horse-racing industry. *See* Pennsylvania Governor's Message, July 31, 2004 (statement of Governor Edward G. Rendell). As of January 2006, the Pennsylvania Gaming Control Board had not yet awarded any operator licenses. The first application deadline was December 28, 2005. See Pennsylvania Gaming Control Board Receives 25 Application Submissions for Operator Licenses, January 9, 2006, at http://www.pgcb.state.pa.us/press/pr_010906.htm (visited May 18, 2006).

6. Florida's Broward County approved slot machines in a racino in March 2005, but voters in Miami-Dade County rejected them. *See* Theresa Walsh Giarrusso, *Go Guide 2005: Seven States Add Slot Machines,* Atlanta Journal and Constitution, March 13, 2005, at K6 (2005 WLNR 3931048).

7. For example, the New Jersey Division of Gaming Enforcement provides the following explanation of its function:

> Licensure is the cornerstone of the regulatory system. Licenses are required of casino owners and operators, casino employees, and companies that do business with casinos in order to assure that those involved with this industry meet the statutory requirements of good character, honesty and integrity and to keep the New Jersey casino industry free from organized crime. The DGE conducts all licensing investigations and provides a recommendation to the Casino Control Commission, which has the power to grant or deny a licensing application

<http://www.state.nj.us/lps/ge/mission&duties.htm>. In Iowa, the Department of Criminal Investigation, Gaming Enforcement Bureau, is "responsible for regulatory enforcement and criminal investigation at all licensed gambling operations in Iowa. The bureau is required to conduct complete and thorough background investigations of business entities and individuals involved in gaming. The bureau maintains an investigatory staff at each of the licensed riverboat casinos and pari-mutuel facilities in Iowa." <http://www.state.ia.us/government/dps/dci/gaming.htm>.

8. *See, e.g.,* <http://www.state.ia.us/government/dps/dci/gaming.htm>

(discussing regulatory functions of Iowa's Department of Criminal Investigation, Gaming Enforcement Bureau).

9. N.J. CONST. ART. 4, § 7, 2.D.

10. For a particularly bleak description of Atlantic City prior to casino gaming, *see* Rutgers School of Business, *The Future Impact of Gaming on Atlantic City 2003–2008* (2003), available at <http://camden-sbc.rutgers.edu/Alumni/Rutgers%20Gaming %20Study>. This study states in part:

> Atlantic City, once revered as America's Favorite Playground, now stood stark and gray against the barren seascape. Decades had passed since its heyday. The former gem of the East Coast had fallen into neglect and disrepair and had become a city long forgotten by tourists and travelers. But the turning point in its revival was drawing near.

Id. at 3. For further history on the constitutional amendment legalizing casino gambling and the enactment of the Casino Control Act, *see* New Jersey v. Trump Hotels & Casino Resorts, Inc., 734 A.2d 1160, 1165–73 (N.J. 1999).

11. CABOT ET AL., *supra* note 2, at 25.

12. N.J. Const. Art. 4, § 7, 2.D.

13. NJ ST 5:12–1

14. *See* Rutgers School of Business, *supra* note 10, at 5.

15. *Id.* at 4.

16. *Id.* at 5.

17. *See id.* at 4.

18. The National Gambling Impact Study Commission distinguishes between convenience gambling and destination resorts in terms of the efficacy for economic development and propensity for problem gambling behavior. *See* NATIONAL GAMBLING IMPACT STUDY COMMISSION REPORT at 7-4 (1999).

19. *See* <http://quickfacts.census.gov/qfd/states/34/34001.html>. It should be noted that the legal age for casino gambling is tewnty-one, so this estimate only approximates the adult population eligible for gaming.

20. *See* <http://quickfacts.census.gov/qfd/maps/new_jersey_map.html> (totaling populations in 2000 for Atlantic, Burlington, Camden, Cape May, Cumberland, Gloucester, and Ocean Counties). Assuming about one-fourth of the population is below the legal gambling age of twenty-one, this would mean that over 1.5 million adults eligible to gamble live in these counties alone.

21. *See* N.J.S.A. § 5:12-71.2.

22. *See* N.J.S.A. § 5:5-65.1.

23. *See* N.J. Admin. Code tit. 19, § 48-2.2.

24. *Id.* § 48-2.2(4).

25. *See id.* at §48-2.3(a).

26. *Id.* at § 48-2.3(b).

27. *See id.* at §§ 48.2-3(c) and (d); 48.2-4.

28. *See* N.J. Stat. Ann. § 5:12-71.2(e).

29. *See* N.J. Admin Code tit. 19, § 48-2.4.

30. *See id.*

31. *See* N.J.S.A. § 5:12-71.3(b).

32. *See id.* at § 5:12-71.3(c).

33. *See id.* at § 5:12-71.2(c).

34. *See id.* at § 5:12-71.3(d).

35. *See* Judy DeHaven, *Few Gamblers Opt for Self-Ban Plan,* NEWARK STAR-LEDGER, January 26, 2003 (2003 WL 10818365).

36. *See id.*

37. See chapter 5 for a discussion of the meaning of the terms *problem gambling* and *pathological gambling.*

38. *See* AMERICAN PSYCHIATRIC ASSOCIATION, DIAGNOSTIC AND STATISTICAL MANUAL OF MENTAL DISORDERS 615 (4th ed. 1994).

39. *See id.* at 617.

40. It should be noted, however, that compulsive shopping is not listed in the American Psychiatric Association's *Diagnostic and Statistical Manual of Mental Disorders.*

41. *See* N.J. Admin. Code tit 19, § 45-1.27A.

42. *See id.*

43. *See* 1989 Iowa Leg. Serv. 73 G.A., S.F. 124, Ch. 67 (West).

44. CABOT ET AL., *supra* note 2, at 59.

45. Iowa Code § 99F.7(2) (1989).

46. *Id.* § 99F.7(1) (1989).

47. *Id.* § 99F.7(5) (1989).

48. *See id.*

49. *See* 1989 Iowa Legis. Serv. 67, S.F. 124, Ch. 67 § 9(6) (April 27, 1989) (enacting Iowa Code § 99F.9(6)).

50. *See* 1989 Iowa Legis. Serv., 75, S.F. 525, § 6 (May 8, 1989) (amending Iowa Code § 99F.9(6)).

51. *See* 1991 Iowa Legis. Serv., ch. 144, S.F. 110, § 1 (May 9, 1991).

52. *See* 1994 Iowa Legis. Serv., ch. 1021, H.F. 2179, § 23 (Marcy 31, 1994).

53. *See* Iowa Code § 99F.9(5).

54. *See id.* § 99F.9(2).

55. *Id.* § 99F.9(4),(5).

56. *See* Iowa Code § 99F.1(8) (1993). This term was deleted from the code in 1994.

57. *See id.* § 99F.4(17) (1989).

58. *See* id. § 99F.7(9).

59. *See Third Gambling Boat Leaves Limited Bets Iowa,* CHI. TRIB., April 1, 1993 (1993 WL 11055799).

60. *See id.*

61. *See, e.g.,* Jeff Lehr, *Gambling Boat Nearly Ready,* HAWKEYE (Burlington, Iowa), November 16, 1994 (1994 WL 3046389); Eva Lego, *Bettendorf Strikes Deal with Lady Luck,* QUAD-CITY TIMES, August 3, 1994 (1994 WL 3071256) (casino boat agrees to return after two-year absence). *See also Iowa Lifts the Restrictions on Riverboat Casino Bets,* CHIC. SUN-TIMES, May 29, 1994 (1994 WL 5556159) (noting that legislation put Iowa's vessels on "same footing" as Illinois vessels).

62. *See* Kathie Obradovich, *Governor Wants More Detail: Davenport Needs to Show More Proof That It Needs Betting Limits Lifted,* QUAD-CITY TIMES, August 10, 1993 (1993 WL 3159488).

63. *See* 1994 Iowa Legis. Serv. 1021 (H.F. 2179), § 11 (March 31, 1994) (amending Iowa Code § 99F.4(17)).

64. *Id.* § 10 (amending Iowa Code § 99F.4(4)).

65. *See* Iowa Code § 99F.9(6) (added by 1994 Iowa Legis. Serv., ch. 1021, H.F. 2179, § 23 (March 31, 1994)).

66. *See* Iowa Code 99F.7(9)(b) (as amended by Acts 2004 80 G.A. ch. 1136, § 45 (effective May 6, 2004)).

67. *See* 1994 Iowa Legis. Serv., ch. 1021, H.F. 2179, § 17 (amending Iowa Code § 99F.7(10)(c)).

68. *See* Iowa Code § 99F.4 to .6.

69. *See id.* § 99F.4 (16), (17).

70. *Id.* § 99F.7(11).

71. *Id.* § 99F.7(11)(e). Legislation in 2004 amended this provision, increasing the previous term limit from two to eight years.

72. *See* Iowa Code § 99F.7(10)(d).

73. *See* <http://www3.state.ia.us/irgc/Referendum.htm> (last visited May 3, 2005) (showing results from 2003–4).

74. *See id.*

75. *See* Racing Ass'n of Central Iowa v. Fitzgerald, 648 N.W. 2d 555, 556–57 (Iowa 2002), *rev'd,* 123 S.Ct. 2156 (2003).

76. *See* Dan Johnson, *It's Been a Bumpy Ride for Prairie Meadows,* DES MOINES REG., August 25, 2002 (2002 WL 23124615).

77. *See id.*

78. *See id.*

79. *See id.*

80. Iowa Code § 99F.5(1).

81. *Id.* § 99F.1(14).

82. *See id.* § 99F.7(2).

83. *See id.* § 99F.10(2).

84. *See id.* § 99F.10.

85. *See id.* §§ 99F.10(4); 99F.10A.

86. *See id.* § 99F.1(1).

87. *Id.* § 99F.11.

88. *See id.*

89. *See* Fitzgerald v. Racing Ass'n of Central Iowa, 123 S.Ct. 2156 (2003), reversing, 648 N.W.2d 555 (Iowa 2002).

90. *See* Racing Ass'n of Central Iowa v. Fitzgerald, 675 N.W.2d 1 (Iowa), cert. denied 581 U.S. 1086 (2004).

91. *See* Iowa Code § 99F.11(2)(b),(c).

92. *Id.* § 99F.11(3).

93. *See id.*

94. *See id.*

95. *See* Iowa Code §§ 99F.11(4); 8.57(5)(e) (diverting amounts in excess of $60 million to other funds). The Vision Iowa fund is discussed later.

96. Iowa Racing and Gaming Commission, Report for Fiscal 2003, at <http://www3.state.ia.us/irgc/FYTD03.pdf>.

97. *See id.*

98. *Cf.* Iowa Code § 99F.7(12) (prohibiting delinquent status in payment of property taxes); (11) (allowing local docking fees to be charged).

99. *Id.* § 99F.6.

100. *See id.*

101. *See id.*

102. *See id.* ("A qualified sponsoring organization shall not make a contribution to a candidate, political committee, candidate's committee, state statutory political committee, county statutory political committee, national political party, or fundraising event as these terms are defined in section 56.2.").

103. <http://www.iowawestfoundation.org/2002annual/pg5.htm> (visited May 3, 2005).

104. *See* <http://www.iowagaming.org/WhatIsTheIGA/nonprofitlicense holders/iowawest.html> ("2003 Grant Recipients").

105. *See* Iowa Legislature Senate File 2447.

106. *See* Iowa Code §§ 15F.102 (defining board composition); 15F.103 (defining board duties).

107. *See id.* § 12.82.

108. *See* <http://www.visioniowa.org/vision.html> (Vision Iowa); <http://www.visioniowa.org/cat.html> (CAT).

109. *See* Iowa Admin Code § 211.4 (2).

110. *See Iowa Gambling Treatment Fund—Revenues, Expenditures, and Redirects,* at <http://www.1800betsoff.org/revenue_redirect.htm> (showing data for 1986–2005 (estimated)).

111. *See* Iowa Gaming Association at <http://www.buyiowafirst.org/Responsible Gaming/responsi.html> (visited May 3, 2005).

112. *See* Chris Clayton, *Gambling Treatment Touted,* OMAHA WORLD-HERALD, November 28, 2002, available at <http://www.responsiblegambling.org/articles/Gambling_treatment_touted.pdf>.

113. *See* William Petroski, *Gambling Treatment Sum to Jump,* DES MOINES REG., August 1, 2004, at 1 (2004 WLNR 16262408).

114. *See id.*

115. *See* Acts 2004 (80 G.A). ch. 1136, § 35 (adding Iowa Code § 99F.4(23)).

116. *See* Iowa Gaming Association Web site, www.iowagaming.org.

117. *See* Uniform Self-Exclusion Form (November 1, 2004), at <http://www.iowagaming.org/ResponsibleGaming/responsi.html>.

118. *See id.*

119. *See* Iowa Code § 99F.4(23) (2004).

120. *See* Iowa Code § 99F.7(16).

121. *See* <http://www.keepthemoneyinnebraska.com/>.

122. Portions of one of these initiatives, which had several parts, were approved, including a provision allowing the state to tax gaming revenues. Whether this reflected voter confusion or a simple desire to impose taxes is open to interpretation.

123. Iowa Acts 2004 (80 G.A). ch. 1136, § 62.

124. *Id.* § 41.

125. *See* William Petroski, *The Lucky Number Is 4,* DES MOINES REG., May 12, 2005, at 1 (2005 WLNR 7575901).

126. Iowa Code § 99F.7(4).

127. For a history of the initial process of legalized casino gaming on riverboats in Missouri, *see* Harris v. Missouri Gaming Comm'n, 869 S.W. 2d 58 (Mo. 1994).

128. *See id.*

129. *See id.*

130. *See id.*

131. *See* Akin v. Missouri Gaming Comm'n, 956 S.W. 2d 251 (Mo. 1997).

132. *See id.*

133. *See* Missouri Stat. Ann. § 313.805(3).

134. MISSOURI GAMING COMMISSION, ANNUAL REPORT TO THE GENERAL ASSEMBLY 8 (2004), available at <http://www.mgc.state.mo.us/annual%20reports/2004/annual2004.pdf> [hereinafter 2004 Annual Report].

135. *Id.* (footnotes omitted).

136. *See* Missouri Stat. Ann. §§ 313.805(13); 313.817(3).

137. *See id.* § 313.805(12).

138. *See id.* § 313.812(9).

139. 2004 Annual Report, *supra* note 134, at 8.

140. *See id.* at 11.

141. *See* MISSOURI GAMING COMMISSION, ANNUAL REPORT TO THE GENERAL

ASSEMBLY (2000) at 19 [hereinafter 2000 Annual Report], at <http://www.mgc .dps.mo.gov> (visited May 16, 2006).

142. *See id.* at 16.

143. *See Free Money,* ST. LOUIS POST-DISPATCH, March 5, 2005 (editorial) (2005 WLNR 3450184) (reporting that the Maryland Heights facility would initiate a $400 million expansion if loss limits were removed).

144. *See* 2000 Annual Report, *supra* note 141, at 9–10. .

145. *See id.* at 18–19.

146. *See* MISSOURI GAMING COMMISSION, ANNUAL REPORT TO THE GENERAL AS-SEMBLY (2001) at 27, at <http://www.mgc.dps.mo.gov/> (visited May 16, 2006).

147. *See id.*

148. *See id.*

149. *See* Missouri. Stat. Ann. § 313.813.

150. 11 MO ADC 45-17.020.

151. *See id.*

152. *See id.*

153. *See id.*

154. *See* Missouri Stat. Ann. §§ 313.842; 313.835(1).

155. *See* Rick Alm, *Gambling and Tourism: House Rules against Disgruntled Gamblers,* KANSAS CITY STAR, May 13, 2003 (2003 WL 19781395).

156. *See* Missouri Stat. Ann. § 313.812 (1).

157. *See* 2004 Annual Report, *supra* note 134, at 11 ("The Commission's practice of waiting to introduce new gaming capacity into a market until there is adequate demand allows Missouri licensees to remain profitable and encourages them to reinvest in Missouri.").

158. *See* 2000 Annual Report, *supra* note 141, at 30–34 (discussing the "St. Louis Expansion Process").

159. *See* Missouri Stat. Ann § 313.812(10).

160. *See id.* § 313.812(1).

161. *See id.* § 313.822 (imposing a 20 percent tax on AGR of gaming establishments).

162. *See id.*

163. *See* 1990 Miss. Laws Ch. 45, § 1 ff (enacting Mississippi Gaming Control Act), codified at Miss Code Ann. § 75-76-1 to -313.

164. *See* Miss. Code Ann. § 75-76-3(2). *See also id.* § 75-76-3(6).

165. *See* Ben H. Stone et al., *Site Approval of Casinos in Mississippi—A Matter of Statutory Construction, Or a Roll of the Dice?* 64 Miss. L.J. 363, 365 n.5 (1995).

166. Miss. Stat. Ann. § 97-33-1.

167. *Cf.* Miss. Gaming Comm'n v. Board of Education, 691 So.2d 452, 455 (Miss. 1997) *with* Miss. Casino Operator's Ass'n v. Miss. Gaming Comm'n, 654 So.2d 892 (Miss. 1995) (overruling gaming commission order allowing site loca-

tion in manmade canal, though recognizing other similar facilities had been approved).

168. Lynne Willbanks Jeter, *Tunica Ranked Third-Largest behind Las Vegas, Atlantic City,* Miss. Bus. J., December 14, 1998 (1998 WL 10300366).

169. *See* Ronald J. Rychlak, *The Introduction of Casino Gambling: Public Policy and the Law,* 64 Miss. L.J. 291, 310 (1995).

170. *See* Miss. Stat. Ann. § 27-109-1.

171. Henry N. Dick III, *Comment, Dockside Gambling and the Federal Maritime Lien Act:Why Dockside Casinos Should Not Be Considered Vessels for Purposes of the Federal Maritime Lien Act,* 64 Miss. L.J. 659, 669 (1995).

172. Rychlak, *supra* note 169, 64 Miss. L.J. at 310 (footnotes omitted).

173. *See id.* at 309.

174. *See, e.g.,* Miss. Gaming Comm'n v. Board of Education, 691 So.2d 452, 455 (Miss. 1997) ("The site, if approved, could and would open the State of Mississippi to inland land-based casino gaming.").

175. *See* 2005 Miss. Laws 5th Ex. Sess. Ch. 16 (H.B. 45) (approved October 17, 2005); *Mississippi to Let Casinos Move onto Dry Land: Governor to Sign Bill to Allow Gambling a Short Distance from Shore,* Associated Press, October 4, 2005.

176. *See* Rychlak, *supra* note 169, 64 Miss L.J. at 308 (noting this approach is unlike every other state except Louisiana). However, in 1996, Louisiana's state constitution was amended to require local parish approval prior to the introduction of gambling in that state. *See* La. Const. Art 12, § 6(c) (1996).

177. *See* Miss. Stat. Ann. § 19-3-79(1).

178. *See id.*

179. *See id.* § 19-3-79 (3).

180. Miss. Stat. Ann. § 19-3-79(2).

181. *See, e.g.,* Miss Stat. Ann. §§ 75-76-67 (suitability determination by board); 75-76-73 (form and contents of license application). Special rules apply to corporate licensees, *see id.* §§ 75-76-201 to -215 (generally); 249-265 (public corporations), and to limited partnerships, *id.* §§ 75-76-219 to -231.

182. *See* Stone et al., *supra* note 165, at 363.

183. *See* Miss. Stat. Ann. 75-76-67.

184. *See* Iowa Code Ann. § 99F.7(1) ("The commission shall decide the number, location, and type of excursion gambling boats licensed under this chapter for operation on the rivers, lakes, and reservoirs of this state.").

185. *See* Missouri Stat. Ann. § 313.812(1).

186. *See* John M. Czarnetsky, *When the Dealer Goes Bust: Issues in Casino Bankruptcies,* 18 Miss. C. L. Rev. 459, 460 (1997).

187. *See id.* at n.7 (citing thirty casinos in Mississippi in 1997); American Gaming Association at www.americangaming.org/Industry/state/statistics.cfm (listing twenty-nine casinos for Mississippi) (visited May 17, 2005).

188. *See id.*

189. *See* U.S. Casino Directory: South Dakota, at www.americancasinoguide .com/southdakota.shtml (visited May 17, 2005).

190. *See* S.D.C.L. 42-7B-1, Commission Note (2005).

191. *See* <http://www.hbo.com/deadwood/about/> (visited May 18, 2005).

192. *See* <http://www.americancasinoguide.com/southdakota.shtml> (visited May 18, 2005).

193. *See* <http://www.legendsofamerica.com/SD-Deadwood2.html> (visited May 18, 2005).

194. *See* <http://www.americancasinoguide.com/southdakota.shtml> (visited May 18, 2005).

195. *See* S.D.C.L. § 42-7B-35.

196. *See id.* § 42-7B-2.1.

197. *See id.* § 42-7B-11 (commission's powers).

198. *See* South Dakota Laws Chapter 374, § 12 (1989).

199. *See* S.D.C.L. § 42-7B-14.

200. *See id.* § 42-7B-16.

201. *See* <http://www.americancasinoguide.com/southdakota.shtml> (visited May 18, 2005).

202. <http://www.state.sd.us/bit/statistics/main_topics/sdcities_a_f.htm>.

203. *See* Barry M. Horstman, *Some Communities Win with Casinos, Some Lose,* Cincinnati Post, September 18, 1997, available at <http://www.cincypost.com/news/1997/gamble091897.html>.

204. *See* S.D.C.L. § 42-7A-38. The statute expresses the maximum credit as no more than $125 per credit value of $0.25 played. This amounts to $1,000 (8 × $0.25 = $2 maximum bet; 8 × $125 = $1,000).

205. *See* S.D.C.L. § 42-7A-37.1 (limited to bars and lounges); § 42-7A-44 (no more than ten per establishment).

206. S.D.C.L. § 42-7A-63.

207. *See* State of South Dakota, *General Fund Condition Statement,* at <http://www.state.sd.us/bfm/budget/rec05/gfcdbud.pdf> (visited May 18, 2005).

208. *See* American Gaming Association, *Industry Information State Statistics,* at <www.americangaming.org/Industry/state/statistics.cfm> (visited May 11, 2005).

209. The vote was 146,428 (46.3 percent) for and 169,642 (53.7 percent) against. *See* S.D. Const. Art. 3, § 25 (reporters note).

210. *See* William Petroski, *Iowa Issues Moratorium on Video Gambling Machines,* Des Moines Reg., January 10, 2006, available at <http://www.desmoinesregister.com>.

CHAPTER 9

1. New State Ice Co. v. Liebman, 285 U.S. 282, 311 (1932) (Brandeis, J., dissenting).

2. *See* Pic-A-State Pa, Inc. v. Reno, 76 F.3d 1294, 1297 (3d Cir. 1996). Other

congressional acts to assist the states in controlling lotteries predate this 1895 statute. For a more complete history of these legislative attempts, *see* United States v. Edge Broadcasting, 509 U.S. 419, 421–22 (1993).

3. 188 U.S. 321 (1903). The text of this act reads as follows:

"§1. That any person who shall cause to be brought within the United States from abroad, for the purpose of disposing of the same, or deposited in or carried by the mails of the United States, or carried from one state to another in the United States, any paper, certificate, or instrument purporting to be or represent a ticket, chance, share, or interest in or dependent upon the event of a lottery, so-called gift concert, or similar enterprise, offering prizes dependent upon lot or chance, or shall cause any advertisement of such lottery, so-called gift concert, or similar enterprise, offering prizes dependent upon lot or chance, to be brought into the United States, or deposited in or carried by the mails of the United States, or transferred from one state to another in the same, shall be punishable in [for] the first offense by imprisonment for not more than two years, or by a fine of not more than $1,000, or both, and in the second and after offenses by such imprisonment only." 28 Stat. at L. 963. U. S. Comp. Stat. 1901, p. 3178.

Id. at 322. Current federal statutes applicable to lotteries include 18 U.S.C.A. §1301 (2003) (transporting lottery ticket); *id.* §1302 (mailing lottery ticket); *id.* §1303 (prohibiting postal employee from acting as agent of lottery).

4. 188 U.S. at 323.

5. *Id.* at 357–58.

6. However, it would later use its regulatory powers to prohibit federally insured banks from participating in lotteries—which arguably reflects an antilottery policy. *See, e.g.,* 12 U.S.C.A. § 25(a) (national banks); 12 U.S.C.A. §339 (state federal reserve member banks); 12 U.S.C.A. § 1829a (state nonmember banks); 12 U.S.C.A. § 1463 (state savings associations).

7. 188 U.S. 375 (1903).

8. *Id.* at 376.

9. *See id.* at 377–78.

10. *See* Pic-A-State, PA v. Pennsylvania, 1993 WL 325539 (M.D. Pa. 1993).

11. *See id.* The challenged statute is currently found at 72 PA. ST. ANN. tit. 72, § 3761-307(c).

12. *Id.*

13. *See generally id.*

14. *Id.* (footnotes 13 and 14 omitted).

15. *Id.*

16. *See id. See also* Pic-A-State PA, Inc. v. Pennsylvania, 43 F.3d 175, 177 (3d Cir. 1994) (summarizing the effect of the district court's memorandum decision). If those taxes proved discriminatory, however, the tax scheme could itself

be challenged. *See, e.g.,* Complete Auto Transit (prescribing tests for validity of discriminatory taxing schemes under Commerce Clause).

17. Pub.L. No. 103-322, 108 Stat. 1796 ("1994 Crime Control Act").

18. *See* Pic-A-State PA, Inc, *supra* note 16, at 176. As the court explained: "One portion of the 1994 Crime Control Act makes it a federal crime to knowingly transmit in interstate commerce information for the purpose of procuring interests in an out-of-state lottery if one is engaged in the business of procuring for a person in one State such a ticket, chance, share, or interest in a lottery . . . conducted by another State (unless that business is permitted under an agreement between the States in question or appropriate authorities of those States)." *Id.* at 177–78 (internal quotation omitted).

19. *See id.* at 179.

20. *See id.*

21. *See id.* at 180.

22. *See also* L.E. Services, Inc. v. State Lottery Commission of Indiana, 646 N.E.2d 334, 344–47 (Ind. App. 1995) (following a similar rationale in upholding an Indiana law proscribing the sale of out-of-state lottery tickets in Indiana).

23. 76 F.3d 1294 (3d Cir. 1996).

24. *See id.* at 1301.

25. *See id.*

26. In support of this conclusion, the court looked to the floor debates and quoted as follows from Senator Specter: "the right of a State to regulate lottery [*sic*] and gambling within its borders must be preserved. Federal gambling laws have traditionally enabled the States to regulate in-State gambling. Federal laws should continue to limit the proliferation of interstate gambling to preserve the sovereignty of States that do not permit certain forms of gambling." *Id.* at 1302 (citation omitted).

27. *Id.* at 1303.

28. *Id.*

29. As discussed in chapter 10, this differentiation between gambling and other forms of entertainment has recently been raised in challenges before the World Trade Organization.

30. 18 U.S.C.A. § 1084.

31. 18 U.S.C.A. § 1953.

32. 18 U.S.C.A. § 1952.

33. 28 U.S.C.A. § 3702.

34. *See* United States v. Borgese, 235 F.Supp. 286, 295–96 (1964); H.R. 967, 1961-2 USCCAN 2631.

35. 18 U.S.C. § 1084(a) (2003).

36. Letter from Robert F. Kennedy to The Speaker of the House of Representatives, April 6, 1961, *reprinted in* 1961-2 USCCAN at 2633.

37. *See id.*

38. Pic-A-State Pa., Inc. v. Pennsylvania, 1993 WL 325539 (E.D. Pa. 1993), *rev'd on other grounds,* 42 F.3d 175 (3d Cir. 1994).

39. *See* United States v. Scavo, 593 F2d 837 (8th Cir. 1979); United States v. Cohen, 378 F.2d 751 (9th Cir.), cert denied, 389 U.S. 897 (1967).

40. *See* United States v. Anderson, 542 F.2d 428 (7th Cir. 1976).

41. *See* United States v. Baborian, 528 F.Supp. 324 (D.R.I. 1981).

42. 18 U.S.C. § 1084(c).

43. 18 U.S.C.A. § 1084(b).

44. H.R. No. 967, 1961-2 U.S.C.C.A.N. 2631, 2632-33.

45. *See, e.g.,* States v. McDonough, 835 F.2d 1103 (5th Cir. 1988).

46. For example, Missouri law contains the following provision:

No licensee shall permit participation by a person in a game conducted in the licensed gaming establishment if such person is not physically present in the licensed gaming establishment during the period of time when such game is being conducted, and all games and the participation of patrons therein shall be entirely located and conducted on the licensed premises. (MS ST § 75-76-101)

47. 18 U.S.C.A. § 1952.

48. *Id.* § 1952(a).

49. *Id.* § 1952(b).

50. *See* Rewis v. United States, 401 U.S. 808 (1971).

51. 18 U.S.C.A. § 1953.

52. 18 U.S.C. § 1953(a).

53. *See id.* § 1953(b).

54. *See* 15 U.S.C.A. § 1171-78, which is also known as the Gambling Devices Transportation Act. *See* United States v. Bally Mfg. Corp., 345 F.Supp. 410 (D. La. 1972).

55. *See* P.L. 102-559, 106 Stat. 4227, *codified at* 28 U.S.C.A. §§ 3701-3704 [hereinafter Sports Protection Act].

56. S. Rep. No. 102-248, at 6 (1992), *reprinted at* 1992 U.S.C.C.A.N. 3553, 3557.

57. *See* 18 U.S.C.A. § 224.

58. *See, e.g.,* United States v. Pinto, 503 F.2d 718, 723 (2d Cir. 1974) (harness racing); United States v. Walsh, 544 F.2d 156 (4th Cir. 1976) (horse racing).

59. For an example of sports bribery prosecution under a state statute, *see* State v. De Paglia, 71 N.W.2d 601 (Iowa 1955) (involving attempted bribery of a basketball player to "shave points" in a Drake versus Iowa State game). The legislative history to 18 U.S.C. § 224 suggests that, although "[s]tate law enforcement agencies have done much to uncover and prosecute these [state] statutes . . . [i]t is felt that more must be done. Bribery of players or officials to influence the results of sporting contests is a challenge to an important aspect of American life—

honestly competitive sports." H.R. Rep. No. 1053 (1964), *reprinted in* 1964 U.S.C.C.A.N. 2250, 2251.

60. S. Rep. No. 102-248 at 5, 1992 U.S.C.C.A.N. at 3555.

61. *Id.,* 1992 U.S.C.C.A.N. at 3556 (emphasis added).

62. *Id.*

63. *Id.* at 7, 1992 U.S.C.C.A.N. at 3558.

64. *Id.*

65. *Id.* at 8, 1992 U.S.C.C.A.N. at 3559.

66. *See id.* at 12–13, 1992 U.S.C.C.A.N. at 3562–63.

67. *Id.* at 14, 1992 U.S.C.C.A.N. at 3564.

68. *Id.,* 1992 U.S.C.C.A.N. at 3565. Senator Grassley's commentary predated the widespread use of the Internet. As discussed in chapter 10, sports betting via the Internet is widely accessible despite the federal ban.

69. *Id.* at 16, 1992 U.S.C.C.A.N. at 3566.

70. *Id.* at 7, 1992 U.S.C.C.A.N. at 3558.

71. *See, e.g.,* Marc Carinci, *London: A Gambler's Paradise,* March 6, 2004, at <http://www.covers.com/covers/mall/articles/london_a_gamblers_paradise.asp>.

72. *See NCAA Steps Up Anti-Gambling Efforts,* ASSOCIATED PRESS, January 7, 2006.

73. *See 2003 NCAA National Study on Collegiate Sports Wagering and Related Behaviors,* available at <http://www.ncaa.org/library/research/sports_wagering/2003/2003_sports_wagering_study.pdf>.

74. *See id.*

75. *See id.*

76. *See id.*

77. *See* National Cable Television Ass'n v. United States, 415 U.S. 336, 341 n.4 (1974) (crediting Chief Justice Marshall with this statement).

78. *See id.* at 341 (footnote omitted).

79. *See* United States v. Hallmark, 911 F.2d 399, 401 (10th Cir. 1990).

80. I.R.C. § 4421(1).

81. *See id.* § 4421(2).

82. *Id.* § 4402.

83. *See id.* § 4401(a)(1).

84. *Id.* § 4411(b).

85. Nevertheless, its potential applicability to tribal gaming in the form of pull-tabs was apparently sufficiently significant to warrant litigation in the Supreme Court. *See* Chickasaw Nation v. United States, 534 U.S. 84 (2001) (upholding application of excise tax provisions to tribal gambling).

86. *See* I.R.C. §§ 4401(a)(2); 4411(a).

87. *See* H.R. Conf. Rep. No. 93-1401, *reprinted in* 1974 U.S.C.C.A.N 6232, 6232–33.

88. 390 U.S. 39 (1968).

89. *See* I.R.C. § 4424.

90. *See* <http://www.onlineblackjackreview.com/Online-Blackjack-Basic-Strategy-Odds.htm> (visited July 7, 2004).

91. *See* Hochman v. Commissioner, 51 T.C.M. (CCH) 311 (1986); GCM 37312 (November 7, 1977).

92. I.R.C. § 165(d); Commissioner v. Groetzinger, 480 U.S. 23, 32 (1987).

93. *See* I.R.C. 165(c)(1).

94. Commissioner v. Groetzinger, 480 U.S. 23, 32 (1987).

95. *See generally* Stephen A. Zorn, *The Federal Income Tax Treatment of Gambling: Fairness or Obsolete Moralism?* 49 Tax Lawyer 1 (1995), for an excellent discussion of these issues.

96. *See* Praytor v. Commissioner, T.C. Memo 2000-282 at n. 2.

97. *See id; see also* Rev. Rul. 54-339, 1954-2 C.B. 89.

98. *See* Commissioner v. Groetzinger, 480 U.S. 23, 32 (1987).

99. *See, e.g.,* Balot v. Commissioner, 81 T.C.M. (CCH) 1409 (2001).

100. *See* Petty v. Commissioner, T.C. Memo 2004-144.

101. *See, e.g.,* I.R.C. §§ 24(b) (child tax credit); 219(g) (retirement contributions for active participants in pension plans); 222(b) (deductions for qualified tuition and related expenses).

102. 1977-2 C.B. 538.

103. *Id.* at § 3.

104. *Id.*

105. *See* Zorn, *supra* note 95, at 7 ("While no one concerned with the effective administration of the tax laws would argue for eliminating the requirement that gamblers substantiate their winnings and losses in some way, the current rules are so out of touch with a realistic expectation of individual behavior as to invite creativity on the part of taxpayers."); 46–50 (discussing cases in this area that appear to relax the standards imposed by the service).

106. *See* Indopco v. Commissioner, 503 U.S. 79, 84 (1992); Norgard v. Commissioner, 939 F.2d 874, 878–79 (9th Cir. 1991).

107. *See* I.R.C. §§ 183; 63(d); 67(b).

108. *See Betting It All on Vegas Roulette Spin,* Reuters, April 8, 2004.

109. *See* <http://wizardofodds.com/games/roulette.html> (visited July 2, 2004).

110. *See id. See also* <http://www.roulette-guru.com/roulette_odds.html> (visited July 2, 2004).

111. *See id.*

112. *See* Petty v. Commissioner, T.C. Memo 2004-144, discussed later.

113. I.R.C. § 6041(a).

114. *See* Lutz v. Commissioner, 83 T.C.M. (CCH) 1446, n. 4 (2002).

115. *See* Treas. Reg. § 7.6041-1.

116. *See id.*

117. *See, e.g.,* Lutz v. Commissioner, 83 T.C.M. (CCH) 1446, n. 4 (2002).

118. *See* I.R.C. §§ 6441; 3402(q).

119. *See, e.g.,* Lyszkowski v. Commissioner, T.C. Memo 1995-235 (discussing legislative history).

120. *See* United States v. Monteiro, 8761 F.2d 204, 211 (1st Cir. 1989).

121. *See* 31 U.S.C. § 1956(a)(1); United States v. Vanhorn, 296 F.3d 713, 717-18 (8th Cir. 2002); U.S. v. Peterson 244 F.3d 385, 390 (5th Cir. 2001).

122. Pub. L. 107-56. Title III, § 302, 115 Stat. 296.

123. Pub. L. 91-508, codified as amended at 12 U.S.C. § 1829b, 12 U.S.C. §§ 1951–1959, and 31 U.S.C. §§ 5311-5332. The applicable provisions governing reporting and disclosure requirements are found at 31 U.S.C. §§ 5311–5332.

124. *See* I.R.C. § 6051I.

125. *See* I.R.C. § 6050I(a).

126. *See id.* § 6050I(d).

127. *See id.* § 6050I(c)(1).

128. *See id.* § 6051I(c).

129. *See* 31 U.S.C. § 5312(a)(2)(X) and 31 C.F.R. § 113.11(n)(7)(i).

130. *See* Treas. Reg. § 1.6050I-1(d)(2).

131. Notice 96-57, 1996-2 C.B. 225. However, reporting requirements remain in effect for nongaming businesses, including shops, restaurants, entertainment, or hotels.

132. *See* Treas. Reg. § 1.6050I-1(d)(2).

133. *See id.*

134. *See* 31 C.F.R. § 103.22(b)(2).

135. *See id.*

136. *See id.; see also* 26 C.F.R. 1.6050I-1(e)(3) (verification requirements under tax provision).

137. *See* Financial Crimes Enforcement Network; Amendment to the Bank Secrecy Act Regulations—Requirement That Casinos and Card Clubs Report Suspicious Transactions, 67 Fed. Reg. 60722-01, 60723, n. 8 (September 26, 2002).

138. *See id.* at 60724.

139. 31 C.F.R. § 103.21(a)(2).

140. *See generally* 67 Fed. Reg. at 60725.

141. *See id.* at 60723.

142. *See id.* at 60725; 31 C.F.R. § 103.64.

143. *See id.* Additional practical guidance for casino compliance was later made available to casino operators. *See* Financial Crimes Enforcement Network, Suspicious Activity Reporting Guide for Casinos (2003), available at <http://www.fincen.gov/casinosarguidancefinal1203.pdf>.

144. 67 Fed. Reg. 67893-03, 2002 WL 31476627 (F.R.).

145. *See* 67 Fed. Reg. at 60728.

146. *See, e.g.,* Posadas de Puerto Rico Assoc. v. Tourism Co., 478 U.S. 328 (1986).

147. 18 U.S.C. § 1304.

148. *See* Greater New Orleans Broadcasting v. United States, 527 U.S. 195 (1999).

149. *See* 18 U.S.C. § 1307.

150. *See* Greater New Orleans Broadcasting v. United States, 527 U.S. 195 (1999).

151. *See, e.g.,* William H. Van Alstyne, *To What Extent Does the Power of Government to Determine the Boundaries and Conditions of Lawful Commerce Permit Government to Declare Who May Advertise and Who May Not?* 51 EMORY L. J. 1513 (2002); Mitchell N. Berman, *Commercial Speech and the Unconstitutional Conditions Doctrine: A Second Look at "The Greater Includes the Lesser,"* 55 VANDERBILT L. REV. 693 (2002); Martin H. Redish, *Tobacco Advertising and the First Amendment,* 81 IOWA L. REV. 589 (1996).

152. 478 U.S. 328 (1986). As a commonwealth of the United States, Puerto Rico is subject to First Amendment protections. *See id.*

153. *Id.* at 332 (citing 1948 Act).

154. *Id.*

155. *See id.*

156. *See id.* at 335–36.

157. *See id.* at 334.

158. *Id.* at 340.

159. *Id.* at 341 (quoting Brief for Appellees at 37).

160. *Id.*

161. *See id.* at 342–43.

162. *See id.* at 344.

163. *Id.* at 346–47 (footnote omitted).

164. 509 U.S. 418 (1993).

165. *See id.* at 425.

166. *Id.* at 426.

167. *See id.* at 434–35.

168. 517 U.S. 484 (1996).

169. *Id.* at 503 (citation omitted).

170. *Id.* at 509–10 (citations omitted).

171. *Id.* at 511 (footnote omitted).

172. *Id.* at 514 (citation omitted).

173. 527 U.S. 173 (1999).

174. *See id.* at 180–81.

175. *Id.* at 185–86 (citations omitted).

176. *See id.* at 187.

177. *Id.* at 190 (citations omitted).

178. *Id.* at 192 (citations omitted).

179. It should be noted that concerns about misleading speech in advertising led the National Gambling Impact Study Commission to recommend a pause in advertising and cooperative efforts at the development and adoption of "best practices" for advertising. *See* NATIONAL GAMBLING IMPACT STUDY COMMISSION REPORT 3-17–3-18 (1999).

180. *See* 44 Liquormart, Inc. v. Rhode Island, 517 U.S. 484, 497 (1996) ("[T]he First Amendment does not protect commercial speech about unlawful activities. *See Pittsburgh Press Co. v. Pittsburgh Comm'n on Human Relations,* 413 U.S. 376 (1973)").

CHAPTER 10

1. GAO, INTERNET GAMBLING: AN OVERVIEW OF THE ISSUES (December 2, 2002) (GAO-03-89).

2. *See* Kurt Eichenwald, *At PartyGaming, Everything's Wild,* N.Y TIMES, June 26, 2005. Bloomberg reports that Christiansen Capital Advisors estimate 2005 online gaming at $8.2 billion. *See Online Gambling Raises the Ante,* BLOOMBERG MARKETS, October 2005.

3. *See* Matt Richtel, *Wall Street Bets on Gambling on the Web,* N.Y. TIMES, Dec. 25, 2005 (reporting estimate from Christiansen Capital Advisors).

4. *See* Carl Blalik, *Lawyers Bid Up Value of Web-Search Ads,* WALL ST. J., April 7, 2004, at B1, c. 2. The term *casino* was sixth on the list of paid placements at $14.97, trailing "mesothelioma attorney" ($70.24), "car accident lawyer" ($50.00), "investment fraud" ($30.00), "Wisconsin mortgage" (19.00), and "conference calling" ($18.22). Though as a technical matter, *casino* might include traditional casino operations, each of the listed ads was for an online operation. As discussed subsequently, government efforts to block online casino ads on sites based in the United States call into question any subsequent estimates based on advertising rates.

5. *See* Eichenwald, *supra* note 2.

6. *See Online Gambling Raises the Ante, supra* note 2.

7. *See* Robin Kelley et al., *GAMBLING@HOME: Internet Gambling in Canada* at 2 (October 2001), available at www.cwf.ca.

8. *See id.* (estimating 1,200–1,400 sites in 2001). A Google search on April 8, 2004, using the term *online casino gambling* returned over 1.1 million Web sites, although many of those sites do not actually contain an online casino. *See also* Michael Totty, *Taming the Frontier,* WALL ST. J. (European ed.), January 31, 2003 (2002 WL-WSJE 3870150) (citing a Bear, Stearns estimate of 1,800 Internet gambling sites).

9. *See* <http://www.gamblinglicenses.com/licensesDatabase.cfm> (accessed January 17, 2006).

10. *See, e.g.,* Jodie T. Allen, *Trump's Latest Chumps,* U.S. NEWS & WORLD REP.,

April 12, 2004, at 35 ("[Trump Hotels & Casino Resorts] the profitless company struggled even to pay interest on its $1.8 billion debt, let alone make the investments needed to keep up with flashy new competitors like the Borgata."); Amy Yee, *Trump Towers Above Casino Debt Issues*, FIN. TIMES, April 8, 2004, at 27 (2004 WL 75248936) ("The worn-out Taj Mahal, Trump Plaza and Trump Marina in Atlantic City, New Jersey are in urgent need of renovation. The casinos are struggling to compete with sleeker casinos like the Borgata, a [$1.1 billion] joint-venture between MGM Mirage and Boyd Gaming that opened last summer.").

11. This issue is addressed in greater detail in chapter 9.

12. The World Sports Exchange, discussed later, is one example.

13. *See, e.g.,* Bambi Francisco, *Yahoo Hits Fresh 52-Week High after Q1,* April 8, 2004, at <http://www.marketwatch.com> (accessed April 14, 2004) (attributing success in part to strength in advertising, including its acquisition of Overture).

14. *See* Mylene Magdalinden, *Yahoo's Revenue Surges 39%, but Earnings Miss Expectations,* WALL ST. J., January 17, 2006, available at www.online.wsj.com.

15. *See, e.g.,* <http://adv.casinoblasters.com/index.php?bamse> (accessed April 12, 2004).

16. *See Casinos Bet on Gambling Addiction Web Site,* at <http://story.news.yahoo .com/news?tmpl=story&cid=573&ncid=573&e=4&u=/nm/20040412/od_nm/ casino_dc> (last visited April 12, 2004).

17. *See* Kelley et al., *supra* note 7, at 3.

18. We are aware of only one exception: Trinidad-based Casino Fortune employs a software-based tool to identify problem gambling patterns to shut down accounts of gamblers manifesting problem behaviors. *See* Amy Eagle, *Taking Chances,* CHI. TRIB., December 15, 2004.

19. *See* <http://mb.winneronline.com/>.

20. *See* Max Drayman, *How PricewaterhouseCoopers Reviews Casino Payouts,* May 24, 2001, at <http://www.winneronline.com/articles/december2000/pwc.htm> (viewed April 12, 2004).

21. *See, e.g., Best Payout Percentages* at <http://www.winneronline.com/ bestpayouts/> (viewed April 12, 2004), showing a ranking of online casinos. It is interesting to note, however, that some of these casinos are also sponsors of the sites, which questions the independence of such listings.

22. 260 F.3d 68 (2d Cir. 2001), *cert. denied.* 536 U.S. 922 (2002).

23. Central Intelligence Agency, THE WORLD FACTBOOK, at <http://www.odci .gov/cia/publications/factbook/fields/2153.html> (accessed April 16, 2004).

24. *See id.* (accessed January 17, 2006).

25. *See* Rebecca Quick, *Entrepreneurs Roll the Dice on a New Site,* WALL ST. J., April 10, 1997, at B18 (1997 WL-WSJ 2416377).

26. *See id.*

27. *See id.*

28. *See id.*

29. *See* United States v. Cohen, 298 F.3d at 70–71.

30. *See id.* at 71.

31. United States v. Cohen, 260 F.3d at 71.

32. 18 U.S.C. § 1084(b)

33. *See* United States v. Cohen, 260 F.3d at 74–75.

34. *See id.* at 75.

35. *See id.* at 74–75.

36. *Id.* at 76. *See also* United States v. Tomeo, 459 F.2d 445, 447 (10th Cir. 1976) (finding it unlikely that Congress contemplated one-way communication in using the term *transmission*).

37. *See* Dean Starkman, *U.S. Charges 14 in Crackdown Bid on On-Line Betting,* WALL St. J., March 5, 1998, at A8 (1998 WL-WSJ 3485072).

38. 18 U.S.C.A. § 1084(a).

39. Other aspects of the Wire Act are discussed in chapter 9.

40. Recently publicized efforts to address the problem of child pornography via the Internet, which has resulted in prosecutions of individuals based on seized credit card records from a domestic processor engaged in handling payments from offshore sites devoted to this material, suggest that prosecution efforts may be feasible where the commitment exists. *See* Cassel Bryan-Low, *Internet Transforms Child Porn into Lucrative Trade,* WALL St. J., January 17, 2006, at A1.

41. *See, e.g.,* In re Mastercard International Inc., 313 F.3d 257, 261–62 (5th Cir. 2002).

42. *See* In re MasterCard, 132 F.Supp. 2d 468, 480 (E.D. La. 2001). *See also* Michael P. Kailus, *Do Not Bet on Unilateral Prohibition of Internet Gambling to Eliminate Cyber-Casinos,* 1999 UNIV. OF ILL. L. REV. 1045, 1060–61 (suggesting that "a plain language interpretation of [§ 1084] would seem to indicate that [it] applies only to wagering on sporting events"). However, this author also states that "a common sense interpretation" would include Internet casinos within the reach of the Wire Act. *Id.* at 1061.

43. *See* People v. World Interactive Gaming Corp., 714 N.Y.S.2d 844 (1999).

44. *See* In Re MasterCard, 132 F.Supp. 2d at 480–81; see also H. R. 4411, The Unlawful Internet Gambling Enforcement Act of 2005, which was introduced in the House on November 18, 2005 but was later referred to the Judiciary Committee where it remains as of May 19, 2006.

45. Brief of the International Financial Sector Regulatory Authority, 2002 WL 32136044 (April 12, 2002).

46. 714 N.Y.S.2d 844 (N.Y. Sup. 1999).

47. *Id.,* 714 N.Y.S.2d at 849.

48. *See id.* at 849–50.

49. *See id.* at 851.

50. 568 N.W.2d 715 (Minn. Ct. App. 1997).

51. *See id.* at 717.

52. *See, e.g.,* Thompson v. Handa-Lopez, Inc., 998 F.Supp. 738 (W.D. Tex. 1998) (finding personal jurisdiction over online casino domiciled in California in breach of contract claim brought by Texas gambler).

53. 128 F.Supp.2d 340, 347–51 (E.D. Va. 2001).

54. *See id.* at 350.

55. *See* 15 U.S.C.A. § 1125(d)(2)(A), (C).

56. *See* 15 U.S.C.A. § 1125(d)(1)(C) ("In any civil action involving the registration, trafficking, or use of a domain name under this paragraph, a court may order the forfeiture or cancellation of the domain name or the transfer of the domain name to the owner of the mark.")

57. *See* Alitalia-Linee Aeree Italiane v. Casinolitalia.com, 128 F.Supp.2d 340 (E.D. Va. 2001) 128 F.Supp.2d at 346, n. 14.

58. *See* Yahoo! Inc. v. La Ligue Contre Le Racisme Et L'Antisemitisme,— F.3d—, 2006 WL 60670 (9th Cir. 2006).

59. *See* 44 Liquormart, Inc. v. Rhode Island, 517 U.S. 484, 497 (1996), discussed in chapter 9.

60. *See* Matt Richtel, *Web Engines Plan to End Online Ads for Gambling,* N.Y. Times, April 5, 2004, at C1, col. 5, at <http://www.nytimes.com/2004/04/05/technology/05yahoo.html>.

61. *See* Matt Richtel, *U.S. Steps Up Push Against Online Casinos by Seizing Cash,* N.Y. Times, May 31, 2004, at <http://www.nytimes.com/2004/05/31/technology/31gambling.html>.

62. *See* Richtel, *supra* note 60.

63. *See* Matt Richtel, *Electronic Arts to Stop Advertising for Online Casinos on Its Website,* N.Y. Times, June 12, 2004, at <http://www.nytimes.com/2004/06/12/business/media/12gamble.html> (visited June 17, 2004).

64. *See generally* Thomas P. Vartanian et al., 21st Century Money, Banking & Commerce 57–59 (1998).

65. *See, e.g.,* <http://www.paymentonline.com/termsandconditions/> (paragraph G) (visited May 3, 2004).

66. For a more extensive account of credit-card industry practices, *see* Cura Financial Services v. Electronic Payment Exchange, Inc., 2001 WL 1334188 (Del. Ch.).

67. *See Paypal Acceptable Use Policy* (Amended November 5, 2005), available online at <http://www.paypal.com/cgi-bin/webscr?cmd=p/gen/ua/use/index_frame-outside>.

68. *See* In re Mastercard International, Inc., 313 F.3d 257 (5th Cir. 2002).

69. *See id.* at 260–61. The civil remedies provision is found at 18 U.S.C. § 1964.

70. *See id.* at 262.

71. *See id.*

72. *See id.*

73. *See id.* at 262, n.14 (citing Kan Stat. Ann. § 21-4304).

74. *See id.* at 260.

75. *See* In re Mastercard International, Inc., 132 F.Supp. 2d 468, 479 (E.D. La. 2001).

76. *See id.*

77. *See* In re Mastercard International, Inc., 313 F.3d 257, 262 (5th Cir. 2002).

78. *See id.* at 260.

79. *See id.*

80. *See, e.g.*, United States v. Kaczowski, 114 F.Supp.2d 143 (W.D.N.Y. 1999) (applying "aiding and abetting" and conspiracy theories to defendants involved in offshore gambling operations).

81. *Internet Gambling Warning,* at <http://www.ksag.org/contents/consumer/internetwarning.htm> (visited May 4, 2004).

82. *See* S. Rep. No. 108–173, 108th Cong., 1st. Sess. 2003, 2003 WL 22437220 (Leg.Hist.) at 15.

83. WTO, *United States—Measures Affecting the Cross-Border Supply of Gambling and Betting Services, Request for the Establishment of a Panel by Antigua and Barbuda,* WT/DS285/ (June 13, 2003).

84. *See* WTO, *supra* note 82, at WT/DS285/1/Add.1 (April 10, 2003) (updating request for consultations dated March 13, 2003, and entered into the record dated March 27, 2003, with a corrected annex of references to U.S. legislation).

85. *See* WTO, *United States—Measures Affecting the Cross-Border Supply of Gambling and Betting Services, Request for Preliminary Rulings by the United States of America,* WT/DS285 (October 17, 2003), at ¶¶ 3–10.

86. *Id.* at ¶ 21.

87. Comments on the United States' Request for Preliminary Rulings by Antigua and Barbuda (October 22, 2003), at ¶ 13. *See also* ¶ 12 ("It is doubtful that anyone could compose a definitive list of all United States laws and regulations that could be applied against cross-border gambling.").

88. *Id.* at ¶ 14.

89. *See* First Written Submission of the United States, November 7, 2003, at ¶ 69.

90. *See id.* at ¶¶ 69–72.

91. *See, e.g.,* AMERICAN GAMING ASSOCIATION, 2003 STATE OF THE STATES: THE AGA SURVEY OF CASINO ENTERTAINMENT 2 (2003) (comparing casino spending and attendance to other entertainment, such as zoos or major league baseball).

92. *See* Second Written Submission of the United States, January 9, 2004.

93. *Id.* at ¶ 34.

94. *See generally id.* at ¶¶ 34, 37–42.

95. *See generally id.* at ¶¶ 43–51.

96. *Id.* at ¶ 53.

97. *Id.* at ¶ 54.

98. *See id.* at ¶ 55.

99. *See id.* at ¶ 114.

100. *See id.* at ¶ 113.

101. *See* WTO, United States—Measures Affecting the Cross-Border Supply of Gambling and Betting Services (WT/DS285/R), (November 10, 2004).

102. *See, e.g.,* Scott Miller & Christina Binkley, *U.S. Ban on Web Gambling Breaks Global Trade Pacts, Says WTO,* WALL ST. J., March 25, 2004, at A2. *See also* Kay Georgi & Phippe Vlaemminck, *WTO Panel Rules Against United States in Internet Gambling Case—What Does It Mean?* COUDERT BROTHERS LLP CLIENT ALERT, March 26, 2004.

103. *See id.* at ¶ 7.2–7.3.

104. *See id.* at § 6.607.

105. *See id.* at ¶ 6.535.

106. *See id.* ¶ 6.589.

107. *See id.* ¶ 6.595–6.600.

108. *See id.* ¶ 7.2–7.4.

109. *See, e.g.,* Miller and Binkley, *supra* note 102; Daniel Pruzin, *WTO Publishes Final Decision on Internet Gambling; U.S. to Appeal,* 9 BNA ELEC. COM. & L. REP. 940 (November 17, 2004).

110. *See* WTO, *United States—Measures Affecting the Cross-Border Supply of Gambling and Betting Services,* AB-2005-1 at ¶ 7 (April 7, 2005).

111. *See id.*

112. *Id.* ¶ 153.

113. *See id.*

114. *See id.* ¶ 213.

115. *See id.* ¶ 303.

116. *See id.* ¶ 310.

117. *See id.* ¶¶ 323–26.

118. *See id.* ¶¶ 360–69.

119. *See* Daniel Pruzin, *WTO Chief Appoints Arbitrator to Determine U.S. Compliance Deadline in Gambling Case,* BNA DAILY REP. FOR EXECUTIVES, July 6, 2005, at A-7.

120. *See* Matt Richtel, *An Industry That Dares Not Meet in the Country of Its Best Customers,* N.Y. TIMES, May 17, 2004, at <http://www.nytimes.com/2004/05/17/business/worldbusiness/17wager.html>.

121. *See* Eichenwald, *supra* note 2.

CHAPTER 11

1. *See* Cherokee Nation v. Georgia, 30 U.S. (Pet.) 1, 20 (1831).

2. *See* United States v. Lara, 541 U.S. 193, (2004).

3. *See id.*

4. *See id.* As the Court also pointed out, some of the federal government's powers over Indian tribes might also be rooted in preconstitutional practices, to the extent that the federal government has inherent powers rooted in its own sovereign status.

5. *See id.*

6. *Id.* (citations omitted).

7. 480 U.S. 202 (1987).

8. *See* 480 U.S. at 207 (citing 18 U.S.C. s 1162(a)).

9. *See id.* at 208.

10. *See id.* at 211.

11. *See id.* at 211.

12. *See id.* at 211. The county ordinance prohibiting card games was similarly defective, as it allowed municipalities to adopt rules that allowed card games, and two cities within the county had, in fact, done so. *See id.* at 212, n.11.

13. *See id.* at 212–14.

14. *See id.* at 214.

15. *See id.* at 217, n.20.

16. *See id.* at 217–22.

17. This concern was raised in the dissenting opinion in *Cabazon Band. See id.* at 224, 226 (Stevens, O'Connor, and Scalia, dissenting).

18. *See id.* at 222.

19. *Id.* at 227.

20. 25 U.S.C.A. § 2702.

21. *Id.* § 2710(a)(1).

22. *Id.* § 2703(6).

23. *See Id.* § 2703(7). Banked card games, in which players bet against the house, are specifically excepted from this definition. *See id.* The statute also grandfathers in certain card games in designated states that may not conform to these requirements. *See id.* at § 2703(7)(C).

24. *See id.* § 2703(7)(B)(ii). However, what constitutes a "slot machine" is a matter for litigation. *See infra.*

25. *Id.* § 2710(b)(1)(A).

26. *See id.* § 2710(b)(2).

27. 317 F.Supp.2d 128 (N.D. N.Y. 2004).

28. 125 S.Ct. 1478 (May 29, 2005).

29. Cayuga Indian Nation of New York v. Village of Union Springs, 390 F.Supp.2d 203 (N.D.N.Y. Oct 05, 2005).

30. *See id.*

31. *See* 25 U.S.C.A. § 2706.

32. 25 U.S.C.A. § 2710(b)(2)(F).

33. *See* 25 U.S.C.A. § 2710(b)(3).

34. *See id.*

35. 25 U.S.C.A. § 2710(b)(3)(D).

36. *See id.* § 2710(c). Regarding financial controls, the commission promulgated regulations in 1999 to provide minimum internal control standards for the industry. *See* 64 Fed. Reg. 590-01 (January 5, 1999).

37. *See* 25 U.S.C.A. § 2703(8).

38. *See, e.g.,* Seminole Tribe v. Florida, 517 U.S. 44, 48 (1996) (Class III is "the most heavily regulated of the three classes").

39. *See* 25 U.S.C.A. § 2710(d)(1)(B).

40. *See id.* § 2710(d)(1)(C). In some states, such as California, the constitution provides for Indian gaming pursuant to a model compact.

41. 25 U.S.C.A. § 2510(d)(3)(C).

42. Arizona Model Compact, ¶ 3(k).

43. *See* American Greyhound Racing v. Hull, 305 F.3d 1015, 1019 n. 3 (9th Cir. 2003) (citing year 2000 amendments to required provisions in compacts).

44. *See, e.g.,* Cheyenne River Sioux Tribe v. South Dakota, 3 F.3d 273, 279 (8th Cir. 1993) ("The 'such gaming' language of 25 U.S.C. § 2710(d)(1)(B) does not require the state to negotiate with respect to forms of gaming it does not presently permit."); Rumsey Indian Rancheria of Wintun Indians v. Wilson, 41 F.3d 421, 427 (9th Cir. 1994) (following 8th Circuit in *Cheyenne River Sioux*); Citizen Band Potawatomi Indian Tribe of Oklahoma v. Green, 995 F.3d 179 (10th Cir. 1993) (video lottery terminals prohibited under Oklahoma law could not be imported for use in a tribal casino).

45. *See* Dalton v. Pataki, 5 N.Y.3d 243 (2005) (holding that state constitutional constraint was preempted by IGRA, thus allowing tribal casino gambling pursuant to compact), cert. denied, 126 S.Ct. 742 (Nov. 28, 2005). The IGRA's language allowing tribal gambling where the state law permits it for "any purpose by any person, organization or entity" was a critical part of this decision. *See id.,* 5 N.Y.3d at 259.

46. *See, e.g.,* McClanahan v. State Tax Commission of Arizona, 411 U.S. 164 (1973) (Arizona could not impose state income tax on tribal member's income earned entirely from reservation sources); Moe v. Confederated Salish and Kootenai Tribes of Flathead Reservation, 425 U.S. 463 (1976) (nixing Montana state taxes on cigarette sales by tribal members on reservations and personal property taxes on motor vehicles).

47. Montana v. Blackfeet Tribe of Indians, 471 U.S. 759, 765 (1985).

48. *See* City of Sherrill v. Oneida Indian Nation, 544 U.S. 197 (2005).

49. 25 U.S.C.A. § 2510(d)(3)(D).

50. 25 U.S.C.A. § 2510(d)(7)(B)(iii)(II).

51. Model Tribal-State Gaming Compact, ¶ E, at <http://www.cgcc.ca.gov/enabling/tsc.pdf> (dated July 14, 2003) (last accessed May 21, 2004).

52. *See* In Re Indian Gaming Related Cases, 331 F.3d 1094, 1105 (9th Cir. 2003).

53. *See id.* at 1105, 1111.

54. *See id.* at 1105–6.

55. *See id.* at 1113.

56. Generic Arizona Compact ¶ 12(b), at <http://www.gm.state.az.us/compact .final.pdf> (last accessed May 21, 2004).

57. *Id.* at ¶ 3(h)(1).

58. *Id.* at ¶ 12(c); A.R.S. § 5-601.02(3).

59. *See* Model Arizona Compact ¶ 12(c); A.R.S. § 5-601.02(4).

60. *See* Veronica Rose, *Compact and Slot Agreement Amendments* (2002-R-0999), at <http://www.cga.state.ct.us/2002/olrdata/ps/rpt/2002-R-0999.htm> (visited May 24, 2004).

61. *See id.*

62. *See id.*

63. *See* In re Indian Gaming Related Cases, 331 F.3d 1094, 1114 n. 17 (9th Cir. 2003).

64. *See* Sault Ste. Marie Tribe of Chippewa Indians v. Engler, 146 F.3d 367 (6th Cir. 1998); *see also id.,* 271 F.3d 235 (6th Cir. 2001).

65. *See id.,* 146 F.3d at 373.

66. *See, e.g.,* Eric S. Lent, *Note, Are States Beating the House? The Validity of Tribal-State Revenue Sharing Under the Indian Gaming Regulatory Act,* 91 GEO. L. J. 451 (2003); Gatsby Contreras, *Exclusivity Agreements in Tribal-State Compacts: Mutual Benefit Revenue Sharing or Illegal State Taxation?* 5 J. GENDER RACE & JUST. 487 (2002).

67. 331 F.3d 1094 (9th Cir. 2003).

68. *See id.* at 1110.

69. *Id.* at 1111.

70. *Id.* at 1113.

71. *See id.* at 1114.

72. *See id.* at 1113.

73. *Id.* at 1115.

74. *See id.* at 1115.

75. *Id.* at 1114, n.17.

76. *See* the subsequent discussion re: tribal lobbying. *See also* Melvin Claxton & Mark Puls, *Tribes Buy Clout with Casino Cash,* DET. NEWS, December 30, 2001, at <http://www.detnews.com/specialreports/2001/chippewa/1230lead/1230lead .htm>.

77. Jan Golab, *Arnold Girds for Indian War,* AMERICAN ENTERPRISE ONLINE (Jan./Feb. 2004), at <http://www.taemag.com/issues/articleid.17819/article _detail.asp>. As for the legal basis for these contributions, Golab further observes: "The Indian Gaming Regulatory Act of 1987 sets forth a list of specific purposes for

which tribal gaming revenues may be used. One of those is 'to promote the economic development of the tribe.' The Indians claim that campaign contributions qualify as 'promoting their economic development.' Critics cry foul." *Id.*

78. *But see* City of Sherrill v. Oneida Indian Nation, 544 U.S. 197 (2005), indicating that purchased lands formerly under state and local government control may still be subject to state and local taxing powers.

79. For an economic analysis of tax impacts, see chapter 4.

80. *See* <http://www.cabazonindians-nsn.gov/cgi-bin/ducs/display/o_content _cms/i_25> (last visted May 21, 2004).

81. *See* <http://www.fantasyspringsresort.com/> (last visited May 21, 2004).

82. *See* Mark Puls & Melvin Claxton, *Power Grab, Money Spur Tribal Expulsions,* DET. NEWS, Aug. 5, 2001, at <http://www.detnews.com/specialreports/2001/ chippewa/sunlead/sunlead.htm> (last visited May 25, 2004).

83. *See* National Indian Gaming Association, Library and Resource Center, Indian Gaming Facts, at <http://indiangaming.org/library/index.html> (last visited May 28, 2003).

84. *See* <http://www.detnews.com/specialreports/2001/chippewa/index .htm> (November 11, 2001).

85. *See, e.g.,* Pueblo of Santa Ana v. Kelly, 114 F.3d 1546, 1549 (10th Cir. 1997) (quoting from IGRA legislative history).

86. *See* 25 U.S.C. A. 2710(d)(5).

87. *See* Artichoke Joe's California Grand Casino v. Norton, 353 F.3d 712, 715 (9th Cir. 2003) (quoting district court decision).

88. *See* 25 U.S.C.A. § 2710(d)(7).

89. *See* Seminole Tribe v. Florida, 517 U.S. 44 (1996).

90. *See* 64 Fed. Reg. 17535-02 (April 12, 1999) (promulgating 25 C.F.R. § 291.1–.15).

91. 25 C.F.R. § 291.3.

92. *See id.* §§ 291.9–11.

93. *See id.* § 291.11.

94. *See* Texas v. United States, 362 F.Supp. 2d 765 (W.D. Tex. 2004).

95. *See* In re Indian Gaming Related Cases, 331 F.3d 1094, 1099 (9th Cir. 2003).

96. *See, e.g.,* United States v. Santee Sioux Tribe of Nebraska, 324 F.3d 607 (8th Cir. 2003).

97. *See generally* 25 U.S.C.A. § 2710.

98. Id. § 2704(4).

99. S. Rep. No. 100-446, at 8 (1988), reprinted in 1988 U.S.C.C.A.N. 3071, 3078.

100. *See* 25 U.S.C.A. § 2719(a)(1). It is possible for reservation lands to surround non-Indian lands, thus allowing expansion "within" the reservation as well as outside of it.

101. *See id.* § 2719(a)(2)(A).

102. *See id.* § 2719(a)(2)(B).

103. *Id.* § 2719(b)(1)(A).

104. 25 U.S.C.A. § 2719(b)(1)(B). Other special exceptions for tribes in Wisconsin and Florida are also included in the IGRA. *See generally* 25 U.S.C.A. §§ 2719(b)(2),(3).

105. 348 F.3d 1020 (D.C. 2003), *cert. denied,* 541 U.S. 974 (2004).

106. *See id.* at 1022.

107. *See id.* at 1022–23.

108. *Id.* at 1023.

109. *See id.* at 1024.

110. *Id.* at 1027.

111. *Id.* at 1029.

112. *See id.* at 1030.

113. *See id.* at 1031.

114. *See Appeals Court Sides with Tribe in Casino Challenge,* SAN DIEGO UNION-TRIBUNE, November 16, 2003, at <http://www.casinoman.net/Content/casino_gambling_news/gambling_news_article.asp?artid=2288> (indicating projected profits of $260 million); *Thunder Valley Deals Mostly Winning Hand,* SACRAMENTO BEE, May 30, 2004, at <http://www.casinoman.net/Content/casino_gambling_news/gambling_news_article.asp?artid=3073> (estimating between 3 and 3.7 million visitors and profits of approximately $300 million).

115. *See* Thomas J. Walsh, *Thunder Valley Casino Opens to Huge Crowds: Bumper-to-Bumper Traffic Greets Formerly Quiet Community of Lincoln,* RENO GAZETTE-JOURNAL, June 9, 2003, at <http://www.rgj.com/news/stories/html/2003/06/09/44205.php> (last visited June 6, 2004).

116. *See Thunder Valley Casino Update—Placer County, California,* at <http://www.placer.ca.gov/news/2003/6-4-03-casino-update.htm> (last visited June 6, 2004).

117. Sac and Fox Nation of Missouri v. Norton, 240 F.3d 1250, 1255 (10th Cir. 2001), cert. denied, 534 U.S. 1078 (2002).

118. *See id.* at 1256.

119. *See id.* at 1254.

120. *See id.*

121. *See id.* at 1255.

122. *See* City of Roseville, supra, 348 F.3d at 1029.

123. *See* Press Release, *Governor Sebelius and Attorney General Kline Take Action Against Wyandotte Casino,* September 9, 2003, at <http://www.accesskansas.org/ksag/contents/news-releases/sep09casino.html>.

124. *See* Mechoopda Indian Tribe of Chico Rancheria, California v. Schwarzenegger, 2004 WL 1103021 (unreported E.D. Cal. 2004).

125. *Id.* at n. 10 (citation omitted).

126. *See generally* Gary Rivlin, *Bet on It: The Tug of the Newfangled Slot Machines,* N.Y. TIMES MAGAZINE, May 9, 2004, at 42ff.

127. *See id.* at 74.

128. *See id.*

129. *See id.*

130. *See* 25 U.S.C.A. § 2703(7)(A)(i).

131. 327 F.3d 1019 (10th Cir. 2003), cert. denied, 540 U.S. 1218 (2004).

132. *See id.,* 327 F.3d at 1025.

133. *See id.* at 1040.

134. *Id.* at 1040–41.

135. 324 F.3d 607 (8th Cir. 2003).

136. *Id.* at 615.

137. *Id.* at 615, n.3 (citation omitted).

138. *See* Ashcroft v. Seneca-Cayuga Tribe of Oklahoma, 124 S.Ct. 1505 (March 1, 2004); United States v. Santee Sioux Tribe of Nebraska, 124 S.Ct. 1506 (March 1, 2004).

139. Brief of Amici Curiae at 1, 2004 WL 161450 (January 21, 2004).

140. *Id.* at 4.

141. *See* <http://www.nigc.gov/nigc/documents/announcements/devclass2505.jsp> (visited January 16, 2006).

142. <http://www.opensecrets.org/industries/indus.asp?Ind=G6550> (visited January 16, 2006).

143. <http://www.opensecrets.org/industries/indus.asp?ind=D&cycle=2006> (visited January 16, 2006).

144. <http://www.opensecrets.org/industries/indus.asp?Ind=H04> (visited January 16, 2006).

145. <http://www.opensecrets.org/industries/indus.asp?Ind=N07> (visited January 16, 2006). For 2006 election-cycle contributions, the gaming industry ranks thirty-eighth among all contributing industries. *See* <http://www.opensecrets.org/industries/mems.asp>.

146. *See 2004 Election Overview: Stats at a Glance,* <http://www.opensecrets.org/overview/stats.asp?Cycle=2004> (visited January 16, 2006).

147. *See* <http://www.choctaw.org/economics/tribal_business_overview.htm> (visited January 17, 2006)

148. *See id.*

149. *See* Thomas B. Edsall, *Abramoff Allies Keeping Distance,* WASH. POST, November 8, 2004, at A23; Andrew Ferguson, *A Lobbyist's Progress,* WKLY. STAND., December 20, 2004, available at <http://www.weeklystandard.com/Content/Public/Articles/000/000/005/022nwtca.asp?pg=2>.

150. The criminal information filed against Abramoff cites "Deprivation of

Abramoff's Clients' Right to Abramoff's Honest Services" regarding "a Native American tribal client based in Mississippi"—which could reasonably be assumed to be the Choctaws. The text of the information is available at www.citizensforeethics.org/filelibrary/abramoff-info.pdf (visited January 16, 2006).

151. Press Release, *Mississippi Choctaws Respond to Abramoff Plea,* January 4, 2006, available at <http://www.choctaw.org/press_room/pr_2006_01_04.htm> (visited January 16, 2006).

152. *See* Texas v. Ysleta Del Sur Pueblo, 220 F.Supp. 2d 668 (W.D. Tex. 2001), aff'd 68 Fed. Appx. 659 (5th Cir. 2002), cert. denied, 540 U.S. 985 (2003). Ysleta Del Sur Pueblo is the formal name for the Tigua tribe.

153. *See id.,* 220 F. Supp.2d at 709–14 (order denying motion for reconsideration of modifying opinion, June 24, 2002).

154. *See id.* at 676–84 (discussing the legislative history of the restoration act).

155. *See id.* at 684–85.

156. *See* Letter from U.S. Representative Sylvestre Reyes (D-TX) to Senator Ben Nighthorse Campbell, Chairman, Indian Affairs Committee, dated September 24, 2004, available at <http://wwwc.house.gov/reyes/news_detail.asp?id=670>.

157. *See* Ferguson, *supra* note 149. The Senate Committee on Indian Affairs has released documents showing the involvement of various Texas and Louisiana tribal interests in the matter of Texas casinos. *See* <http://www.indian.senate.gov/exhibits2.pdf>. These include an e-mail dated November 12, 2001, from Abramoff associate Michael Scanlon to general counsel of the Couchattas, J. VanHorne, providing an article from the *Houston Chronicle* on November 11, 2001, as background on the litigation.

158. *See* Ferguson, *supra* note 149.

159. *Id.* (e-mail from Ralph Reed to Abramoff, November 14, 2001).

160. *See* Paul West, *Christian Rightist Seeks Georgia Office,* SAN FRAN. CHRON., March 27, 2005, available at www.sfgate.com.

161. *See* Ferguson, *supra* note 149. One open question about such a plan would be whether the tribe would have an insurable interest in older tribal members. It is easy to envision public policy objections, not to mention moral objections, to such a scheme.

162. *See Operation Open Doors,* WASH. POST, December 3, 2004, at A26, available at <http://www.washingtonpost.com/wp-dyn/articles/A30123-2004Dec2.html>.

163. *See GOP Congressman Latest Casualty in Abramoff Scandal,* at <http://indianz.com/News/2006/012026.asp>.

164. *See* United States Senate Committee on Indian Affairs, Oversight Hearing on Lobbying Practices, Exhibits Released to the Public November 17, 2004, available at <http://www.indian.senate.gov/2005hrgs/111705hrg/111705exhibits.pdf> (e-mail dated January 22, 2002).

165. *See id.* ("Contact Information for guests of September 24, 2001 dinner party" hosted by CREA).

166. *See id.* (various e-mails).

167. *How Abramoff Spread the Wealth,* WASH. POST, December 12, 2005, available at <http://www.washingtonpost.com/wp-dyn/content/graphic/2005/12/12/GR2005121200286.html>.

CHAPTER 12

1. *See* National Council on Problem Gambling, *Problem Gambling Resource and Fact Sheet* at <http://www.ncpgambling.org/media/pdf/eapa_flyer.pdf> (visited June 3, 2005).

2. See chapter 5.

3. *See* Earl L. Grinols & David B. Mustard, CASINOS, CRIME, AND COMMUNITY COSTS 88 REVIEW OF ECONOMICS AND STATISTICS 28 (February 2006), discussed in chapter 5.

4. *See* United States Department of Health and Human Services, Office of Child Support Enforcement, Table 11: Total Amount of Arrearages Due FY 2003, available at <http://www.acf.hhs.gov/programs/cse/pubs/2004/reports/preliminary_data/table_11.html> (accessed June 3, 2005).

5. Professor Grinols chronicles many of these reports in his recent book, GAMBLING IN AMERICA 146–66 (2004).

6. *See generally* GAO, IMPACT OF GAMBLING: ECONOMIC EFFECTS MORE MEASURABLE THAN SOCIAL EFFECTS (GGD-00-78, April 27, 2000), available at <http://www.gao.gov/new.items/gg00078.pdf>.

7. *See* <http://www.keepthemoneyinnebraska.com/> (visited June 4, 2005).

8. *See* <http://www.gamblingwiththegoodlife.com/> (visited June 4, 2005).

9. *See id.*

10. *See* www.keepthemoneyinnebraska.com (visited June 4, 2005) (emphasis added).

11. *See* Robynn Tysver, *Another Try at Casinos Eyed,* OMAHA WORLD-HERALD, January 17, 2006, at 1.

12. Florida Stat. Ann. § 100.371(a)(6).

13. Advisory Opinion to the Attorney General re Authorizes [*sic*] Miami-Dade & Broward County Voters to Approve Slot Machines in Parimutuel Facilities, 880 So. 2d 689 (Fla. 2004).

14. *See* Official General Election Ballot, Miami-Dade County, November 2, 2004, at <http://elections.metro-dade.com/mdgen-eng.html> (accessed November 24, 2004).

15. *See* Amy Sherman, *Courts Now Get a Spin at the Slots,* MIAMI HERALD, May 25, 2005, at A1 (2005 WLNR 8244850).

16. 2004 Pa. Legis. Serv. Act 2004-71 (H.B. 2330) (PURDON'S) (approved July 4, 2004).

17. *See* David Nitkin, *Gambling Industry Puts Their Money on State Lobbyists,* BALT. SUN, June 1, 2005, at 2B (2005 WLNR 8671813).

18. *See id.*

19. *See Safe Bet,* BALT. SUN, June 9, 2005, at 14A (2005 WLNR 9156122).

20. *See* Donald Wittkowski, *Trump Hotels Postpones Emergence from Bankruptcy,* PRESS ATL. CITY, May 13, 2005, at <http://pressofatlanticcity.com> (accessed May 31, 2005).

21. *See* David Littlejohn, *Steve Wynn's $2.7 Billion Gamble,* WALL ST. J., May 17, 2005, at D10.

22. See chapter 2.

23. *See* John Curran , *New Jersey Gamblers Prefer LV, Study Says,* LAS VEGAS REV.-J., May 26, 2005, at <http//www.reviewjournal.com/lvrj_home/2005/May-26-Thu-2005/business/1885362.html>.

24. See chapter 4.

25. As discussed in chapter 11, tribal and commercial casino interests are both involved in political spending. *See also* Campbell Lynn, *$9.6 Million Contributed in Illinois in 10 Years,* DES MOINES REG., May 30, 2004 (2004 WL 74844624).

26. Iowa Acts, House File 2302, section 61.

27. *See Request for Proposals for a Study of the Socioeconomic Impact of Gambling on Iowans,* at <http://www.legis.state.ia.us/Contracts>.

28. *See* William Petroski, *Per Mar Withdraws from Iowa Gambling Study,* DES MOINES REG., October 22, 2004, at B1 (2004 WL 90800014); *see also* William Petroski, *Gambling Study Firm Has Ties to Casinos,* DES MOINES REG., October 19, 2004, at A1 (2004 WL 90799696); *State Should Walk Away,* DES MOINES REG., October 20, 2004, at A16 (2004 WL 90799026); William Petroski, *Gaming Critic Fears Study Will Be Biased,* DES MOINES REG., October 11, 2004, at B1 (2004 WL 90799242).

29. *See* Petroski, *Gambling Study Firm, id.*

30. *See* William Petroski, *State Approves Expansion of Casino in Council Bluffs,* DES MOINES REG., November 19, 2004, at B8 (2004 WL 100489586).

31. *See* Joel J. Smith, *Compulsive Gamblers Triple at Detroit Casinos,* DET. NEWS, October 14, 2004.

32. *See* Amy Eagle, *Taking Chances,* CHI. TRIB., December 15, 2004.

33. The Justice Department's recent decision to reduce the claim for punitive damages against the tobacco industry from more than $130 million to only $10 million further reinforces the view that political decisions can change the fortunes of an industry. *See* Eric Lichtblau, *Political Leanings Were Always Factor in Tobacco Suit,* N.Y. TIMES, June 19, 2005, at 1.

34. 379 F.3d 654 (9th Cir. 2004).

35. *Id.* at 663.

36. *See id.* at 660.

37. *See id.* at 661.

38. *See id.* at 664.

39. *Id.* at 665.

40. *Id.*

41. *See id.* at 665–66.

42. *See id.* at 666–67.

43. Liz Benston & Cy Ryan, *Gaming Industry Wins Key Ruling in Lawsuit,* LAS VEGAS SUN, August 11, 2004, at <http://www.lasvegassun.com/sunbin/stories/gaming/2994/aug/11/517321932.html>.

44. 261 Mich. App. 534, 683 N.W.2d 200 (2004).

45. 320 F.3d 729 (7th Cir. 2003).

46. *Id.* at 730.

47. *Id.* at 732. The court also cited Hakimoglu v. Trump Taj Mahal, 70 F.3d 291 (3d Cir. 1995), a case arising out of New Jersey in which the Third Circuit refused to create a private cause of action where a gambler suffered gaming losses while intoxicated.

48. *See id.* at 732–33.

49. *See, e.g.,* John Warren Kindt, *The Costs of Addicted Gamblers: Should the States Initiate Mega-Lawsuits Similar to the Tobacco Cases?* 22 MANAGERIAL & DECISION ECON. 17 (2001); John Warren Kindt, *Subpoenaing Information from the Gambling Industry: Will the Discovery Process in Civil Lawsuits Reveal Hidden Violations Including the Racketeer Influenced and Corrupt Organizations Act?* 82 OREGON L. REV. 221 (2003).

50. *See* THE DEVELOPMENT OF THE LAW OF GAMBLING: 1776–1976 at 416, n.8 (1977), commissioned by the National Institute of Law Enforcement and Criminal Justice and the Law Enforcement Assistance Administration of the United States Department of Justice (citing Act of March 5, 1877, ch. 103, Nev. Laws 173).

51. *See id.*

52. *See, e.g.,* Narragansett Indian Tribe v. National Indian Gaming Com'n, 158 F.3d 1335, 1340 (D.C. 1998), in which neither the parties nor the court was willing to treat gambling as a fundamental right.

53. *See id.*

54. See chapter 5.

55. *See* 11 U.S.C. § 525(a).

56. *See* In re Christmas, 102 B.R. 44 (D. Md. 1989) (quoting H.R.Rep. No. 95-595, 95th Cong., 1st Sess., *reprinted in* 1978 U.S.Code Cong. & Admin.News 5963, 6126).

57. *See id.* at 459.

58. *See* 11 U.S.C. § 707 (effective October 17, 2005).

59. *See* Joseph M. Kelly, *Compulsive Gambling in Britain,* 4 J. GAMBLING. BEHAV. 291 (1988).

60. Neil Humphrey, *Rich Island, Poor Island,* TODAY, Marcy 27, 2004, at <http://www.wildsingapore.com/sos/media/040327-1.htm> (last visited June 27, 2005).

61. *See* Chad Skelton, *Knowing When to Fold 'Em: Problem Gamblers I—The Nether-lands Has a Solution*, Vancouver Sun, November 20, 2004.

62. See chapter 8.

63. I. Nelson Rose, *Gambling and the Law—Update 1993*, 15 Hasting Comm./Ent. J. 93, 104 (1992).

64. *See id.*

INDEX